SMALL BUSINESS MANAGEMENT

THE WILEY SERIES IN MANAGEMENT

SMALL BUSINESS MANAGEMENT

SECOND EDITION

HAL B. PICKLE
St. Edward's University

ROYCE L. ABRAHAMSON
Southwest Texas State University

John Wiley & Sons
New York • Chichester • Brisbane • Toronto

The designs used on the cover represent internationally recognized symbols for many of the world's businesses, shops and services.

Production supervised by Ellen P. O'Neill
Cover and text design by Laurie Ierardi
Copyedited by Deborah Herbert

Library of Congress Cataloging in Publication Data:

Pickle, Hal B
  Small business management.

  (The Wiley series in management ISSN 0271-6046)
  Includes bibliographical references and index.
  1. Small business—Management. I. Abrahamson, Royce L., joint author. II. Title.
HD62.7.P52   1981   658′.022   80-25071
ISBN 0-471-06218-9

Printed in the United States of America

10 9 8 7 6 5 4 3 2 1

To Coy, Mattie Laura, Sherry, Kristine, and Rachel

PREFACE

This book is intended for prospective small business entrepreneurs and for persons who are operating small business firms and want to improve their operations. Its format enables the instructor to use one of several teaching methods: lecture, lecture with case write-up before class, case discussion in class, or a combined case-lecture method in class.

The second edition is more practice oriented than the previous one. It contains a substantial expansion of the techniques and methods of day-to-day management of the small business enterprise, which is reflected in the new chapter format. Moreover, two chapters from the first edition, "Small Business and Its Environment" and "The Entrepreneur" have been combined into one chapter, "Entrepreneurship," and the two descriptive chapters, "Retail and Service Firms" and "Wholesalers and Manufacturers" have been eliminated. Material from these chapters has been greatly condensed and included in other chapters.

A new chapter "Computers in Small Business," has been added concerning an important and rapidly expanding area of small business management. The cost of microcomputers has decreased at such an accelerated rate that they are now within the price range of most small businesses. This new chapter provides information about the value and application of computers to the small business manager.

The informal style of the first edition is retained. In addition, each chapter now contains at least two cases that illustrate the text discussion and at least one new case based on a "real world" small business situation. Many new illustrations and applications have been included throughout the book. Some of them are listed below.

Material included in a corporation's articles of incorporation and bylaws.

An expanded section of subchapter "S" corporation with some of the benefits to be derived from them.

An explanation of physical and psychological market barriers.

The basic process to use in determining location.

S. B. A. eligibility requirements.

S. B. A. ineligible applicants.

The procedure for loan application of new and existing businesses.

Accounts receivables and methods of handling them.

Simplified sales journals covering both cash and accrual basis accounting.

A combined monthly income and cash flow statement keyed to the journals.

A "request for not in stock" method.

Cost of insurance protection.

Adjustable life insurance.

Burglar alarm systems.

The importance of price image and its relationships.

Markup as a percentage of selling price.

A bid, actual cost, and variance system.

Considerable expansion of the bank credit card section.

Collection methods, including the four steps of collection.

A description of each area of the Uniform Commercial Code.

Various negotiable instruments and their use.

Various "consumer protection laws."

Legal rights of prospective franchisees.

The Code of Ethics of International Franchising Association.

Increased coverage of franchise information.

The expansion of franchising in international markets.

The most recent information on legislation affecting small business owners, such as the Civil Rights Act and the Occupational Safety and Health Administration Act.

More coverage on the training of personnel in the small business.

A description of employee compensation plans.

Greater coverage of the management functions.

An expanded coverage of organization change, employee discipline, and employee communication.

Purchasing policies and procedures.

Considerations in make or buy decisions of small businesses.

Flowchart of the purchasing decision process.

Economic Order Quantity (EOQ).

An expanded coverage of international marketing.

Addition of a telephone survey technique for use as a tool for collecting marketing research data.

Advertising budget expenditures as percent of sales for selected types of businesses.

A checklist for promotional advertising in newspapers.

A guide for improving salesperson's performance.

For reviews and suggestions, we sincerely thank Professor Arthur Zenner, Oscar Rose Junior College; Professor Richard Hodgetts, Florida International University and Professor Francis MacKenzie, Idaho State University.

Hal B. Pickle
Royce L. Abrahamson

CONTENTS

9 PERSONNEL MANAGEMENT IN THE SMALL BUSINESS

18   CONSUMER BEHAVIOR AND PERSONAL SELLING   425

19   ADVERTISING AND SALES PROMOTION IN THE SMALL BUSINESS   453

20   CONSUMER CREDIT   481

SECTION SIX THE GOVERNMENT AND SMALL BUSINESS   497

21   LEGAL CONSIDERATIONS   499

22 GOVERNMENT CONTROL AND ASSISTANCE   515

PREVIEW OF THIS CHAPTER   SHERMAN ANTITRUST ACT, 1890
CLAYTON ACT, 1914   FEDERAL TRADE COMMISSION ACT, 1914
ROBINSON-PATMAN ACT, 1936   FOODS, DRUG, AND COSMETIC
ACT, 1938   OCCUPATIONAL SAFETY AND HEALTH ACT
CONSUMER PROTECTION LAWS   GOVERNMENT ASSISTANCE
TO SMALL BUSINESS   DISCUSSION QUESTIONS
STUDENT PROJECT   CASE A PULVER'S OFFICE SUPPLY
CASE B FEDERAL TRADE COMMISSION EXPERT

SECTION

ONE

SMALL BUSINESS, ENTREPRENEURS, AND OWNERSHIP

1

ENTREPRENEURSHIP

PREVIEW OF THIS CHAPTER

1. In this chapter, you will learn what entrepreneurs do and their importance to a private enterprise economic system.

2. You will find out what personal characteristics contribute to small business success.

3. You will learn what a small business is and the various ways of defining a small business.

4. You will discover the role and scope of small business in our economic system.

5. You will recognize the advantages and limitations of the small business enterprise.

6. You will learn that there are many rewards in addition to profit that entrepreneurs derive from small business ownership.

7. You should be able to increase your chances for success in small business because of your increased awareness and understanding of the common problems faced by small business firms.

8. You will understand that many small businesses are a family operation.

9. You will discover that a commitment to social activity is required of both the entrepreneur and spouse in many small businesses.

10. You will be able to understand these key words:

Small business	Analytical thinking
Small Business Administration	Human relations ability
Small business manager	Communications ability
Entrepreneur	Oral communication
Drive	Written communication
Mental ability	Technical knowledge
Creative thinking	Empathy

Profit	Status
Satisfying work	Family business
Ego involvement	Social activity

Each year thousands of individuals, motivated by initiative and high expectations, launch out into the world of work in search of fulfilling their goal of success. In our society, individuals choose how they will attempt to achieve their goal of success. Many thousands will pursue their goals by starting some type of business, and most of these businesses will be "small businesses." These individuals will become entrepreneurs. An entrepreneur is "one who organizes a business undertaking, assuming risk, for the sake of profit."[1]

Entrepreneurs are a keystone in the American free enterprise system. They discover new ideas and business opportunities, bring together funds to estab-

These young entrepreneurs are awaiting customers to buy the eggs they are selling at the open-air market on New York City's Ninth Avenue.

[1]Webster's *New World Dictionary of the American Language.*

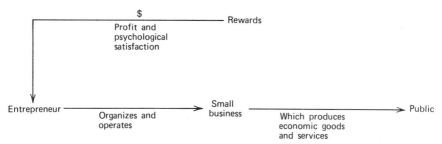

Figure 1-1 Entrepreneurs organize and operate small businesses for profit and psychological satisfaction.

lish a business, organize the business, and often manage the business operation to provide economic goods and services for the public. Without a doubt, much of the success of the United States has resulted from the vast energy and innovations of its entrepreneurs operating in an environment of private enterprise.

Small business owners are in every way entrepreneurs. Usually, the owners of small businesses organize even the smallest aspects of their business. They also assume risk. Perhaps the only deviation from the definition of an entrepreneur might be in terms of profit. In addition, the psychological satisfaction owners derive from their business often rivals the profit satisfaction. (See Fig. 1-1.)

CHARACTERISTICS THAT CONTRIBUTE TO BUSINESS SUCCESS

Extensive research has been conducted in an attempt to identify the personality characteristics that contribute to business success. To date, no general agreement has resulted from this search. One research study of 97 small business managers did produce a correlation of .63 between success and five general characteristics: (1) drive, (2) mental ability, (3) human relations ability, (4) communications ability, and (5) technical knowledge.[2] (See Fig. 1-2.)

DRIVE

In general terms, drive is a person's motivation toward a task. It is comprised of such personality traits as responsibility, vigor, initiative, persistence, and

[2]Hal B. Pickle, *Personality and Success: An Evaluation of Personal Characteristics of Successful Small Business Managers*. Small Business Administration, Washington, D. C., 1964.

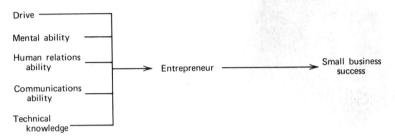

Figure 1-2   Contributors to small business success.

ambition. An entrepreneur must exert considerable effort in establishing and managing his/her small business. The manager who works hard planning, organizing, coordinating, and controlling his/her small business is more likely to have a successful business than the manager who is lax and haphazard.

Of course, many entrepreneurs work long hours in their businesses at menial tasks, such as cooking in a restaurant, and still do not succeed because they fail to perform the more difficult management functions of planning, organizing, directing, and controlling. In fact, some small business managers perform menial chores in order to avoid managerial tasks because they feel inadequate or lack the knowledge necessary for functioning as an effective manager. By staying busy in the menial tasks, they convince themselves they don't have time to perform many management functions. It is not unusual to hear such comments as "I know I should be doing that, but I just don't have time."

MENTAL ABILITY

Mental ability that contributes to the success of the small business entrepreneur-manager consists of overall intelligence (IQ), creative thinking ability, and analytical thinking ability. Small business managers must be reasonably intelligent, able to adapt their actions to the needs of the business in various situations (creative thinking), and able to engage in analysis of various problems and situations in order to deal with them (analytical thinking). (See Fig. 1-3.)

The small business manager who is able to recognize his problems and create ways of solving them is much better equipped to succeed in small business than the individual who is unable to perform these functions adequately. For example, some small business managers in retail establishments use their intelligence to create unique promotional campaigns that are very effective in increasing patronage of their stores.

This is not to imply that a person with a high IQ will automatically be a

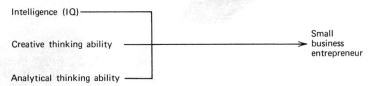

Figure 1-3 Mental ability is important to the entrepreneur.

success in a small business. It means that adequate intelligence, creative thinking, and analytical thinking are among the contributors to a person's success in small business management. Many people who have less than average intelligence have succeeded in small businesses, and many people with very high levels of intelligence have failed in small businesses.

HUMAN RELATIONS ABILITY

Personality factors, such as emotional stability, personal relations, sociability, consideration, and tactfulness, are important contributors to the entrepreneur-manager's success in small business. One of the most important facets of human relations ability is one's ability to "put himself/herself in someone else's place" and know how the other person feels. This is the ability to practice empathy.

Small business managers must maintain good relations with their customers if they are to establish a relationship that will encourage them to continue to patronize the business. They must also maintain good relations with their employees if they are to motivate them to perform their jobs at high levels of efficiency. In addition, they must be aware of the needs and motivations of customers if they are to adequately train employees to maintain good customer relations.

The entrepreneur-manager who maintains good human relations with customers, employees, suppliers, creditors, and the community is much more likely to succeed in business than the individual who does not practice good human relations.

COMMUNICATIONS ABILITY

Communications ability is the ability to communicate effectively in both written and oral communications. Good communication also means that both the sender and the receiver understand and are being understood. Two individuals may converse with each other and never really communicate because of psychological and/or semantic barriers.

The employee who tells the boss what he/she thinks the boss wants to hear rather than what he/she considers to be bad news is not communicating because of a psychological barrier. In addition, a person's environmental background often produces a personal value system and perception that may be entirely different from another person's value system and perception. To one person, belonging to a certain organization may mean social acceptance and be considered a favorable factor. To another person, it may mean conformity for the sake of conformity and be considered unfavorable. Words also have different meanings for different people. For example, the words "good" and "bad" have different meanings for different individuals.

Effective written communications are much more difficult to achieve than effective oral communications. The receiver does not have the sender's tone of voice and facial expressions to provide meaning. Also, there is not immediate feedback from the receiver to the sender to aid in clarification. To illustrate, a teacher might walk into his class and in a pleasant voice, with a smile, say, "This class can go jump in the lake." Very few students would be offended, although they might be puzzled. On the other hand, if the instructor wrote the same message on the blackboard and left it for the class to discover, he/she would probably receive a wide range of reactions, from anger to amusement.

The small business manager who can effectively communicate with customers, employees, suppliers, and creditors will be more likely to succeed than the manager who does not. For example, a business firm may send out to a good customer, who has forgotten to make a payment on time, a form letter that says, "We have not received your monthly payment; please remit at once." The business intends only to remind the customer; however, the customer may take it as a dun and an implication that he is not meeting his debts. Some individuals may be offended enough to stop trading with the business, and the firm would never know why.

TECHNICAL KNOWLEDGE

The small business must provide an acceptable product or service if it is to succeed. The small business entrepreneur who establishes a hamburger stand may be motivated, have mental ability, be able to practice good human relations, and be effective in communications; however, if he/she doesn't make a good hamburger, he/she will fail.

Technical knowledge is the one ability that most people are able to acquire if they try hard enough. If an entrepreneur is going to start a hamburger stand, it is wise that he/she work in one for a period of time to learn the technical aspects, such as hamburger production, equipment, and suppliers.

Small business entrepreneur-managers who have high levels of drive, mental ability, human relations ability, communications ability, and technical knowledge stand a much better chance of success than their counterparts who possess low levels of these same characteristics.

This neighborhood bakery is typical of the thousands of small businesses in the United States.

WHAT IS A SMALL BUSINESS?

Answers to the question, ''What is your definition of a small business?'' would likely reflect a wide range of understandings. No doubt some would consider a business small if it had no more than a specified number of employees (i.e., 5 or 10). Others would likely believe that a small business is one that limits its scope of operations to the local market area. Others frequently classify businesses as small by the nature of the firm, such as the local drugstore, clothing store, service station, barbershop, or jewelry store.

In order to provide a framework of understanding of what a small business is, two of the more common definitions are presented. The Committee on Economic Development (CED) offers a definition which states that a business will be classed as a small business if it meets two or more of the following criteria:

1. Management is independent. (Usually the managers are also owners.)
2. Capital is supplied and ownership is held by an individual or a small group.
3. The area of operations is mainly local. Workers and owners are in one home community. Markets need not be local.
4. Relative size within the industry—the business is small when compared to the biggest units in its field. The size of the top bracket varies greatly so that what might seem large in one field would be definitely small in another.[3]

The Small Business Administration (SBA), created by the Small Business Act of 1953, is an agency of the federal government with the designated purpose of assisting the small business owner-manager. The SBA's definition of small business states that a small business firm is "one which is independently owned and operated and not dominant in its field of operation."

The CED and the SBA definitions are similar in scope. Both use qualitative guidelines for size classification. Each emphasizes independent ownership and management and relative small size in the field of operation as guidelines for defining a business as small. These guidelines are appropriate for our definition of a "small business" as used in this text.

Until 1980, the SBA used a quantitative size classification based on sales receipts to determine if a firm was eligible for a loan through the SBA. Manufacturers were not included, however, as they were classified according to number of employees. These standards were:

Retail   Any retailing concern is classified as small if its annual receipts do not exceed $2 million.

Services   Any service concern is classified as small if its annual receipts do not exceed $2 million.

Construction   Any construction concern is small if its average annual receipts do not exceed $9.5 million averaged over the preceding three (3) fiscal years.

Transportation and warehousing   Any concern primarily engaged in passenger and freight transportation or warehousing is classified as small if its annual receipts do not exceed $1.5 million.

Wholesale   Any wholesaling concern is classified as small if its annual receipts do not exceed $9.5 million.

Manufacturing   Any manufacturing concern is classified as small if its number of employees does not exceed 250 persons and large if its number of employees exceeds 1500 persons. If employment is between 250 and 1500, a size which is standard for the industry is used.

[3]*Meeting the Special Problems of Small Business*. (New York: Committee for Economic Development, 1947), p. 14.

However, the proposed new SBA guidelines seek to simplify loan eligibility and use only one measure, the average number of full-time and part-time employees over a 12-month period. Varying size standards are set for 750 industries. For example, for industries in which there is considerable competition, the guidelines for being classed as small would be 15 or fewer employees.

In the text, we frequently refer to the manager, management, owner-manager, entrepreneur, entrepreneur-manager. Whenever such titles are used, they are a reference to the person in charge of a small business in either of the following situations: (1) where the owner is also the manager, or (2) where the manager is a paid employee.

IMPACT OF SMALL BUSINESS IN THE ECONOMY

Small businesses make significant contributions to our economy. The SBA identifies 10.4 million businesses as small. This means that nearly 97 percent of all businesses in the United States—sole proprietorships, partnerships, corporations, part-time businesses, and unincorporated professional activities—are small businesses. Nearly a third of all small businesses are in service industries and nearly a quarter are in retailing. As a source of employment, small businesses provide jobs for about 58 percent of the American work force, excluding farm employment. In terms of output, small businesses account for approximately 43 percent of the gross national product. Other dramatic influences of small business are underscored below.

Small firms account for nearly $8 out of every $10 made by construction firms.

Small firms account for nearly $7 out of every $10 made by retailers and wholesalers.

Members of minority groups own 4.4 percent of all U. S. businesses. Most minority owned businesses are small. Women own 4.6 percent of all U. S. businesses and 5.7 percent of all U. S. small businesses. Nearly all women-owned firms are small.

The livelihood of more than 100 million Americans is provided directly or indirectly by small business.

The small business sector creates more jobs than any other sector.

Between 1969 and 1976, 14 million Americans joined the labor force and in that same period, 9 million jobs were created. During that time, there was no increase in employment among the nation's top 1000 corporations, which had approximately 16 million employees both in 1969 and 1976. Of the 9 million individuals in the new jobs, 3 million went to work for state governments but the remaining 6 million worked for small firms.[4]

An additional measure of the prominence of small businesses is indicated by the fact that some 95.6 percent of all manufacturing concerns are classed as small, using SBA guidelines.

REWARDS AND ADVANTAGES OF SMALL BUSINESS OWNERSHIP

The small business owner-manager realizes distinct rewards and advantages that relate directly to the size and form of ownership.

PROFIT SERVES AS SALARY

A key incentive for small business entrepreneurs is that, being their own bosses, they are working for themselves. Thus, the profit derived from the company operations serves as one of the primary rewards of successful small business entrepreneurs. Some small businesses are extremely profitable. Profit is an important product of successful small business because it provides the owners with funds that can contribute to their families' comfort and well being. To a great extent, small business entrepreneurs control the size of their income by the type and quality of decisions they make, by the effort they expend, and by their managerial expertise. Thus, earning a profit is one of the strongest motivators for initiating a private business venture. As is shown in Figure 1-4, however, profit is certainly not the only reward small business entrepreneurs may receive from their successful small business.

EXPECTATIONS OF FUTURE WEALTH

Many small business entrepreneur-managers work more for the future of their business than for their present well-being. Their dreams of building their business to achieve future wealth and status motivates them and contributes considerable personal satisfaction. Many never realize their dreams, but some do. J. C. Penney, Henry Ford, and King C. Gillette are just a few of the entrepreneurs who saw their small business grow into modern corporate giants.

The classic example of the small business owner who turned his company into a corporate giant is H. Ross Perot. Perot started his company, Electronic Data Systems, Inc., when he was 32 years old with $1,000 and an idea. Just seven years later, he was worth over $1 billion.

[4]"Small Facts," *Enterprise*, March 1980, p. 15.

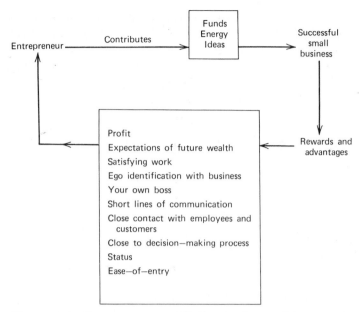

Figure 1-4   Entrepreneur contributions and rewards.

Many small business firms are operated as part-time activities by people who support themselves, and often their business, working at other full-time employment. They create and operate these part-time businesses in expectation of creating a full-time business for themselves. Some realize their dreams and others just go on supporting their part-time businesses for years with income from their full-time employment.

It should be noted that expectations of dreams for some people are more satisfying than the actual realization of the dreams. In this sense, small business firms that are not successful may provide considerable satisfaction to their creators for long periods of time.

SATISFYING WORK

Most people spend a third or more of the hours they are awake in the work environment. Unfortunately, many people in the world derive little satisfaction from their work. Some even detest their type of work to the extent that they continually look forward to the weekends and dread the next work week. Some individuals even suffer psychological illnesses as a result of their dislike for their work environment. People who really enjoy their work generally realize more out of life than people who do not.

Many small business managers are able to realize considerable satisfaction from work in their business. The television repairman who owns his own shop may derive a sense of accomplishment every time a broken set is fixed. In addition, he may derive even greater satisfaction in the management of the business. The challenge of creating a business and achieving the various tasks involved in its operation and growth can be very exhilarating to many people.

EGO IDENTIFICATION WITH THE BUSINESS

Most owners of small businesses started the firms themselves, often as a result of considerable sacrifice and work. As a result, it is understandable that most of them feel a close ego identification with their business. Many entrepreneur-managers feel the firm is, in a sense, an extension of their own being. The authors realized early in their consulting experience with small business firms that any criticism of the operations of the firm had to be handled very tactfully because it was common for the entrepreneur-manager to take strong personal offense.

Almost all small business entrepreneur-managers who have established a successful small business exhibit a very strong sense of personal pride in their business, which is certainly justified. In fact, it is not at all uncommon for the entrepreneur-managers to want their children to carry on the family business because of personal pride.

ENTREPRENEUR-MANAGERS ARE THEIR OWN BOSS

Entrepreneur-managers of a small business are their own boss. This provides personal satisfaction to many individuals. Making decisions for the business is not only a continuing challenge but can also be a strong source of satisfaction to many people. Entrepreneur-managers, in a sense, feel that they control their own destiny and do not have to answer to anyone for their actions. In addition, the rewards they receive are in direct proportion to how well they perform in business. Being their own boss is a common reason given by small business entrepreneur-managers for starting their own business and would appear to be a strong motivator for many individuals.

Some small business entrepreneur-managers have continued to operate their own small businesses for years even though they could have made considerably more money working for someone else. Areas of personal satisfaction, including being their own boss, are undoubtedly primary motivators for these individuals.

SHORT LINES OF COMMUNICATION

Since there is usually only one level of management in the small business enterprise, face-to-face, direct contact is possible between the manager and the employees when giving instructions or discussing specific problems relating to the business. The one-to-one communication relationship significantly increases the chances of reducing or eliminating many common communications problems encountered in larger firms. In larger firms, for example, messages ordinarily must pass from the sender through several other persons in the chain of command before the person for whom the communications are intended finally sees or hears them. In this relaying process messages can easily become distorted or misinterpreted.

Even though lines of communication are short and direct in small businesses, managers must exercise great care in communication. As we have already mentioned, they must be aware that it is quite possible for such common communication problems as semantic barriers, psychological barriers, and selective perception to persist even in face-to-face communication.

The small business owner-manager should recognize these barriers and take advantage of the opportunities they have to avoid them as a result of their strategic position in the communication chain. Furthermore, they should realize that direct oral communication with employees can eliminate much of the confusion or misinterpretation that so often results from written instructions.

In the small enterprise, effective use can be made of communication upward from the employees to the owner-manager. This bottom to top communication process is an effective method for improving understanding within the organization.

Effective utilization of the short lines of communication will enable the small business owner-managers to reduce many of the human problems caused by faulty communication between themselves and their employees. On the other hand, poor communication will have a negative influence on the organizational environment and consequently increase human relations problems.

CLOSE CONTACT WITH EMPLOYEES AND CUSTOMERS

Small business owners have the opportunity to develop and maintain harmonious working relationships with their employees. Since there is usually only one level of management (with the owner and manager often the same person), direct interaction is possible between the manager and employees. Through this relationship, they have the opportunity for greater understanding of employee needs and wants. Likewise, employees can gain a greater measure of understanding for the manager's position. Problems can be worked out on a face-to-face basis, and as noted above, communication problems can be significantly reduced because of direct relationships. The employees and the manager often work side by side on an informal rather than a formal basis. In this way, each participant learns to respect each other's position and viewpoints. Furthermore, in the small firm, it is vital that all the members cooperate to form an effective work team.

One of the particular advantages of the small business firm is that it provides the type of environment in which close personal customer relationships can be cultivated. This condition is ordinarily not possible in larger companies. Customers may even become known on a first name basis, and the manager knows what they are buying. Customers can be given personal, individualized consideration to fit their specific needs since the small businessman recognizes the value of such relationships to the success of the business. Customers like this preferential treatment and it is often a major reason why they return frequently to make additional purchases. The manager is also able to handle customer complaints directly. By recognizing the opportunities they have and by dealing fairly with their customers, small business owners can do much to insure their future success.

CLOSE TO DECISION-MAKING PROCESS

As we have stated, there is often only one level of management in the small firm; thus, the small business owner is directly involved in all decisions affecting the on-going business concern. Whereas the manager of a larger firm often has to refer matters upward in order to get a decision, the small firm manager can make needed decisions on the spot. This is an especially important advantage where time is a critical factor.

STATUS

In most communities, the entrepreneur-manager ranks high on the work status hierarchy. There is a wide range of status even within the small business group. For example, the principal stockholder-president of the local bank is usually assigned a higher status in the community than the service station owner-manager. In spite of this range of status, the community usually perceives a higher status for the small business entrepreneur group than most forms of blue collar and white collar employment. In fact, in many small communities, small business owners are often assigned to the top of the status scale.

It should also be pointed out that perceived status is more important to an individual's satisfaction than actual status assigned by other people. Many small business entrepreneur-managers feel they have high levels of status in their communities and derive considerable satisfaction from this impression, regardless of whether or not it is actually true.

EASE OF ENTRY

An attractive feature of the small business operations, particularly the single proprietorship, is the ease with which one can go into business. All that is required to open the doors for business is a location, any special operating licenses required by city or state government, and some capital. No other restrictions are normally placed on entrance into small business.

SOME LIMITATIONS OF SMALL BUSINESS FIRMS

Several limitations which should be considered in conjunction with small business ownership are discussed below.

LACK OF SPECIALIZATION

In a large business firm, specialists are hired to perform critical functions and activities. Accountants maintain company financial records, salespeople actively make contacts in the field to sell the company's products, members of the personnel staff actively recruit the type of qualified persons needed to fill job vacancies. Larger firms have the financial resources available to enable them to hire individuals who possess the expertise needed to staff the variety of positions in the firm—professional managers, staff personnel, and the like. In the small business, entrepreneur-managers generally perform all or most of these activities since their monetary resources are limited. Hence, they must be generalists rather than specialists. They must be familiar with all phases of the firm's operations—general management, accounting, sales management, production management, personnel management and any other necessary functions that must be performed. Because they have many duties to carry out, they frequently do not have enough time to devote to long-range planning of the firm. Instead, most of their time is spent in dealing with the current day's activity or crisis. Thus, a disadvantage to many small firms is their inability to hire and utilize specialists in the functional areas.

CONFINING, LONG HOURS OF WORK

Considerations on the positive side of owning one's own business included being your own boss and profit serving as salary. One disadvantage is that managers of the small business must do most of the work themselves. Very often, entrepreneur-managers are the first to arrive in the morning and the last to leave at night. If they become ill, they cannot call in sick to their boss. They cannot take off a few days without making special arrangements for someone to operate the business for them. And if someone from outside the family is hired, an added expense is incurred.

It is not uncommon for such firms to be open six days a week, and many are open seven days a week (such as restaurants, ice cream parlors, drugstores). Owners work 60, 70, and often more hours each week. For example, a steakhouse owner is open for business from 11 A.M. to 9 P.M. seven days a week, or a 70-hour week. And this does not include the additional preparation that must be done prior to opening and closing. An auto parts wholesaler who has no employees keeps his shop open six days a week, from 7 A.M. to 7 P.M., and occasionally it is open Sundays for a few hours. The only break he has in his day's routine is when his wife takes over for him for a 30-minute lunch break. Hours of operation must be adjusted to correspond to the times it is convenient for his customers.

RISK OF FUNDS

While there is the advantage of profit making, there is the risk of losing funds. This disadvantage is noted since funds invested in the firm are largely the owner's own funds or borrowed funds. Thus, the owner may be personally liable for any and all debts. Hence, it is possible that the small business owner-manager may not only lose a lifetime of personal savings but may also build up liabilities that will take years to pay off.

COMMON PROBLEMS OF SMALL BUSINESS FIRMS

While walking down the street of a city or town, large or small, one sometimes sees a "going out of business" sign hanging in a store window. Certainly the small business owner did not intend this to happen when the store opened for business.

A successful small business offers too many rewards to owners for them to be discouraged by the historical failure rate of small businesses. In this section, some of the common problems encountered by small business owners are examined. We were apprehensive about covering the topic of business failures so early in the text. However, by analyzing the causes of these problems, prospective small business managers can adequately prepare themselves in management knowledge and skills and thus prevent these problems from arising in their business firms.

A business for sale and a store for rent.

Each year, Dun & Bradstreet reports on the causes of business failure for all sizes of businesses. These causes are shown in Figure 1-5. Knowledge of the causes of failure should enable small business owners to eliminate or avoid all the causes of small business failure. The monetary and psychological rewards that can be derived from small business ownership and management should not be passed up because of the existence of a high failure rate. Rather, armed with adequate knowledge, the small business owner-manager can avoid the usual pitfalls. It is the intention of this text to provide that knowledge.

As the data indicate, over 90 percent of the business failures were directly attributed to the owners' lack of managerial skill. Inadequate management was demonstrated through lack of business experience and through incompetence. Only a small percentage of business failures are attributed to neglect, fraud, or disaster. The cause for a small percentage of failures was not available.

COMMON PROBLEMS OF SMALL BUSINESS

CAUSES		PERCENT OF TOTAL FAILURES
Inadequate management		93.1
Lack of experience in line	16.4	
Lack of managerial experience	14.1	
Unbalanced experience	21.6	
Incompetence	41.0	
Neglect		1.6
Fraud		1.3
Disaster		0.6
Reason unknown		3.4

Figure 1-5 Some common causes of business failure. (*Source.* Dun & Bradstreet.)

INADEQUATE MANAGEMENT

In the dynamic business environment that exists today, managers of small firms must be alert to the rapid changes that occur. Changes in clothing styles, eating habits, and energy supplies all have a tremendous impact which owners must recognize and to which they must react.

Failure to identify and respond to changing social, economic, and environmental conditions will lead to serious problems or eventual failure of the firm. A number of problems faced by small business managers caused by inadequate management are discussed below.

Lack of Experience in Line

Sometimes owner-managers may lack experience in the line of business they enter. They may have a strong background in one line of business but be unsuccessful in another due to their unfamiliarity with the specific problems of the new line of business. A case in point is the mortician who sold his mortuary business and purchased a jewelry store. Within a year the jewelry store closed. The primary cause of this unsuccessful business venture was that the owner lacked experience in this completely different line of business.

Lack of Management Experience

Another form of inexperience is shown by a lack of management experience. There is a vast difference between being the best machinist, mechanic, or salesperson and being able to manage a machine shop, an auto repair shop, or a retail store. While the manager of the firm usually has a specific job skill, the possession of a particular job skill in no way guarantees success in the new role as manager. Without proper management training, the skills and techniques necessary for effective management will not likely be attained.

Overconcentration of Experience

An overconcentration of experience in one function may present a problem to the small firm owner-manager. Owner-managers must have the ability to view the firm conceptually. This means they should be able to perceive the need for, interrelationship of, and contribution of each activity of the firm. If owner-managers concentrate a major portion of their time and energy on the one function which is their interest and speciality—either sales, production, or finance—and neglect the others, this approach will likely have an adverse effect on the total firm. For example, managers may focus their efforts on sales. In order to complete a sale, they may promise delivery of merchandise by certain dates when they know the firm does not have the productive capacity to meet such deadlines. When the firm fails to make delivery on the scheduled date, they alienate the customer, the lifeblood of the firm. Thus small business managers must recognize that the health and vitality of the firm depend in large measure on giving balanced attention to all functions of the firm. In addition, the above illustration underscores the need for small business managers to be honest with their customers. Ethical dealings with customers help to build repeat sales and enhance the small business owner-manager's image in the business community.

Incompetence of Management

The major hazard of the small firm is the incompetence of the manager. From the standpoint of the firm, owner-managers are incompetent because they do not possess the leadership ability and knowledge necessary to operate their own firms.

Weak Competitive Position

Competition is the bulwark of our economy. Firms that cannot efficiently compete in such areas as services offered, prices charged, or quality of merchandise sold definitely have difficulty surviving. For example, a small restaurant manager may lower the price of the hamburgers served in order to match lower prices charged by competing firms. However, while lowering the price, the owner-manager may have to use a lower grade of meat or a thinner meat patty. If this kind of action is taken to remain competitive, the outlook for the firm is bleak. Since most business firms, and especially small firms, must depend on repeat customer patronage for continued survival and growth, lowering the quality of the product is likely to encourage customers to patronize competitors.

Lack of Proper Inventory Control

Since small business managers are generalists, they may lack an understanding of the importance of proper inventory control. Too large an inventory results in such common problems as the owner's money being tied up or waste through spoilage or obsolescence. An inadequate inventory means that goods are unavailable for delivery to customers when they are demanded. For example, a farm equipment dealer in a small town had a policy of maintaining a bare minimum of merchandise in stock. He made no effort to determine which parts had a high turnover. Most customers, when they needed a part for replacement, required it immediately. However, the dealer was unable to supply the parts. Instead, he would offer to order the parts from the manufacturer, a process requiring several days for delivery. Since customers couldn't wait this long for replacement parts, they were forced to go to the neighboring city 17 miles away where there was a farm equipment dealer who could supply their needs. As a result of the first dealer's inventory policy, he lost many sales and customers and is no longer in business, while his competitor in the nearby town has a very active, flourishing business.

Inadequate Credit Control

A common problem facing small business managers is whether or not to extend credit. Those firms that do grant credit must protect against the practice of extending too much credit. One small firm had at one time $10,000 worth accounts receivable on its books. Much of this credit had been extended to "friends" of the owner. When these bills became due, most of them were never collected since the "friends" had disappeared. And while it was difficult or impossible for the owner to collect his accounts, he could not postpone payment of his bills or purchase of new stock for inventory, despite his financial predicament resulting from his inadequate credit policy. Fortunately the firm was able to survive. Survival was made possible by a complete turnabout in policy. The owner of the firm no longer extends any credit; all sales are for cash only. And while the owner of the firm was uncertain as to the effect this would have on his business, the results have been positive. Today, the small firm is on sound financial ground.

Low Sales Volume

For all lines of business—manufacturing, wholesaling, retailing, construction, and commercial service—inadequate sales represents a common problem of the small firm. Income for the firm is generated by sales. Without income, the result is obvious—failure of the business. Many reasons contribute to a poor sales record. Some of the most commonly identified factors include a poor location, inferior products, ineffective advertising, prices out of line with those of competitors, and poor service.

Poor Location

Site selection frequently is not accorded the attention it should receive. Too often, a location is selected for some superficial reason, such as the availability of a building to rent or to buy, closeness of a facility to one's home, heavy traffic flow, or any other of a myriad of reasons. Yet none of these reasons may be the salient locational factors necessary to help make the business a success. For example, a heavy flow of pedestrian traffic past a site does not guarantee that shoppers will drop in, much less purchase merchandise. It is possible that the traffic flow is heavy simply because people are rushing by on their way to a bus stop or to their place of work and do not have time to stop and shop.

NEGLECT

While only a small percentage of firms fail because of neglect, neglect is a particular problem of the small business owner-manager. Since the owners are frequently the managers, they must guard their firm against personal neglect. Common reasons for neglecting the business include improper use of time, poor health, laziness, marital problems, or apathy. Sometimes managers become too involved and devote too much time to community or other outside activities. While these activities have merit, owner-managers must be careful not to place these activities ahead of the firm's interest. The owner-managers should establish priorities for themselves relative to their business. They must keep in mind the objectives of the firm and not become easily diverted by too many outside activities or disenchanted by minor business or personal setbacks.

FRAUD

Fraud is the deliberate misrepresentation of the status of the business by the owner-manager in order to deceive others. Some means by which fraud is committed include using a misleading name for the company, issuing false and misleading financial statements, and disposing of the assets of the firm in an irregular manner.

DISASTER

There are some circumstances over which the owner may have little or no control. Natural disasters, such as an earthquake, flood, or hurricane may wipe out the small business owner. In February 1971, southern California was struck by a devastating earthquake, causing millions of dollars in damage to business firms. Hurricane Agnes, in June of 1972, was the most destructive storm in U.S. history. Some $3 billion in property damage was reported, with many thousands of businesses damaged or destroyed. Hurricane Frederick caused some $2 billion damage along the Gulf coast in 1979. Fire, labor problems, burglary, and theft of merchandise by employees are further examples of types of disasters that confront the small business owner.

A store selling baby clothes and furniture suffered $10,000 damage to the store and its contents when the driver of an auto pushed the accelerator rather than the brake, causing the auto to jump the curb and crash through the show window into the building.

A convenience store had damages of $15,000 caused by the driver of an auto that crashed into the store front.

A lawnmower repair-rental firm burned on Christmas weekend, causing $25,000 damage to the store building, some 50 lawnmowers, tools, and accessories.

The bookkeeper of a small restaurant supply firm was arrested and charged with embezzling $23,591 over a 10-month period.

Insurance coverage and bonding of employees can provide some measure of protection against these occurrences and thus help to ease some of the burden of financial loss.

INCREASED VOLUME OF GOVERNMENT REPORTS

While not a problem identified in the Dun & Bradstreet data and not a problem limited solely to the small business, the increased volume of required reports is placing a proportionally heavier burden on small firms, due primarily to their limited financial and personnel resources. One government source estimates that of the $40 billion annual paperwork cost, half is borne by small businesses. One small manufacturer spends between $12,000 and $15,000 annually responding to required government requests for information. Another small business owner estimates that one-fourth of her time is spent in filling out required reports, leaving much less time to manage the firm. Currently, several congressional committees are studying this problem and seeking remedies.

The foregoing discussion of common problems emphasizes that 9 of every 10 failures are due to incompetence, unbalanced experience, and lack of managerial experience. Hence, the alarm signal should be sounded for persons planning to operate their own business. Equipped with this information, they should be able to learn from the unfortunate experience of others. With adequate preparation in and consideration of these significant areas, small business owner-managers will greatly enhance their chances for a successful business venture.

A FAMILY OPERATION

Many small businesses are a family operation, and the business plays an important role in the daily existence of the family. Often, all members of the family spend at least some time working in the business, and business matters are discussed by the family at the dinner table.

It is common for the wife to work in the business. In service firms, she usually answers the phone, takes orders and messages, and keeps the books of the business. In retail establishments, she usually performs these same functions in addition to waiting on customers.

Sometimes the wife is the entrepreneur-manager of a small business. The female entrepreneur-manager has traditionally been active in such areas of small business as dress, gift, and floral shops. Often the wife is the entrepreneur-manager while the husband works as a full-time employee for someone else. In these cases, the husband's role in the business is usually in physical-type activities, such as maintenance of the store. Based on the current trend in female sentiment and movement, it seems realistic to expect female entrepreneur-management in a wide range of small businesses in the future.

Children of small business owners often perform some duties in the family business as soon as they are old enough. Making deliveries, cleaning up, waiting on customers, and operating a cash register are common tasks for children to perform. In skilled trades, children of the owner often learn trade skills as apprentices to their father. It has been common practice, in all nations throughout history, for many skilled trades to be passed down from father to son. In addition, small business firms are often passed down from parents to their children, and some have operated in the same family for generations.

There are many small businesses that are in operation and providing a service to customers that could not exist except as family operations. The profit of the firm is in reality a salary for the family. If many small business firms were

A family-operated business.

forced to pay salaries to other people for work being performed by the family, it would be financially impossible for them to continue to exist.

SOCIAL ACTIVITY

It they are to be successful, many small business entrepreneur-managers and their spouses must make a commitment to social activity to promote their business. Social activity is an excellent means of promoting contact. For example, the owner of an insurance agency usually depends on his social contacts to provide many of his potential policy holders. The owner of a retail store often builds customer patronage for his/her store from acquaintances he/she meets socially. The advantages of social activity are particularly important to owners of service and retail establishments in small towns.

Many small business managers find it desirable to belong to such organizations as the local Chamber of Commerce, country clubs, and various civic organizations. Many spouses of small business managers also help the small business by belonging to various clubs and organizations. The wife or husband of a small business owner-manager can usually contribute considerably to customer patronage through social activity. It is not at all uncommon to find the small business manager and/or spouse engaged in various community projects sponsored by civic organizations.

In the final analysis of this chapter, we must conclude that the entrepreneur is vital to the economic well-being of the nation. In exchange for his/her services, the successful entrepreneur is rewarded by profit and various forms of personal satisfaction.

THE FUTURE OF SMALL BUSINESS

What is the outlook for the continued growth of the small business firm, and the opportunities it provides for individual freedom and development, as a vital force in the business community? If this question is answered based only on past performance of small firms, it is apparent that the small enterprise has an essential role to play. Not only does the small firm provide avenues through which opportunities are opened to individuals, permitting them to develop and express themselves, but taken collectively, the small business community also makes a significant contribution to our total economic system.

In Congressional hearings before a House Small Business subcommittee, one of the major conclusions was that the reliance of the U. S. economy on small businesses is growing rapidly. Small business is providing most of the new jobs and most of industry's scientific and technological development.

The Small Business Administration reports that in the last eight years, U.S. employment increased by 9.5 million. The top 1000 manufacturers provided less than one percent of the growth–74,897 new jobs. State governments added three million, the services sector half a million, and small businesses the other six million.

In the area of research, the Office of Management and the Budget showed that while the small business sector received only 3.5 percent of the federal research and development dollars, it accounts for more than half of all scientific development.

Most of our economic growth has come from innovation. The first airplane, the jet engine and the helicopter, the office copying machine, the instant camera, and air conditioning—these and the industries surrounding them are among the breakthroughs that came from the workshops of small business people. A National Science Foundation study found evidence that small firms are producing four times as many innovations for each R & D dollar as medium-sized firms and 24 times as many as the largest firms.

DISCUSSION QUESTIONS

1. What functions do entrepreneurs perform, and why are they important in a private enterprise economic system?
2. Why are the following personality characteristics important contributors to the success of the small business entrepreneur-manager?
   Drive
   Mental ability
   Human relations ability
   Communications ability
   Technical knowledge
3. What are the different ways of defining a small business?
4. Discuss the importance of small business to the economic system of the United States.
5. Is profit the only reward an entrepreneur derives from a small business? Explain.
6. What is the status level of the small business entrepreneur?
7. Explain the advantages and limitations of the small business.
8. Identify the common problems of business failure. Which problems are the major cause of most failures?
9. Why is a family operation important to many small businesses?
10. List some of the tasks the spouse and children of the entrepreneur-manager perform in a family-operated business.
11. Is social activity important to some small business owners? Explain.

STUDENT PROJECTS

1. Prepare a short written report outlining the reasons why you would like to go into business for yourself. In addition, list three to five types of business in which you would be interested.

2. Prepare a list of reasons against going into business for yourself.
3. Interview the owner-manager of a local small business and obtain the following information.
   A. Why did he/she start the small business?
   B. Find out which of the personality characteristics he/she feels are his/her strong points and which need to be improved.
      1. Drive
      2. Mental ability
      3. Human relations ability
      4. Communications ability
      5. Technical knowledge
   C. List in order of importance the following advantages he/she receives from small business ownership.
      1. Profit
      2. Expectations of future wealth
      3. Satisfying work
      4. Ego identification with business
      5. Your own boss
      6. Short lines of communication
      7. Close contact with employees and customers
      8. Close to decision making process
      9. Status
      10. Ease of entry
   D. Does any member of the owner-manager's family work in the business? If so, what are their tasks?
   E. Does the owner and the owner's spouse engage in social activity? Does the owner feel that this increases customer patronage?

CASE A

REFLECTIONS OF A SMALL BUSINESS OWNER

The following letter, written by a small business owner, are his reflections after 10 years of successful business operation.

As with most other things, the advantages and disadvantages of small business have drastically changed in the past 10 years. Many years ago there was more money to be made by owning your own small business than working for someone else and, since you were your own boss, there was more freedom as far as time off. Today many large companies, particularly those which are government subsidized, are in a position to pay larger salaries, give more time off and offer more benefits than the small business owner. Many changes have affected the potential profit for small business, some of which are higher minimum wage (normally with little or no additional volume or profit), the collection and disbursement of various taxes (sales taxes, etc.) which is costly at higher hourly wages and no profit, so much additional bookkeeping and reports required by government (small business cannot afford computers and many new aids because of cost). The trend now is to consumer protection which has made it more difficult to meet their regulations on a small budget and small volume. Many of these regulations have actually increased the price to the consumer since the cost of complying with these rules and regulations must be added to the price, with little or no benefit to the consumer. The trend as far as laws governing credit collection has also been to protect the consumer; therefore, the small business owner has more problems trying to collect when people refuse to pay for their purchases.

The advantages of owning and managing a small business as compared to working for a large concern are less in number but probably more satisfying personally. There is a sense of accomplishment which could not be attained otherwise. The small businessman has more opportunity to "do his thing" by expressing himself in advertising, etc. The good manager is in a position to enjoy constant income when faced with illness or a necessity for being gone.

If I had it to do over again, I would still own my small business because of the personal satisfaction.

Very truly yours,

Question

As a student of small business, evaluate what this small business owner is saying about the status of small business ownership.

CASE B
ERNEST BOSWELL

Ernest Boswell has been employed for the past 15 years as a traveling salesman for the Tender Meat Company. His work involves calling on selected meat market managers of grocery stores in a city of 250,000 as well as meat markets and grocery stores in smaller towns within a 100-mile radius of the larger city.

Gauged by the annual dollar volume of his sales efforts, Ernest has been one of the most successful salesmen in the company's 50-year history. A large degree of his success is attributed to the fact that he has excellent knowledge about meat (cuts, quality, etc.), and this ability has earned him the respect of market managers. Ernest also feels that he has learned a good bit about managing a market, based on the conversations he has had with his customers and his own personal observations gathered during his sales calls.

Part of his sales territory extends into a number of surrounding smaller cities. During one of his calls on the Southside Meat Market, he learned from the owner that he is considering selling the market. Ernest has been calling on this market for 10 years, and he knows that this is the only meat market in town and that it has an established clientele.

Recently, Ernest has grown tired of traveling. He wonders if this might not be the opportunity he has been seeking to "settle down" in one place.

Questions

1. Does Ernest's background as a successful meat sales person assure him of success as a meat market owner?
2. Discuss some of the major problems he is likely to encounter as an owner.
3. What advantages should he be aware of if he purchases his own business?
4. Explain the disadvantages to Ernest of owning his own business.

CASE C

BROGAN'S BARBECUE

Bill Brogan has worked for a large cereal manufacturer as a salesman for six years, but he doesn't like his job. Some of the things Bill doesn't like about his job are:

1. He doesn't like his boss.
2. He is the top salesman, and he feels he works harder than any salesman, but is not getting ahead as fast as he feels he should.
3. He has suggested several changes and promotional ideas that made the company a considerable amount of money, but he never received anything for his ideas.
4. He feels being a salesman has little status.
5. He feels the work is not challenging.

Bill does like his contact with the customers, and they all seem to like him.

Bill and his wife like to entertain and they often have people over for barbecue cookouts. He has also been the organizer of several barbecue dinners to raise funds for two of the civic organizations to which he belongs. Everyone tells Bill that he makes the best barbecue they have ever tasted and he should go into the business. Bill has started to consider these comments seriously as a means of getting out of his present job. He is thinking about establishing a western type barbecue restaurant in the town of 30,000 where he now lives.

Bill has found what he considers a good location for rent. It would require very little work to adapt it to a western atmosphere for a barbecue restaurant. Bill has also talked to an equipment distributor and found that his savings would be sufficient to purchase the equipment the distributor says he would need and still have some money left.

Bill has no experience in small business and is hesitant to invest his life savings even though he would like to quit his present job. His wife likes the idea and says she could help in the business.

Questions

1. Do you feel Bill has the personality characteristics that contribute to success in small business? Explain.
2. Do you feel Bill could be happy running a small business? Explain.
3. What are some of the tasks his wife could perform in helping him run the barbecue restaurant?
4. What are some of the positive factors that would indicate Bill might be a success in the small business?
5. What are some of the negative factors? How could Bill overcome them?
6. Would you advise Bill to establish the barbecue restaurant?

2
OWNERSHIP

PREVIEW OF THIS CHAPTER

1. In this chapter, you will learn that the needs and characteristics of the business determine which form of ownership best fits the business.

2. You will discover the advantages and disadvantages of the sole proprietorship.

3. You will also discover the advantages and disadvantages of the partnership.

4. You will understand the difference between general and limited partners.

5. You will learn about stocks and bonds and the difference between preferred and common stock.

6. If you ever wondered about corporations, you will be interested in the advantages and disadvantages of the corporation as a form of ownership.

7. You will understand how a joint venture functions and where it is used.

8. You will learn how businesses cease to function through dissolution and bankruptcy.

9. If you ever go into business for yourself, you will be interested in the ways different forms of ownership are taxed and how Subchapter "S" can save you money.

10. You will be able to understand these key words:

Sole proprietorship	Dividends
Partnership	Preferred stock
Corporation	Common stock
Articles of copartnership	Par value
General partner	Cumulative dividends
Limited partner	Joint venture
Interest	Stockholders

Bonds	Corporation tax
Dissolution	Subchapter "S" corporations
Bankruptcy	

There are three forms of business ownership: (1) the sole proprietorship, (2) the partnership, and (3) the corporation. In addition, the joint venture, technically an adaptation of the partnership form of ownership, is increasing in usage.

Small business owners often ask which is the best form of ownership. There is no one answer to this question because it depends entirely on the individual business. The corporation form of ownership is usually not suited to a "mom and pop" operation, and the sole proprietorship form of ownership would be completely impossible for a giant firm like American Telephone and Telegraph.

The needs and characteristics of each business dictate which form of ownership is most suited to that business (see Fig. 2-1). Some of the factors that should be considered when selecting a form of ownership are:

1. The problems of creating the form of ownership.
2. The amount of capital needed in the business.
3. The amount of profit available for distribution.
4. The authority relationship in operating the business.
5. The length of life of the business and need for continuity of the business.
6. The extent of liability to the owners.
7. Legal restrictions of the form of ownership.
8. Taxation

THE SOLE PROPRIETORSHIP

The sole proprietorship is the most common form of business ownership in the United States today, as shown in Figure 2-2. The sole proprietorship is owned by one person and has distinct advantages and disadvantages relative to other forms of ownership.

ADVANTAGES OF THE SOLE PROPRIETORSHIP

The advantages of the sole proprietorship are as follows.

1. It is the easiest form of ownership to establish. All the owner must do to create this form of ownership is to acquire the assets (permits are sometimes

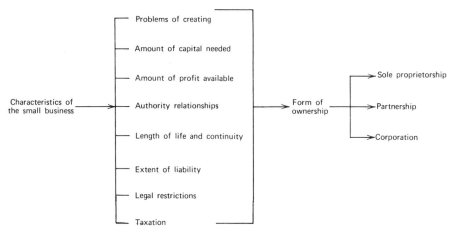

Figure 2-1 Characteristics of each small business determine best form of ownership.

required, such as a liquor license for a tavern) to begin his or her business and it is automatically a sole proprietorship.

2. All profits earned by the business belong to the owner and do not have to be shared with anyone else.
3. The owner of the business has total authority over his business.
4. There are no special legal restrictions on the sole proprietorship form of ownership. Only those general areas of civil and criminal law that apply to all forms of business ownership apply to the sole proprietorship.

DISADVANTAGES OF THE SOLE PROPRIETORSHIP

1. The amount of capital available to the business is limited to the assets and credit of the one owner. The degree of the problem rests with the amount of capital needed in the business. Many people in the United States could finance a small hot dog stand in a rented building. However, no one could amass the wealth necessary to sustain General Motors which has assets valued at over $30 billion.
2. Length of life of the business is dependent on the owner. In general terms, the owner may close his doors and go out of business at any time he chooses. In addition, technically, if he dies, the business ceases to exist. Of course, the assets are still in existence. It may be sold or a relative may take over the firm, at which time it then becomes a new sole proprietorship.
3. The owner has unlimited liability. The owner is liable not only for the amount he has invested in the business but also for all other assets he owns. In cases of bankruptcy or legal judgments, all assets, with the exception of

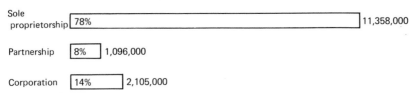

Figure 2-2 Number of sole proprietorships, partnerships, and corporations in the United States. (*Source:* Statistical Abstract of the United States, 1979.)

his homestead and other items specified by state law, may be taken from him to satisfy legal claims.

THE PARTNERSHIP

A partnership consists of two or more people. The partnership may be established almost on any basis the partners may wish.

Although it is not required legally, it is best for partners to have legal counsel draw up an instrument called "articles of copartnership" (see Fig. 2-3). This agreement should state what each partner is to contribute to the partnership, what authority each partner has, and how the profit or loss is to be shared. If an articles of copartnership agreement is not created, the laws of the state in which the partnership exists determine distribution of authority, profit, and loss in cases of dispute.

Articles of copartnership should contain the following general information.

1. Effective date of the partnership.
2. Name of the firm.
3. Names and addresses of the partners.
4. Nature and scope of business activity of the partnership.
5. Location of all business activity.
6. Period of time the partnership is to exist.
7. Contributions of each partner.
8. Distribution of profit and loss.
9. Withdrawals and salaries of the partners.
10. Contribution of time by the partners to the business.
11. Authority relationship of the partners.
12. Partners access to books and records of the partnership.
13. Terms and method of withdrawal of any partners.
14. Distribution of assets and name of business if dissolved.
15. A provision for arbitration of disputes.

107—Article of Co-Partnership.

JULIUS BLUMBERG, INC., LAW BLANK PUBLISHERS
80 EXCHANGE PLACE AT BROADWAY, NEW YORK

Articles of Agreement,

Made the *day of* *one thousand nine hundred and*

BETWEEN

WITNESSETH: *The said parties above named have agreed to become co-partners and by these presents form a partnership under the trade name and style of*

for the purpose of buying, selling, vending and manufacturing

and all other goods, wares and merchandise belonging to the said business and to occupy the following premises:

their co-partnership to commence on the *day of* *19*
and to continue

and to that end and purpose the said

to be used and employed in common between them for the support and management of the said business, to their mutual benefit and advantage. AND *it is agreed by and between the parties to these presents, that at all times during the continuance of their co-partnership, they and each of them will give their attendance, and do their and each of their best endeavors, and to the utmost of their skill and power, exert themselves for their joint interest, profit, benefit and advantage, and truly employ, buy, sell and merchandise with their joint stock, and the increase thereof, in the business aforesaid.* AND ALSO, *that they shall and will at all times during the said co-partnership, bear, pay and discharge equally between them, all rents and other expenses that may be required for the support and management of the said business; and that all gains, profit and increase, that shall come,*

Figure 2-3 A section of a standard form for creating articles of copartnership.

TYPES OF PARTNERS

There are two basic categories of partners in a partnership—the general partner (sometimes called ordinary) and the limited partner (sometimes called special).

General Partner

There is no legal limit to the number of general partners a partnership may have, but there is usually a requirement that it have at least one. The general partner has unlimited liability. He may be held liable not only to the extent of his investment in the business but also any other assets he may own (excluding certain homestead items specified by state law). The general partner must also take an active part in the operations of the business.

Limited Partner

There is no legal requirement that a partnership must have any limited partners, and there is no limit to the number it may have. The primary difference between the general partner and the limited partner is that the limited partner has limited liability. The limited partner can lose only his investment in the partnership. Other assets he may own cannot be seized to satisfy debts of the partnership. Also the limited partner may or may not take an active part in the management of the business. In some cases, customers and the general public may not even know the limited partner is a partner in the business.

ADVANTAGES OF THE PARTNERSHIP FORM OF OWNERSHIP

1. Creation of the partnership form of ownership requires little effort and involves little cost. Usually, the only cost in creating the partnership form of ownership is a legal fee for drawing up and recording the articles of copartnership.
2. Profit may be divided in any manner prescribed by the partners. Sometimes, formulas are created to divide profit on the basis of funds invested in the business or time spent in the business.
3. Usually, more capital may be raised by the partnership than by the sole proprietorship. The amount of capital that can be raised by the partnership is limited to the assets and credit of all the partners.
4. The partnership allows for limited partners who have limited liability. This is important not only to the limited partners but also to the capital-accumulating ability of the partnership. The protection of limited liability makes it easier to obtain investment funds from people who would not become general partners because of the risk involved.

5. Any type of authority relationship may be established in the partnership. Often, it allows people of widely diverse talents and skills to enter into a business. For example, one person may be a highly skilled technician in the production of a product but not have sales or management skills. Another person may have sales ability and management skills but not have sufficient technical skills to produce the product. Together in a partnership, they may be very successful, where alone they may have failed.
6. Usually, no special legal restrictions exist for partnerships that do not exist for the sole proprietorship.

Advantages offered by the partnership not offered by the sole proprietorship are (1) its ability to combine capital and/or skills of more than one person, and (2) the limited liability of being a limited partner.

DISADVANTAGES OF THE PARTNERSHIP FORM OF OWNERSHIP

1. While the partnership usually has greater capital accumulating ability than the sole proprietorship, it usually has far less potential than the corporation.
2. There is great potential for authority disputes in partnerships. Although the articles of copartnership generally spell out the authority of each partner, it is impossible to make allowances for all contingencies. There are usually areas of overlap of authority where conflict may arise. In addition, it is unusually difficult for even two people to function in the operations of a business without some friction. The addition of each person to the partnership geometrically increases the potential of friction. It is not at all unusual for a highly successful partnership to break up because of personality clashes in the operations of the business.
3. General partners contribute a limited life to the partnership. The withdrawal or death of any general partner terminates the partnership. The remaining partners may settle claims of the withdrawn partner and start a new partnership. However, it can often be a real problem to obtain enough funds to buy the ownership of a partner. Limited partners aid continuity of the business because they may withdraw, die, or sell their ownership in the partnership without terminating the partnership.
4. The unlimited liability of the general partners can be a serious disadvantage to the general partners. For example, suppose a person with extensive property holdings goes into business with another person to produce canned specialty food items. Also, imagine a negligent employee allowing canned fish to go out of the plant without sufficient cooking and causing several deaths (accidently uncooked food products causing death has actually occurred in two instances). Court judgments against the parntership could cause the individual to lose all of his wealth and put him into debt for the rest

of his life. Of course, insurance and other methods of dealing with risk (Chapter 14) can help reduce losses.

Primarily, the partnership has disadvantages the sole proprietorship does not have in that it must generate sufficient profit for more than one person and there is considerable potential for dispute.

JOINT VENTURES

A joint venture is a specialized type of partnership. In the regular partnership, persons join together in a *continuous operation* of a business. In a joint venture, individuals join together in co-ownership for a *given limited purpose.*

For example, three men who purchase a tract of land for the sole purpose of developing it with apartments and then selling it for a profit would be engaging in a joint venture. On the other hand, if the three men contributed funds to the purchase and operation of a store on a continuous basis, it would be the creation of the usual partnership.

While not nearly as common as other forms of ownership, joint ventures are increasing in frequency, particularly in real estate developments. The joint venture is taxed as a partnership. In addition, a formal, signed agreement should be drawn up by legal counsel to avoid future problems and disputes.

THE CORPORATION

The corporation form of ownership consists of three or more owners (in most states) who are known as stockholders. The corporation is in a legal sense an artificial being in that it may own property, enter into contracts, be liable for debts, sue and be sued, and conduct day-to-day business.

The corporation form of ownership comprises only 14 percent of all businesses; however, it accounts for 83 percent of all business receipts (Fig. 2-4).

Corporations are created by obtaining a charter from one of the 50 states. State laws vary in their requirements and taxation of corporations. Among other things, states usually require that a corporation have three or more stockholders, that the stockholders elect a board of directors, and that records are maintained at a designated location. The board of directors has overall responsibility for operating the corporation. The board of directors also appoints the officers of the corporation and establishes overall policy for the corporation.

The Articles of Incorporation usually contain such information as:

1. Name of the corporation
2. Period of time the corporation will exist (usually, perpetual)

Sole
proprietorships | 9% | $375 billion

Partnerships | 4% $160 billion

Corporations | 87% | $3,606 billion

Figure 2-4   Receipts of business by form of ownership (*Source:* Statistical Abstract
of the United States, 1979.)

3. Purpose of the corporation
4. Number of shares of stock the corporation can issue and their par value
5. Initial address of the corporation
6. Names and addresses of the initial Board of Directors
7. Names and addresses of incorporators

   The corporation must also have its own by-laws, which give such information
as:

1. Stockholders meetings
   a. Place and time
   b. Means of calling special meetings
   c. Means of establishing a voting list
   d. What constitutes a quorum
   e. Voting of shares
2. Board of Directors
   a. Number and means of election
   b. Term of office
   c. Means of removal
   d. Method of filling vacancies
   e. Quorum at meetings
   f. Regular and special meetings—time, place, notification
3. Officers of the corporation
   a. Titles and duties of principal officers
   b. Means of removal and filling vacancies
   c. Method of fixing salaries
4. Contracts, Loans, Checks, and Deposits
   a. Who may enter into contracts for the corporation
   b. Why may borrow money for the corporation
   c. Who may write checks and drafts
   d. Place of deposit of corporation money
5. Certificates for shares and their transfer (stock)
   a. Form of stock certificates
   b. Methods of transfer of stock

6. Fiscal year of the corporation (when it starts and ends)
7. Dividends (how they are declared and paid)
8. Description of the corporation seal
9. Amendment of by-laws

Corporations accumulate funds by selling stock (certificates of ownership) and/or bonds (certificates of debt).

STOCK

Ownership in a corporation may exist in two basic forms: preferred stock and common stock. Both preferred stock and common stock may be issued by the corporation with an almost unlimited combination of features available to them. However, most stocks issued do have certain features in common.

Stockholders receive payment from the corporation in the form of dividends. The board of directors of the corporation determine if a dividend will be paid and the amount of the dividend if it is paid. There is no legal requirement under normal circumstances that a corporation must pay dividends. One exception to this general rule occurred when stockholders forced Henry Ford to pay dividends after they proved in court that he was unreasonably holding back large profits to the detriment of the stockholders.

Some corporations have never paid a dividend. In fact, some stockholders do not want their corporation to pay dividends. They prefer to have earnings plowed back into the corporation to increase the value and growth of the corporation. This, in turn, almost always increases the value of their stock. Individuals must pay income taxes on all dividends received and the dividends are treated as current income. This may be as much as 70 percent for some persons with large incomes. By holding the stock more than six months and selling it for more than they paid for it, they are required to pay income taxes on only 40 percent of the gain because it is considered a capital gain.

Preferred Stock

Preferred stock has several distinct characteristics, some of which, as its name implies, provide benefits that common stock does not receive. However, preferred stock usually has to give up some desirable features to obtain these benefits.

Par or No-Par Feature   Preferred stock may be either par or no-par stock. Par value of a stock is an arbitrary amount of value that is printed on the face of the stock certificate. Preferred stock with a par value usually exists in units of $100. The par value of the stock has no relationship to either the market value (the price it can be sold for on the open market) or book value (all assets minus all liabilities equals book value of all stock). For all practical purposes, it is simply a record-keeping device. Preferred stock may also exist as no-par, that is, it does not have a stated value printed on the certificate.

Preferred Payment of a Stated Amount of Dividend   Preferred stock usually has a stated amount of dividend that must be paid to the stockholder before any dividends can be paid to common stockholders. Usually this stated dividend exists in the form of a stated percent of par value. For instance, it is relatively common for the dividend rate of preferred stock to be 6 percent of par. If the stock is 6 percent, $100 par, then the preferred stockholder must be paid $6.00 before common stock may receive any dividends. If the preferred stock is no-par, then the certificate will contain a statement as to a standard dividend that must be paid first. For instance, it may state on the face of the certificate that the preferred stockholder must receive $6.00 before any payment can be made to common stockholders.

Cumulative or Noncumulative   Preferred stock may be cumulative or noncumulative in terms of dividends. A cumulative feature is the most common. Since there is no requirement that dividends be paid to stockholders each year, it would be possible for a corporation dominated by common stockholders to hold back all dividends for several years and then pay preferred stockholders for only one year and distribute the rest to the common stockholders. The cumulative feature prevents this in that it requires the corporation to pay not only the current year's dividend but also all past years' unpaid dividends to preferred stockholders before common stock can receive any dividends. Of course, noncumulative means that previous years' dividends that were not paid do not have to be paid before common stock receives dividends.

Voting or Nonvoting   Preferred stock usually does not have voting rights. It is a feature that is usually reserved for common stock. However, there is no legal requirement that prevents preferred stock from having voting rights, and it does have this privilege in some corporations. Stockholders in corporations often sign proxies which give another person the right to cast their vote in the corporation. Proxies are usually solicited by the existing board of directors.

Common Stock

There is more common stock than any other type of stock in most corporations, and in most small businesses it is the only type of stock.

Common stock usually has full voting rights. In addition, it usually is paid only after preferred has been paid. As a result, it is a higher risk stock than

A common-stock certificate.

preferred. However, in a corporation with large profits, it often receives much larger dividends and/or increases in price per share than preferred.

Common stock, as with preferred stock, may also be par or no-par. Also, it is an arbitrary figure that exists only for record-keeping purposes. More common stock has a par value of $1.00 per share than any other denomination. In fact, it is not unusual for a common stock to have a par value of $1.00 per share and have a market value of several hundred dollars per share. Some common stocks do not have an arbitrary value assigned to them and, as a result, are no-par common stock.

Bonds

Bonds are a certificate of long-term debt owed by a corporation. They are usually issued in amounts of $1000 each. Bonds have a maturity date at which

An example of a registered bond.

time the corporation must pay the face amount of the bond to the owner of the bond. In addition, the bond has an interest rate printed on the face of the bond. The corporation must pay the amount of the interest to the bondholder at the prescribed periods of time, usually once a year. For example, a bond with $1000 value and carrying an 8 percent interest rate must pay the bondholder $80 each year and $1000 at maturity. In addition, just because the bond has a face value of $1000 does not mean it is sold for that amount. Depending on the current interest rate, most bonds are sold at either above or below this face value. However, the face value is the amount that must be paid at maturity regardless of how much it brought when first sold.

The bondholders do not have voting rights unless the corporation fails to pay its yearly interest or its face value at maturity. In cases of forfeiture, bondholders usually assume full voting rights and all forms of stock lose their voting rights until the debt is satisfied.

	SOLE PROPRIETORSHIP	PARTNERSHIP	CORPORATION
Creation of form of ownership	One person starts a business	Two or more people sign articles of copartnership	Three or more people obtain state charter
Ability to accumulate capital	Assets and credit of one person	Assets and credit of all partners	Sale of stocks and bonds
Profit sharing	All to owner	To partners based on agreement	Stockholders
Authority	All to owner	Based on articles of copartnership	Board of directors
Life and continuity	Depends on owner	Depends on general partners	Usually perpetual life and transfer of stock provides continuity
Liability	Unlimited liability	Unlimited liability to general partners	Limited to amount of stockholder investment
Legal restrictions	No special ones	No special ones	Several state and federal restrictions

Figure 2-5 Features of the sole proprietorship, partnership, and corporation form of ownership.

ADVANTAGES OF THE CORPORATION FORM OF OWNERSHIP

1. The primary advantage of the corporation is its ability to accumulate capital. Many corporations have accumulated vast amounts of money for investment into assets through the sale of stocks and bonds. General Motors is an excellent example in that it has more than 1 million stockholders and assets in excess of $30 billion.
2. The length of life of the corporation is established in its charter. Most charters specify the life of the corporation to be to perpetuity (i.e., their life is without end). Ownership of corporations in the form of stock makes it easy to transfer ownership without disturbing the corporation. A father who owns a business may find it very hard to divide his business among his children under the sole proprietorship and partnership forms of ownership. In the corporation form of ownership, all he must do is divide the shares of stock.
3. In general, the corporation has limited liability, that is, all a stockholder can lose is the money he paid for his stock. There are some exceptions to this general rule. If a very small corporation borrows money, lenders often require the owners to sign personal liability notes in order to obtain the loan. This means that the owners must repay the note with their own assets if the corporation is unable to repay the note. Another somewhat rare exception occurs when a stockholder is also an officer of the corporation and is guilty of fraud or neglect.

DISADVANTAGES OF THE CORPORATION FORM OF OWNERSHIP

1. Creating the form of ownership of the corporation requires greater time and money than any other form of ownership. However, it is not an unreasonable amount in most cases. A charter must be obtained from the state. This requires time, legal fees, and state fees. It usually takes several weeks to process the charter application. The cost for attorney and state fees usually is from $500 up, depending on the state.
2. Taxation is sometimes a serious disadvantage which will be discussed later in this chapter.
3. There are a wide range of legal restrictions on corporations. States have various legal requirements of corporations such as charter limitations, right to do business in other states, and some government supervision which usually requires reporting to various agencies of the state. The federal government also has various legal restrictions on corporations that engage in interstate commerce. The corporation is also subject to all usual civil and criminal aspects of law to which the sole proprietorship and partnership are subject. Individuals operating the corporation are subject to the law in terms of their conduct in operating the corporation. For example, a few years ago

several officers of electrical manufacturers were sentenced to terms in prison for price fixing in violation of the Sherman Antitrust law.

DISSOLUTION AND BANKRUPTCY

The form of ownership of a business may be terminated by either dissolution or bankruptcy. Although in a technical sense the business is dissolved in bankruptcy, dissolution is usually considered terminating the business when it is solvent. On the other hand, bankruptcy is always an act of terminating the business because of insolvency.

DISSOLUTION

Dissolution of the sole proprietorship may result because of the death of the owner or as an act of the owner. The partnership form of ownership may cease due to withdrawal of a general partner (such as by death), some condition stated in the articles of copartnership (such as a time limit for the partnership to exist), or by consent of the partners. A corporation may be dissolved because of a charter limitation (i.e., time limit) or vote of the stockholders (the charter usually specifies the number of votes necessary for dissolution, such as majority or two-thirds).

State laws prescribe the order to which various claims against the assets of the business are satisfied. Generally, they are satisfied in this order:

1. Any wages or claims of employees.
2. Any taxes due government agencies.
3. Creditors' claims.
4. Owners of the business.

In the case of the corporation form of ownership, creditor's claims would include all bondholders. Also, the par value (in the case of no-par, the value carried on the books) of the preferred stockholders would be paid first and then common stockholders would receive all monies that are left after the sale of assets.

BANKRUPTCY

Stated simply, the conditions exist for bankruptcy when the total amount of all liabilities exceed the total value of assets. Or stated in another way, it is when there are not sufficient assets to pay all debts.

In a technical sense, a business is not bankrupt until it is declared to be bankrupt. A petition to the courts to declare the business bankrupt may be made by owners of the business (voluntary bankruptcy) or by creditors (involuntary bankruptcy). In cases of declared bankruptcy, the courts appoint a trustee who sells all assets of the business and divides it according to the order listed in dissolutions. The trustee receives a fee for his work which is deducted from the total funds before any are distributed.

In cases of bankruptcy, it should be remembered that the sole proprietor and general partner have unlimited liability, while the stockholder in the corporation has limited liability to the extent of his investment in the corporation.

TAXATION OF THE FORMS OF OWNERSHIP

There are some areas of government taxation that are common to all types of business ownership. Some of these common forms of taxation are local business licenses, licenses for sale of alcoholic beverages, property taxes (real estate and personal property), and payroll taxes.

In addition to these common areas of taxation, there are some taxes that vary according to the form of ownership.

TAXATION OF SOLE PROPRIETORSHIPS

Usually, the only type of tax the sole proprietorship is subject to, other than those listed as common taxes above, is the federal income tax. All profit of the sole proprietorship is considered current income to the individual owner. All profit from the business is listed as "income other than wages, dividends, and interest" in his personal income tax report. All profit of the business is taxed in this manner even if he has not withdrawn it from the business. It is never considered as a salary and, therefore, is not an expense to the business.

TAXATION OF PARTNERSHIPS

Partnerships are usually taxed differently from other forms of business ownership only in the area of federal income taxes. All profit earned by the partnership is considered personal income to the partners in the proportion of share of profits specified by the articles of copartnership. It does not matter whether or not the profits are withdrawn from the business. Even when the articles of copartnership specify a salary to one or more partners, it is still considered a distribution of profit rather than wages in the computation of federal income taxes. This treatment of federal income taxes is the same for both general and limited partners.

TAXATION OF CORPORATIONS

The corporation is subject to taxes that are not common with partnerships or sole proprietorships. One of these is the state corporation tax. State laws vary widely in their method and amount of taxation of corporations. However, most states tax corporations on profit and some on the basis of assets.

Corporations are also subject to a federal corporation tax. The corporation income tax is computed on the basis of 17 percent of the first $25,000, 20 percent on the next $25,000, 30 percent on the next $25,000, 40 percent on the next $25,000, and 46 percent on all income above $100,000. For example, if a corporation had taxable income this year of $200,000, the tax would be computed as follows:

$$
\begin{array}{lcr}
17\% \text{ of } \$25,000 & = & \$4,425 \\
20\% \text{ of } \$25,000 & = & 5,000 \\
30\% \text{ of } \$25,000 & = & 7,500 \\
40\% \text{ of } \$25,000 & = & 10,000 \\
46\% \text{ of } \$100,000 & = & \underline{46,000}
\end{array}
$$

Total corporation tax = $72,925

Salaries of all employees and officers, regardless of whether or not they are stockholders, are considered an expense to the corporation. However, the salary of the officer or employee is considered wages in his personal income tax computation. In addition, all dividends distributed by corporations are considered personal income to the individual. In a sense, this amounts to double taxation in that profit of the corporation is subject to a corporate income tax and the dividends distributed from the remaining profit is also taxed as current income to the stockholder.

This double taxation of the profits of the corporation would seem to be a serious disadvantage of the corporation form of ownership. Sometimes it can be an advantage to certain persons. For example, an entertainer may earn enough in fees for his services to place him in the maximum personal income tax bracket of 70 percent. By incorporating and allowing his fees to become income to the corporation, he is able to draw a salary that takes him to the 46 percent bracket and then leave all additional profit in the corporation for reinvestment. His salary is counted as an expense to the corporation. The profit is then subject to the corporation tax which only goes to 46 percent. Of course, to obtain a tax advantage, he must reinvest the excess amount, because if he declares it as dividends, it is taxed as personal income.

SUBCHAPTER "S" CORPORATIONS

In an attempt to assist small businesses, Congress added Subchapter "S" to the internal revenue code. Subchapter "S" permits corporations under certain conditions to be taxed as a proprietorship or partnership. These conditions are:

1. It must be a domestic corporation (A corporation chartered by one of the 50 states).
2. It can not have more than 10 shareholders.
3. It can not be a member of an affiliated group of corporations.
4. All shareholders must be individuals or estates (not corporations or partnerships).
5. No stockholder can be a nonresident alien.
6. It has only one class of stock.

People are often confused by the title "Subchapter S corporation." They mistakenly think it is a special form of corporation. It is a regular corporation chartered by one of the fifty states. It is eligible for and does elect to be taxed under Subchapter S of the Internal Revenue Code. In a year in which the corporation elects to be taxed under Subchapter S, all profits of the corporation (whether distributed or not) are *not* subject to the regular corporation tax. The shareholders (stockholders) have their share of the profit added to all their other income and are then taxed as individuals. Subchapter S can be of considerable value to a small business. The business gets to keep all the desirable features of the corporation form of ownership without the double taxation disadvantage. For example, if you had considerable wealth but still wanted to enter into a high risk business, you could possibly lose everything as a sole proprietor or general partner. However, if the corporation is a Subchapter S corporation you would only risk your investment and still be taxed as an individual.

Some of the other potential benefits are:

1. Income splitting. In a high profit year, a father may give stock to his children to take advantage of his lower income tax bracket without giving up control of the corporation.
2. Shifting income to a lower income year. If the corporation tax year (e.g., starts July 1) is different from the owners' personal income tax year (starting January 1), the dividends may be declared to shift income from high income years to low income years.
3. Being taxed as a Subchapter "S" corporation may be elected and terminated at will. This makes possible the use of Subchapter "S" corporation taxation during years when it is an advantage and not during years when it is not an advantage.
4. Availability of fringe benefits for the stockholders. Employee benefit plans are often not available to sole proprietors and partners simply because they are employers, not employees. Fringe benefits to stockholders as employees (life and health insurance, pension plans, etc.) are a deductible expense to the corporation. Also, some executives may be uninsurable as individuals

	TAXED
Sole proprietorship	As individual
Partnership	As individuals
Corporation	Corporation tax
	Dividends taxed to individuals
Subchapter "S" corporations	Under certain conditions small corporations taxed as partnership

Figure 2-6 Taxation by form of ownership.

but insurable under group plans because all employees must be accepted in the plan.
5. A tax-free death benefit can be provided selected stockholders. The company can provide up to $5,000 to an employee's family at the time of the employee's death. The company can restrict the benefit to one or as many employees as the company chooses.

Subchapter S is rather complex and technical and the potential for tax savings so diverse, that no one should become a Subchapter S corporation without the advice and guidance of an accountant or attorney. On the other hand, the potential benefits are so great to many businesses that almost everyone operating a small business should investigate its potential for his or her business.

In conclusion, all the factors presented in this chapter must be considered by each individual business before an effective decision can be reached as to the best form of ownership for that business.

DISCUSSION QUESTIONS

1. Since more businesses are sole proprietorships than any other form of ownership, the sole proprietorship must be the best form of ownership for small businesses. Evaluate this statement.
2. When would you use the sole proprietorship form of ownership?
3. Would you have articles of copartnership if you formed a partnership? Explain.
4. Explain the two different types of partners.
5. When would you use the partnership form of ownership?
6. If you started a corporation, what instruments might you use to raise capital
7. Would you issue preferred or common stock?

8. When would you use the corporation as a form of ownership?
9. When would you use a joint venture?
10. What type of taxes must the various forms of ownership pay?
11. What is a Subchapter "S" corporation and why is it important to some small businesses?

STUDENT PROJECT

Find three businesses in your community—a sole proprietorship, a partnership, and a corporation.

1. Ask each business why they have their form of business ownership.
2. Ask the partnership what type of partners they have in the business.
3. Ask the corporation from what state they obtained their charter.
4. Find out if the corporation uses Subchapter "S".
5. Find out what types of securities the corporation has outstanding.
6. Find out if the partnership has articles of copartnership.

CASE A
SAM TUTTLE AND SONS

Sam Tuttle started an air conditioning and heating firm shortly after World War II on borrowed funds. Sam is particularly proud of his business because it has always been successful. He has obtained a reputation for providing a quality product and good service at a reasonable price.

Sam has two children, both sons, who are 20 and 22 years of age. Both sons are single and are currently working in the business. Sam would like to leave his business to them when he retires in five years. The business has been very profitable, but Sam is not sure it will continue to provide sufficient profit to provide a very comfortable living for both sons when they marry and have their own families.

Sam has discovered that he can obtain an exclusive distributorship in a nearby town for the same brand of equipment he is now using. He has thoroughly investigated the potential of the new business and is firmly convinced it will equal the present business in profit. Sam has found a suitable location and feels he has sufficient funds to finance the new location.

Sam is presently wondering if he should change the form of ownership of his business. He knows very little about the various forms of ownership and has asked your help.

Questions

1. Should Sam retain both businesses as a sole proprietorship?
2. Should Sam create a partnership? If he does, what types of partners would you suggest he establish?
3. Should Sam create a corporation? If he does, what type of securities should he issue?
4. Would a joint venture be advisable for this type of business? Explain.
5. Would you advise Sam to use Subchapter ''S'' if he sets up a corporation?

CASE B
A COSMETIC AND TOILETRY BUSINESS

Jean and Murray Kenedy are thirty-seven and have been married for 14 years. They have two adopted children ages 10 and 12. Jean obtained her college degree in chemistry and has worked as a sales representative for a large chemical firm since leaving college. She is one of the company's best salespersons and has consistently earned above average in sales commissions. Murray obtained his college degree in business administration and is now the assistant plant manager in a medium sized manufacturing plant that produces retail store shelves and counters.

Jean and Murray began talking about starting their own business even before they were married. The challenge of creating a business and making it grow appeals very much to them. Since the second year of their marriage, they have lived on Murray's salary and invested Jean's salary (after paying taxes on it) with the idea of obtaining enough money to start the business. They now have $215,000 and are ready to make their move into their own business.

They have investigated several ventures over the years and have changed their minds several times about what kind of business they wanted to create. About three years ago, Jean began to investigate the possibility of producing a limited line of cosmetics and toiletries. They are now convinced it offers them a good potential. Jean has formulated the following items to be their products:

Women's Products
Face cream
Hair rinse
Two perfumes
Hand cream
Hair spray
Shampoo

Men's Products
Hair tonic
Shaving cream
After shave lotion
Men's cologne

Jean has attempted to make these products as allergy safe as possible. These products appealed to both Jean and Murray because the manufacturing process is basically mixing and filling containers. The same general purpose machinery needed to produce any one of these products will also produce the rest. As a result, it is possible to produce all of them with a limited investment. Murray has leased a building that will fit their needs. He has also placed orders with manufacturers of the machinery they will need. His estimates show they will have $20,000 left to use as working capital after they have paid for everything required to produce the product.

Murray has turned in his resignation notice effective next week. Jean will keep her job as a safety factor until the business can get off the ground and produce a profit. The last month has been hectic for both of them trying to get everything lined up to get the business going. It has just occurred to them that they have never decided on the form of ownership they want for the business.

Questions

1. Would you select the sole proprietorship form of ownership? Explain your answer.
2. Would you select the partnership form of ownership? Explain your answer. If you did select this form of ownership, what type of partners would you use?
3. Would you select the corporation form of ownership? Explain your answer. If you did select the corporation form, would you issue bonds, preferred stock, and/or common stock? Why?
4. Could things happen in the future that would cause a need for a change in the form of ownership? Explain your answer.
5. Could they be a Subchapter "S" corporation under IRS regulations? Could it be to their benefit to do so?

3

FRANCHISING

PREVIEW OF THIS CHAPTER

1. In this chapter, you will learn the definition of franchising.

2. You will be aware of the impact that franchising has on the distribution of goods and services.

3. You will be able to identify many of the advantages and limitations of franchising.

4. You will learn what kinds of assistance franchisors provide franchisees.

5. You will learn how much it costs to acquire a franchise.

6. You will be made aware of the types of retail franchise operations you may invest in.

7. You will learn the scope of franchising in international markets and minority ownership.

8. You will learn about the laws designed to protect the franchises.

9. You will be provided with a number of questions for evaluating a franchising opportunity.

10. You will be able to understand these key words:

Franchise	Lessor
Franchisor	Lessee
Franchisee	Exclusive distributorship
Leasing	

HISTORY OF FRANCHISING

Franchising is not a new marketing concept. The term "franchising" comes from the French, and the original meaning was to be free from servitude.

Franchising has long been an effective form of marketing, used primarily by manufacturers whose product lines were especially suited for exclusive or highly selective distribution.

Historically, the concept of franchising as we know it today in our own country dates back to 1898 and had its beginning in the auto industry. It was then that an independent dealer was licensed to service and sell electric and steam automobiles. Franchise operations were confined primarily to auto manufacturers, oil refineries, and soft-drink companies until as late as the 1940s. However, the early history of franchising is almost completely overshadowed by the recent upsurge of franchising as a retailing institution. About 90 percent of the current franchisors have started their businesses since 1954. During the 1960s and 1970s franchising has had its greatest impact in the United States. Not only has there been a significant change in the types of franchising outlets but also in the volume of goods and services sold through this type of retailing institutions. Figure 3-1 underscores franchising's impact on retail sales.

One of the best known franchises is Kentucky Fried Chicken, Inc. Its story illustrates the fantastic growth that has been enjoyed by the franchise industry since World War II.

Harlan Sanders opened a small service station in Corbin, Kentucky, and also served meals to tourists at his family's dinner table in order to make ends meet during the depression. His reputation for food (especially his fried chicken) soon spread, and food preparation became the dominant business. Incidentally, he was made a Kentucky Colonel in the 1930s in recognition of his contribution to the state's cuisine.

While catering for a banquet, he added an unusual combination of 11 herbs and spices to his special cooking process which sealed in the natural juices and flavor. In order to properly single out his fried chicken from "southern fried chicken," he designated his product "Kentucky Fried Chicken."

Kentucky fried chicken became his restaurant's specialty item. His restaurant grew to a capacity of 150 seats and prospered until the mid-1950s. Then, a new interstate highway was planned which rerouted tourist traffic away from his restaurant. With this turn of events, he auctioned off his business at a loss, paid his debts, and began living on Social Security benefits.

Dissatisfied with retirement and with confidence in the quality of his fried chicken, the Colonel went into the chicken franchising business. In 1955, at the age of 65, he took his first Social Security check, $105, and began traveling cross-country by car from restaurant to restaurant. He cooked his fried chicken using his special recipe and utensils for the restaurant owner and employees. If their reaction was favorable, they entered into a handshake agreement which gave the Colonel a profit of a nickel for each chicken sold. The first franchise was opened in Salt Lake City, and by 1963, there were more than 600 Kentucky Fried Chicken franchised outlets. In 1964, Colonel Sanders sold his interest in

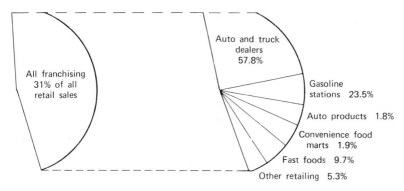

Figure 3-1 Franchising share of retail sales (percentages).
(*Source:* U.S. Department of Commerce.)

the U.S. company but retained ownership of his Canadian company. He now serves as a goodwill ambassador, promoting Kentucky Fried Chicken through national advertising and personal appearances.

About 1.5 million meals are sold daily through Kentucky Fried Chicken franchises. Kentucky Fried Chicken now has more than 4,500 food outlets, opening one new outlet a day, and annual sales of over $1 billion. This phenomenal growth has occurred in less than 20 years from its origin, and it all started with an investment of a $105 Social Security check.

DEFINITION OF FRANCHISING

Franchising is a form of licensing. The owner (franchisor) of a product, service, or method obtains retail distribution through affiliated dealers (franchisees). The franchisee often has exclusive access to distribute the franchising product in a specific geographic area.

The franchisee sells the product, service, or method which carries the franchisor's brand name, but the franchisor maintains control of the distribution methods used. Frequently, the franchise operation is similar to a large chain operation in that all franchise outlets have an identifying trademark, standard symbols, equipment, storefronts, standardized services or products, and maintain uniform practices that are outlined in the franchise agreement.

The International Franchise Association defines franchising as "a continuing relationship in which the franchisor provides a licensed privilege to do business, plus assistance in organizing, training, merchandising, and management in return for a consideration from the franchisee."

ADVANTAGES OF FRANCHISING

A number of the specific advantages that are inherent in the franchising distribution method are discussed below.

MANAGEMENT TRAINING

In Chapter 1, reference was made to the fact that some 90 percent of all business failures are attributed to poor management. Franchise operators receive training in management skills and knowledge prior to opening for business from the franchisor. Follow-up training is provided on a continuing basis after the franchise is opened for business. The training covers a broad range of topics relating to franchise operation. Many training seminars are usually held at the franchisor's home office. Owners of new franchises are instructed in proper methods of franchise operation. Such topics as store management, accounting, sales, advertising, and purchasing are thoroughly covered. For example, new owners of a McDonald's franchise receive ten days of intensive instruction at its "Hamburger University" prior to opening. Shakey's Pizza Parlors offer its dealers and parlor managers both classroom and in-parlor instruction at Shakey University in St. Louis. This program allows the participants to learn in an operating parlor atmosphere. Topics include all aspects of parlor operations and management functions. Shakey's maintains a training department to assist franchisees in understanding Shakey's philosophy and increasing their management skills. Shakey's continually seeks to develop new training methods and techniques to enable the parlor manager to operate his franchise as professionally and profitably as possible.

Furthermore, training continues after the franchisee begins operation. Kentucky Fried Chicken, for example, provides assistance and training in such activities as customer service, general restaurant management, quality control, and accounting methods. The training may be conducted at the franchise location. Or, selected franchise personnel may attend a training session at a selected model store near the franchise location. Some franchisors bring franchisees together at regional meetings where they may exchange views and opinions and receive management advice.

Franchisors recognize the contribution that management training and consultation provide franchise owners as a major reason for each franchisee's success. Individuals with a minimum of business experience are given the opportunity to learn the management skills necessary for operating their own business successfully. And the success of the franchisor is reflected in the success of the franchisees.

Franchise names, such as McDonald's, are familiar to millions of customers both in the United States and in foreign countries.

ESTABLISHED BRAND NAME OR SERVICE

When franchisees are licensed, they acquire the right to use the nationally known brand name or trademark of the franchisor. The identification with an established name provides the franchisee with the distinct advantage of the drawing power of well-known products or services. Customers recognize a certain characteristic—the "Golden Arches" of McDonald's—and quickly identify that attribute as a symbol of courteous service, quality food, and cleanliness. These associations are important factors when consumers are deciding on which firm to patronize.

STANDARDIZATION OF PRODUCTS OR SERVICES

Since the franchise owner uses the brand name or trademark, the franchisor's national reputation depends to a large degree on the quality of his product or service provided by the dealer. To assure uniformity of goods or services nationwide, the franchisor assists the owner in maintaining his standard quality of performance. For example, Shakey's provides an operations manual to its parlor owners that details the following:

1. Pizza construction and ingredient specifications.
2. Other food products (salad, chicken and potatoes).
3. Personnel (dress, hiring, training, managing).
4. Customer service.
5. Parlor maintenance and sanitation.
6. Equipment (purchase and maintenance).
7. Management and cost controls.
8. Use of Shakey's Incorporated trademarks and service marks.

Franchisees must adhere to the standard operating rules if the franchisor's goal of uniform product and services are to be achieved and the national image enhanced. The operations extend to all phases of a franchise's activity.

NATIONAL ADVERTISING

Effective advertising is an essential requirement for those selling brand name products or services. Association with a nationally known franchisor permits franchise owners to benefit from the widespread promotion of his products or services.

National advertising campaigns are made possible by each franchise owner's contribution of a stated percentage of monthly sales or a flat monthly rate to the franchisor. These funds are used for cooperative advertising. This cooperative advertising effort allows national television and magazine advertising to be used, which is obviously beyond the scope of any individual franchisee. The advertising is prepared by a central advertising agency, which means that the ad will be uniform throughout the market area whether seen or read in Boston or San Diego.

To supplement the national advertising program, franchisors require local dealers to spend a minimum amount or percentage on local advertising. Franchisors also give assistance to the franchisee in planning and designing their local ads.

FINANCIAL ASSISTANCE

A characteristic of franchise businesses is that the financial requirement may be less than needed for the same type of operation started on an independent basis. Becoming affiliated with a franchising company offers the franchisee several advantages in the area of financial assistance.

In some cases, qualified franchisees may obtain partial financing from the franchising company. The following are illustrative of the variety of financing arrangements available:

An auto repair franchise will arrange for financing of one-third of total requirement.

A retail store selling high quality domestic and imported cheeses and sausages will finance up to $15,000 on equipment needs.

A general employment agency will finance up to 50 percent of the equity capital needed.

Franchising companies also provide guidance to franchisees on how to establish good relationships with banks and on seeking financing for sites and buildings through conventional means. Because affiliation with a franchisor permits access to the franchisor's business know-how, the franchisee often is able to obtain more favorable credit terms with the bank or other lending agency.

Other financial assistance may be provided in the form of short-term credit for the purchase of certain food and paper supplies if the franchisee elects to purchase these items from the franchising company. One major franchisor offers both short- and long-term financing arrangements to franchisees whose credit rating qualifies them. The advantages to this method of financing includes a lower down payment than required by outside lending agencies, competitive interest rates, flexible repayment terms, and preparation of all necessary paperwork by the franchisor at no cost to the franchisee.

PROVEN METHODS OF DOING BUSINESS

An outstanding benefit of franchising operations is that the dealer does not have to start and build the operation from the ground up. Instead of relying solely on individual know-how, he/she has available the combined knowledge and skills of an on-going business firm which is based on good business management practices. Thus, he/she is able to avoid many of the common pitfalls of independent operators. He/she is buying into a business firm that already has an established record for success. Additionally he/she profits by being able to capitalize on the franchisor's developmental work, which has already been done to build goodwill, establish a consumer-accepted image, design store fixtures, and provided established products and services.

Reliance on the proven methods of operation and experience of the franchising company gives the franchise owner the opportunity to reduce the risk of failure. Furthermore, the assistance received from the franchisor in organizing and promoting the business product or service permits the franchisee to concentrate more attention on managing the business in the most efficient way.

CHAIN BUYING POWER

Selling standardized products enables the franchisor to use centralized buying. Volume purchases enable the franchisor to obtain merchandise at lower prices. These lower prices can then be passed on to the franchisee when he purchases merchandise from the franchisor. This practice enables these quasi-chains to enjoy the buying power that chain stores enjoy.

LOWER RISK OF FAILURE

While the owner of a franchise is not immune to failure, the risk of failure is much lower than that for the small businessman who starts out on his own. The International Franchise Association emphasizes that over 90 percent of franchised businesses succeed while only about 13 percent of all new businesses succeed.

FAVORABLE INCOME POTENTIAL

In general, the franchisee has a favorable income potential. Association with a company with a proven business system, plus the owner's initiative, can adequately reward the owner. For example, McDonald's average revenue per store is $800,000 with a pretax profit of 18.90 percent; Wendy's is $510,000 and a pretax profit of 20.15 percent; and Burger King's revenue is $496,000 and pretax profit of 10.60 percent.[1]

ASSISTANCE IN RECORD KEEPING, ACCOUNTING, AND INVENTORY CONTROL

Frequently, franchisors develop reporting procedures and forms to assist the franchisee in financial control. This service may include systems to be used for maintaining control of inventory, and preparation of operating statements and tax returns. This assistance facilitates the franchisee's control over his operation and provides standardized accounting and reporting procedures.

TERRITORIAL PROTECTION

Many franchises have a policy of assigning and protecting the territory of the franchise. Others do not. An area of a city, an entire city, or a larger territory may be designated for a franchise outlet. This procedure protects both franchisor and franchisee interests.

[1]*Source:* Blyth, Eastman, Dillon and Co., Inc.

LIMITATIONS OF FRANCHISING

As with any business undertaking, there are limitations that must be recognized. Some of these are discussed below.

FRANCHISE FEES AND SHARING OF PROFIT

The initial financial requirements vary for the type of franchise and also within franchising companies. These variations depend on the size of operations that a franchisor desires to build. One franchisor's equity capital requirements range from $5 to $10,000. A national motel requires equity capital of $250,000 and a net worth of $1.5 million.

One franchisor's requirements include a dealership license fee, down payment on equipment, signs, furniture, and start-up operating capital. Operating capital expenditure covers supplies and inventory, wages and expenses while training key people, promotion and advertising of opening, franchise operating cash reserves, licenses and fees (health permits, business licenses), and other deposits such as insurance and utilities. Within this same franchise, the typical total investment depends on the size of the franchise operation. The investment for a smaller outlet is $115,500 and for a full-size outlet it is $208,500.

In addition, continuing fees (or profit sharing with the franchisor) must be paid to the franchisor for continuation of use of the franchising company's trademarks, service marks, trade names, and other items. This profit sharing is a stated percentage of monthly or annual sales or a flat annual fee. For example, one franchise agreement calls for the dealer to pay 5.5 percent of the monthly food sales for the life of the dealership to the franchisor. Other fees are also involved. To illustrate, a specific amount or percentage must be set aside for both national and local advertising. One franchise agreement requires the franchisee to spend a minimum of 3 percent of gross food sales on local advertising. Other fees are paid to the franchisor to cover continuing operational advisory services, such as purchase of the merchandise and financial management. Rental fees may be required if the franchisor owns the land on which the franchise is located.

STRICT ADHERENCE TO STANDARDIZED OPERATIONS

Although franchisees own the business, they do not have the autonomy to run the firm as do independent business owners. The franchisor ordinarily exercises varying degrees of continuing control over the franchisee's operation in order to assure the quality and uniformity standards of products and services at each outlet. This control extends to the franchising company's personnel visiting and inspecting each outlet to determine its compliance with company standards for operations and quality control. If the franchisee does not perform up to standard, it can result in loss of the franchise. For example, if the franchisee purchases and serves an inferior quality of food, this reflects on the image of the firm in the eye of the consumer, and has the possibility of negatively affecting all franchises.

RESTRICTED FREEDOM IN MAKING PURCHASE DECISIONS

Under the terms of some franchise agreements, the franchisee must purchase certain merchandise (food or nonfood items) from the franchisor or from suppliers licensed by the franchisor. To the extent that this policy exists, the franchisee's independence in purchasing merchandise is limited. In some cases this eliminates the competitive purchasing advantage a franchisee could have by using other suppliers who offer equal quality but at a lower cost.

LIMITED PRODUCT LINE

The franchisor controls the products or services that may be sold through the outlet. The franchisee cannot introduce other products or services except as they are introduced by the franchisor or approved by the company.

A summary of the advantages and disadvantages of franchising is presented in Figure 3-2.

ADVANTAGES	LIMITATIONS
Management training	Franchise fees and sharing of profit
Established brand name or service	Strict adherence to standardized operations
Standardization of product or service	Restricted freedom in making purchase decisions
National advertising	Limited product line
Financial assistance	
Proven method of doing business	
Chain buying power	
Lower risk of failure	
Favorable income potential	
Assistance in record keeping, accounting, and inventory control	
Territorial protection	

Figure 3-2 Advantages and limitations of franchising.

CODE OF ETHICS OF INTERNATIONAL FRANCHISE ASSOCIATION

The International Franchise Association is a nonprofit association which is an industry organization of franchisors. The Code of Ethics is designed to enhance mutual trust and confidence between franchisor and franchisee. Specifically, the Code of Ethics includes the following.

CODE OF ETHICS

(International Franchise Association)

Each member company pledges:
1. No member shall offer, sell or promote the sale of any franchise, product or service by means of any explicit or implied representation which is likely to have a tendency to deceive or mislead prospective purchasers of such franchise, product or service.
2. No member shall imitate the trademark, trade name, corporate name, slogan, or other mark of identification of another business in any manner or form that would have the tendency or capacity to mislead or deceive.
3. The pyramid or chain distribution system is inimical to prespective investors and to the franchise system of distribution, and no member shall engage in any form of pyramid or chain distribution.
4. An advertisement, considered in its totality, shall be free from ambiguity and, in whatever form presented, must be considered in its entirety and as it would be read and understood by those to whom directed.
5. All advertisements shall comply, in letter and spirit, with all applicable rules, regulations, directives, guides and laws promulgated by any governmental body or agency having jurisdiction.
6. An advertisement containing or making reference, directly or indirectly, to performance records, figures or data respecting income or earnings of franchisees shall be factual, and, if necessary to avoid deception, accurately qualified as to geographical area and time periods covered.
7. An advertisement containing information or making reference to the investment requirements of a franchise shall be as detailed as necessary to avoid being misleading in any way and shall be specific with respect to whether the stated amount(s) is a partial or the full cost of the franchise, the items paid for by the stated amount(s), financing requirements and other related costs.
8. Full and accurate written disclosure of all information considered material to the franchise relationship shall be given to prospective franchisees a reasonable time prior to the execution of any binding document and members shall otherwise fully comply with Federal and state laws requiring advance disclosure of information to prespective franchisees.

Source: Franchise Opportunities Handbook, 1979. U. S. Department of Commerce, pp. xxvii and xxix.

9. All matters pertaining to the franchise relationship shall be contained in one or more written agreements, which shall clearly set forth the terms of the relationship and the respective rights and obligations of the parties.
10. A franchisor shall select and accept only those franchisees who, upon reasonable investigation, appear to possess the basic skills, education, personal qualities, and financial resources adequate to perform and fulfill the needs and requirements of the franchise. There shall be no discrimination based on race, color, religion, national origin or sex.
11. The franchisor shall encourage and/or provide training designed to help franchisees improve their abilities to conduct their franchises.
12. A franchisor shall provide reasonable guidance and supervision over the business activities of franchisees for the purpose of safeguarding the public interest and of maintaining the integrity of the entire franchise system for the benefit of all parties having an interest in it.
13. Fairness shall characterize all dealings between a franchisor and its franchisees. To the extent reasonably appropriate under the circumstances, a franchisor shall give notice to its franchisee of any contractual breach and grant reasonable time to remedy default.
14. Franchisor should be conveniently accessible and responsive to communications from franchisees, and provide a mechanism by which ideas may be exchanged and areas of concern discussed for the purpose of improving mutual understanding and reaffirming mutuality of interest.
15. A franchisor shall make every effort to resolve complaints, grievances and disputes with its franchisees with good faith and good will through fair and reasonable direct communication and negotiation. Failing this, consideration should be given to mediation or arbitration.

ASSISTANCE TO DEALERS

A significant part of the franchisor-franchisee relationship is the kind of assistance which the dealer receives. Obviously, the type and magnitude of assistance varies among franchisors. However, listed below are representative kinds of support offered to dealers by franchisors.

Conduct market survey of proposed location of franchise.
Assist in site selection.
Aid dealer in negotiating purchase or lease.
Provide financial assistance.
Provide building plans at no cost.
Assist in obtaining building permits.
Give each dealer a manual of operations.
Conduct training seminars for dealers prior to franchise opening.

Provide consultant to assist in opening of franchise.

Make continuing, follow-up management counseling available.

Distribute to dealers information about company plans, policies, new products through periodic reports and bulletins.

Control and maintain quality of products sold.

Provide continuing research and development.

Assist in planning advertising and sales promotion.

FRANCHISE INFORMATION

The *Franchise Opportunities Handbook* published by the Department of Commerce provides information on hundreds of franchises. Data for a select number of franchises are shown as they are presented in this publication.

AAMCO TRANSMISSIONS, INC.
408 East Fourth Street
Bridgeport, Pennsylvania 19405
Ron Smyth, Vice President, Franchise Sales

Description of Operation: AAMCO centers repair, recondition and rebuild transmissions for all cars. This is done by specially trained mechanics. Franchisees do not need to have a technical background, but should have a strong business background.

Number of Franchisees: 765 in 50 States and across Canada.

In Business Since: 1958

Equity Capital Needed: $35,000.

Financial Assistance Available: A total investment of $72,500 required to open an AAMCO center in a major market. A total of $60,000 is required in a secondary market. Company can arrange financing for 1/2 of total requirement, if franchisee has good credit references. Franchisee has the option to arrange own outside financing.

Training Provided: A comprehensive 6 week training course is provided at the company headquarters. In addition field training is provided at the opening of the operation to see that franchisee is properly launched.

Managerial Assistance Available: A consulting and operation division continually works with each center on a weekly basis to insure proper day-by-day operation. Monthly area meetings are held.

MIDAS-INTERNATIONAL CORP.
222 South Riverside Plaza
Chicago, Illinois 60606
William Strahan, Vice President

Description of Operation: Automotive exhaust system, brake, shock absorbers, and front end alignment. Shops offer fast service "while you watch" in clean, pleasant, modern surroundings.

Number of Franchisees: 1,100 in 50 States, Canada and Puerto Rico.

In Business Since: 1956

Equity Capital Needed: $100,000 investment for inventory, equipment, sign, furniture, fixtures, fees and working capital.

Financial Assistance Available: Franchisee receives complete assistance in obtaining necessary financing from appropriate lending agencies with which Midas has working arrangements.

Training Provided: Both a dealer orientation program and on-the-job training programs are initially provided, followed by continuous in-the-shop field counseling and periodic dealer seminar-type meetings on all aspects of shop operations. Provide formal training program at National Training Center, Palatine, Illinois.

Managerial Assistance Available: A shop operator's manual is provided along with record keeping and accounting manual. Training received from regional directors covers all aspects of management, marketing, and sales.

KAMPGROUNDS OF AMERICA, INC.
P. O. Box 30558
Billings, Montana 59114
Harold Lloyd, Vice President

Description of Operation: Kampgrounds of America, Inc. (KOA) is America's largest system of campgrounds for recreational vehicles. The average campground contains 100 sites equipped with water and electrical hookups; many sites have sewer hookups. Each campground features clean restrooms with hot showers, a convenience store, laundry equipment and playground equipment. Many have swimming pools.

Number of Franchisees: 840 in the United States and Canada.

In Business Since: 1964

Equity Capital Needed: $55,000 minimum

Financial Assistance Available: KOA does not provide direct financing to franchisees for campground construction. However, it does provide assistance in obtaining financing such as, assisting the franchisee in preparing his prospectus, developing operating projections, and meeting with potential lenders.

Training Provided: KOA provides formal classroom training in campground development and campground operations for franchisees and their personnel. Each school (development and operations) last three days and several sessions are conducted throughout the year.

Managerial Assistance Available: KOA provides formal classroom training and continual management services for the life of the franchise in such areas as development, general operations, advertising and merchandising. In addition, complete manuals of development, operations and supply catalogs are provided. Regional consultants are available in all regions to work closely with franchisees. Each campground is visited regularly to insure conformance with standards and to assist franchisees in solving problems. KOA publishes a Kampground Directory annually and sponsors an annual meeting of franchisees.

DUNKIN' DONUTS OF AMERICA, INC.
P. O. Box 317
Randolph, Massachusetts 02368
Robert Rosenberg, President
Thomas Schwarz, Executive Vice President

Description of Operation: Franchised and company-owned coffee and donut shops with drive-in and walk-in units. Sale of over 52 varieties of donuts and Munchkins at retail along with coffee, soup, and other beverages. Franchises are sold on the basis of individual stores and also area franchises for one or more stores in selected market areas. Franchisor encourages development of real estate and building by the franchisee, subject to approval of Dunkin' Donuts of America, Inc. Franchisor also develops locations for franchising and for company operations.

Number of Franchisees: 956 (113 company) in 42 States plus stores in Canada, Japan and Puerto Rico.

In Business Since: 1950

Equity Capital Needed: Franchise Fee, $22,000 or $27,000 depending on geographical area. Working capital, approximately $11,000. Franchise fee reduced by 1/3 when franchisee develops real estate.

Financial Assistance Available: Equipment package may be financed for three years through the franchisor. Signs may be financed directly through sign companies.

Training Provided: 5 week training course for franchisees at Dunkin' Donuts University in North Quincy, Massachusetts consisting of production and shop management training. Initial training of donutmen and managers for franchisees and retraining is carried out at Dunkin' Donuts University without additional charge.

Managerial Assistance Available: Continuous managerial assistance is available from the District Sales Manager assigned to the individual shop. The Company maintains quality assurance, research and development and new products programs. The franchisee-funded marketing department provides marketing programs for all shops. The marketing programs are administered by an area marketing manager who develops plans on a TV market basis.

MCDONALD'S CORPORATION
1 McDonald's Plaza
Oak Brook, Illinois 60521
Licensing Manager

Description of Operation: McDonald's Corporation operates and directs a successful nationwide chain of fast food restaurants serving moderately priced menu. Emphasis is on quick, efficient service, high quality food, and cleanliness. The standard menu consists of hamburgers, cheeseburgers, fish sandwiches, french fries, apple pie, shakes, breakfast menu, and assorted beverages.

Number of Franchisees: 4,495 in the United States, 739 internationally (including Canada).

In Business Since: 1955

Equity Capital Needed: $100,000 to $125,000 and ability to acquire outside financing —$125,000 to $200,000.

Financial Assistance Available: None

Training Provided: Minimum of 150 hours pre-registration and 300 plus post-registration; eleven days of basic operations training and 2 weeks managerial training at Hamburger University in Elk Grove, Illinois.

Managerial Assistance Available: Operations, training, maintenance, accounting and equipment manuals provided. Company makes available promotional advertising material plus field representative consultation and assistance.

LEASING

Small business owners may enter into a leasing agreement with the manufacturer. A lease is a contract between the property owner (lessor) and the tenant (lessee). The contract allows tenants the right of possession and use of the leased property for which they pay the property owner rent. The lease specifies the rights of the parties to the lease.

As one example, in the distribution of gasoline and related products, oil companies frequently build stations and lease these stations to independent operators. The producer sells the station operator the brand name products as well as offering managerial assistance and guidance through periodic individual and group meetings with the company's distributors in a sales territory.

For use of the physical facilities, the operator must make a rental payment. This payment may be a specific amount or a flat fee plus a stated percentage of the gross or net income.

The lease arrangement enables the owner to avoid a large cash outlay required for purchasing a building. Hence, leasing may help the small business owner overcome some of the problems of obtaining financing.

EXCLUSIVE DISTRIBUTORSHIP

A somewhat different distribution method from franchising is the exclusive distributorship, an extreme form of selective distribution. Under an exclusive distributorship arrangement, a manufacturer makes a contract with a dealer (wholesaler, agent, or retailer). The terms of this agreement specify that the manufacturer will sell goods or services within a particular geographic area only through a single dealer, an exclusive distributorship. A joint distributorship exists when more than one dealer represents a seller in a specific territory. In addition to restricting the sales territory, a manufacturer may provide the dealer with additional services, such as sales training or assistance in advertising. In return, the dealer agrees to certain stipulations of the manufacturer. The dealer may agree to maintain a satisfactory inventory level, charge prices set by the manufacturer, or not stock competing products.

This arrangement gives manufacturers greater control over maintaining the image and prestige of their products. Likewise, marketing costs can be reduced since products are distributed through fewer outlets. This form of distribution is common to the auto industry as well as some major appliance industries.

TYPES OF FRANCHISES

To an investor interested in a franchise operation, the following list identifies many types of retailing outlets available as franchise operations.

Automotive products/services
Auto/trailer rentals
Beauty salon/supplies
Business aids/services
Campgrounds
Children's stores/furniture/products
Clothing stores
Construction/remodeling materials/
  services
Cosmetics/toiletries
Drug stores
Educational products/services
Employment services
Equipment/rentals
Foods—donuts
Foods—grocery/specialty stores
Foods—ice cream/yogurt/candy/
  popcorn/beverages
Foods—pancakes/waffle/pretzel
Foods—restaurants/drive-ins/
  carry outs
General merchandising stores

Health aids/services
Hearing aids
Home furnishings/furniture-retail/
  repair/services
Laundries/dry cleaning services
Lawn and garden supplies/service
Maintenance/cleaning/sanitation/
  supplies
Motels/hotels
Paint and decorating supplies
Pet shops
Print shops
Real estate
Recreation/entertainment/
  travel services
Security systems
Soft drinks/water-bottling
Swimming pools
Tools/hardware
Vending
Water conditioning

FRANCHISING IN INTERNATIONAL MARKETS

Economic growth in many foreign markets is opening new doors for franchise expansion, especially in the services sector. Many international markets are characterized by more disposable personal income and stronger demand for consumer goods and services.

There are distinct advantages in international markets, such as (1) entry into the international market with a minimum risk, (2) minimum investment of time and capital, and (3) maximum opportunity for new business ventures.[2]

Canada, Great Britain, and Japan are the dominant markets for franchising operations. Fast food restaurants and auto and truck rental franchises account for the largest share of the franchised operations.

While opportunities abound, some problems faced by the franchising industry in foreign markets should be identified. They include:

Official limitations on royalty payments or licensing and trademark contracts. In some cases royalties on trademarks and brand names are taxable and payable by the franchisor whether he is domiciled in or out of that particular country.

Problems may exist in the protection of trademarks as no facility exists for their registration.

In some cases franchising arrangements remain solely the concern of contracting parties and there are no regulations to safeguard franchising agreements. Tie-in arrangements are discouraged and sometimes forbidden.

In some countries, a significant percentage of ownership share of the business activity is required by local nationals; in others, aliens cannot own real estate property and in others, they cannot own retail businesses.

There are also import restrictions on equipment. This may impose a significant problem with respect to equipment or systems considered essential to the distinctiveness of the end-product or the end-service.

Wide economic variation as a result of inflation and currency valuation, exchange controls, and price ceilings on products pose problems affecting various types of franchising business categories.[3]

MINORITY-OWNED FRANCHISES

Two common drawbacks to small investors, especially minority entrepreneurs, is the lack of managerial skills and inadequate financing. Franchising has made it possible to lessen these drawbacks because of the services provided franchisees, such as continued management training and financial assistance. Thus, franchising is an avenue open to minority group members for business success. Most minority-owned franchises are owned by blacks and persons with Spanish surnames.

Franchises most popular among minority entrepreneurs are automotive products and services, fast food restaurants, food retailing other than con-

---

[2]*Franchising in the Economy, 1976–78*, U.S. Department of Commerce, p. 5.
[3]*Franchising in the Economy, 1976–78*. U.S. Department of Commerce, p. 7.

Many women have taken advantage of opportunities for minority franchise ownership.

venience stores, convenience stores, and construction, home improvement, and maintenance and cleaning services.

FRANCHISING AND THE LAW

Franchising opportunities must be tempered with a recognition of some of the risks and problems associated with this fast growing field. For example, franchising has become the focal point of regulation in 14 states. In addition, a regulation enacted by the Federal Trade Commission seeks to put an end to some abuses by franchisors, such as unsubstantiated profit claims and arbitrary terminations of franchises.

The Federal Trade Commission regulation requires franchisors in all states to provide disclosure statements to prospective franchisees. This disclosure statement provides detailed information on 20 areas that may influence the decision to invest or not to invest in the franchise. The areas covered are:

1. Information identifying the franchisor and its affiliates, and describing their business experience.
2. Information identifying and describing the business experience of each of the franchisor's officers, directors and management personnel responsible for franchise services, training and other aspects of the franchise program.
3. A description of the lawsuits in which the franchisor and its officers, directors and management personnel have been involved.
4. Information about any previous bankruptcies in which the franchisor and its officers, directors and management personnel have been involved.
5. Information about the initial franchise fee and other initial payments that are required to obtain the franchise.
6. A description of the continuing payments franchisees are required to make after the franchise opens.
7. Information about any restrictions on the quality of goods and services used in the franchise and where they may be purchased, including restrictions requiring purchases from the franchisor or its affiliates.
8. A description of any assistance available from the franchisor or its affiliates in financing the purchase of the franchise.
9. A description of restrictions on the goods or services franchisees are permitted to sell.
10. A description of any restrictions on the customers with whom franchisees may deal.
11. A description of any territorial protection that will be granted to the franchisee.
12. A description of the conditions under which the franchise may be repurchased or refused renewal by the franchisor, transferred to a third party by the franchisee, and terminated or modified by either party.
13. A description of the training programs provided to franchisees.
14. A description of the involvement of any celebrities or public figures in the franchise.
15. A description of any assistance in selecting a site for the franchise that will be provided by the franchisor.
16. Stastical information about the present number of franchises; the number of franchises projected for the future; and the number of franchises terminated, the number the franchisor has decided not to renew, and the number repurchased in the past.
17. The financial statements of the franchisors.
18. A description of the extent to which franchisees must personally participate in the operation of the franchise.

19. A complete statement of the basis for any earnings claims made to the franchisee, including the percentage of existing franchises that have actually achieved the results that are claimed.
20. A list of the names and addresses of other franchisees.[4]

The Federal Trade Commission regulation prescribes a number of legal rights to the prospective franchisee. They are:

1. The right to receive a disclosure statement at your first personal meeting with a representative of the franchisor to discuss the purchase of a franchise; but in no event less than 10 business days before you sign a franchise or related agreement, or pay any money in connection with the purchase of a franchise.
2. The right to receive documentation stating the basis and assumptions for any earnings claims that are made at the time the claims are made; but in no event less than 10 business days before you sign a franchise or related agreement, or pay any money in connection with the purchase of a franchise. If an earnings claim is made in advertising, you have the right to receive the required documentation at your first personal meeting with a representative of the franchisor.
3. The right to receive sample copies of the franchisor's standard franchise and related agreements at the same time as you receive the disclosure statement, and the right to receive the final agreements you are to sign at least 5 business days before you sign them.
4. The right to receive any refunds promised by the franchisor, subject to any conditions or limitations on that right which have been disclosed by the franchisor.
5. The right not to be misled by oral or written representations made by the franchisor or its representatives that are inconsistent with the disclosures made in the disclosure statement.[5]

A violation of the federal law could result in a penalty to the franchisor of up to $10,000 for each violation. If a prospective franchisee has been injured by a violation, the Federal Trade Commission may be able to provide a remedy for the injury suffered, such as compensation for any money lost or the setting aside of future contractual obligations.

However, your best protection as a prospective franchisee is to thoroughly

---

[4]*Source: Franchising Opportunities Handbook, 1979.* U.S. Department of Commerce, pp. xxv and xxvi.
[5]*Source: Franchising Opportunities Handbook, 1979.* U.S. Department of Commerce, pp. xxvii and xxviii.

investigate the franchisor, evaluate your own abilities, and to be aware of your legal rights.

FRANCHISE ANALYSIS

One set of guidelines suggested for the prospective franchisee is provided below. These 25 questions should be answered when evaluating the potential franchise.

CHECKLIST FOR EVALUATING A FRANCHISE

The Franchise

1. Did your lawyer approve the franchise contract you are considering after he studied it paragraph by paragraph?
2. Does the franchise call upon you to take any steps which are, according to your lawyer, unwise or illegal in your state, county or city?
3. Does the franchise give you an exclusive territory for the length of the franchise or can the franchisor sell a second or third franchise in your territory?
4. Is the franchisor connected in any way with any other franchise company handling similar merchandise or services?
5. If the answer to the last question is "yes" what is your protection against this second franchisor organization?
6. Under what circumstances can you terminate the franchise contract and at what cost to you, if you decide for any reason at all that you wish to cancel it?
7. If you sell your franchise, will you be compensated for your good will or will the good will you have built into the business be lost by you?

The Franchisor

8. How many years has the firm offering you a franchise been in operation?
9. Has it a reputation for honesty and fair dealing among the local firms holding its franchise?
10. Has the franchisor shown you any certified figures indicating exact net profits of one or more going firms which you personally checked yourself with the franchisee?
11. Will the firm assist you with:
    (a) A management training program?
    (b) An employee training program?
    (c) A public relations program?
    (d) Capital?
    (e) Credit?
    (f) Merchandising ideas?
12. Will the firm help you find a good location for your new business?
13. Is the franchising firm adequately financed so that it can carry out its stated plan of financial assistance and expansion?

14. Is the franchisor a one man company or a corporation with an experienced management trained in depth (so that there would always be an experienced man at its head)?
15. Exactly what can the franchisor do for you which you cannot do for yourself?
16. Has the franchisor investigated you carefully enough to assure itself that you can successfully operate one of their franchises at a profit both to them and to you?
17. Does your state have a law regulating the sale of franchises and has the franchisor complied with that law?

You—the Franchisee

18. How much equity capital will you have to have to purchase the franchise and operate it until your income equals your expenses? Where are you going to get it?
19. Are you prepared to give up some independence of action to secure the advantages offered by the franchise?
20. Do YOU really believe you have the innate ability, training, and experience to work smoothly and profitably with the franchisor, your employees, and your customers?
21. Are you ready to spend much or all of the remainder of your business life with this franchisor, offering his product or service to your public?

Your Market

22. Have you made any study to determine whether the product or service which you propose to sell under franchise has a market in your territory at the prices you will have to charge?
23. Will the population in the territory given you increase, remain static, or decrease over the next 5 years?
24. Will the product or service you are considering be in greater demand, about the same, or less demand 5 years from now than today?
25. What competition exists in your territory already for the product or service you contemplate selling?
    (a) Nonfranchise firms?
    (b) Franchise firms?

OUTLOOK FOR FRANCHISING

The outlook for franchising as a viable force for distributing goods and services in our economic system is very promising. Franchising's growth is expected to be quite strong in the 1980s. Franchising is one of the most successful methods of distribution in our economy.

Fast food restaurants will likely retain their leadership role in franchising. Currently, one-third of food dollars are spent for eating out. It is predicted this may change to 1 out of every 2 in the 1980s as lifestyles change (more women

Source: Franchising Opportunities Handbook, 1979. U.S. Department of Commerce, pp. xxix and xxx.

in the workforce, higher population mobility), as there is more advertising, and as increased emphasis is placed on the sale of quality food.

Business services franchises are expected to show strong growth. Real estate franchising is a fast growing area as well.

DISCUSSION QUESTIONS

1. What is franchising?
2. Discuss the advantages and limitations of franchising operations.
3. What types of assistance does the franchisor make available to franchisees?
4. What is leasing?
5. What is an exclusive distributorship?
6. Identify the different types of franchises.
7. What are some problems in international franchising?
8. Discuss the franchising opportunities for minority group members.
9. Discuss some legal factors involved in franchising.

STUDENT PROJECTS

1. In your city or specific trading area of your city, make a survey to determine the number of franchised operations located there.
   A. Identify the franchise by name.
   B. Identify them by kind of franchise (fast food, motel, rent-a-car, etc.).
2. Review the business classified ads under "business opportunities" and make a list of a number of types of franchises available.
3. Select a specific franchise and write to obtain information about what it takes to start the franchise and the types of service the franchisor provides the franchisees.
4. Interview a franchisee and have him/her explain the assistance provided by the franchisor.

CASE A
MIDWEST RESTAURANT*

Fred Wilson was a labor union leader in a Midwest steel town, with 16 years of seniority on his job. He was well liked by his fellow workers, and found his

*Source: Franchising: Instructor's Manual, Management Development Program, prepared by the Small Business Administration.

dealings with management at the bargaining table interesting and challenging. But Fred did feel that he could go no farther in his job, and he and his wife talked often about a business of their own.

A newspaper advertisement of a drive-in restaurant franchise attracted Mrs. Wilson, and at her urging, Fred inquired about it. A meeting was arranged with a company representative, at which time the Wilsons were exposed to the company's management, sales territories, advertising policies, cost and profit projections, and financing arrangements. At the conclusion of the meeting, the Wilsons were convinced this was their golden opportunity.

The Wilsons did not have very much capital because Fred's salary had been invested in paying off the mortgage on their home as rapidly as possible, and they enjoyed the luxury of a fine automobile each year. However, the Wilson's credit was excellent, and they borrowed what they lacked from their local bank, setting up a rapid repayment schedule, just as they had done with their home. The projected income figures indicated to Fred that this was feasible.

Less than a month later, the former steel worker was listening to marketing experts, food technicians, and experienced accountants explain the franchise operation. The training period was brief, but quite thorough, and Fred decided that whatever he didn't quite understand at the moment he would learn as he went along. Filled with enthusiasm, Fred returned home, eager to enter into his new business.

In the initial few days of operation, a company representative helped him operate the business. Store traffic was excellent—Fred's enormous circle of friends began to patronize the establishment immediately, and the pleasure of being the "boss" masked the strain of the long hours in the new enterprise.

When the company's representative left, Fred and his wife both worked in the restaurant, and, although the traffic of the first few days slackened a bit, the Wilsons were still working a good 16-hour day. After the first 2 months, Fred and his wife felt that the strain on them was too great—Mrs. Wilson had not worked previously, and Fred was quite used to his comfortable 40-hour week. So the Wilsons made a decision to hire additional help to ease their burden.

Two new employees were hired and given a 2-day on-the-job training course by a franchisor company representative. By the end of the week, Fred was convinced that the new employees could handle the job, and he let them take over the evening shift.

After 2 weeks, it became apparent that this system wouldn't work—and the Wilsons split up the workday—Fred and one employee took one shift, and Mrs. Wilson and the other employee took the other shift. The system seemed practical—the customers were being served properly, and all looked well . . . until the Wilsons looked at their accounts.

The additional costs of the help, on top of the financial obligations the Wilsons faced to repay their initial investment, was not leaving them very much.

They were working very hard, and realizing less money than Fred had earned at his previous job. The only decision the Wilsons could make was to let the help go, and continue to do all the work themselves, on a 6-day week, 16 hours a day. By the time the sixth month had rolled by, Fred was searching earnestly for a buyer for his restaurant.

Questions

1. Based on the supplied information, what do you feel was the principal reason for the Wilson's disenchantment with their franchise?
2. How compatible was Fred Wilson's background with the type of business he entered?
3. What financial arrangements could have been made to ease the Wilson's financial burden? Explain.
4. What would you suggest as a solution to the problem facing the Wilsons?

CASE B
RON SCHULTZ*

Ron Schultz had been an insurance salesman, modestly providing for his wife and two sons. They resided in a modest Philadelphia neighborhood, and lived on the strict budget that many families find necessary with a limited income.

Schultz had been looking for a new field to enter—one that would permit him to expand his income base. One of the opportunities he investigated was a franchise with one of the country's largest automatic transmission repair services, headquartered near his home.

Careful investigation revealed a growing market potential with very little competition. New car dealers were only equipped to handle the one make of transmission that they sold. And, because of their high overhead structure, transmission repair prices were quite high. Neighborhood garages that took in transmission repair work were farming it out to small shops that varied in quality, time, and cost. The potential was evident. But Ron was concerned with yet another problem—his lack of a mechanical background.

The franchisor's training program was designed to overcome just such preliminary doubts. An intensive 4-week program, the course consisted of 48 hours per week, covering employee recruiting, pricing, customer service, advertising, cost control and other vital details. The end result was to familiarize the franchisee with all aspects of the transmission service business, with an

*Source: Franchising: Instructor's Manual, Management Development Program, prepared by the Small Business Administration.

emphasis on *managing* transmission specialists, rather than teaching the actual mechanical work.

At the franchisor's suggestion, Ron selected several names at random from a list of the company's franchisees, and visited several of them at his convenience. Each of the franchisees seemed very pleased with his own business, and encouraged Ron to seek his own franchise with the company.

Further inquiry indicated that the location for the new franchise could be right in Ron's area. The tentative location was in a location that boasted 40,000 registered automobiles within a 30-minute ride of the shopsite. The initial cash investment that would be required for this franchise was $21,000, and the franchisor was ready to aid Ron in securing the financing. This investment would provide initial rental, substantial parts inventory, specialized tools, outdoor signs, utility deposits, office supplies, workbench, and shelving.

Continuing assistance offered by the franchisor included montly conferences for all area franchise operators to review various phases of operations, weekly parts deliveries from the franchisor's warehouse, and a weekly review of sales progress and business proficiency.

The essential requirements Ron had to meet—besides his initial cash investment—were a strong desire to earn money and an ability to communicate with people.

Questions

1. List the advantages you can see in the franchisor's offer.
2. List the principal disadvantages you can see in the franchisor's offer.
3. What additional information can Ron obtain to aid him in making his decision?
4. What course of action would you recommend for Ron Schultz, based on the above information? Explain.

CASE C

LEEROY KING

LeeRoy King has been employed by an agency of state government for 10 years. He works in the personnel section, and his duties are primarily limited to interviewing personnel for jobs with this state agency. Recently, LeeRoy has begun to feel frustrated and boxed-in in his position. He sees only limited opportunities for advancement in his present position, yet he knows he has other obligations to his wife and 5-year-old child.

At slack times during the day, LeeRoy finds himself looking out his office window, daydreaming about new opportunities that would be challenging, satisfying, and rewarding. He has given serious thought to resigning from his present job to strike out on his own, using the $5000 in savings he has been able to set aside. He realizes that his business experience is limited and doesn't know if he has sufficient background to go it alone.

At their coffee break this morning, he and several of his fellow workers talked about the opportunities of independent business ownership versus franchise ownership. While LeeRoy had considered opening his own business, he had not given any thought to franchising.

That evening, while reading his newspaper, LeeRoy turned to the business section. Under franchising opportunities he read the following:

1. Investment opportunity in fast growing group of children's fashion shops. Excellent location available in new shopping center in this area. Equity capital needed: approximately $45,000.
2. America's number one camping host has a campground franchise available in this area. The site will have 100 sites for water and electrical hookups for recreational vehicles. $25,000 minimum equity capital.
3. Opportunity to purchase franchise specializing in reconditioning and rebuilding automatic transmissions for all cars. Absolutely no mechanical experience necessary. Minimum cash requirement is $12,500.

Questions

1. Explain what franchising is to LeeRoy.
2. Explain the advantages of franchising, especially since he has limited business experience.
3. Explain some of the drawbacks he might encounter.
4. Where can he get financial assistance?
5. Study the business section of your own newspaper and determine other franchise opportunities for LeeRoy.
6. What type of franchise would you recommend to him?

SECTION
TWO
ESTABLISHING THE FIRM

4

BUY AN EXISTING FIRM OR START A NEW ONE

PREVIEW OF THIS CHAPTER

1. In this chapter, you will learn the advantages and disadvantages of buying an existing business.

2. You will find that there are advantages and disadvantages to starting a new business.

3. If you plan to buy an existing business you will find you must analyze (1) why the owner wants to sell, (2) the physical condition of the business, (3) the market in which the business exists, (4) the financial condition of the business, and (5) legal aspects of the purchase in order to arrive at a true value of the business.

4. You will discover that you are buying future profit of the business and learn how you can capitalize this yearly profit to arrive at a guideline for a fair price.

5. If you ever plan to start a new business, you will be interested to learn that the feasibility study should include investigation of (1) location, (2) market, (3) physical facilities, (4) operations and personnel, and (5) projected financial statements.

6. You will understand why you must spend time, effort, and money in investigating business opportunities to lessen the risk of business failure.

7. You will be able to understand these key words:

Composition of population	Financial condition
Customer attitudes	Legal aspects
Physical facilities	Capitalization
Travel time	Rate of return
Customer attitude surveys	Feasibility study
Market barriers	

The entrepreneur has many decisions to make once he decides to become engaged in a small business venture. One of the first, and one of the most important decisions, is whether to start a new business or buy an existing business. The answer to this question may vary in each case, and there are many factors to consider.

This chapter investigates the advantages and disadvantages of both buying an existing firm and starting a new one. In addition, the chapter provides an overview of the information needed to arrive at a realistic decision when buying an existing firm or starting a new one.

In some respects, information required for buying or starting a business, and the methods of obtaining this information, are a part of the entire field of small business management. Consequently, specific knowledge and methods of obtaining information are contained throughout the entire book. Therefore, this chapter serves as an overview and introduction to the knowledge necessary to perform adequate investigation for purchasing an existing business or starting a new one.

BUY AN EXISTING BUSINESS

There are both advantages and disadvantages to buying an existing business. If the small business entrepreneur decides to buy an existing business, then there are many things he must investigate and analyze about the business if he is to make a good purchase decision.

ADVANTAGES

There are several factors that may make an existing business an attractive purchase.

1. It is a proven business, which reduces the risk, and often, makes it easier to finance.
2. The business often has well-established customer goodwill.
3. Lines of supply and credit have already been established.
4. Employees have already been hired and trained.
5. The physical facilities are sometimes available for rent, rather than purchase, which reduces the amount of capital necessary to buy the business.
6. Sometimes, it is difficult to find potential buyers for business firms because of lack of skills, lack of interest, or lack of capital. Consequently, one may find an existing business that is being sold at a very low price relative to the value of the business. This is often true of manufacturing firms, which are sometimes sold far below the replacement value of the building, machinery, and equipment.

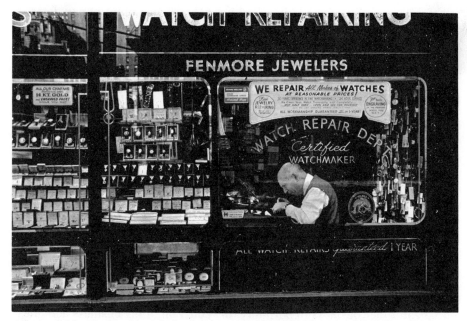

A potential buyer for this existing business would need very special skills.

DISADVANTAGES

There are also several factors that may make an existing business unattractive as a purchase.

1. The business may be offered for sale because it is losing money. The buyer of an existing business must be very careful to determine the true reason why the business is being sold. The reason the seller gives may not be the real reason.
2. Customer, supplier, and creditor ill will, rather than goodwill, may have been established and carry over to the new owner.
3. The employees working in the firm may not be desirable employees, and it may be difficult to get rid of them because of unionization or other reasons. Also, firing undesirable employees often has an adverse effect on the morale of good employees in situations where they don't know what to expect when a new owner takes over the business.
4. It may not be the best location for the business.
5. The facilities may not be completely suited to the needs of the business. If remodeling is required, the cost may be excessive.
6. Innovations in the business may be difficult due to present facilities. For

example, the size of the building may prevent the addition of new lines of products that would help sales.

7. There may not be a business for sale of the type you are looking for in a given market, or it may cost an excessive amount of money to purchase one.

FACTORS TO INVESTIGATE AND ANALYZE

To arrive at a wise purchase decision, the small business entrepreneur must investigate various aspects of the existing business. He must analyze and evaluate (1) why the owner wants to sell, (2) the physical conditions of the business, (3) the market in which the business exists, (4) the financial condition of the business, and (5) legal aspects of the purchase, in order to arrive at (6) a true value of the business. (See Fig. 4-1.)

Why Does the Owner Want to Sell?

There can exist an almost endless list of reasons why a business is up for sale. Sometimes the reason the seller gives for selling the business is the real reason and sometimes it is not. The owner may wish to sell because of such reasons as retirement, other business opportunity, or reduction of his business activities. On the other hand, he may wish to sell because the business is losing money, there is a continued trend of decreasing sales, new competition, legal problems, or excessive effort is required for the level of profit being produced.

When the reasons for selling are factors that will ultimately mean the failure of the firm, the reason given for selling is usually not the real motivation. Few people would volunteer information that would automatically preclude anyone

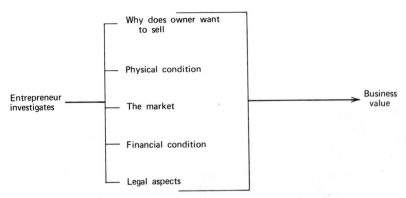

Figure 4-1 Factors to investigate when buying an existing firm.

buying the business. For example, one individual looking for a small business to buy was offered a small grocery-gasoline store at a price that seemed very reasonable. An income statement provided by the owner indicated a very profitable business. However, a careful examination of sales and purchase records showed the firm to be making much less profit than claimed. In addition, talking to people in the nearby town revealed a new highway was being planned which would eliminate a large part of the store's business.

Rather than end up with a failing business and losing savings, any prospective buyer should expend considerable energy in evaluating the business.

Physical Condition of the Business

The physical condition of the business is an important part of the total value of the business and the amount of capital that will be needed in the business.

The age and condition of such items as the building, equipment, and even inventory determine how much money must be spent in addition to the purchase price to get the business in proper operating condition. A buyer that must spend considerable money in remodeling the business that he just bought should make sure that he has or can obtain the necessary funds when he purchases the business. He should consider the cost of remodeling a part of the total cost of the business.

Old machinery and equipment may have to be replaced soon after the purchase, and the buyer must consider total cost and availability of funds for this before he makes the purchase. Inadequacy or obsolescence of inventory is also an expense and should be considered. In addition, if the buyer decides to purchase the business, he should include a complete list of all inventory and equipment in the purchase/sale agreement. There have been instances when a person agrees to buy a business at a specific price and then finds, on taking over the business, that the former owner has sold a large part of the inventory without replacing it. This reduction in inventory may represent a loss of thousands of dollars.

The prospective buyer must also evaluate the appearance of the business to determine if it provides an adequate image to customers. For example, a restaurant that is badly in need of paint does not produce an image of cleanliness to customers, and the cost of painting should be considered before purchasing the business.

Another consideration is that of adequacy of equipment. The manufacturing firm that has machinery and equipment that is not efficient and causes high labor costs may not be a good buy. In retail and service firms, the location of the business is an important factor to sales and should be evaluated during the purchasing decision.

The Market

To evaluate the market in which the business exists, the entrepreneur must determine (1) the composition of the population, (2) competition, and (3) attitudes of customers.

Composition of the Population   The first step in analysis of the composition of the population is to define the market in terms of where it exists. It may exist as the entire town, a large section of the town, or as a neighborhood. Studying maps, lists of customers, traffic patterns, and travel times (this is achieved by traveling major traffic arteries from the store at legal speed limits and marking the time it takes to reach various points on a map) help define the normal market area of the business.

Often looking for natural or psychological barriers helps define the market for a small business. Expressways, highways, and rivers with few crossings are examples of natural and psychological barriers. Figure 4-2 shows how highway and expressway locations in one town define the market for many small businesses in the area.

Once the market area has been defined, the composition of the population should be determined to help identify the number of potential customers in the market. The following information about the population of the market area should be collected and analyzed.

1. Characteristics of the population—such as income, education, unemployment, ethnic composition, average family size, and size of age groups.
2. The trend of size of the population over the past years.

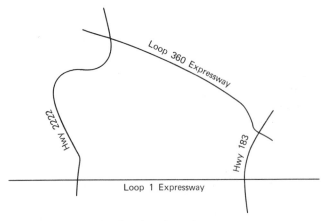

Figure 4-2   Market barriers in a city area.

3. Identify any significant changes in characteristics of the market area over the past 10 years.
4. Attempt to predict any future changes in size or characteristics of the market area.
5. Estimate the number of potential customers for the business from the population data collected.

Some of this information can be found from census tracts in U.S. Bureau of Census publications (found in many public libraries). However, it may be out of date (the census is only taken every 10 years) in areas that are growing or changing.

Sometimes, much of this data is available from local groups, such as city governments, local chambers of commerce, or other civic organizations. In other cases, little or none of the information is available and must be collected by statistical sample techniques (discussed in Chapter 16). Often, this information may be collected at the same time that customer attitude surveys are conducted.

Competition   The prospective buyer should measure competition of the business in the market area by obtaining the following information.

1. How many direct competitors are there in the area (stores of the same type).
2. How many indirect competitors are there in the area (stores that are different types, but handle some of the same merchandise)?
3. How many competitors have gone out of business in the past 5 years?
4. How many new competitors have entered the area in the past 5 years?
5. What is the volume of business of competition in the market area as compared to the store being investigated?
6. What are the pricing policies of the competition?
7. What customer services do competitors offer?
8. How much and how effective is the sales effort (including advertising and promotion) of the competition?
9. What is the appearance of the competition? Is their establishment attractive?
10. Identify and rank all competition as either strong or weak.

Most of this information concerning competition can be obtained by either direct observation or by talking to merchants and people in the marketing area. Many competitors will answer some questions themselves.

Customer Attitudes   The attitude of previous and current customers of the business is important to the prospective buyer. Goodwill of customers has value and definitely affects the purchase price of the business. A negative attitude, on the other hand, decreases the value of the business and should be studied to determine if the new owner can reverse these opinions.

The prospective buyer should perform a sample survey of people in the market area to obtain information about their attitudes toward the business. Often, this can be one of the most important types of information the buyer can obtain because it identifies actions he should take if he purchases the business. A discussion of the method of taking statistical customer attitude surveys is contained in Chapter 16. A sample customer attitude survey device is presented in Chapter 18.

Financial Condition of the Business

There are several financial areas of the business that should be investigated. Some of the questions that should be answered are:

1. What has been the trend of profit over the past 10 years?
2. Has profit been consistent each year or are there wide fluctuations in profit?
3. What has been the trend of sales for past years?
4. Are assets valued realistically in the balance sheet? Significant amounts of intangible assets (goodwill, organization costs, etc.) and unrealistic depreciation may distort the true value of the assets.
5. Will there be sufficient funds after the purchase to meet current expenses and debt?
6. Are the expenses listed in the income statement realistic, or are there some that could be eliminated without harming the business?
7. Do you feel the profit record of the business is in line with the purchase price?

The prospective purchaser of the business should insist on at least the previous 5 years' (1) balance sheets, (2) income statements, (3) income tax returns, and (4) cash flow statements (accounting statement analysis is discussed in Chapter 11). Unfortunately, many small business firms do not maintain cash flow statements (Chapter 11) in spite of the fact that it is so important to a prospective buyer. However, cash flow statements can be almost always created from the records of the firm by an accountant if adequate records have been kept. The wise buyer will have this function performed by an accountant.

The wise buyer should also remember that the accounting statements provided by the seller may not be correct because of error or dishonesty. In addition, the income tax return is only a copy of the original and may not be accurate. The buyer should verify at least the latest year of each different statement by examining sales, expenditures, and inventory records.

Legal Aspects

There can be many legal aspects to consider when a business is being investigated for possible purchase. Some of these are:

1. The prospective buyer should investigate evidence of ownership of the business. It is wise to purchase title insurance since the title insurance company will conduct a complete search of legal records to make sure the buyer receives a clear title.
2. Is the business location zoned properly? Sometimes, businesses are in existence when zoning is created by the community, and they are allowed to continue in a nonconforming status. The nonconforming status prohibits additions to the business and can be a serious block to growth of the business.
3. Are there any liens or liabilities outstanding against the business that will be assumed by the new owner?
4. Does the business have the required licenses and permits, and will these be available in the future?
5. Are patents, trademarks, copyrights, and trade names protected under the law? Can an adequate defense of these be made if contested? (Defense of these must be made in court by the holder if contested.)
6. Does the firm have any exclusive dealerships and do they pass on to the new owner? When do these agreements expire, and what are the terms of the agreements?
7. Does the firm have a union contract and what does it specify?
8. Does the business have employment agreements with any other person or persons?
9. Obtain copies of all leases on buildings, equipment, and so forth, and study the terms of the leases.

The prospective buyer must obtain complete information about all legal aspects concerning the business because failure to do so can result in loss of thousands of dollars or even failure of the business.

Value of the Business

All the previous areas of investigation discussed make a definite contribution to the value of a business. However, they contribute to the value of the business in that they help determine the future profitability of the business. A prospective buyer, in reality, is buying the future profit of the firm. In a very real sense, future profit is the return on his investment in money, time, and effort.

A fair return on investment is also dependent to some degree on the amount of risk sustained. For example, a government security (one of the safest investments available) may provide a 5 or 6 percent return on investment. To obtain a return of $20,000 per year, an investor would have to buy $400,000 worth of government securities having a 5 percent return ($20,000 ÷ 5%). If a buyer wishes to obtain the same $20,000 per year from an investment in a blue chip corporate bond (a higher risk than government securities but still considered a good risk) that returns an average of 10 percent per year, he would have to pay $200,000 ($20,000 ÷ 10%).

Investment in most small business firms is usually much more risky than either government securities or blue chip corporation bonds and stocks. The capitalization of the yearly profit of a firm usually varies between four and eight times the yearly profit figure (this would be from 12.5 percent to 25 percent return on investment). Consequently, a firm that was expected to produce a profit of $20,000 per year should reasonably expect to bring a price of between $80,000 and $160,000 depending on the degree of risk involved. Of course, price is established by the buyer and the seller and what is paid often has no relationship to this capitalization guideline. However, a wise buyer will generally follow this guideline on future profit expectations in determining what price he is willing to pay.

Many prospective buyers do not expend the time, effort, and money necessary to adequately evaluate the purchase of a business. This is definitely a mistake. It is far better to expend some time, effort, and money to make sure that the buyer is getting a fair deal than to take a chance that the purchase will turn out all right. If the prospective buyer does not perform an adequate analysis, he stands a strong chance of losing his savings and being in debt for some period of time in the future. It also helps him to operate the business more effectively once it is purchased, because he has a considerable amount of information on which to base operating decisions. The buyer should be conservative and realistic in his analysis. In addition, he should avoid being unrealistic about what he can do to improve the business.

START A NEW BUSINESS

Starting a new business also has advantages and disadvantages. Starting a new business also requires extensive investigation and analysis if the business is to have the best chance of success.

ADVANTAGES

Factors that may make it attractive to start a new business rather than purchase an existing business are:

1. Location is many times one of the most critical decisions for a business firm.

This entrepreneur is capitalizing on the current popularity of bicycles.

It can be the difference between success and failure in many businesses. Often, the only way to obtain the best location is to start a new business.

2. Physical facilities can be constructed to conform to the most efficient use for the business planned. Existing buildings seldom can be arranged to provide the most efficient work flow possible, particularly in manufacturing firms, without having wasted space.

3. Innovating in a new business is much easier than in an existing one because of physical limitations of the existing business.

4. All phases of the new business can be established by the owner without having to change something as when buying an existing business.

5. Existing businesses sometimes have ill will of some customers, suppliers, creditors, and employees. The existing business may also have an image (such as a price image) that the new owner does not want. Starting a new business allows the entrepreneur to establish whatever image he desires.

6. In many cases there just are not any businesses of the type that fit the capabilities of an entrepreneur. Consequently, the only alternative left is to start one.

DISADVANTAGES

Factors that may make it undesirable to start a new business rather than buy an existing business are:

1. There is a higher risk factor in starting a new business.
2. It often takes considerable time and expenditures of funds for a new business to build its customer patronage.
3. Funds are usually harder to obtain to start a new business than to buy an existing, successful firm.
4. It usually takes time to work out the "bugs" in a new business, both in facilities and procedures.
5. Lines of credit and supply must be established.
6. An existing business has sales, expenditures, and profit records to help project future profit. These must be estimated when starting a new business. This makes them much less accurate and dependable.

The Feasibility Study

Investigation and analysis of a new business is much more difficult and much less accurate than studying the purchase of an existing firm. Past records of the business operations are not available with which to make evaluations of the business. The feasibility study should include investigation of (1) location, (2) market, (3) physical facilities, (4) operations and personnel, and (5) projected financial information. (See Fig. 4-3.)

As mentioned earlier, methods and sources of collecting information concerning areas of the feasibility study are discussed in detail in many chapters of this book. The following discussion of the information needed in a feasibility study is intended to give an overview of some of the information and entrepre-

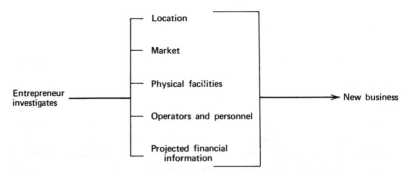

Figure 4-3 Factors to investigate when starting a new business.

neur must analyze in order to arrive at a realistic evaluation of the proposed firm's chances of success. This information is also necessary to good planning and successful establishment of the business. It should also be noted that much of the information needed for a feasibility study of a new business is related to the information needed to evaluate the purchase of an existing firm.

Location

Selection of the site for the business will usually require information which will include:

1. Determining who your customers are and what causes them to buy the product(s) and/or services you plan to offer. For example, if you were going to sell imprinted tee shirts, you would know that most of your customers would be below 35 years of age and generally buy this product on impulse. Consequently, the best location for your store would be in a high customer traffic area. A mall which was visited by a high percentage of young people would be an ideal site. Also, comparing the characteristics of your customers (age, education, income, etc.) with the distribution of these characteristics in city areas would show which would provide the most customers. Generally, retail, service, wholesale, and manufacturers like to locate as near as is practical to their customers.
2. Determine who are your potential competition, how effective they are, and where they are located. A comparison of the areas which have the most customers with areas which have the most competition will provide insight into which is the best area for your new business.
3. Decide to build, buy an existing building, or rent based on the needs of the business, the amount of capital available, and the availability of adequate sites and structures.
4. A list of all available sites and their cost. Local realtors are a good source of this information. Location site is often a tradeoff between desirability of site, cost, and available capital.
5. Identification of the major traffic arteries.
6. A traffic survey of automobiles and pedestrians (depending on the type of business) at the best sites.
7. Zoning information from the city on the various possible sites.

The Market

In many types of business, selection of a good location also depends to a large degree on the market. Some of the information that should be collected and analyzed includes:

1. Population size and characteristics (income, education, age groups, etc.).
2. Projections of population size and characteristic changes in future years.
3. Number, effectiveness, and characteristics of competition in the market.
4. A statistical customer survey should also be conducted in the selected market area in order to determine where people currently buy products the new business will offer. The survey should also determine why they buy at these businesses and what they like and do not like about them. A careful study of all completed questionnaires can be very valuable in arriving at a projected sales forecast for the new business.

Figure 4-4 presents the national average of number of inhabitants per store by type of business. The data in this figure provide an excellent guideline when measuring the adequacy of the market to support a new business.

Physical Facilities

If the decision is to build, rather than to rent or purchase an existing building, the following information must be acquired.

1. Determine work flow and layout of equipment.
2. Determine building specifications and type of construction.
3. Establish amount of parking space needed based on number of employees and customers. Cities usually require a minimum number of parking spaces based on the type of business and size of the building.
4. Identify the type of and access to loading and unloading facilities needed by the business.
5. Based on the type of business, arrive at the type and cost of equipment needed.
6. Obtain city building requirements.
7. Design a floor plan for the business.

Operations and Personnel

Some of the information needed to arrive at operations and personnel planning are:

1. Create job descriptions for all personnel needed in the business.
2. Draw up an organization chart showing lines of authority and responsibility.
3. Set a salary schedule for each job position based on current wage rates in the community.

4. Establish a work schedule showing hours and days worked for each position.
5. Establish a list of products to be carried with the amount of each that will be carried in initial inventory.
6. Determine sources of supply for all inventory items.
7. Determine if there will be any seasonal patterns of sales or if there will be seasonal items carried in inventory.
8. Establish price policies for all merchandise. Determine markups and obtain prices of competitors.
9. Create a plan for opening promotion and advertising.
10. Establish policies for amount and type of advertising to be conducted regularly after opening.

Projected Financial Information

Using the information gathered in the previous investigations create the following financial information.

1. Create a projected budget for the first year of operation. Try to estimate all income and expense items as accurately as possible.
2. Create a projected balance sheet based on all assets you have determined the business will need, plus all debts you plan to incur as a result of financing.
3. Create a projected cash flow statement for the first year's operations using income, expense, asset, and financing data.
4. If possible, draw a breakeven chart.
5. Determine your source of funds by contacting banks and other financial sources listed in Chapter 7.

Figure 4-5 presents some of the more common items for which the cost or estimated cost must be obtained before starting the business. It also shows into which accounting statement these costs are entered.

The financial statements in Chapter 11 can be used as guides.

As with the investigation of buying an existing business, the feasibility study for establishing a new business requires the expenditure of time, effort, and money. However, this expenditure of time, effort, and money greatly enhances the chances of success of the new firm. If a feasibility study is not made, the entrepreneur stands a very real risk that much more time, effort, and money will be lost as a result of failure of the business. Very few entrepreneurs perform adequate feasibility studies. If they did, the high failure rate of new business firms during the first year of operations would be reduced drastically. Most of the waste of business failure could be avoided.

KIND OF BUSINESS	NUMBER OF INHABITANTS PER STORE
RETAIL	
Building materials, Hardware, Garden supply, and Mobile home dealers	
Building materials and supply stores	5,339
Hardware stores	8,008
Retail nurseries, lawn and garden supply stores	26,028
Mobile home dealers	20,823
General merchandise group stores	
Department stores	26,029
Variety stores	9,465
Food stores	
Grocery stores	1,073
Meat, fish stores	12,248
Fruit stores and vegetable markets	26,028
Candy, nut, and confectionery stores	16,018
Retail bakeries	10,959
Automotive dealers	
Motor vehicle dealers, new and used cars	6,407
Motor vehicle dealers, used cars only	6,548
Auto and home supply stores	5,480
Gasoline service stations	921
Apparel and accessory stores	
Women's clothing	5,368
Men's and boys' clothing and furnishings stores	9,053
Family clothing stores	11,568
Shoe stores	7,712
Furniture, Home furnishings, and Equipment stores	
Furniture and home furnishings stores	3,107
Household appliance stores	10,411
Radio, television, and music stores	6,941
Eating and drinking places	
Eating places	823
Drinking places (alcoholic beverages)	1,964
Drug stores and Proprietary stores	4,004
Miscellaneous retail stores	
Liquor stores	4,957
Used merchandise stores	6,310
Automatic merchandising machine operators	16,017
Fuel and ice dealers	10,412
Florists	8,676
Cigar stores and stands	52,058
Sporting goods stores and bicycle shops	9,053

Figure 4-4 National average of number of inhabitants per store by type of business, retail and service. (*Source:* Computed from Bureau of Census publications.)

KIND OF BUSINESS	NUMBER OF INHABITANTS PER STORE
Book stores	26,028
Stationery stores	34,705
Jewelry stores	8,329
Hobby, toy, and game shops	20,823
Camera and photographic supply stores	41,646
Gift, novelty, and souvenir stores	8,465
Luggage and leather goods stores	115,683
Sewing, needlework, and piece goods stores	11,568
SERVICE	
Hotels, motels, trailer parks, camps	
Hotels	14,873
Motels	4,658
Sporting and recreational camps	28,920
Trailering parks and campsites for transients	15,199
Personal services	
Coin-operated laundries and dry cleaning	6,589
Photographic studios, portrait	6,948
Beauty shops	1,101
Barber shops	2,263
Shoe repair, shoeshine, and hat cleaning	16,141
Funeral service and crematories	9,963
Automotive repair, services, and garages	
General automotive repair shops	2,896
Top and body repair shops	6,548
Automotive rental and leasing	19,869
Automobile parking	19,812
Miscellaneous repair services	
Radio and television repair shops	5,983
Reupholstery and furniture repair	8,499
Amusement and recreation services	
Motion picture production, distribution, services	24,326
Motion picture theaters	16,396
Billiard and pool establishments	35,594
Bowling alleys	24,643
Dental laboratories	24,383
Legal services	1,442

Figure 4-4 (Continued)

ITEM	BUDGET	BALANCE SHEET	CASH FLOW STATEMENT
Salaries and wages	X		X
Rent	X		X
Advertising	X		X
Delivery expense	X		X
Supplies	X		X
Telephone and telegraph	X		X
Other utilities	X		X
Utility deposits		X	
Insurance	X		X
Taxes (property and other)	X		X
Payroll taxes	X		X
Interest expense	X		X
Maintenance (including janitorial costs)	X		X
Legal fees	X		X
Fixtures, equipment, and furnishings	D*	X	P**
Decorating and remodeling	D*	X	P**
Installation of fixtures, machinery and equipment	D*	X	P**
Starting inventory	X	X	X
Licenses and permits	X		X
Advertising and opening promotion	X		X
Accounts receivable		X	
Cash as working capital		X	
Counters	D*	X	P**
Storage, shelves, cabinets	D*	X	P**
Cash register	D*	X	P**
Safe	D*	X	P**
Bad debts	X	X	X
Window display fixtures	D*	X	P**
Special lighting	D*	X	P**
Signs	D*	X	P**
Cars and trucks	D*	X	P**
Land		X	P**
Buildings	D*	X	P**
Travel	X		X
Entertainment	X		X
Dues	X		X
Accounting services	X		X
Postage and freight	X		X

Figure 4-5 Cost items and where they are entered. (*Depreciation of item is entered. **Entered when purchased only.)

DISCUSSION QUESTIONS

1. Give three advantages and disadvantages of buying an existing business firm.
2. Why would an owner want to sell his small business?
3. What would be some factors of population in the market area you would want to investigate when deciding whether or not to buy an existing business firm?
4. What are some legal aspects to look for when buying an existing business?
5. How does a small businessman determine the value of an existing firm he plans to buy?
6. Give three advantages and disadvantages of starting a new business.
7. How should a person go about deciding whether or not to start a new business?
8. Why should a person spend time, money, and effort investigating the purchase of an existing business or the feasibility of starting a new business?

STUDENT PROJECT

Select a small business in your community and do the following:

1. Ask the owner, if he or she were to sell the business, what price he or she would ask for it.
2. Ask questions to determine, in general, physical condition of the business, the market, financial condition of the business, and legal aspects of the business.
3. Decide if you would purchase the business and, if so, set a price that you believe is a fair one. Compare this price with the owner's price.

CASE A

QUALITY APPLIANCE STORE

John Jacobs recently inherited $50,000 from an uncle and wants to go into business with the money. John is currently a salesman for a well-known appliance manufacturing concern. One of his accounts is the Quality Appliance Store which is for sale. The Quality Appliance Store has been in business for 15 years and has always stressed the quality of the appliances and service after the sale. The owner says he has other business interests and wants to sell the appliance store to spend more of his time on them. He has provided John with balance sheets and income statements for the past 5 years. The balance sheet shows assets of $40,000 (none of which are intangible assets) and liabilities of $10,000. The income statement shows that he has consistently made from $20,000 to $22,000 profit each year for the past 5 years. The owner is asking $40,000 for the business.

John feels he is well qualified to operate the business firm and feels he could even increase the sales of the business by good promotion and advertising techniques. It does bother him that the owner is asking $10,000 more than the net worth of the business. He has even considered starting a new business of the same type in the same market, rather than pay the extra $10,000.

Questions

1. What are some of the major factors John should investigate before he decides whether or not to buy the Quality Appliance Store?
2. What are some of the major factors John should investigate before deciding to start a new store?
3. What do you think of the owner's reasons for selling the store?
4. Do you consider the price the owner of the Quality Appliance Store is asking for the business to be a fair price?
5. Would you recommend that John purchase the existing business or start a new business in the same market? Explain your recommendation.

CASE B

SUSIE Q

Susan Quintas has been interested in music for many years. She is twenty-six, unmarried, and has $150,000 in municipal bonds inherited from one of her aunts. Susan tried a musical career as a pop singer (Susie Q) for three years after she graduated from the local college. Her singing career never amounted to much so she decided to try some other career. She would now like to start a stereo store selling medium and high quality stereo equipment.

Susan divided the town into five sections based on the location of physical and psychological barriers. She then created a customer questionnaire and hired several college students to conduct a survey. Her survey revealed that customers who bought the most stereo equipment were between the ages of 18 and 35, had incomes between $15,000 and $35,000, and had a high school or higher education. When medium- and high-quality stereo owners revealed where they had bought their stereo equipment, three stores (we will call them X, Y, and Z) accounted for about 72 percent of the sales. Customers listed equipment specifications as the first reason for their selection, with price a close second.

Susan has obtained information from census tracts, the city government, and the local Chamber of Commerce. She has broken this information down into the five areas of her survey.

SECTION	MEDIAN INCOME	AVERAGE AGE	AVERAGE YEARS OF EDUCATION	COMPETITION	CHARACTERISTICS OF SECTION
1	$18,000	30	12	Firm X—Discount image	Fastest growing
2	24,000	24	13	Firm Y—High price line	Old, established
3	40,000	38	14	Two minor stores	Old, established
4	12,000	30	13	Firm Z—Discount image	Old, becoming industrial
5	25,000	25	13	Three minor stores	New, growing

Firm Y is located in a shopping mall while X and Z are located in stores on major streets. A new shopping mall is being built in section five.

Questions

1. Which section of town would you pick in which to locate? Why?
2. Outline the steps Susan must go through to start her store.

5

LOCATION ANALYSIS FOR THE SMALL BUSINESS

PREVIEW OF THIS CHAPTER

1. In this chapter you will learn why location is a vital concern for the small business owner.

2. You will be made aware of many of the factors that must be considered when studying the potential of a trading area.

3. You will learn that accessibility to a site is important to the store's success.

4. You should be able to distinguish between consumer goods, shopping goods, and specialty goods.

5. You will be able to discuss why adequate parking is an important criteria in store location.

6. You will understand the differences between various sites: central business district, neighborhood locations, shopping centers/malls, suburbs, and wayside locations.

7. You will be able to comprehend the importance of site economics.

8. You will be aware of why zoning laws are important to the small business owner.

9. You will learn why a small business owner should conduct an automobile and pedestrian count of the proposed store location.

10. You will be able to understand these key words:

Accessibility of site	Pedestrian traffic count
Trade area	Site economics
Convenience good	Traffic count
Shopping good	Central business district
Specialty good	Neighborhood location
Vehicle traffic count	Shopping center/malls

Neighborhood shopping center	Regional shopping center
Community shopping center	Zoning
	Retail affinity

IMPORTANCE OF LOCATION ANALYSIS

The selection of the business location has been singled out as a strategic factor in the success or failure of a new business venture, especially for retail firms. For the owners of on-going businesses, site analysis is an equally important management decision-making activity affecting the economic health of the firm. Owners must choose the course of action best suited to the firm. For example, if the present store site is leased, should the lease be renewed or should the business be relocated? If the owner plans to add another store, location analysis is essential for the expansion venture.

Most small business owners choose to locate in their hometown or neighborhood. As suggested earlier, the decision for selecting a particular location is frequently based on the fact that an existing building is vacant or the site's proximity to the owner-manager's place of residence. Clearly, these convenience factors should not be considered sufficient reasons for choosing a specific site without a thorough investigation of the site's potential.

In the ensuing discussion, our attention is focused on site analysis for retail and service firms. While the material is concerned with starting a new business, it can easily be adapted to the needs of the owner of the on-going business contemplating relocation or expansion.

TRADE AREA AND ITS POTENTIAL

In evaluating where to locate the business, the owner needs to realize that site selection involves finding answers to three major questions.

1. First, what town or city presents the greatest opportunity for the type of business selected?
2. Second, what area within the selected town or city demonstrates potential for survival or growth?
3. Third, in the area selected, what site best meets the needs of the planned business?

In weighing answers to these questions, the owner-manager tries to determine the economic feasibility for the proposed business in a particular area. Some of the main considerations in this search are highlighted below while a detailed site-location checklist is presented later in the chapter.

SELECTION OF THE TOWN OR CITY

Analysis of a trading area should begin with an economic feasibility study of the town or city. This evaluation aids in determining the appropriateness of the trading area for the proposed business. Some of the strategic factors to be considered in studying the potential market in a trading territory include population trends, nature of the competition, and community attitudes.

Population Trends

Analysis of the town or city should reveal economic indicators of the area's business potential. One immediate concern centers on the trend of the area's population. Population studies should make it possible to establish a profile of important indicators of the area's population, such as age distribution and family makeup. Do young people find employment in the local area after graduation or do most relocate to find employment? Are the families chiefly younger families with children or older families? To illustrate, analysis of population of a fast growing city to determine its suitability for a franchise operation revealed the following: in 1970, the population was 2,800; in 1980, it increased to 13,000; and it is projected to increase to 30,000 by 1990. The greatest percentage of people moving into the area are young married couples with children. This market represents a strong potential market for homebuying and related furnishing as well as other types of businesses.

A second important indicator is the income levels in the trading area. This measures the disposable personal income of residents. Disposable personal income is the amount of money that consumers have available to spend and is a measure of purchasing power.

Purchasing power for an area can be estimated from several sources. First, information may be derived from data supplied by local sources, such as the chamber of commerce or trade associations. Second, a valuable resource is *Sales and Marketing Management Magazine's* "Survey of Buying Power" which reports annual data on individual and family purchasing power. Third, the Census Bureau publishes a great amount of data.

For example, assume a small business manager is considering whether or not to open a new grocery store in an area. Figure 5-1 illustrates how a forecast of an area's purchasing power may be obtained as well as the potential for a new grocery store.

Local population	812,500
× Per capita disposable income	$5952
= Total disposable income	$4,837,000,000
× Percent of disposable income spent for food	18%
= Total food sales potential for area	$850,660,000

Figure 5-1 Estimate of purchasing power for a food store in San Diego, California. (*Source:* Local population and per capita disposable income are derived from *Sales and Marketing Managment Magazine,* July 23, 1979, p. c-24.)

Individual purchasing power can be multiplied by the size of the local population to determine total purchasing power. By multiplying the total purchasing power by 18 percent (the average nationwide expenditure for food), the small business manager is able to obtain an estimate of the yearly food expenditure for the area. From a local trade association group, such as the Retail Grocer's Association, it may be found that retail grocery sales are $825,000,000. This is somewhat less than the potential sales for the area, estimated to be approximately $850,660,000 as shown in Figure 5.1. If this condition exists, then the small business manager must evaluate the area as to its potential to provide sufficient sales and profit over and above what it will cost to operate the business (advertising, rent, salaries, etc.) to justify another grocery store.

A third indicator is the occupational analysis. The occupational survey should disclose the types of employment predominant in the area. To illustrate, it should identify the proportion of total employment in each of the categories shown in Figure 5-2. These data aid in evaluating the stability of employment for the area. For example, if a high percentage of the area's work force is employed in jobs that are of a seasonal nature, this would indicate an unstable employment picture for the area and thus involve more risk for a new firm.

The educational level of the population under consideration should also be evaluated. Knowledge of the above factors will help the owner to decide the type of merchandise carried, prices, and method of business operation.

Competition

Another concern is the quality and quantity of competition found in an area. Evaluating the competitive situation should enable the small businessman to obtain a clearer picture of the overall business environment of the area. An important result of this evaluation is that trends in the business community can be detected. For example, it will be possible to determine if new, competing stores are opening their doors for operation and, if so, how many and what size. This survey should also provide perspective on what is happening to estab-

INDUSTRY DIVISION	PERCENTAGE OF EMPLOYED PERSONS
Mining	0.1
Contract construction	8.3
Manufacturing	17.4
Transportation and public utilities	4.7
Wholesale trade and retail trade	26.3
Finance, insurance, real estate	6.8
Services	19.9
Government	16.5

Figure 5-2 Percentage of employed persons in Phoenix, Arizona, on nonagricultural payrolls, classified by industry division. (*Source: Employment and Earnings,* Bureau of Labor Statistics, U.S. Department of Labor, Vol. 27, No. 3, March 1980, pp. 78–79.)

lished competitors in the area. Are these stores expanding their operations or are they closing?

Information on the number of competing stores in the area will make it possible to forecast chances of survival. However, the existence of a few competitors in an area does not necessarily mean there is an open door for your business. It may be that the city or town cannot or will not support any more firms of that type.

Community Attitude

The prevailing attitude in a community toward new business firms is a significant factor. Community attitudes have a major impact on shaping the future of the town or city. Positive attitudes can encourage growth through aggressive programs designed to stimulate the economy of the specific trading area. Programs designed to attract new businesses or to promote growth of existing firms are a major factor in evaluating a city. Community attitudes that discourage new business obviously present an immediate roadblock to selecting a specific area and hence discourage growth of the community.

SELECTING THE SPECIFIC AREA OF THE TOWN OR CITY

Once the town or city has been selected, the business manager must choose the specific part of the town or city where the business will be located. Again, this decision will be influenced by many factors, such as the nature of the business as well as the quantity of traffic needed to sustain it. For example, a drugstore usually does not generate enough traffic to support itself as does a department store or supermarket. Instead, much of the drugstore's traffic comes from surrounding stores. As a result, most drugstores pay particular attention to locating in or near areas where they can benefit from heavy traffic. Drugstores locate in areas of heavy traffic—downtown areas or neighborhood shopping centers. Others locate in the same building with medical clinics or in office buildings where doctors and dentists are housed.

Some businesses depend on heavy pedestrian traffic, such as neighborhood grocery stores, barber shops, and other types of personal service shops. Hence, this requirement means they must locate within walking distance of their prospective customers. Other firms can locate some distance from their customers since they cater to a more mobile customer.

In selecting the area of town, the small business manager needs to examine many of the same factors considered in selecting the city. The number of competitors operating in the area should be determined as well as how large an area of town they draw from, the volume of their sales, and sales forecasts.

Another factor is the clientele of the local area. Again, the business manager must evaluate whether the area's population is growing or declining, as well as determining the direction of expansion of both the residential and the business district. Also to be determined are such factors as the occupational groupings represented by the area population, the income levels, and the age categories of the local populace.

Other important factors to consider are the cost of rent, transportation facilities to and from the location, the availability of parking facilities, and the general appearance and store vacancy rate of the business district.

SELECTING THE SPECIFIC SITE

In smaller towns, the choice of the specific site may be limited to whatever building or site is available. In larger towns, there will probably be a choice of sites available. Again, the vital issue of the potential of the trade area must be studied, using the same criteria discussed before. These criteria include competition, traffic flow, parking facilities, street location, building availability and suitability, accessibility of transportation to the site, and the type of goods sold in the area.

In selecting a location for a retailing outlet, the small business owner needs to evaluate the site in light of the type of goods to be sold. For example, retailers sell consumer goods (goods purchased by the ultimate consumer for personal use). Goods are classified into three categories.

Convenience Goods

Convenience goods are sold through many outlets and usually the per unit price is low. They are advertised nationwide and customers buy them frequently and give little thought to the purchase of these items or where they are purchased. Convenience goods include such items as soft drinks, candy, gum, and cigarettes.

Shopping Goods

Shopping goods are sold through a selected number of outlets. The per unit cost is usually substantial, so customers normally make both quality and cost comparisons. These items are purchased infrequently and have a relatively long life expectancy. It also takes a concerted effort to sell these goods. Shopping goods include refrigerators, ranges, TVs, stereos, autos, and furniture.

Specialty Goods

Specialty goods refer to items that have a special quality or characteristic. Price is not a factor in the purchase of specialty goods, and they are sold through only a restricted number of outlets. An attribute of specialty goods is that customers will go out of their way to purchase them. Some examples of specialty goods are specific brands, exotic perfumes, jewelry, cameras, and special types of foods.

Studies of specific sites show that one side of the street is preferable for retail stores. This is especially true in sections of the country that have long, hot summers. More people tend to walk on the cooler side of the street, and it permits more effective window use for displays. Corner locations are beneficial in that they provide more window display space as well as being accessible to two distinct flows of traffic.

ACCESSIBILITY OF SITE

For many types of businesses, such as apparel shops, accessibility or the ease with which customers can reach a particular site plus the traffic movement past the site are the most important factors in selecting a location.

In site selection, care must be taken to identify the factors that could impede the traffic flow, including both pedestrian and vehicle traffic, to and from the site. These limitations must be considered in relation to the specific area chosen: downtown area, shopping centers, or drive-ins along heavily traveled streets.

Small business owners must analyze their unique situation to determine if there are factors that would limit the flow of traffic to and from their site. Traffic congestion is often a factor that discourages a shopper from patronizing a particular store, especially in downtown business districts. Another important consideration is how easily autos can enter and leave a particular site. If the entrance or exit poses a hazard to the driver, getting on or getting off a shopping center lot may deter many shoppers from patronizing a store. This is also the case for drive-ins. Furthermore, if a site has only limited access or is located at an intersection, these impediments can inhibit the smooth flow of traffic and thus discourage shoppers.

In the same manner, accessibility must also be considered for pedestrian traffic. The small business manager must identify any potential hazards to pedestrian traffic. The availability of sidewalks and ease of entrance into the business firm are positive factors in accessibility. Ease of entry and exit are vital to pedestrian traffic, since pedestrians desire to avoid congestion just as the driver of a vehicle does. If customers have to follow a circuitous route, such as climbing stairs to a site, chances are reduced for them frequenting the store.

Another matter to consider is how accessible is the site by the other modes of transportation serving a city, such as bus, streetcar, or even subway. Convenient transportation services to and from all residential areas make it easier for the customer to decide to shop in a particular store or business area.

Studying the traffic pattern and traffic arteries allows small business owners to determine the accessibility of his specific location. They are also able to develop a time travel map detailing peak periods of traffic that assist them in deciding on their hours of operation. Accessibility to a site is one of the best ways of ensuring that a firm will survive and grow in a competitive environment.

In analyzing the accessibility of a site, the small business manager must consider the traffic interruption factors. These interruptions disrupt the pattern of traffic flow and can have an adverse effect on a site's potential. The following six negative factors should be considered.[1]

1. Dead spots where a shopper loses interest in going farther.
2. Driveways and other physical breaks in the sidewalks.
3. Cross traffic, either vehicular or pedestrian.
4. Areas that are identified with hazard, noise, odor, unsightliness, or other pedestrian inhibiting qualities.
5. Businesses that generate traffic in the form of trucks, public vehicles, private automobiles, or pedestrians who are not shoppers, and which tend, therefore, to create congestion.
6. Businesses whose customer's average parking time is extremely long.

[1]Richard L. Nelson, *The Selection of Retail Locations.* (New York: F. W. Dodge Corporation, 1958), p. 346.

Shopping centers build huge parking areas to help attract customers.

PARKING

In our highly mobile society, even with energy shortages, people still depend primarily on the automobile as their basic form of transportation for doing their shopping. As noted above, accessibility is a key factor for business firms. Another essential element is the adequacy of parking facilities. A major problem of downtown store locations, especially in the larger cities, has been the absence of adequate parking. Driving around the block hunting for a parking space is extremely frustrating and easily discourages the prospective customer. Sometimes merchants even park their cars in front of their own businesses, especially in smaller towns. Customers are inconvenienced when they try to find a parking space and are forced to park some distance away from the stores in which they want to shop.

Customers expect, even demand, that adequate parking facilities be close to the store. Downtown merchants have recognized this fact. As a result, old, dilapidated buildings have been razed and replaced by parking lots and garages. Many merchants even provide free parking in the downtown parking lots or garages. Shopping centers have been able to overcome many of the problems posed by inadequate parking by building huge parking areas.

There are no uniform means for determining parking adequacy for all retail and service establishments. Instead, each store owner-manager must determine the parking space needed according to the type of store operation. For example, one study of shopping centers indicated that a supermarket can use 12 spaces for each 1000 square feet of floor space, whereas small retail and specialty shops require no more than 4 to 5 spaces per 1000 square feet.[2] Basic considerations in determining parking adequacy include the following:

1. Type of neighborhood in which the site is located.
2. Frequency and length of store visitation by shoppers.
3. Pattern of business through time (variations or fluctuations in daily, weekly, or seasonal sales volume).[3]

SITES

In many small towns, there may be only a single business district. However, the decision-making process is more complex in cities or towns with larger or multiple business districts. Ordinarily, there are several kinds of locations available, each having their own advantages and disadvantages. Basically, the choices to be considered are:

1. Central business districts.
2. Neighborhood locations.
3. Shopping centers/malls.
4. Suburbs.
5. Wayside.
6. Near competition.

CENTRAL BUSINESS DISTRICTS

The downtown business district has been the traditional center of a town or city's shopping area because of the early development of this section of town and the convergence of the transportation systems in the central area. A business locating in a central business area has the advantage of being able to draw customers from the entire trading area of the city. On the positive side, many small businesses are able to take advantage of the drawing power of the

[2]Richard G. Thompson, *A Study of Shopping Centers*. Research Report #16, Real Estate Research Program, Institute of Business and Economic Research, University of California, Berkeley, 1961, p. 30.
[3]Ronald R. Gist, *Basic Retailing*. (New York: John Wiley & Sons, 1971), p. 151.

Heavy pedestrian traffic helps a retail location.

larger stores and the employment in the many offices in the downtown locations. While the larger stores prevail, the small businessman can take advantage
of the large volume of shoppers drawn by the large downtown stores as well as
the traffic produced by people who work in the downtown area. Convenience
good stores as well as shopping goods and specialty goods stores are found in
the downtown locations.

However, certain drawbacks are associated with a downtown location. One
disadvantage is that this location usually has higher operating costs and higher
rental rates. Furthermore, competition is usually very keen in the downtown
area. With increased traffic congestion, downtown locations have had some
difficulty in attracting customers. To counteract these problems, some cities
have initiated programs to revitalize the downtown business areas to make
them more appealing. Building renovations and the creation of pedestrian
walkways are part of the plan to encourage new business life for the downtown
areas.

Revitalized downtown areas encourage lunchtime strolling and shopping.

NEIGHBORHOOD SHOPPING AREAS

Within most cities are found clusters of several stores scattered throughout the residential areas. Ordinarily, these stores are convenience type stores. Stores located in neighborhood shopping areas include drugstores, hardware stores, grocery stores, and small variety stores. Service establishments (barber, beauty shops, dry cleaners) also find neighborhood locations attractive.

Neighborhood shopping area stores depend largely on the patronage of people who live in the area immediately surrounding the location. Compared to downtown locations, neighborhood stores have lower operating costs and lower rental rates. A distinct advantage of neighborhood locations is the opportunity afforded the owner-manager to enjoy direct, personal contact with customers. Through personal attention, such as knowing customers by name, the small business manager is able to promote repeat patronage for the store. Neighborhood stores are usually small, with annual sales of $50,000 or less.

SHOPPING CENTERS AND MALLS

The decade of the 1950s ushered in the period when large segments of the population moved to the suburbs. As the population shifted, it also became more mobile, chiefly as a result of the automobile. With the movement away from the central cities to the suburbs and the increased traffic congestion in the downtown areas, fewer shoppers patronized the downtown businesses. Instead customers found it more accessible to shop in planned shopping centers.

Basically, there are three categories of shopping centers. These are: (1) the neighborhood shopping center, (2) the community shopping center, and (3) the regional shopping center.

Neighborhood Shopping Center

This center usually serves a population of from 3,000 to 20,000 living within 6 to 10 minutes driving time of the center. A supermarket is usually the main store of this center and is responsible for drawing most of the traffic to the center. In addition to the supermarket, the small businesses located in this center sell convenience goods (foods, drugs, sundries) or offer personal services (barber shop, beauty shop, dry cleaning, shoe repair shops). Usually, the neighborhood center is small, with from 3 to 12 stores, arranged in a strip design.

Community Shopping Centers

These centers are larger, with from 12 to 50 stores. The trading area usually overlaps with other trading areas, so the population served ranges from 20,000 to 150,000. In addition to convenience goods stores and personal services shops, these centers also have many stores that carry shopping goods which enable shoppers to make price and quality comparisons in the center. The major store in this type of center may be a junior department store or a variety store and supermarket. If the main store is a department store, the apparel and furnishings store should locate as near it as possible to take advantage of its traffic. Stores that depend on fast turnover of traffic, such as dry cleaners or barber shops, should be located where there is always available parking.

Regional Shopping Centers

Regional centers cater to a much larger trading area. The area may extend 10 to 15 miles or more in all directions. The trading area depends on the location of competitors as well as travel time to reach the center (usually 20 to 40 minutes driving time). These centers have 50 to 100 or more stores. They have more than one major department store as the prime customer draw. There are many

Attractive enclosed malls make shopping convenient and pleasant.

shops normally attracted to these centers. Other features that serve to attract customers into the shopping center include community rooms, theatres, medical clinics, and banks and postal services.

Many of the regional shopping centers have enclosed, weather-controlled malls. These centers provide the added advantages of making it convenient and pleasant for customers to shop at all times, since a consumer can complete all shopping under one common roof. These centers have other features, such as fountains and landscaped interiors that add to their attractiveness.

Shopping center locations are advantageous in that occupants of a center can pool their advertising efforts and take advantage of group sales promotions. Further, shopping centers offer ample parking close to the stores and shops and have modern, attractive interiors and exteriors.

Suburbs

The population shift also opened the suburbs as a choice location for independent business owners who did not locate in planned shopping centers. Smaller stores, specialty shops, and service businesses are ordinarily found in suburban locations, with patronage drawn from the local trade area. While competition is keen in these locations, an advantage is that operating costs are usually lower.

Wayside Locations

Wayside locations along heavily traveled thoroughfares offer very satisfactory locations for some small businesses. Fruit stands, drive-in grocery stores, ceramic pottery stores, auto parts sales, and eating establishments are a few of the types of businesses found at wayside locations. Merchandise is usually lower priced at these locations and there is ordinarily ample parking space. Rent and other operating costs are usually lower for wayside locations also.

NEAR COMPETITION

Analysis of competitors in relation to various factors is an important criteria of site selection. In considering whether to locate near competitors (stores that are similar or complementary in type), the advantages must be weighed against the disadvantages. Specifically, a store owner-manager must consider not only how many competitors there are in an area but also the types of customers to which they cater. The size and financial strength of the competitors should also be evaluated. These two matters should point up the size of the potential market as well as buying power of those prospective customers. If the firms have a much stronger financial base and larger size, it may be a disadvantage for the smaller store. Another area of investigation should center on a comparison of the quality of goods and services offered by competitors. An economic survey of the area should reveal if the area demands the quality of your product as compared to the quality of merchandise sold by competition.

Locating near competition makes it easier for shoppers to do comparison shopping. Hence, it becomes possible for competing stores to pull more customers than it would be possible to do individually.

This analysis makes it possible to pinpoint both strengths and weaknesses of competitors. The small business manager can then imitate the positive aspects of the competition and either avoid their weaknesses or implement policies to fill the void not served by competitors. Another factor to consider is how many customers would be lost to competing stores. If more customers are lost than gained, such a close location would be a negative decision. Hence, another critical issue to be analyzed is how strongly the stores complement each other.

Many types of stores have a strong affinity to one another either because they sell similar or complementary merchandise. For example, department stores often locate close to one another, as do antique shops, theatres, and variety stores. Other examples of retail affinity include:

1. Men's and women's clothing stores and variety stores frequently locate near department stores.
2. Restaurants, barber shops, and candy, tobacco, and jewelry stores are commonly located near theatres.
3. Florists usually are grouped with shoe stores and women's clothing stores.
4. Paint, home furnishings, and furniture stores are generally located near each other.
5. Drugstores may be found in any of the above groupings.

SOME FACTORS IN JUDGING A LOCATION FOR A SMALL DRIVE-IN RESTAURANT

Described below are some factors to be considered in choosing a location for a drive-in restaurant.

How many families are there in the market area? What is the age range, average income, general occupational group? Are most of them young married couples, retirees, or middle aged? How many teenagers are there?

For this sort of information, ask the school board, the churches, the city or county government, the chamber of commerce, real-estate firms, stores, credit bureaus, and perhaps newspapers.

- How far is the site from surrounding or nearby residential areas? Is it 3 minutes, 10 minutes, 20 minutes driving time?
- How far will you be from suppliers? Can they serve you without delay and extra charges?
- How far from your location are other drive-in restaurants? If they are near, will they compete for the same customers—are they the same type of drive-in as the one you are planning? Or can you coexist—will they perhaps even attract customers to your drive-in?

- What types of business are in the immediate area? What is the general appearance of the buildings? Are they well kept or run down? Talk to the proprietors of the stores regarding business trends.
- Are there any churches in the area? Will churchgoers stop by your drive-in after services?
- Are there any special social or ethnic groups in the community? Will they be attracted to a drive-in, or are they persons who would not normally patronize one?
- Get the following information about traffic on the streets adjacent to the drive-in site:

1. What is the auto traffic flow on the streets? You can usually get this from state or country offices.
2. Are there traffic control lights?
3. Will traffic congestion be a problem?
4. What is the speed limit on the streets?
5. Are any streets one-way streets?
6. Are there centerline dividers on the streets?
7. What sort of pedestrians and auto passengers pass the location? Male, female, business employees, students, housewives? Are they transients? Are they en route from school, college, offices, industrial plants?
8. Can the site be seen from all directions? If so, from how far away?
9. What percent of your drive-in business will be morning, lunch-hour, afternoon, evening, night business?
10. Is the site near any interstate highway or city beltway?
11. Are the general surroundings of the area pleasant, dismal, or just average?
12. Will you be able to find employees in the area or nearby?[4]

SITE ANALYSIS CHECKLIST

The detailed checklist presented in Figure 5-3 serves as an extremely useful guide for the small business owner in location analysis. By rating the appropriate items, it is possible to develop a conceptual view of the suitability of alternative sites. Each factor can be rated with a plus (+) which would be a favorable vote for a specific site, a minus (−) which would be an unfavorable vote, or a zero (0) which would be neutral, not significant to the business.

[4]Source: *Starting and Managing a Small Drive-in Restaurant,* The Starting and Managing Series. (Washington, D.C.: Small Business Administration, 1972), pp. 17–19.

	Rating $(+, -, 0)$
I. City or town	
A. Economic considerations	
1. Industry	
a. Farming	_____
b. Manufacturing	_____
c. Trading	_____
2. Trend	
a. Highly satisfactory	_____
b. Growing	_____
c. Stationary	_____
d. Declining	_____
3. Permanency	
a. Old and well established	_____
b. Old and reviving	_____
c. New and promising	_____
d. Recent and uncertain	_____
4. Diversification	
a. Many and varied lines	_____
b. Many of the same type	_____
c. Few varied lines	_____
d. Dependent on one industry	_____
5. Stability	
a. Constant	_____
b. Satisfactory	_____
c. Average	_____
d. Subject to wide fluctuations	_____
6. Seasonality	
a. Little or no seasonal change	_____
b. Mild seasonal change	_____
c. Periodical—every few years	_____
d. Highly seasonal in nature	_____
7. Future	
a. Most promising	_____
b. Satisfactory	_____
c. Uncertain	_____
d. Poor outlook	_____
B. Population	
1. Income distribution	
a. Mostly wealthy	_____
b. Well distributed	_____
c. Mostly middle income	_____
d. Poor	_____

Figure 5-3 Checklist for locating a store. (*Source:* Small Business Administration, *Small Business Location and Layout.* Washington, D.C., U.S. Governmental Printing Office.)

Figure 5-3   (Continued)

2. Trend
   a. Growing   _____
   b. Large and stable   _____
   c. Small and stable   _____
   d. Declining   _____
3. Living status
   a. Own homes   _____
   b. Pay substantial rent   _____
   c. Pay moderate rent   _____
   d. Pay low rent   _____

C. Competition
   1. Number of competing stores
      a. Few   _____
      b. Average   _____
      c. Many   _____
      d. Too many   _____
   2. Type of management
      a. Not progressive   _____
      b. Average   _____
      c. Above average   _____
      d. Alert and progressive   _____
   3. Presence of chains
      a. No chains   _____
      b. Few chains   _____
      c. Average number   _____
      d. Many well established   _____
   4. Type of competing stores
      a. Unattractive   _____
      b. Average   _____
      c. Old and well established   _____
      d. Are many people buying out of community?   _____

D. The town as a place to live
   1. Character of the city
      a. Are homes neat and clean or rundown and shabby?   _____
      b. Are lawns, parks, streets, etc., neat, modern, attractive?   _____
      c. Adequate facilities available
         1. Banking   _____
         2. Transportation   _____
         3. Professional services   _____
         4. Utilities   _____
   2. Facilities and climate
      a. Schools   _____
      b. Churches   _____
      c. Amusement centers   _____
      d. Medical and dental services   _____
      e. Climate   _____

Figure 5-3 (Continued)

II. The actual site
  A. Competition
    1. Number of independent stores of same kind as yours
      a. Same block   ————
      b. Same side of street   ————
      c. Across street   ————
    2. Number of chain stores
      a. Same block   ————
      b. Same side of street   ————
      c. Across street   ————
    3. Kind of stores next door   ————
    4. Number of vacancies
      a. Same side of street   ————
      b. Across street   ————
      c. Next door   ————
    5. Dollar sales of nearest competitor   ————

  B. Traffic flow
    1. Sex of pedestrians   ————
    2. Age of pedestrians   ————
    3. Destination of pedestrians   ————
    4. Number of passers-by   ————
    5. Automobile traffic count   ————
    6. Peak hours of traffic flow   ————
    7. Percent location of site   ————

  C. Transportation
    1. Transfer points   ————
    2. Highway   ————
    3. Kind (bus, streetcar, auto, railway)   ————

  D. Parking facilities
    1. Large and convenient   ————
    2. Large enough but not convenient   ————
    3. Convenient but too small   ————
    4. Completely inadequate   ————

  E. Side of street

  F. Plant
    1. Frontage—in feet   ————
    2. Depth—in feet   ————
    3. Shape of building   ————
    4. Condition   ————
    5. Heat—type; air conditioning   ————
    6. Light   ————
    7. Display space   ————
    8. Back entrance   ————
    9. Front entrance   ————
    10. Display windows   ————

Figure 5-3 (Continued)

G. Corner location—if not, what is it?   _____

H. Unfavorable characteristics
    1. Fire hazards   _____
    2. Cemetery   _____
    3. Hospital   _____
    4. Industry   _____
    5. Relief office   _____
    6. Undertaker   _____
    7. Vacant lot—no parking possibilities   _____
    8. Garages   _____
    9. Playground   _____
    10. Smoke, dust, odors   _____
    11. Poor sidewalks and pavement   _____
    12. Unsightly neighborhood buildings   _____

I. Professional men in block
    1. Medical doctors   _____
    2. Dentists   _____
    3. Lawyers   _____
    4. Veterinarians   _____
    5. Others   _____

J. History of the site   _____

SITE ECONOMICS

Another criteria of location analysis is the determination of the cost of the site. If the site selected is the best available on all other factors previously mentioned, but the cost is excessive, then it may be that another site with lower occupancy costs should be selected.

Occupancy of a building site may be either on an ownership or lease basis. Most initial entrants into business lease their buildings. Some rent on a monthly basis but the more common practice is for a longer term lease for which they pay a fee, called rent. If the building is owned, then the maintenance and depreciation as well as mortgage and tax payments are a cost of occupying the store.

Each store owner-manager must analyze his specific store's requirements to evaluate the economic feasibility of the site relative to the occupancy cost. For example, stores that sell convenience goods, such as drugstores or cigar stores, usually require and must pay a premium for occupying a corner location. Service type operations, such as barber shops or dry cleaners, usually do better on inside locations.

	RATING			
	EXCELLENT	GOOD	FAIR	POOR
Site	_____	_____	_____	_____
Area—square feet (or acres)	_____	_____	_____	_____
Sale price or lease rate	_____	_____	_____	_____
Real estate tax rate (if land to be purchased)	_____	_____	_____	_____
Other annual assessments and costs	_____	_____	_____	_____
Total annual taxes (or rent) and other costs	_____	_____	_____	_____
Estimated volume expectancy	_____	_____	_____	_____
Ratio of total costs to volume expectancy	_____	_____	_____	_____
Stability of tax or rental costs in area	_____	_____	_____	_____
Trend in expansion of schools and other tax-supported improvements in area	_____	_____	_____	_____
Cost of building	_____	_____	_____	_____
Other	_____	_____	_____	_____

Figure 5-4 Site economics-cost and return analysis—vacant-land sites (*Source:* Richard L. Nelson, *The Selection of Retail Locations,* New York: F.W. Dodge Corporation, 1958, p. 346.)

The two checklists presented below can serve as guidelines in analyzing the economics of a site (see Figs. 5-4 and 5-5).

When considering renting a building, the small businessman should evaluate the characteristics of stores appropriate for high rent areas and low rent areas, as shown in the following listing.[5]

High Rent Area

1. High value of merchandise in proportion to bulk
2. Window display highly important
3. High rate of turnover
4. Low gross margin per item
5. Pickup or convenience goods sold
6. Appeal to transient trade
7. Little newspaper advertising
8. Price and convenience stressed
9. Low overhead

[5]Small Business Administration, *Small Business Location and Layout.* (Washington, D.C., U.S. Government Printing Office.)

	RATING			
	EXCELLENT	GOOD	FAIR	POOR
Site	___	___	___	___
Area—square feet	___	___	___	___
Sale price or rental	___	___	___	___
Real estate tax rate (if building to be purchased)	___	___	___	___
Other annual assessments and costs	___	___	___	___
Total annual taxes (or rent) and other costs	___	___	___	___
Estimated volume expectancy	___	___	___	___
Ratio of total costs to volume expectancy	___	___	___	___
Stability of tax or rental costs in area	___	___	___	___
Trend in expansion of schools and other tax-supported improvements in area	___	___	___	___
Cost of razing, additions, or other remodeling	___	___	___	___
Cost of cleaning and other improvement	___	___	___	___
Cost of heating	___	___	___	___
Cost of light and other utilities	___	___	___	___
Other	___	___	___	___

Figure 5-5 Cost and return analysis—building sites (building existing on property). (*Source:* Richard L. Nelson, *The Selection of Retail Locations,* F.W. Dodge Corporation, New York, 1958, p. 346.)

Low Rent Area

1. Low value of merchandise in proportion to bulk
2. Large amount of floor space for interior display
3. Low rate of turnover
4. High gross margin per item
5. Shopping lines sold in addition
6. Established clientele
7. Much advertising
8. Uses features of various kinds to attract customers
9. High overhead

Analysis of these characteristics should assist the small business manager in determining the rental fee that is economically feasible for a site. The final decision in selecting a specific site must be guided in part by the expected sales volume compared to the rental fee.

ZONING

In the search for a site for the business, the owner-manager must be aware of the zoning regulations in the area under consideration. Zoning refers to the division of a city or county into districts in order to control the location and use of buildings, land, and construction. The three broad categories of zoning include residential, business or commercial, and industrial, although there may be subcategories within the major classification, In cities or counties, a governing body, called either a zoning commission or a city or county planning commission, establishes zoning regulations that define the purpose for which land or buildings are to be used. This commission can also bring action to prevent or restrain the construction or remodeling of a building or the use of a building or land that violates the city or county zoning regulations.

A basic aim of zoning laws is to ensure a degree of consistency in the types and uses of buildings in a given area. The owner-manager must be aware that zoning laws affect not only the type of business that may be permitted to be established in an area but may also determine the kind of building that may be constructed as well as its height and size.

For example, an individual purchased a home in an area zoned residential with the expectation of starting a small beauty parlor business in the home. She applied to the zoning commission for a change in zoning category which would have permitted the overlapping of commercial and residential zones areas. Her application was denied on basis of objections from the neighbors as well as on basis of traffic and parking problems that would have been caused.

This case directs a word of caution to small business owners about the prospective site. They must ascertain that the intended business will not violate the zoning laws of an area. Hence, a site may be a good location, but city or county zoning regulations may prohibit locating there. Thorough investigation into zoning laws are an essential part of the site selection process. A zoning map of the city and surrounding territory can be useful in determining location and boundaries of zoning categories in a city or county.

Although it may be possible to get a site rezoned, the small business owner should not purchase a site until the site's classification has been changed. Too often, a site is purchased with no assurance, only hope, that it can be rezoned. Purchasing on the expectation that it may be rezoned is at best a risky business venture and fatal to the business if a reclassification cannot be obtained.

TRAFFIC ANALYSIS

It was stated earlier that for many types of businesses, such as apparel shops, the ease with which customers can reach a particular site plus the traffic movement past the site are most important factors in deciding on a location. For these businesses, a traffic count can measure the amount of pedestrian and vehicle traffic past a site which could be considered potential customers of the store.

The traffic count is a valuable tool in location analysis for two reasons. First, it reveals how many cars or people pass a given location. Second, the traffic study yields an indication of what kinds of people pass a given site. This information is extremely useful in the decision-making process for site selection.

PEDESTRIAN TRAFFIC COUNT

To make a pedestrian traffic count, it must be decided who is to be counted, when the count will take place, and where the count should be made. The purpose is to attempt to establish the amount of traffic on a normal shopping day.

Prior to making the count, decide on who is to be included in order to make the count more reliable. The finding of a heavy volume of traffic passing a site is of little or no value if the traffic obviously does not include the type of people to whom the store caters. By failing to establish who is to be counted, it is possible to end up with either too high or too low estimates. For example, a heavy volume of pedestrian traffic represented by workers entering a nearby office building would give misleading results if attention was focused only on the basis of volume without consideration of kind of traffic. A ladies' wear shop would be more interested in the number of female passersby, men's clothing stores in the number of male passersby, and drugstores in the total traffic volume. Another useful way for counting could include the age categoreis of pedestrians.

Furthermore, pedestrians should be classified according to their purpose in passing. A man rushing to catch a bus is not a good prospect for purchasing a suit. Hence, it is necessary to study the traffic movement during the shopping hours if a more reliable indication of potential customers during a normal shopping day is to be obtained. People passing early in the morning are ordinarily on their way to work, people passing at noon are usually on their way to lunch, and late afternoon passersby are on their way home. The in-between hours represent the best times to make a count of prospective shoppers. For example, more people enter a downtown store between the morning hours of 10 and 12 and afternoon hours of 1 and 3, thus representing times to study passersby. However, shopping center traffic would be heavier during evening hours because the center is open then. Moreover, care must be taken to include any local customs or other factors that would cause deviations.

Other considerations in determining traffic flow are the season as well as the month, week, and day. Traffic normally is much heavier before holidays and during the latter part of the week.

When a day with normal traffic flow has been selected, it is a good policy to divide the day into half-hour and hour intervals. This enables traffic to be counted and recorded for each half-hour interval that the store is open for business.

Another factor in pedestrian traffic counting is to establish where the count will be made. Will all traffic passing near the site or just the traffic passing in front of the site be counted? Care must also be taken so as not to count people twice, such as when customers enter and leave a store.

AUTOMOBILE TRAFFIC COUNT

Many firm's sales depend on drive-in customers. The same technique used in counting pedestrian traffic may be employed in establishing auto traffic flow. Determination must be made of who, when, and where in counting. Data on traffic flow along major streets may be available from city or state government agencies or outdoor advertising companies. However, you should not rely solely on these sources, since your business may have special needs.

Auto traffic may be classified on the basis of the kind of trip taken: work trip, planned shopping trip, or pleasure trip. Retailers and service establishments seek locations that enable them to take advantage of the kind of customer they are striving to reach. For example, in work trip traffic, the dry cleaner would prefer a location on the side of the street where people go to work, while the drive-in grocery prefers the location on the side of their homeward trip. Location analysis shows that a good retailing location for planned shopping trip traffic is on the right-hand side of the main street going into a shopping district and next to streets carrying traffic into, out of, or across town. Motels, service stations, and restaurants attract customers by locating along heavily traveled freeways with easy exit and access back to the freeway.

By analyzing pedestrian and auto traffic, it becomes possible to develop a time-travel map. This map facilitates developing a picture of the quality and quantity of traffic flow during normal shopping hours and is one major element in deciding if the site would generate enough business volume to operate profitably.

Traffic analysis is more significant in location evaluation for some types of outlets than for others when considered on the basis of the type of consumer goods sold. Outlets distributing convenience goods must rely on the quantity of pedestrian and auto traffic as the most important measure. Drive-in stores that sell convenience goods are more attractive to consumers if they are located close to their residence.

Shopping goods outlets depend more on quality than quantity, since people who visit these stores usually make a deliberate effort to shop there. Specialty goods outlets are usually able to locate in a more out of the way site, since customers seek them out. Hence, traffic analysis is not as essential as it is for convenience and shopping goods stores.

LOCATION ANALYSIS FOR SMALL WHOLESALERS

Wholesalers are middlemen. Their sales are usually made to retailers or to other wholesalers. Small wholesalers usually serve a local market, such as the wholesale grocer supplying merchandise to grocery stores in the immediate town or making deliveries to nearby towns.

Briefly stated, the small wholesaler has to consider many of the same location factors we have outlined earlier for retailing and service establishments. However, they must be evaluated in light of his unique requirements.

For example, the small wholesaler must consider the trading area's potential when evaluating sites. In most towns or cities, there is a wholesaling district that must be determined as far as its suitability and accessibility. Recently, some wholesalers have begun to locate on the edge of towns to provide more flexibility.

LOCATION ANALYSIS FOR THE SMALL MANUFACTURERS

As with the retailing and service establishments, location of the small manufacturer is also one of the keys to its success or failure. Hence, the small manufacturer must consider many of the same factors in determining the proper location as for other types of business. Factors to be considered are outlined in the checklist given in Figure 5-6.

DISCUSSION QUESTIONS

1. Why is location such an important matter for small business owners?
2. Discuss some of the factors that should be considered in analyzing the trading area.
3. Explain why accessibility of site is a major criteria for locating the small business.

FACTOR	EXCELLENT	GOOD	FAIR	POOR
1. Accessibility to market served	____	____	____	____
2. Quantity and quality of labor supply available (short and long term)	____	____	____	____
3. Available supply of raw materials	____	____	____	____
4. Tax burden of business in the community	____	____	____	____
5. Community attitudes toward business	____	____	____	____
6. Availability of transportation	____	____	____	____
7. Suitable climate	____	____	____	____
8. Community services and facilities (housing, schools, police and fire protection, hospitals)	____	____	____	____
9. Adequacy of utilities (gas, water, electrical power)	____	____	____	____
10. Potential for expansion and growth	____	____	____	____
11. Evaluation of site chosen in relation to competition	____	____	____	____

Figure 5-6   Rating sheet for a small plant.

4. Identify the three types of consumer goods.
5. What are some of the chief factors to consider when evaluating the parking facilities of a proposed site?
6. Explain the advantages and disadvantages of the central business district.
7. What is site economics? Why is it important?
8. What are some of the factors to be considered in evaluating whether to rent in a high rent area or a low rent area?
9. What is zoning?
10. Discuss the factors to consider in making a pedestrian and automobile traffic count.

STUDENT PROJECTS

1. Select a line of business (grocery, hardware, florist, etc.) and obtain an estimate of your area's purchasing power for the potential of this line of business.
2. Consult Bureau of Census data and determine the percentage and/or number of people employed industry by industry for your city, county, and/or state.
3. Interview a small business owner to determine the factors he/she considers most important in selecting a location for the business.

CASE A

WESTON ANIMAL CLINIC

When Dr. Alice Weston graduated from the State University with a Doctor of Veterinary Medicine degree, she joined the Taylor Animal Clinic which was owned and operated by Dr. Samuel Taylor. Two years later when Dr. Taylor retired, Dr. Weston bought the clinic and changed its name to Weston Animal Clinic. Now she operates it as a sole proprietorship.

The Weston Animal Clinic is located in a small town near a large lake. The area is a popular recreational area for boating, camping, and fishing. The nearest veterinarians are located about 30 miles away. The clinic serves a population of some 10,000 people in the lake area, where most of the people reside at the southern end of the lake. There are also many weekend visitors and summer residents who come to the area to enjoy the camping and water sports.

Most of the animals treated at the clinic are small animals (pets). The relatively few large farm animals that are treated must be cared for away from the clinic because of the lack of space.

During the past two years the clinic's revenue has grown, with net income before taxes as a percent of gross revenue being 46 percent and 53 percent, respectively, for each of the two years.

Dr. Weston prefers to make this area her permanent residence. Her objectives for the business are to expand the veterinary practice and at some future time add a partner.

Dr. Weston currently is considering expanding the clinical facilities. This may necessitate relocation. The specific reasons for expansion are the increased demands to treat larger animals and the increased demand for kennels for smaller animals for boarding and medical treatment. If the clinic is expanded, this would provide additional work for the anticipated partner. One factor that hinders the expansion objective is the space in the current building.

Three choices are available to Dr. Weston.

1. The building in which Dr. Weston is located contains three separate businesses: a florist, a dentist, and the clinic. The clinic has an area of 1100 square feet, 800 of which are used for the clinic and the remaining 300 used for kennels. Dr. Weston has a two-year lease for $200 a month. There is the possibility the building could be purchased and remodeled. However, the construction of the building is not of the quality that would warrant a long term investment and it is set on a small lot that would not allow adequate expansion.
2. A second choice is to try to locate an existing building that is more suitable.

A concern with this choice would be the need for remodeling to convert the building into a functional animal clinic.

3. The third choice is to purchase property and build a new clinic. Dr. Weston feels that a facility of 2000 square feet would be large enough immediately—1100 for the clinic and 900 for kennels and stalls to house animals. There is also the need for future expansion. This option would cost approximately $55,000 for the land and to construct the facility. Mortgage payments would be $630 per month compared to the current lease of $200 monthly.

One location that is available for purchase is about a mile from a small town and is close to a small shopping center which has a convenience store, post office, and hardware store. A medical clinic is being planned for the area.

Question

Analyze Dr. Weston's choices and recommend the one most suitable for the objectives stated for the business.

CASE B

WANDA'S FLOWER SHOP

Edward and Wanda Morris own and operate a flower shop in a city of 25,000. They prepare floral arrangements for all occasions. Their competition consists of three other floral shops in the city. Edward, a high school teacher, and Wanda gave much thought to planning the shop prior to its opening. Now that it is open, it is operated by Wanda and a part-time employee who works five mornings a week making deliveries and helping in the shop, including taking telephone orders.

The only available space that they could afford at the time of their opening was a small, separate area in a relatively new building. It has its own entrance and a small show window. An electrician's shop occupies the major portion of the building. While it is a relatively new building, its location is inconvenient for their floral shop. It is located three miles from downtown on an access road along a major interstate highway, away from the mainstream of the city's traffic. A large percentage of their customers telephone in their orders, or they must make an effort to drive out to their shop. At the current location, there is no chance of walk-in customers.

With a minimum amount of newspaper advertising as well as word-of-mouth recommendations from satisfied customers, the floral shop has enjoyed a steady growth of business. Consequently, the current physical facility is now too small to be able to serve more customers adequately. Furthermore, the Morris's want to move to a location where pedestrian traffic passes by, thus increasing the chances for walk-in customers.

Question

Outline the factors that Edward and Wanda should consider in deciding where to relocate their floral shop.

6

PHYSICAL FACILITIES OF THE SMALL BUSINESS

PREVIEW OF THIS CHAPTER

1. After reading this chapter, you will understand why the physical facility is important for the business firm.

2. You should be aware of the issues to be considered in choosing between a new facility and an existing structure.

3. You will be able to comprehend the factors in deciding whether to buy or lease a building.

4. You should recognize the factors to be considered in determining the size and type of facility needed.

5. You will be able to identify the factors that should be evaluated pertaining to the exterior of a bulilding.

6. You will be able to explain the important features of a building's interior of which the small business owner should be cognizant.

7. You will understand the importance of store layout.

8. You will recognize the difference between process layout and product layout in a factory.

9. You will understand the difference between merchandising and processing service establishments.

10. You will be able to explain these key words:

Display window	Product layout
Recessed front	Grid layout
Layout	Free flow layout
Process layout	

IMPORTANCE OF THE PHYSICAL FACILITY

The specific appearance of a building appropriate to the type of business housed therein has been recognized by many as an aid in attracting customers. Customers recognize the unique features of a building and associate them with the firm's goods or services. This is a main reason why franchisers stress uniform building design for their franchised outlets.

Planning the store's physical facility is essential in order for the firm to effectively serve customers or manufacture a product.

The suitability of each building must be considered in view of any specific requirements a business might have.

In the preceding chapter, criteria for locating a satisfactory site for the business were presented. In this chapter, we examine some of the considerations in determining the physical facilities of the small business.

DECISIONS INVOLVED IN CHOOSING A PHYSICAL FACILITY

In choosing a physical facility, small business owners are faced with decisions of whether to construct their own structure or occupy an already constructed building and whether to buy or lease the facility.

CONSTRUCT A NEW FACILITY

The ideal situation for small business owners is to determine the building requirements and design the facility from the ground up. The advantage of this approach is that modern features can be incorporated into the building plans. The exterior design as well as the interior and layout can be arranged to suit the special needs of the small business owner. In addition, the physical location can be chosen.

OCCUPY AN EXISTING FACILITY

Most small business owners occupy buildings that are already constructed. In evaluating the existing building or space in a shopping center, small business owners must not only determine if the location is suitable but also if the available building will meet their requirements or can be remodeled to meet the required specifications.

To illustrate, since the energy shortages beginning in the early 1970s, some 56,000 gasoline service stations have closed. Many of these stations have been sold to franchisees and other small business owners and have been converted into adequate facilities for other types of businesses. The net result is that the cost of remodeling the building is considerably less than constructing a new building and the remodeling process is faster than constructing a new facility.

A typical conversion can take as little as 45 days and cost from $10,000 to $65,000. It is less if the project is done by the owner-manager. One Houston couple turned an old Texaco station into an exotic plant boutique for $500. In addition, many facilities have good locations with large, paved parking lots and utilities in place and sometimes even landscaping.[1]

Fast-food operations have been especially successful in converting service stations into satisfactory facilities. Service stations have also been converted into dry cleaning plants, print shops, used-car lots, muffler shops, bookstores, doughnut bakeries, pawn shops, and various types of repair shops.

BUY OR LEASE

After the decision has been made to locate the business in an existing structure or build a new one, the choice of renting or buying the building must be made.

In smaller towns or in areas where real estate values are not too high, small business owners may own their building. Another alternative is to lease the facility, either on a stated dollar rental fee per month or year or on the basis of paying rent as a percentage of the firm's annual sales or gross profit.

When choosing between leasing and buying, small business owners should weigh the following advantages and disadvantages.

Advantages of Buying

When owner-managers buy their building, they have the option to maintain it in the way they desire. They do not have to obtain permission from the building's owner if they wish to modernize the structure in any way. Furthermore, by owning the building, small business owners do not have to be concerned about being evicted as long as the business is solvent. Another advantage of ownership is that if the property appreciates in value, the small business owner reaps the benefit. Still another advantage is that building depreciation is an expense of business operations for income tax purposes, as are taxes and interest payments.

Disadvantages of Buying

On the other side of the coin are the negative factors of ownership. Property may decline in value if a business district becomes run down. A large initial

[1]Peter Mohr, "Life After Death Along Gasoline Alley," *Fortune,* November 1979, pp. 86 and 88.

capital outlay is required if the building is purchased plus the cost of regular interest and mortgage payments. Additionally, ownership limits the mobility of the owner. If owners want to relocate, they must dispose of the owned building in some manner. In addition, there are substantial costs involved in taxes and maintenance and repairs that may limit the amount of working capital for other on-going business operations.

Advantages of Leasing

Leasing offers several advantages to small business owners. By leasing, the owners do not have to make a large initial cash outlay as they would if they purchased a building. Hence, more funds are available for current operations. Leasing also increases the mobility of owners if they decide to move when the lease expires. By leasing, they do not suffer the financial loss if the building declines in value. For income tax purposes, rent is also an expense of doing business. The lease agreement may also stipulate that the building owner pay for all or part of any renovation desired by the building occupant.

Disadvantages of Leasing

A disadvantage of leasing is that the owner of the building may not renew the lease, forcing small business owners to lose a valuable site when the lease expires. The owner's permission must be obtained to make modifications and such permission may not be granted. One small business owner leased a building and upon reading the fine print of the contract after signing it discovered that the lease prohibited the displaying of any type of store sign on the property. This small business owner had to rent a porta-trailer display board and place it away from the building's property line.

The small business owner should carefully weigh the pros and cons of leasing versus buying before the final decision.

SIZE AND TYPE OF FACILITY

When the business is initially established or when it is to be relocated, small business owners must find an existing physical facility that is adequate or construct one that meets their specific requirements.

Determining the size of the facility is extremely important to the small business owner. Yet it is also one of the more difficult requirements to accurately gauge. Defining space requirements requires projecting the firm's needs into the future, which clearly involves the issue of uncertainty. If the estimation of size needs is understated, then a new facility or building addition may soon be required, resulting in increased cost and inconvenience both to customer and owner. Overestimating space needs means inefficient use of space and added cost until the volume of business activity matches space availability.

The initial size of the facility should be adequate to meet current needs but should also provide for a kind of construction that can easily and economically be expanded when growth of the firm justifies it. For example, in selecting a building for locating a men's specialty shop, initial spatial requirements must be established for the retail selling area as well as storage area. But the existing structure also needs to be evaluated in terms of its flexibility for modification. For example, are there existing walls that can be easily removed if future growth requires more selling and display area?

The type of building should be functional for the specific type of business housed in it. However, the building should also be attractive in appearance. The small business owner should be aware of the zoning regulations governing building design codes and fire codes for the particular site. Specifically, owners must know the exact requirements as far as wall and roof construction, entrances, exists, and occupancy. Some specific questions to be answered in regard to the type of building are presented below.

1. What type of exterior walls are best suited for the type of business?
2. What type of roof will be required?
3. What is the best type of insulation for the roof and walls?
4. What type of structural frame will be most appropriate?
5. Will the architectural design be appropriate for the particular business district?
6. What type of floor is required?

Before reaching a final decision, the small businessman should seek the advice of a professional builder or architect in analyzing the building requirements for specific building needs.

BUILDING EXTERIOR

The outside appearance of the building gives a valuable assist in setting the appeal of the store to the customers' eye. Often, a distinctive exterior can give one business owner a competitive edge. For the physical facility that is to be constructed as a separate facility, the building architecture can be designed to meet specific requirements. In planned shopping centers, the theme of the entire center is uniform throughout. However, as we have already stressed, most small business owners find it advantageous to occupy a building already constructed. Many of these buildings must be modernized before they are suitable structures. The factors discussed below are representative of building exterior features that should be considered, especially if remodeling is necessary.

BUILDING ARCHITECTURE

The exterior greatly aids in helping to create the type of store image the owner wishes to project. The exterior may be designed along simple, modern lines of design. Or, it may be of an ornate design. The trend is toward the more simple, functional type of building design, with features of pleasing colors and special facades.

STORE FRONT

The small business owner must decide what type of exterior facade will be used to dress up the appearance of the store. A variety of building materials are used for the store front. The type used often depends on the funds available. More expensive materials, such as brick, fieldstone, highly finished tile, or less ex-

A well-planned store front includes attractive window displays and store signs which clearly identify the small business.

pensive materials, such as aluminum sheathing, stainless steel, or special types of structural glass, may be used. The materials and store front design selected should reflect the image of the store. Modernization of the store front can make even an old building look totally different and refreshing.

DISPLAY WINDOWS

"Window shopping" is a favorite pastime for many Americans. The small business owner should make use of this knowledge as plans are made for the display windows of the store. (See Fig. 6-1.) Attractive window displays present the kind of merchandise sold in the store and serve to project its image. Window displays of merchandise often catch the customers' eye and interest, causing them to come in and purchase the items displayed. When analyzing the display window in the building, the merchant should take care to note how it can be used most effectively. Many small business owners recognize the importance of window displays and install plate glass windows across the entire

---

I. Merchandise selected

    1. Is the merchandise timely?
    2. Is it representative of the stock assortment?
    3. Are the articles harmonious—in type, color, texture, use?
    4. Are the price lines of the merchandise suited to the interests of passersby?
    5. Is the quantity on display suitable (that is, neither overcrowded nor sparse)?

II. Setting

    1. Are glass, floor, props, and merchandise clean?
    2. Is the lighting adequate (so that reflection from the street is avoided)?
    3. Are spotlights used to highlight certain parts of the display?
    4. Is every piece of merchandise carefully draped, pinned, or arranged?
    5. Is the background suitable, enhancing the merchandise?
    6. Are the props well suited to the merchandise?
    7. Are window cards used, and are they neat and well placed?
    8. Is the entire composition balanced?
    9. Does the composition suggest rhythm and movement?

III. Selling power

    1. Does the window present a readily recognized central theme?
    2. Does the window exhibit power to stop passersby through the dramatic use of light, color, size, motion, composition, and/or item selection?
    3. Does the window arouse a desire to buy (as measured by shoppers entering the store)?

Figure 6-1 A checklist for window displays. (*Source.* John Wingate and Seymour Helfant, *Small Store Planning for Growth,* Small Business Management Series No. 33, Small Business Administration, Washington, D.C., 1977, p. 77.)

front of their business. This enables potential customers to see into the store without any barriers to their line of vision. Merchants also use show windows to display announcements about a special sale.

Display windows should be designed to fit the merchandise sold. Displays should be between waist and eye levels, depending on the type of merchandise sold. For example, rings, watches, and other jewelry items are small in size and should be displayed higher from the floor.

Small business owners must realize that unattractive window displays can dampen customer interest in a store and even influence shoppers to go elsewhere.

ENTRANCES AND EXITS

Entrances to the store are important because they determine how smoothly customer traffic moves into and out of the building. In the previous chapter, we stressed the importance of accessibility to the store. Obstacles that hinder traffic flowing smoothly into and out of the store often drive customers away, thus reducing sales. Careful planning can alleviate these obstacles. Some obstacles that may discourage customers are hard-to-open doors, poor location of doors or too narrow doors, steps up to the entrance, or poor condition of a sidewalk leading up to the entrance. Entrances should be designed so that customers can easily enter the store. Some stores use automatic opening doors. Entrances should also be clearly marked and well lighted. Awnings over entrances may add to shoppers' convenience if they are of the proper height.

RECESSED FRONT

Many retail outlets use a recessed store front which enables the customer to casually look at the merchandise displayed in the show window, yet be off the street and out of the mainstream of pedestrian traffic. The small business owner should consider whether this feature is important to the particular business.

OUTSIDE SIGNS

Properly placed signs pointing to the store are an important aspect of the store's exterior and are useful landmarks for guiding the customer to the store, just as a lighthouse guides a ship. Shoppers may become frustrated when they are looking for a specific store and are not able to find it because a sign does not clearly mark its location. The small business should be aware of some of the common problems encountered with respect to outside signs. These include improperly designed signs, signs placed in a poor position, signs that are the wrong size, signs that are illegible (faded out), signs that are in poor condition, or signs that are a poor color.

BUILDING INTERIOR

Shoppers tend to have favorable attitudes toward shopping in stores where the interior is both appealing and inviting. The small business owner should pay special attention to those features that help to create a favorable shopping environment: floors, walls and ceilings, lighting and fixtures, color scheme, and year round temperature control.

FLOORS

Flooring should be sturdy enough to handle traffic as well as the weight of materials that will move over it. In a factory, a painted concrete floor may be satisfactory. For a retailing firm, flooring should have a type of covering that matches the decor of the store and also be safe and comfortable for the customer. This may include various kinds of tile, hardwood, carpet, linoleum, or terrazzo. The condition of the flooring should be considered also. Some questions need to be answered regarding flooring. How difficult is it to maintain the floor? Is the floor covering unsuitable or dangerous (does it become slick if it gets damp?) Is the floor covering an unsuitable color or of poor material? Does the flooring add to the noise or reduce the noise in the store? Is the flooring durable? What is its cost?

WALLS AND CEILING

Like flooring, the walls and ceiling are an essential part of the store's overall appearance. Walls should be of sufficient strength to support the requirements of the building, such as holding up shelving as well as matching the color scheme of the store. Partitions are useful in that these movable walls allow for variety in the arrangement of the store. Likewise, the ceiling requirements must be analyzed. Will it be plaster or acoustical tile? By using a suspended acoustical tile ceiling, some flexibility in ceiling height can be obtained. Lowering the ceiling can also reduce the cost of operation, such as lower heating and cooling costs. Inclusion of fireproof partitions can also help to reduce insurance costs. Use of the proper type of paint on the interior walls and partitions helps to reduce maintenance costs.

LIGHTS AND FIXTURES

Adequate lighting aids the shopper. Lighting requirements must be analyzed for each type of store. A proper lighting system enhances the environment of the store. Equally as important, proper lighting enables the customer to see merchandise quickly and clearly and makes selection of desired items easier. Insufficient lighting can cause customers to shy away from a store. Glaring or obscure lights are examples of this problem. In the factory, lighting must be adequate for workers to perform their job efficiently. Lights should be bright but not glaring.

A lighting system must be designed which is energy efficient. It must also be a flexible system so that it can be increased at some future time if the need arises. It must also have the proper appearance, be maintained easily and inexpensively, and be sturdy in construction.

COLOR SCHEME

Colors can be used to advantage to give the store specific appeal. Paint manufacturers suggest that different colors can create certain visual effects. For example, certain colors can be used to make a building appear larger. Painting the rear walls a darker color creates the illusion of making a long, narrow building seem wider.

The owner should use colors wisely in the selling space and in fixtures. It is best to avoid using bright shades of color. While they are attention getters, they may overpower the merchandise. Loud colors and strong color contrasts should be used only in the proper environment, such as a store specializing in youth-oriented apparel.

Soft pastel shades lend themselves to overall store decor, while darker colors can be used for accents. The color scheme should enhance the merchandise displayed. Blue, green, gray, and black are best used with displays of more expensive merchandise. Low-priced bargain merchandise displays use bright shades of yellow, orange, and red with white to make them stand out. Colors can also be used to brighten a store or factory and make it more appealing to customers and more conducive to promoting employee efficiency. Certain colors reflect light. Hence, they help to reduce lighting needs and save electrical energy.

AIR CONDITIONING AND HEATING

Year-round temperature control is a valuable feature for the small business. Many stores, especially those in warmer climates, are air-conditioned. Air conditioning is accepted as necessary for customer shopping convenience. Employees seem to perform better in air-conditioned facilities. Care must be taken to install equipment that meets the needs of the building. It must be both adequate in size (not too large or too small) and efficient in operation. Heating and heating equipment must also be evaluated for its adequacy.

ADDITIONAL AND SPECIAL BUILDING FEATURES

For any special building features that may be required to meet the specifications of the small business, the manager must determine whether the facility has them or if the building can be modified to provide them. It should also be determined whether the existing facilities are adequate for present needs or if they are adaptable for expansion if future growth requires it. The additional features that should be evaluated include:

Electric wiring—adequate for present needs and adaptable to expansion at a later date; any special wiring needed to operate business equipment

Gas piping—adequacy and condition of piping

Plumbing—adequacy

Absence of structural obstacles (columns and posts will not interfere with store operations)

Restroom furnishings and equipment

Shelves and wall cases

Transportation for personnel, freight, and merchandise—elevator, escalator, conveyors

Water fountains

Burglar alarms

Fire extinguishers and other fire equipment—sprinkler system

Location of loading docks as well as their size and type

Availability of protective covering to go over merchandise in the loading and unloading docks

Waste disposal facilities—incinerator, dispose-all, trash room

Public address system

Drainage facilities

LAYOUT

Layout in the retail store or in the factory should be analyzed by the small business owner, as it plays a key role in making the business a success. Layout means the planned physical arrangement of the business firm's interior. Much deliberation and planning should go into determining the best layout design for the specific type of business activity, since the type of arrangement varies from firm to firm.

The purpose of retail store layout is to attract customers and to aid in the

Proper store layout facilitates customer shopping.

efficient operation of the business. The attainment of these two goals is facilitated by effective use of proper climate control, lights, color scheme, and ease with which premises and stock can be cleaned and maintained. In determining the store configuration, a number of factors need to be evaluated.

TYPE OF MERCHANDISE OFFERED

In developing the physical arrangement, the type of merchandise offered for sale should be considered. For the retailer, the store's success is dependent almost entirely on selling. Properly designed store layout makes the products available to the consumer in the most efficient way possible. The layout of the selling floor should be planned with customer convenience uppermost in importance. Related merchandise should be displayed close together to ensure ease of shopping. For example, shirts, slacks, ties, shoes, belts should be located in adjacent areas.

If feasible, merchandise should be displayed openly so that customers can examine it. For some types of merchandise, such as jewelry or cameras, open displays are not practical. Items likely to be purchased on impulse need to be displayed near the store's entrance or where there is heavy customer traffic.

Figure 6-2 presents a classification of goods as well as a suggested location of merchandise in the small retail store.

I. Impulse goods	II. Convenience Goods
Bought:	**Bought:**
As a result of attractive "visual merchandising" displays	With frequency and in small quantities
Should Be Placed:	**Should Be Placed:**
Near entrance in small store—on main aisle in larger stores	In easily accessible feature locations along main aisle
III. Necessities or Staple Goods	IV. Utility Goods
Bought:	**Bought:**
Because of an actual need	For home use—brooms, dust pans, etc.
Should Usually Be Placed:	**Should Be Placed:**
To the rear of one-level stores—on upper floor of multilevel stores (not an infallible rule)	As impulse items up front or along main aisle

V. Luxury and Major Expense Items

Bought:

After careful planning and considerable "shopping around"

Should Be Placed:

At some distance from entrance

Figure 6-2 Classification and arrangement of merchandise in small retail stores. (*Source:* Small Business Administration. *Small Business Location and Layout*, Administrative Management Course Program, Topic 13, U.S. Government Printing Office, Washington, D.C.)

SIZE OF STORE

A properly planned layout makes it possible to use the store's total area efficiently. Space needs for storage, office, and selling area must be determined. In a retail store, selling is the most important activity. Hence, nonselling and office activities, while they are essential, should not take up valuable selling space. Rather, they should conform to the store size.

CUSTOMER VOLUME AT PEAK HOURS

In planning the store arrangement, thought should be given to how many customers will be in the store at the peak hours and how readily these customers can be served. Fast, efficient service is especially important in retail and service establishments. Locating cash registers close to the selling area reduces the amount of time a sales clerk must spend walking to and from the sales floor; hence, customer service is improved. More customer traffic can be accommodated if self-service fixtures (display cases, counters) are arranged for customer convenience. By using a counter with several tiers, it is possible to use vertical space efficiently. Stock areas should be located as near the selling area as practical to reduce the amount of time a sales clerk must be away from the selling area getting additional stock. In a shoe store, for example, the shoe stock is ordinarily located on shelves immediately behind the displayed stock. Since only a limited stock can be displayed, the sales clerk ordinarily must go to the stockroom to obtain the size and style of shoe desired. The sales person merely steps through a curtained opening, selects the shoes requested, and is back on the sales floor in a very short time. By considering such factors, the small business owner will be able to serve his customers at the peak hours of business and, in turn, increase store sales.

STORE FIXTURES

Fixtures are an integral part of effective layout design. A useful guide for deciding on the kind of fixtures needed is that the most practical and economical fixtures permit merchandise to be displayed in proper arrangement for each line of merchandise with maximum exposure and minimum amount of distractions.

Before deciding on fixtures, the small business owner should determine the kind of merchandise to be displayed on them as well as how much space is needed on each display fixture to display different kinds of merchandise. Fixtures should not be too large. Crowding together of display fixtures in small and crowded aisles where customers must push and shove defeats the purpose of even the best designed displays.

Other factors that must be considered in determining store layout are

Building construction
Fire and security protection measures
Number of employees and facilities
Service to customers (restrooms, fitting rooms)

A checklist for evaluating the interior arrangement and display of a retail store is given in Figure 6-3.

INTERIOR LAYOUT ARRANGEMENTS

A basic function of layout is to make merchandise accessible to the customer. In considering layout, the retailer should establish the type of internal arrange-

	Yes	No
I. Layout		
1. Are your fixtures low enough and signs so placed that the customer can get a bird's-eye view of the store and tell in what direction to go for wanted goods?	____	____
2. Do your aisle and counter arrangements tend to stimulate a circular traffic flow through the store?	____	____
3. Do your fixtures (and their arrangement), signs, lettering, and colors all create a coordinated and unified effect?	____	____
4. Before any supplier's fixtures are accepted, do you make sure they conform in color and design to what you already have?	____	____
5. Do you limit the use of hanging signs to special sale events?	____	____
6. Are your counters and aisle tables not overcrowded with merchandise?	____	____
7. Are your ledges and cashier/wrapping stations kept free of boxes, unneeded wrapping materials, personal effects, and odds and ends?	____	____
8. Do you keep trash bins out of sight?	____	____
II. Merchandise emphasis		
1. Do your signs referring to specific goods tell the customer something significant about them, rather than simply naming the products and their prices?	____	____
2. For your advertised goods, do you have prominent signs, including tear sheets at entrances, to inform and guide customers to their exact location in the store?	____	____
3. Do you prominently display both advertised and nonadvertised specials at the ends of counters as well as at the point of sale?	____	____
4. Are both your national and private brands highlighted in your arrangement and window display?	____	____
5. Wherever feasible, do you give the more colorful merchandise in your stock preference in display?	____	____
6. In the case of apparel and home furnishings, do the items that reflect your store's fashion sense or fashion leadership get special display attention at all times?	____	____
7. In locating merchandise in your store, do you always consider the productivity of space—vertical as well as horizontal?	____	____
8. Is your self-service merchandise arranged so as to attract customers and assist them in selection by the means indicated below:		
a. Is each category grouped under a separate sign?	____	____
b. Is the merchandise in each category arranged according to its most significant characteristic—weather, color, style, size, or price?	____	____
c. In apparel categories, is the merchandise arranged by price lines or zones to assist the customer in making a selection quickly?	____	____
d. Is horizontal space usually devoted to different items and styles within a category (vertical space being used for different sizes— smallest at the top largest at the bottom)?	____	____
e. Are impulse items interspersed with demand items and not placed across the aisle from them, where many customers will not see them?	____	____

Figure 6-3 Checklist for interior arrangement and display. (*Source*. John W. Wingate and Seymour Helfant, *Small Store Planning for Growth*. Washington, D.C.: Small Business Administration.)

The interior layout of this department store is designed to make merchandise easily accessible to customers.

ment best suited for the store to facilitate traffic movement and shopping. In the retailing store, the grid and the free-flow arrangements are two basic designs.

GRID LAYOUT

The grid layout, or rectangular arrangement, features a main aisle and secondary aisles which are located at right angles to the main aisle. (See Fig. 6-4.) Main aisles carry a large share of the traffic and provide the best location for convenience goods, impulse items, or seasonal merchandise. Shopping goods are displayed on the secondary aisles, and specialty goods may be located in a less traveled area. An essential element for consideration is that the store area that contributes most to sales is located in the front quarter of the store near the entrance and checkout counter. As much as two-thirds of the store's annual sales may be made in the front quarter of the store. An advantage of this arrangement is the ease with which customers can find their way around the store.

FREE FLOW LAYOUT

Store owners using the free-flow layout recognize that customers normally move to their right when they enter the store. This layout may be arranged in

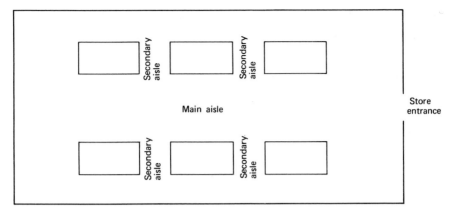

Figure 6-4 Grid layout.

circular, octagonal, or U-shaped patterns. Unlike the grid layout, the free-flow layout plan has no uniform pattern. It has more flexibility since display counters can be rearranged without disrupting the layout pattern. Another advantage of this plan is that it may encourage customers to move easily from one area of the store to another and thus give the customer greater exposure to merchandise.

Ordinarily, the grid layout is less expensive and probably better suited to the needs of the small business. However, some owner-managers use the free flow arrangement to create a distinct store personality.

PLANT LAYOUT

Layout in the plant refers to the efficient arrangement of the manufacturing facilities and employees. In the plant layout, attention is centered on how the equipment is to be set up as well as the location and space requirements of support services, such as maintenance, receiving and shipping, and storage. Some of the benefits of good factory layout are listed below.

1. Lower cost of manufacturing.
2. More efficient use of floor space.
3. Reduced manufacturing bottlenecks.
4. More effective control.
5. Better quality of products.
6. Better service to customer.
7. Minimized material handling.
8. Less time needed to manufacture goods.

TYPE OF FACTORY LAYOUT

Two basic patterns of layout of the plant are process layout and product layout.

Process Layout

Process layout, shown in Figure 6-5, is usually found in plants where many different kinds of products are produced or are produced for customer specifications. It is often called job order production and is characteristic of many small plants.

Process layout means that similar equipment is located in one area or department of the plant. Hence, all lathes or drills would be in one area. In this arrangement, all work of a specific kind is sent to the specific department or area. All lathe work required in the factory would be sent to the lathe machine area.

The advantages of the process layout are:

- Superior control of intricate processes.
- Greater utilization of machinery.
- Lower capital investment in equipment.
- Increased flexibility; readily adaptable to frequent rearrangement of operational sequence.
- Steadier operation; production can be maintained better during absenteeism. Machine breakdowns are not serious since work may be routed to other machines.
- Improved service; maintenance requirements of equipment can be grouped for specialized service.
- Lower unit cost; more economical where volume of work is too small to justify a production line.
- Best stuited for items requiring a flexible sequence of operations.

Storage area for raw materials	Saws	Lathes	Finishing area	Storage area for finished products
	Drills	Grinding and sanding machines	Assembly area	

Figure 6-5   Floor diagram of process layout in small factory.

Product layout is the most efficient arrangement for this manufacturing process.

- Reduced equipment; fewer duplicate machines necessary to meet production requirements.
- Production stimulated; more incentive to workers to increase production through incentive plans.[2]

Product Layout

Plants where product layout is used ordinarily manufacture products in large quantities. (See Fig. 6-6.) This type of layout has all manufacturing equipment necessary to produce the product arranged in sequence. Hence, as the raw material moves through the manufacturing process, all operations are per-

[2]Raymond Newton, *Principles of Plant Layout for Small Plants*, Technical Aids for Small Manufacturers. (Washington, D.C.: Small Business Administration, 1971), p. 3.

Storage raw materials	Product A Saws	Drills	Sanding machines	Assembly	Painting	Storage finished product
Storage raw materials	Product B Lathes	Milling	Sanding machines	Assembly	Varnishing	Storage finished product
Storage raw materials	Product C Saws	Lathe	Heat treating	Plating	Assembly	Painting	Storage finished product

Figure 6-6 Floor diagram of product layout in small factory.

formed until the finished product "rolls off the assembly line." In product layout, different types of machines are located in a work area so that they can perform the operations necessary to complete their function in the assembly line. Hence, there is a good deal of duplication of kinds of machinery located throughout the plant.

Product layout is usually too sophisticated and expensive a system for the small businessman, being adaptable to requirements of the larger, mass-production industries. This system is especially suitable for automated manufacturing processes.

Advantages of product layout include:

- Simplifies controls and reduces cost accounting.
- Reduces materials-handling costs.
- Provides smoother flow of materials.
- Reduces floor space required for goods in process.
- Cuts production time.
- Reduces investment in work in process.
- Develops efficient labor through job specialization.
- Provides better overall supervision and reduces paper work.
- Reduces floor space required per unit produced.[3]

[3]Ibid.

SERVICE ESTABLISHMENT LAYOUT

The layout for the service establishment is determined primarily by whether it is a merchandising or processing establishment.

Merchandising service establishments include barber shops, beauty shops, and motels. Layouts in these establishments must center on customer convenience and attractive physical appearance of the facility.

Processing type service establishments include tailor shops, laundries, and print shops. These businesses have their processing operations separated from where customers' orders are taken. A small print shop, for example, takes customer orders in front and the printing equipment is in the back of the building. The separation of work area and service area makes for more efficiency in work performance.

ASSISTANCE IN PLANNING THE LAYOUT

The small business owner should seek as much assistance as possible in determining the layout design of the business. Many sources are available to provide this assistance. Retail trade associations provide planning services to their members. Manufacturers of store equipment and fixtures will also provide assistance. Other valuable resources are contractors, financial advisors, architects, interior designers, business suppliers, and government agencies, especially the Small Business Administration. Much of this service is offered free or at a minimal cost. Carefully thought-out plans can avoid unnecessary waste and expense later in relation to store or plant layout.

DISCUSSION QUESTIONS

1. What decision does the small business owner have to make when choosing a physical facility?
2. What factors should be evaluated when deciding whether to buy or lease a facility?
3. Identify some of the issues that need to be studied when determining the size and type of facility.
4. List and explain the important features of exterior design.
5. Briefly discuss the interior building features that should be evaluated by the small business owner.
6. What is the meaning of layout?

7. What items need to be considered when determining a retail store layout?
8. What is the difference between a grid layout and a free-flow layout?
9. Explain the difference between process and product layout of a factory.
10. Discuss the difference between a merchandising service establishment and a processing service establishment.

STUDENT PROJECTS

1. Select a small retail store and evaluate the store's interior and exterior features.
   A. Building exterior
      1. Type of building architecture
      2. Store front
      3. Display windows
      4. Entrances
      5. Outside store signs
   B. Building interior
      1. Flooring
      2. Walls
      3. Ceiling
      4. Lights and fixtures
      5. Color schemes
      6. Temperature control
      7. Special features
2. Draw the floor plan of the layout of the store and describe the layout plan.

CASE A
HOUSE'S JEWELRY STORE (A)

House's Jewelry Store is a small, single unit retail jewelry store located in the downtown shopping area of a city of 10,000 population. The business opened in 1959 in a smaller store but moved to its present location in 1969. The location has been good and rental payments are relatively low. There is one other competitor in the downtown area.

Floor space is 3,000 square feet. One-fourth of the floor space is allocated to repair facilities, clerical space, and storage areas. The remaining floor space is divided into four areas. Diamonds, expensive gemstones, and wedding sets comprise one-fourth of the selling area. Watches, gold necklaces and bracelets, gold-filled jewelry, and other assorted pieces occupy about one-fourth of the selling floor. Gift items, pottery and china, silver and pewter serving pieces, and stemware utilize another one-fourth of this space. The remaining floor space is aisle space.

In addition to the owner and his wife, three full-time employees and one part-time employee work in the store. Each person performs a wide range of duties in the store. The watch repair department is a leased-out service department designed to increase sales by attracting additional customers to the store. The store's downtown competitor has no in-store watch repair service. All watches brought in for repair are sent out of town.

During the past two years, the Houses have been evaluating whether to move the business to a new shopping center located at the edge of the city. Population shifts, the movement of other retailers, the deterioration of the downtown area, and the favorable atmosphere at the shopping center area have been the factors which have made them decide to move.

There is a suitable location in the new center. The Houses want their new store to have an efficient, well planned layout.

Specifically, they want the following to be incorporated into their design layout.

1. A workshop area located in the store rather than behind the store as is the case with the present location. This would allow the owner to have closer contact with actual store operations.
2. Pieces of jewelry that have a similar function, such as watches, bracelets, and chains should be placed in close proximity to each other. This arrangement will facilitate customer shopping.
3. Use track lighting to enable displays to be mobile and to add to the flexibility of the layout.
4. All display cases should be lined with materials of a related color scheme to allow jewelry to be accentuated by reflection of light on its surface.

The proposed store layout is shown below.

Proposed Layout:
  Area (30 feet by 60 feet)
  Space allocation:
    Space should be divided into departments
    Dropped ceilings over certain areas will enhance different items
    Wall space should be used for display
  Layout spaces
    Record room (6 x 8 feet) for security files
    Workshop (10 x 20 feet) for jewelry repair and casting
    Watch repair room (6 x 8 feet)
    Checkout stand placed at back of store

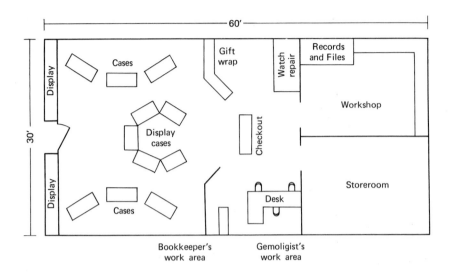

Gift wrapping area
Desk and working area for bookkeeper
Desk and diamond salon for owner (desk—L shaped with 3 chairs)

Question

Evaluate the store layout as to its suitability for the new jewelry store.

CASE B

CLIF'S APPAREL SHOP

Clif Waterman graduates from college this semester. At college, Clif majored in business administration. Many of Clif's friends have already accepted employment with various business firms. However, Clif has other personal ambitions. He has wanted for a long time to be his own boss, and he has planned to fulfill this ambition by opening his own retail business.

While attending college, Clif worked part-time during the school year in one of the large department stores in the city. He earned enough through his part-time employment to pay for his college expenses. In the summer, he worked full-time in the same store and was able to save enough money so that, with a small bank loan, he has sufficient capital to open his retail store. In addition, Clif feels that his past work experience should be invaluable to him.

Clif's dream has been to open his own men's and boys' clothing store, appropriately called "Clif's Apparel Shop." He plans to carry a complete line of merchandise (suits, slacks, sports jackets, shirts, shoes, socks, and other accessories). He hopes to cater to teen-agers and adults of all ages.

Clif is not only anxious to select the right location for his clothing store but he also realizes that the physical facility that will house his store is important. A site available in a shopping center is new; his would be the first business to occupy it. Its appearance conforms to the general design of the shopping center.

On the other hand, a vacant building downtown is available, but it is an older building, having been constructed in the 1940s. A number of businesses have previously occupied the site, including a small drugstore, a fabric shop, and more recently, a small appliance store. This building will have to be modernized to meet Clif's own store needs.

Both sites are available for long-term lease, or the downtown store may be bought outright.

Questions

1. What factors should Clif evaluate before deciding whether to buy or to lease?
2. What factors should Clif consider with regard to the store's exterior?
3. What are the interior features that Clif must consider?
4. What type of layout would you recommend for Clif for his retail store?
5. Where can Clif get assistance in getting advice on store layout?

7

SOURCES OF FUNDS

PREVIEW OF THIS CHAPTER

1. In this chapter, you will learn that the small business has many needs for money.

2. You will understand the difference between short-term capital needs and long-term capital needs.

3. You will find out that equity capital comes from personal savings, partners, and/or sale of stock.

4. You will discover that commercial banks, vendors, equipment manufacturers and distributors, factors, sales finance companies, insurance companies, private investors, small business investment corporations, and the Small Business Administration are sources of debt capital for the small business.

5. You will probably be surprised to find out that commercial banks make several different types of loans: traditional bank loans, installment loans, discount accounts receivable, discount installment contracts, and have lines of credit for business firms.

6. You will learn that vendors and equipment manufacturers and distributors finance purchases for the small business.

7. You will understand how factors and sales finance companies finance customer credit for small business firms.

8. You will discover that insurance companies and private investors make limited loans to small businesses.

9. You will learn how Small Business Investment Corporations provide funds to small businesses.

10. If you have ever planned to go into small business, you will be interested in the many different types of financial assistance the Small Business Administration provides small business firms.

11. You will discover who is eligible for a SBA loan and how you go about making application for one.

12. You will learn what sources provide funds for different types of needs.

13. You will be able to understand these key words:

Capital

Customer credit

Equity capital

Debt capital

Commercial banks

Vendors

Equipment manufacturers and distributors

Factors

Sales finance company

Insurance company

Private investor

Small Business Investment Corporation

Small Business Administration

Short-term loan

Long-term loan

Traditional bank loan

Installment sales contract

Line of credit

Accounts receivable

Loan guarantees

Pool loans

Economic opportunity loans

Development company loans

Disaster loans

Loan application

The small business failure rate discussed in Chapter 1 indicates that many small business entrepreneurs make fatal mistakes when they start their business. It also indicates that one of the major causes of business failure is the lack of sufficient capital when the business is first started. The high failure rate of small businesses also makes it difficult to borrow funds to start a new firm. Knowing the correct amount of capital needed and the possible sources where these funds may be borrowed is extremely important to the small business entrepreneur.

AMOUNT OF CAPITAL

Many small business entrepreneurs mistakenly feel that if they are able to rent a store, purchase equipment, and purchase the initial inventory, they have sufficient funds to start the business. These are major items requiring capital, but they are certainly not all that are required. There are many other costs that require a considerable amount of money. For example, most businesses are not immediately profitable, and the owner must sustain himself and his family until the business can provide him a living. Also, he may have to finance customer credit until it begins to turn over and produce funds for the business. Figures

7-1 and 7-2 show worksheets that indicate the amount and type of capital that is usually needed by a new business. Please note that the entrepreneur must have funds to cover several months of expenses that recur each month. Most firms sustain greater cash payments than cash receipts during the first several months of operations.

In addition to the list in Figures 7-1 and 7-2, if the owner borrows money to start the business, he must also pay back the principal and interest of all loans. The amount of the payments of these loans is very important to the small business owner. It is not uncommon for a small business entrepreneur to establish a business that produces a good profit but have it fail because he had very large monthly payments on loans. What normally would be sufficient profits are drained into repaying the loan.

The amount of the monthly payments is subject to three factors: (1) the total amount of money borrowed, (2) the time in which the loan must be repaid, and (3) the interest rate charged by the lender.

AMOUNT

The more he must borrow, the greater the burden it becomes to repay. For example, if the following amounts are borrowed at 10 percent interest for 10 years, the payments will be:

AMOUNT	MONTHLY PAYMENT	TOTAL INTEREST PAID
$ 10,000	$ 125.35	$ 5,042.00
25,000	313.37	12,604.40
50,000	626.74	25,208.80
100,000	1,253.47	50,416.40

TIME

The length of time in which the loan must be repaid can be critical to the success of the business. For example, if a small business entrepreneur borrows $50,000 at 10 percent interest to start a business, he would have to repay the following amounts depending on the length of repayment time:

TIME TO REPAY	MONTHLY PAYMENT	TOTAL INTEREST PAID
5 years	$ 1,045.14	$ 12,708.40
10 years	626.74	25,208.80
15 years	487.27	37,708.60
20 years	417.53	50,207.20

Estimated Monthly Expenses

Item	Your estimate of monthly expenses based on sales of $_____ per year		Your estimate of how much cash you need to start your business (See column 3.)	What to put in column 2 (These figures are typical for one kind of business, you will have to decide how many months to allow for in your business.)
	Column 1		Column 2	Column 3
Salary of owner-manager	$		$	2 times column 1
All other salaries and wages				3 times column 1
Rent				3 times column 1
Advertising				3 times column 1
Delivery expense				3 times column 1
Supplies				3 times column 1
Telephone and telegraph				3 times column 1
Other utilities				3 times column 1
Insurance				Payment required by insurance company
Taxes, including Social Security				4 times column 1
Interest				3 times column 1
Maintenance				3 times column 1
Legal and other professional fees				3 times column 1
Miscellaneous				3 times column 1

Starting Costs You Only Have to Pay Once		
Fixtures and equipment		Fill in Figure 7-2 and put the total here
Decorating and remodeling		Talk it over with a contractor
Installation of fixtures and equipment		Talk to suppliers from whom you buy these
Starting inventory		Suppliers will probably help you estimate this
Deposits with public utilities		Find out from utilities companies
Legal and other professional fees		Lawyer, accountant, and so on
Licenses and permits		Find out from city offices what you have to have
Advertising and promotion for opening		Estimate what you'll use
Accounts receivable		What you need to buy more stock until credit customers pay
Cash		For unexpected expenses or losses, special purchases, etc.
Other		Make a separate list and enter total
Total Estimated Cash You Need to Start with	$	Add up all the numbers in column 2

Figure 7-1 Capital needs worksheet. (*Source. Checklist for Going into Business*, Small Business Administration, 1973, p. 7.)

List of Furniture, Fixtures, and Equipment

Leave out or add items to suit your business. Use separate sheets to list exactly what you need for each of the items below.	If you plan to pay cash in full, enter the full amount below and in the last column.	If you are going to pay by installments, fill out the columns below. Enter in the last column your downpayment plus at least one installment.			Estimate of the cash you need for furniture, fixtures, and equipment.
		Price	Downpayment	Amount of each installment	
Counters	$	$	$	$	$
Storage shelves, cabinets					
Display stands, shelves, tables					
Cash register					
Safe					
Window display fixtures					
Special lighting					
Outside sign					
Delivery equipment if needed					
Total Furniture, Fixtures, and Equipment (Enter this figure also in Figure 7-1 under "Starting Costs You Only Have to Pay Once.")					$

Figure 7-2 Fixtures and equipment worksheet. (*Source. Checklist for Going into Business*, Small Business Administration, 1973, p. 12.)

Of course this does not mean that the small business owner should always take as long to repay a loan as possible. The longer it takes to repay a loan, the more the borrower will pay in interest. For example, the 5-year loan above would pay $12,708.40 in total interest, while the 20-year loan would pay $50,207.20 in total interest.

INTEREST RATE

Interest rates may fluctuate widely over a period of time and have a definite effect on how much an entrepreneur must pay for borrowed money. For example, if an entrepreneur borrows $50,000 to be repaid in 10 years at the following interest rates, the monthly payments and total amount of interest paid on the loan will be:

INTEREST RATE (%)	MONTHLY PAYMENT	TOTAL INTEREST PAID
5	$ 521.70	$ 12,604.00
7	563.72	17,645.40
9	605.73	22,687.60
11	647.74	27,728.80
13	689.76	32,771.20

Of course, all three factors together determine the payment amount. For example, borrowing a smaller sum of money for a longer period of time than planned could still result in the same payment amount. (See Fig. 7-3.)

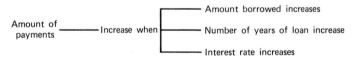

Figure 7-3 Factors that increase loan payments.

SOURCES OF EQUITY CAPITAL

Equity capital (ownership) may come from personal savings, partners, or by selling stock in a corporation. The best and most common source of funds to start a business is from a person's own savings. As a general rule, most small business authorities suggest that the small business entrepreneur provide at least 50 percent of the starting funds in the form of equity capital. Usually, any amount under 50 percent requires a level of borrowing that creates payments which are extremely difficult, if not impossible, to meet.

If the small business entrepreneur does not have sufficient equity capital himself, he may consider taking in a partner or selling stock in a corporation. He may take in a general or a limited partner, but he must remember that he may have to give up some control over the business. If he incorporates and sells stock, he obtains the features of the corporation form of ownership (which may or may not be good for him) and he may have to give up some control of the business. In addition, if he decides to add a partner or sell stock, he must be sure that there will be sufficient profits in the business to sustain himself while providing funds for the equity investors.

SOURCES OF DEBT CAPITAL

Possible sources of debt capital (borrowed funds) for the small business entrepreneur are commercial banks, vendors, equipment manufacturers and distributors, factors, sales finance companies, insurance companies, private investors, Small Business Investment Corporations, and the Small Business Administration.

COMMERCIAL BANKS

Commercial banks are primarily a source of short-term loans. In fact, they lend more short-term funds than any other type of financial institution.

The bank receives both demand (checking accounts) and savings deposits from their customers and lends out a percentage of these deposits to businesses and individuals. Generally, 5 years is the maximum length of time of any loan a commercial bank makes and usually it doesn't exceed 3 years. However, banks do participate in loans with the Small Business Administration that are for longer periods of time.

As a rule, commercial banks usually do not lend funds for long-term fixed assets such as buildings and land. Often, it does lend money for the purchase of equipment and inventories and for financing customer credit.

The commercial bank may lend money in several ways, by traditional bank loans, installment loans, line of credit, discounting accounts receivables, and discounting installment sales contracts. (See Fig. 7-4.)

Traditional Bank Loan

The traditional bank loan may extend for a few days to finance such things as taking advantage of a cash discount. Also, it may extend for several months or

A small commercial bank which is an important source of loans for local small businesses.

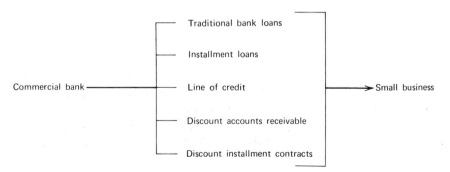

Figure 7-4 Commercial banks financial assistance to small business.

years to finance various purchases or to provide working capital. Interest is calculated on the amount borrowed, subtracted from the total, and the balance is loaned for a specific period of time. No installment payments are involved and the total loan is repaid at maturity. For example, if a businessman borrowed $1,000 at 10 percent interest for a month, the bank would subtract the interest of $8.33 and give the borrower $991.67. He would then be required to repay the $1,000 a month after the date of the loan.

Installment Loans

Installment loans are made to businesses by commercial banks usually to finance purchases of equipment and other fixed assets. Generally, they are for a year or more in time. For example, a business might borrow $9,000 for 3 years from a commercial bank to purchase a panel delivery truck. At 12 percent interest, the business would be required to pay the bank $296.25 per month for 3 years. The actual or true interest rate on this type of loan is almost always higher than the interest rate on the traditional bank loan for the same borrower.

Line of Credit

The line of credit is not a true type of business loan, but rather an established limit of credit a business may automatically borrow. All loans above an amount established by a bank must go to a committee made up of officers of the bank for approval. To avoid delay and save effort, a commercial bank's loan committee will usually establish a line of credit for a business firm. The business may then simply notify the bank that it is borrowing the money, and it is automatically made available.

Discount Accounts Receivable

This is a method by which commercial banks help businesses finance customer credit. The bank loans a business a percentage of the amount of its accounts receivable and the business pledges its accounts receivable as collateral. For example, a business, to provide working capital, might take $10,000 worth of customers' 30-day accounts to the bank for discounting. The bank would make an estimate of the collectability of the accounts and lend a percentage of the total amount, for instance, $8,000. The business would receive cash immediately to use as working capital. As the business receives cash from customers on these accounts receivable, they turn them over to the bank until the entire loan plus interest is repaid. After the bank is repaid, the business retains any additional funds it collects. If it does not collect enough accounts to repay the bank, it must make up the difference.

Discount Installment Contracts

Commercial banks also assist businesses in their customer credit by discounting installment sales contracts. To illustrate, a customer makes a purchase of merchandise and signs an installment contract with a business. The businessman then takes the contract to the bank where he receives money for the contract.

Most customer installment sales contracts contain an effective or true interest rate of 18 percent. Banks usually will loan the business the full face value of the contract. The interest charged in the installment sales contract is then their fee for making the loan. The bank or business then collects the payments from the customer, which go to the bank to repay the businessman's loan. If the customer fails to repay the contract, the business must reimburse the commercial bank.

VENDORS

Vendors can be an important source of short-term credit for small business firms. Firms that sell inventories to a business usually will finance the purchase of these goods for short periods of time, usually from 30 to 90 days. For example, a drug wholesaler might sell merchandise to a drugstore on credit, with the store having 30 days to pay. For 30 days, the drugstore would then be selling merchandise for which it had not paid. At the end of the 30-day period, the drugstore would then take money that it had received from the sale of the merchandise and pay the amount owed the drug wholesaler.

Vendors also have needs for working capital, so it is common practice for them to offer their business customers a cash discount. When they offer a cash discount, the terms of the purchase, such as "3/10 n/30," means that the total amount of the purchase is due in 30 days; however, if the customer will pay the total amount of the purchase within 10 days, they are allowed to subtract 3 percent from the total amount. Business firms often find that they can borrow money from a commercial bank for 20 days to take advantage of this discount and the cost of the loan is less than the cash discount.

EQUIPMENT MANUFACTURERS AND DISTRIBUTORS

To encourage businesses to purchase their equipment, manufacturers and distributors often will finance the purchase. Usually, this loan exists in the form of an installment sales contract. The manufacturers or distributors may actually carry the note themselves or discount the installment sales contract with a financial institution. Machinery, equipment, display shelves, cash registers, and office equipment are some of the more common items financed by manufacturers and distributors.

FACTORS

Factors are financial firms that finance accounts receivables for business firms. They may either purchase or discount accounts receivable.

If they discount accounts receivable, they function exactly as the commercial bank example discussed previously. They will lend a certain amount of money based on their analysis of the collectability of the accounts, and the business turns them over to the factor until the original amount borrowed plus interest is repaid. All remaining collections are kept by the business firm. If the small business fails to collect the amount owed the factor (including interest), it must make up the difference.

When a factor purchases accounts receivable, he makes an analysis of the collectability of the accounts and pays the business firm a percentage of the total amount. The business firm (sometimes the factor) then collects the accounts and turns all collections over to the factor. It is very important to the factor that he judges the collectability of the accounts with considerable accuracy because the total he collects must cover what he loans and his expected profit. If he collects less, then he must suffer the loss.

SALES FINANCE COMPANIES

Sales finance companies purchase installment sales contracts from business firms. The customer will sign an installment sales contract, after which the business firm sells the contract to the sales finance company. Usually, the business firm will receive the full face value of the contract, and the profit of the sales finance company is derived from the interest of the contract.

Sales finance companies also engage in what is known as "floor planning." Floor planning is common in the retail automobile trade and in retail sales of large appliances. To illustrate, the sales finance company finances the purchase of the dealer's stock of automobiles. In return for this financing, the dealer then pays the sales finance company interest on the loan until the car is sold. When the car is sold, the dealer then turns the contract over to the sales finance company and receives the full amount of the purchase. The sales finance company then collects principal and interest in montly installment payments from the automobile purchaser. The automobile serves as collateral to the sales finance company until the loan is repaid.

INSURANCE COMPANIES

Insurance companies make some long-term loans to small businesses for the purchase of fixed assets. Insurance companies collect premiums on their policies and then invest them in stocks, bonds, and business loans. Insurance companies are regulated by both state and federal agencies, and the type of loans they are able to make are controlled to some degree by government agencies in order to protect the policy holders. Insurance companies usually loan funds to small businesses that have high value collateral to pledge to ensure the repayment of the loan. Loans for shopping malls and apartments are common business loans made by insurance companies. Other than these types of loans, insurance companies are a limited source of small business loans.

PRIVATE INVESTORS

Private citizens that lend their savings are often a source of capital for small business. They usually lend their funds for a time period of 1 to 5 years. The private investor is generally an individual who is willing to risk his or her funds for a higher interest rate than he or she would be able to obtain from savings and loan associations or bonds. The interest rate they charge is usually above that of most financial institutions. It often is in the range charged by small loan companies who make consumer loans.

The small business owner should investigate private sources to make sure that he is not dealing with someone who is associated with crime and/or usury.

SMALL BUSINESS INVESTMENT CORPORATIONS

Small Business Investment Corporations (SBIC) are privately owned financial corporations that are licensed, regulated, and promoted by the Small Business Administration, an agency of the federal government. SBICs may only loan or invest money in small businesses according to the SBA (Small Business Administration) definition of a small business. They themselves may obtain loans or guarantees of loans from the SBA to lend and invest in small businesses. An SBIC must have a minimum initial investment of at least $150,000. Often, the investment exceeds more than $1 million. The SBIC may obtain loans or guarantees (the SBA guarantees the financial institution making the loan that the loan will be repaid) of loans that amount to twice the SBIC's paid-in capital and surplus with a $7.5 million maximum.

The SBIC then take the funds they have invested and funds obtained through the SBA and either (1) make loans that must exceed 5 years to small businesses or (2) invest in small businesses. They often invest in small businesses but are prohibited from obtaining controlling interest in the businesses. Many SBICs provide management consulting to the business firms to protect their investment.

In 1969, the SBA established a program of SBICs to aid minority enterprises. These are called MESBICs (Minority Enterprise Small Business Investment Corporations).

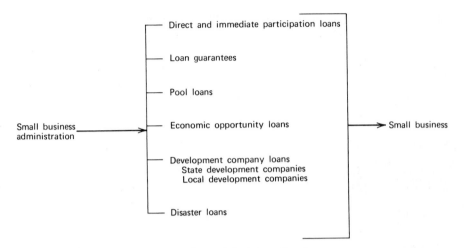

Figure 7-5   Types of Small Business Administration loans.

SMALL BUSINESS ADMINISTRATION

The Small Business Administration (SBA) was established as an agency in the Department of Commerce in 1953 to help promote small business. The SBA engages in various types of activities that assist small businesses, including financial assistance (other types of assistance will be discussed in Chapter 22).

The basic types of loans the SBA engages in are (1) direct and immediate participation loans, (2) loan guarantees, (3) pool loans, (4) economic opportunity loans, (5) development company loans, and (6) disaster loans.

Eligibility Requirements

The SBA makes loans only to small businesses. The SBA's definition of what is a small business differs according to type of business.[1] (See also Chapter 1.)

1. Manufacturing—number of employees may range up to 1,500, depending on the industry.
2. Wholesaling—yearly sales not over $2 million to $22 million, depending on the industry.
3. Services—yearly sales less than $2 million to $8 million, depending on the industry.

[1]SBA Business Loans, Small Business Administration, March 1978.

4. Retailing—yearly sales less than $2 million to $7.5 million, depending on the industry.
5. Construction—yearly receipts of less than $9.5 million for last three years.
6. Agriculture—yearly sales of less than $1 million.

The SBA does not compete with financial institutions in making loans. If the applicant can obtain sufficient money at a private financial institution, federal law does not allow the SBA to make that person a loan. Before applying to the SBA, the applicant must seek private financing at a local bank or other lending institution. If the applicant lives in a city of more than 200,000 people, he/she must apply to two lending institutions.

The SBA also specifies six general credit requirements.[2]

1. The applicant must be of good character.
2. The applicant must show ability to operate the business successfully.
3. The applicant must have enough capital so that, with an SBA loan, he/she can operate on a sound financial basis.
4. The applicant must show the proposed loan to be of sound value or secured so as to reasonably assure repayment.
5. The applicant must show the past earnings or future prospects indicate ability to repay the loan out of profit.
6. The applicant must be able to provide funds to have a reasonable amount at stake to withstand possible losses during early stages if the venture is a new business.

Ineligible Applicants

The SBA cannot make loans in certain circumstances.[3]

1. When funds are otherwise available at reasonable rates.
2. When the loan is to "(a) pay off a loan to a creditor or creditors of the applicant who are inadequately secured and in a position to sustain loss, (b) provide funds for distribution of payment to the principals of the applicant, or (c) replenish funds previously used for such purposes."
3. When the loan is for speculation in any kind of property.
4. When the applicant is a nonprofit organization.
5. When the applicant is a newspaper, magazine, or book publishing company.
6. When any of the gross income of the applicant is derived from gambling.
7. When the loan provides funds to lending institutions.
8. When the loan is used to purchase real property to be held for investment.

[2]Ibid.
[3]SBA Business Loans, Small Business Administration, March 1978.

Direct and Immediate Participation Loans

The SBA can make a loan directly to the small business or it can participate in loans with private financial institutions. When it is a participating loan, the SBA lends part of the funds and the private financial institution puts up part of the loan. The maximum amount that can be loaned by the SBA in either type of loan is $150,000. The interest rate charged by the SBA is set by law, based on a formula that relates to the cost of money the government is currently borrowing. The interest rate usually is between 6½ and 8 percent. Within certain limitations banks set the interest rate on their part of the loan. Direct and participating loans comprise a very small percentage of the total financing made possible by the SBA.

Loan Guarantees

The SBA is allowed by law to guarantee up to 90 percent of a loan to a financial institution, with a maximum of $350,000 ($500,000 in special situations). The lending institution lends all the money, but the SBA guarantees a specific percentage repayment. If the borrower defaults on the loan, the SBA then reimburses the lending institution the amount of the loan guarantee.

Guaranteed loans comprise a large percentage of the total financing by the SBA. The bank can charge any interest rate up to a rate maximum set by the SBA. It usually is about ½ percent above the prime rate charged by large New York banks. The SBA prefers guaranteed loans rather than direct or participation loans because it allows them to make many times more money available to small businesses.

Pool Loans   Small businesses sometimes pool their purchasing power by forming corporations for the purpose of purchasing raw material, equipment, inventories, supplies, or research. For example, several small retail stores may form a corporation to purchase all or part of their inventory in order to obtain better prices from quantity purchases, such as in carload lots. The SBA is allowed to make loans to these corporations, the maximum being $250,000 multiplied by the number of small businesses in the pool.

Economic Opportunity Loans   The SBA makes economic opportunity loans to disadvantaged persons (1) whose total income is not sufficient for needs of the family and (2) who are unable to acquire financing through other lending institutions at reasonable terms. The maximum economic opportunity loan is $100,000 for up to 15 years. Economic opportunity loans historically have been high risk loans with almost no collateral in an attempt to aid disadvantaged persons.

Development Company Loans The SBA makes long-term loans to both state and local development companies, which they, in turn, lend to businesses for the purchase of land, buildings, machinery, and equipment.

State Development Companies   The SBA is able to lend a state development company an amount equal to all loans from other sources for as long as 20 years.

Local Development Companies Local development companies may be either profit or nonprofit corporations established to assist local economic growth. It must have at least 25 stockholders or members. The SBA is able to lend up to $350,000 for each small business the local development corporation assists.

Disaster Loans The SBA is allowed by law to make low interest loans to small businesses that are damaged due to some form of disaster, such as a hurricane or flood. Disaster loans to small businesses are limited to $500,000 and may be for periods of up to 30 years.

Loan Application

Business that are in existence follow different steps than an entrepreneur trying to start a new business.[4]

FOR ESTABLISHED BUSINESSES

1. Prepare a balance sheet (see Chapter 11) listing all assets and liabilities of the business (not personal items).
2. Prepare an income statement (see Chapter 11) for the previous full year and the current year to the date of the balance sheet.
3. Prepare a current personal financial statement of all owners (excluding stockholders who hold less than 20 percent of the stock).
4. Prepare a list of all collateral to be offered as security for the loan with present market value of each.
5. State the amount of the loan desired and the purposes for which it will be used.
6. Take all this material to a bank and apply for a loan. If the loan is refused, ask about a guaranteed loan or participation loan. If the bank is interested, have them contact the SBA. Remember, you must go to two banks if the city has more than 200,000 population.
7. If a guaranty or a participation loan is not available, write or visit the nearest SBA office.

[4]Ibid.

ENTREPRENEURS STARTING A NEW BUSINESS

1. Describe in detail the type of business you wish to start.
2. Describe your experience and management capabilities.
3. Prepare a statement of how much you or others have to invest in the business and how much you need to borrow.
4. Prepare a current financial statement listing all personal assets and liabilities.
5. Prepare a detailed projection of earnings for the first year of operation.
6. Prepare a list of all collateral to be offered as security and your estimate of the current market value of each.
7. Take all this material to a bank and apply for a loan. If the loan is declined, ask about a guaranty or participation loan. If the bank is interested, have them contact the SBA. You must go to two banks if the city has more than 200,000 population.
8. If a guaranty or participation loan is not available, write or visit your nearest SBA office.

SOURCES OF FUNDS BY TYPE OF CAPITAL NEED

Small business firms have various types of short-term and long-term needs. Short-term needs may include such items as working capital, customer credit, and inventories. Long-term needs include such items as land, buildings, machinery, fixtures, furniture, and equipment. Very few sources extend loans for all these needs. Most financial institutions specialize in lending money for only one or two areas of these needs. Figure 7-7 presents various sources of capital for small business listed by the general areas of needs for which they specialize in providing funds.

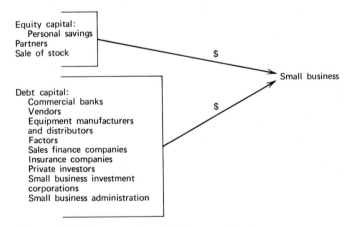

Figure 7-6 Sources of capital for small business.

SHORT-TERM CAPITAL		
Working capital (Salaries and other expenses)	Customer credit	Inventories
Commercial banks	Commercial banks Factors Sales finance companies	Commercial banks Vendors
LONG-TERM CAPITAL		
Land and buildings	Machinery, fixtures, furniture, and equipment	
Insurance companies Private investors	Commercial banks Equipment manufacturers and distributors Private investors	
ALL TYPES OF CAPITAL NEEDS		
Private sources	Government sources	
Small Business Investment Corporations	Small Business Administration	

Figure 7-7   Sources of funds by type of capital needed.

DISCUSSION QUESTIONS

1. What are some of the items for which a small business needs money?
2. Where may a small business obtain equity capital?
3. If you wanted to finance customer credit using a commercial bank, what types of loans might you ask for at the bank?
4. How do vendors help finance small businesses?
5. How do equipment manufacturers and distributors help finance small businesses?
6. How does a factor operate?
7. How does a sales finance company operate?
8. Where do insurance companies get money to lend and what type of loans do they usually make to small businesses?
9. Why do private investors lend money to small businesses?
10. What is a small business investment corporation?
11. What type of loans does the Small Business Administration lend?
12. If you were a small business owner, where would you look for funds to purchase machinery and equipment?

STUDENT PROJECT

Interview a small business owner and find out the following:

1. What were the sources of his or her starting capital? What percent was equity capital and what percent was debt capital?
2. Does he or she use any of the following financial sources? Are they used for short-term or long-term funds? What does he use them to finance?

   Commercial banks
   Vendors
   Equipment manufacturers and distributors
   Factors
   Sales finance companies
   Insurance companies
   Private investors
   Small business investment corporations
   Small Business Administration

CASE A

HARRY'S MAD MOD THREADS

Harry Butler plans on opening a clothing store in a city of 300,000 population when he graduates from college next month. In fact, he has already chosen a name for the store, "Harry's Mad Mod Threads." He has $12,000 in savings.

He has located a store for rent at $200 per month that he feels is suited to his needs and has made a list of various things he will need to open and their price.

Merchandise	$8000
Shelves, racks, and displays—free installation	4000
Remodeling	2000
Cash register (used)	400
Checkout counter	200
Used desk	100
Adding machine	200
Office supplies (3 months supply)	100
Telephone:	
Deposit	75
Installation fee	25
Rate per month	16

Utilities:
Deposit	200
Estimated monthly bill	40

Harry has made some other estimates and plans as follows:

1. He can completely turn over his inventory every 4 months.
2. He plans a 100 percent markup on cost of all merchandise.
3. He plans to hire a part-time clerk at $50 per week.
4. He feels he can get by on $600 per month for himself.
5. He plans to spend $1,000 on opening promotion and advertising.
6. He feels he can get by with $100 a month advertising thereafter.
7. Harry estimates that 75 percent of his sales will be on credit in the form of 30-day accounts.

Questions

1. Estimate how much money Harry will have to obtain by filling in a worksheet similar to Figure 7-1.
2. Should Harry try to obtain equity or debt capital? Explain.
3. Which of the following sources could Harry use and for which items.

Source   *Money For*
Commercial bank
Vendors
Equipment manufacturers and distributors
Factors
Sales finance companies
Insurance companies
Private investors
Small Business Investment Corporations
Small Business Administration

4. Which sources would you advise Harry to use and for what uses?

CASE B

MARVIN MATLOCK

Marvin Matlock has operated a restaurant in a town of 18,000 for the past 10 years. His restaurant is located at one of the off ramps of a major highway and his sign and building are visible for several hundred yards. He features "down home cooking" at reasonable prices with fast service. During the past 10 years he has been in business, Marvin has gone to considerable effort to make sure the quality of his food stays constant and the appearance of his establishment is always clean and neat. As a reward for his efforts, profits have always been good. The past two years the business has cleared about $40,000 per year.

Two weeks ago someone left a burner on under a skillet filled with grease. This resulted in a fire that completely destroyed the restaurant. Marvin had taken out fire insurance when he first started 10 years ago. The agent had asked Marvin on several occasions if he wanted to increase his insurance due to increased costs, but Marvin had never done anything about the value of the policy.

The fire insurance policy paid Marvin $150,000. After checking with contractors and equipment dealers, Marvin finds that a new building will cost him $175,000 while equipment and furniture will cost another $60,000. Even with his savings and the insurance money, Marvin only has $180,000. It will take five months to get back into business. Marvin feels he must have at least $1,500 a month to meet his personal needs. He has estimated that he needs about $65,000 more to get him back into business and provide enough money for working capital to get him going again.

Marvin lists his needs as follows:

Building	$ 175,000
Equipment	40,000
Furniture	20,000
Personal draw	7,500
Working capital and miscellaneous expenses	2,500
Total funds needed	$ 245,000
Funds on hand	−180,000
Additional funds needed	$ 65,000

Marvin wants you to help him find the money.

Questions

1. Examine all sources of small business financing and determine which might give Marvin a loan and for what purpose.
2. Which sources would you suggest Marvin borrow from and how much should he borrow?

SECTION
THREE
MANAGEMENT CONTROL

8

MANAGEMENT AND EMPLOYEE RELATIONS IN THE SMALL BUSINESS

PREVIEW OF THIS CHAPTER

1. You will understand what management is.

2. After reading this chapter, you will be aware that the small firm has a number of objectives.

3. You will be able to identify the functions of the small business manager.

4. You will learn why employee relations are so important in the small firm.

5. You will have an understanding of the internal organizational environment of a small business.

6. You will be able to identify the needs of the individual.

7. You will be able to explain the "hierarchy of needs" concept.

8. You will understand what employee morale is as well as the indicators of employee morale.

9. You will understand some of the problems of employee discipline.

10. You will learn some of the guides for effective communication.

11. You will be able to explain these key words:

Manager	Morale
Organization chart	Autocratic leader
Planning	Free-rein leader
Organizing	Participative leader
Directing	Social needs
Controlling	Ego needs
Staffing	Self-realization needs
Employee relations	Safety and security needs
Internal organization	Employee discipline
environment	Formal status
Hierarchy of needs	Informal status
Motivation	Hot-stove rule

If the small business is to survive and prosper in the competitive business environment, owner-managers must recognize and capitalize on the opportunities afforded them. The presence of competent managers is one of the surest ways of attaining the goal of growth. As shown in Chapter 1, the major cause of business failure is inadequate management. Hence, the need for qualified managers is paramount for strengthening the firm's position in the business community.

MANAGING THE SMALL BUSINESS

The fundamental description of managers is that they supervise the work activities of employees in order to see to it that they accomplish their specific tasks. The work of a manager clearly distinguishes between doing and managing. However, in the small business this distinction is not so definite. Owner-managers ordinarily work side by side with employees. It is essential that owner-managers recognize their responsibilities for management activities, and not concentrate on activities to the neglect of managing.

FUNCTIONS OF MANAGERS

The management responsibilities of small business managers involve coordinating the firm's human, physical, and financial resources to accomplish specific results. Managers accomplish these responsibilities by performing the functions of management: planning, organizing and staffing, directing, and controlling.

PLANNING, SETTING OBJECTIVES, AND DECISION MAKING

The planning function is the process of setting objectives and then deciding the future courses of actions the firm will follow to reach its objectives. Thus, the initial phase of planning for small business owners is to develop objectives for the firm. Objectives define the desirable future goals of the firm.

We live in an age where change is continual. Change has a tremendous impact not only on how objectives are set but also on how they are achieved. Business objectives also provide the guidelines for setting specific policies for accomplishing objectives, decision making, and the actions taken by owner-managers.

The objectives of the business should be set down in writing and evaluated on a regular basis. Objectives must reflect concern for the various parties-at-interest to the firm: ownership (sole proprietorship, corporation, stockholders);

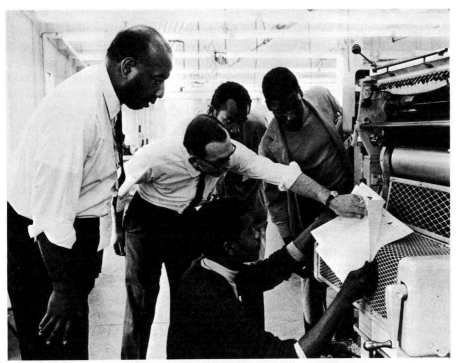

Teamwork between the small business owner-manager and employees in this print shop is essential as they plan their next project.

employees; customers; and the community at large. Objectives must also take into account the interrelatedness of short term and long term objectives as well as the interdependence of the basic functions of the firm—finance, sales, production, and personnel.

Representative objectives that recognize the various constituencies of the firm may include:

1. To earn a satisfactory level of profit for owners
2. To pay a fair, competitive wage or salary to employees
3. To provide quality products and services to customers
4. To be a socially responsible member of the community at large

Planning involves the two essential phases of long-range planning and short-range planning. First, long-range planning determines the overall direction of the company. Short-range planning deals with the specific measures necessary to reach long-range goals. Most small business managers spend the greater portion of their time on short-range, day-to-day planning, usually as a result of job pressures that arise daily. However, immediate business pressures should not preclude the manager from being concerned about longer range plans in order that the firm can remain properly oriented toward attaining its objectives.

Planning, of necessity, is a continuous process due to the dynamic nature of the business environment. Changing external market conditions as well as internal changes demand that long-range and short-range plans be regularly evaluated and updated.

Another planning activity of owner-managers is continually making decisions. The quality of the decisions affects the success of the firm. The four essential, interrelated steps in the decision-making process are discussed below.

Define the Problem

Initially, the manager evaluates the current status of the business. The essential concern at this stage is to identify the real problem correctly. If a wrong problem is defined, solutions, no matter how well thought out and applied, will fail. For example, a retail apparel store owner realized that store sales had leveled off for the past year. The owner-manager knew that if she was to remain competitive, store sales would have to be increased by at least 5 percent a year for the next three years (after accounting for inflation). The issue was how the problem of lagging sales could be increased to reach the goal.

Developing Alternatives

To consider how the goal was to be reached, the owner-manager developed a number of possible alternatives as well as the pros and cons of each. Possible alternatives considered for increasing sales included:

1. Increase the amount of advertising
2. Use a variety of media for advertising
3. Have more special sales
4. Add additional lines of merchandise
5. Offer more customer services
6. Provide sales personnel with additional training in sales techniques
7. Offer bonuses to sales personnel
8. Move to a new location in a new shopping mall

Evaluating Alternatives

After preparing a rather complete list of alternatives, she evaluated each to determine its feasibility. Those that did not appear to offer a contribution to the goal of increased sales were shelved for consideration later. In this case, it was not possible to add more merchandise lines or move to a new location at this time.

Implementing the Plan of Action

The evaluation process should indicate which plan or combination of alternatives are appropriate courses of action to achieve increased sales. Usually several alternatives are incorporated into the plan of action. In this case, the owner-manager chose to begin advertising selectively on television to announce special sales. In addition, store personnel were given additional training in selling techniques. The net effect has been to increase sales (in real growth terms) by 6 percent the first year.

ORGANIZING AND STAFFING

Organizing is the management function of coordinating and integrating the human, financial, and physical resources of the firm so that they follow the planned course needed to reach the firm's objectives. Included in the organizing function are the following related activities.

Identify the Jobs To Be Performed

The initial activity in the organizing function is to define the jobs which must be performed if the firm is to realize its goals. It is also useful at this stage to draw up an organization chart of the formal organization, even if it is a very simple structure and chart. Organizing also includes the concept of division of work. Insofar as is possible in small firms, it is desirable to divide the jobs and group them into logical units, such as departments or sections, usually on the basis of similarity. Each department is responsibile for a particular phase of the opera-

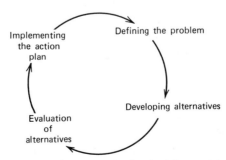

Figure 8-1 The four steps in the decision-making cycle.

tion. For example, all sales functions would be grouped together and all record keeping activities would be grouped together.

Staffing

Once the tasks have been identified, the need is to match personnel to jobs. The goal of staffing is to see that employees are selected and placed in tasks for which they are qualified. This activity is discussed more completely in Chapter 9.

Define Authority and Responsibility

How much authority and responsibility each employee has should be clearly defined. Even in the small firm, it is preferable that this information be in writing. Authority is the right of persons to take action and make the necessary decision for completing the tasks assigned to them. Responsibility is the obligation employees have to perform the tasks assigned to them to the best of their ability.

In the small business, the owner-manager has complete and final authority and responsibility. As often happens, however, owner-managers find that they do not have time to devote to every detail in the company. Effective managers realize that one of the most practical methods of running a successful company is to delegate some authority to their employees. Delegation of authority enables employees to make decisions in areas where they are qualified. It also allows the manager to devote extra time to more important matters. Delegation encourages key employees to take initiative. In addition, employees can have authority delegated to them to keep the company running if the owner-manager must be away from the business. When authority is delegated, employees are responsible for performing the tasks satisfactorily.

One small manufacturer recognized the necessity for establishing the formal organization. He divided the firm into three departments: production, sales, and administrative.

He then designated the responsibilities for each department manager. The production manager was given authority and responsibility for manufacturing, packing, and shipping. The sales manager's authority and responsibility was for advertising, attracting new customers, and customer service. The administrative department manager's authority and responsibility was for accounting, purchasing, and personnel activities.

After working together with department managers, the owner-manager was able to establish the job procedures and to avoid the overlapping of authority and responsibility between departments. All these procedures were then written down. Thus, managers had specific information on what decisions they

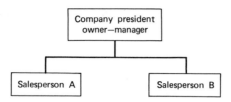

Figure 8-2 Organization chart of a small retail store.

could make and which actions needed approval by the owner. The owner also designated the production manager to be in charge during the owner's absence.

Determining Authority-Responsibility Relationships

The authority and responsibility relationships among the personnel need to be clearly defined to avoid confusion and overlapping authority. The organization chart is a useful device for representing graphically the authority relationships among people and departments and their responsibilities. The chart can also delineate the channels of communication and the lines of decision making in the company. Usually the organization chart is quite simple in the small business. At the outset, there is usually one manager. Figure 8-2 depicts the organization of a small retail store.

As the firm grows, additional employees are hired and an assistant manager may be added at a later date. Figure 8-3 shows this revised chart.

DIRECTING

Directing involves the owner-manager with employees on a daily, face-to-face basis. Directing includes the activities of leadership, communication, and motivation. The quality of the face-to-face supervision that the owner-manager has

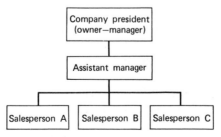

Figure 8-3 Organization chart of a small retail store showing addition of employees.

with employees is a major factor in determining the success of the firm. Employee relations are treated in more detail later in this chapter.

CONTROLLING

The control function's purpose is to provide managers with the information necessary to determine if current events conform to plans and objectives. Control is the means of monitoring what is happening in the business and provides managers with feedback on company progress toward achieving objectives. The control function is a continuous process which involves four basic stages.

1. Set standards of performance (establish acceptable levels of employee output, such as monthly sales quotas for salespersons).
2. Check performance at regular intervals (hourly, daily, weekly, monthly, annually).
3. Determine if there are any deviations from the standards.
4. If there are deviations, take corrective action, such as retraining or more training. If no deviations exist, continue the activity.

EMPLOYEE RELATIONS IN THE SMALL BUSINESS

Of the many issues that confront the owner-manager, one of the more challenging is found in the area of employee relations. Small business managers often possess a high level of technical skills, such as being a top-notch salesperson, or have the ability to work with things, such as machine shop equipment, computers, or accounting procedures. However, as an owner-manager, one of the most valuable skills is human relations, or the ability to work effectively with people to achieve individual and company goals.

In our text, "employee relations" refers to the daily interpersonal relationships which exist between small business managers and employees at work. The state of the interpersonal relationships defines the type of internal organization environment or climate which exists in the firm. The internal organization environment is shaped by the following factors in the workplace.

1. Social factors (group interaction, superior-subordinate relationships)
2. Physical work conditions (lighting, layout, equipment, other facilities in the workplace)
3. Economic factors (salary, wages, fringe benefits)

The perception that employees have of these factors influences, either directly or indirectly, their attitudes, behavior, expectations, and productivity toward the company's objectives, policies, working conditions, superiors, subordinates, and peers.

Most firms have at least a few employees on the payroll. A primary goal of managers is to get employees to work together as a team rather than as individuals. Teamwork stresses mutual understanding and cooperation for goal achievement.

Managers seek to understand employees, their motivation, and what causes them to act and respond as they do. In this section, we will explore some of the prominent issues of employee relations which should provide a basis for increasing the manager's understanding of employee behavior. This concern is very real in the small business where there are usually only a few employees, and each employee needs to perform his/her tasks to benefit both employee and the company.

THE INDIVIDUAL IN THE ORGANIZATION

Since employees spend a substantial portion of their lives at work, owner-managers should realize that the workplace has a profound impact on the lives of individuals. Modern managers recognize that each individual is unique with his/her own physical makeup, values, feelings, interests, needs, and emotions. Each individual's behavior in the workplace is shaped by several factors. The individual "is a product of . . . (1) his physical and social environment, (2) his physiological structure, (3) his wants and goals, and (4) his past experiences."[1]

EMPLOYEE NEEDS

All individuals have a unique set of needs. In our discussion, needs are all the things people must have in order to survive as well as the things they want. Human behavior is directed toward need satisfaction. It is of strategic importance that owner-managers strive to identify what employees want from a job in order to more clearly understand the reasons they are motivated. Motivation is the inner drive that ignites behavioral action to satisfy needs. Employee motivation may be positive or negative. Positive motivation occurs when employees strive toward a goal, such as putting forth extra effort on the job to gain a promotion, recognition, or a salary increase. Negative motivation results from such reasons as fear of failure or frustration and causes an employee's motivation to be aimed toward protection of self. Negative motivation may result in an employee rejecting new work methods or a promotion.

[1]David Krech, Richard S. Crutchfield, and Egerton Ballachey, *Individual in Society* (New York: Mc-Graw-Hill Book Company, Inc., 1962), pp. 17–18.

When owner-managers more fully comprehend employee needs, it leads to more constructive employer-employee relations because owner-managers then understand "why" employees respond as they do on the job.

Figure 8-4 presents a diagram of the need satisfaction process. For example, an employee has the desire to be promoted (need identification). In order to satisfy this need, the employee undertakes the actions which he/she feels will result in the job promotion (motivation to act). When the employer recognizes the employee's outstanding performance and rewards him/her with a promotion the need is satisfied (satisfaction of needs). The need satisfaction process is on-going within individuals.

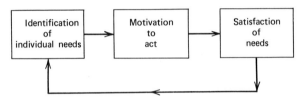

Figure 8-4   The need satisfaction process.

HIERARCHY OF NEEDS

A hierarchy of needs has been suggested by Abraham Maslow to indicate which needs are most important for an individual at a given time. This need hierarchy suggests a priority in which one level of needs must be reasonably well satisfied before the next higher need becomes prominent. The need hierarchy aids in understanding and explaining why employees behave the way they do on the job. In addition, knowledge of the need hierarchy is beneficial to managers, since they can use this information to build an organization environment that will offer opportunities for the higher order needs to be satisfied. Where employees are provided with opportunities to fulfill their needs, they will tend to respond with more favorable attitudes toward the organization and their work assignments. The need hierarchy is shown in Figure 8-5.

Physiological Needs

The basic needs are what an individual must have in order to survive. These needs include food, air, shelter, and water.

Safety and Security Needs

The second order of needs is safety and security. Safety needs are fulfilled in one sense by removal of dangerous conditions on the job. For example, by

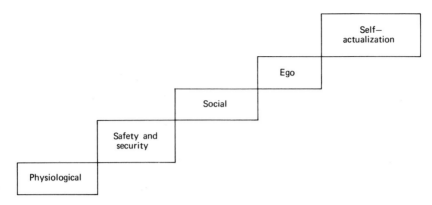

Figure 8-5 The hierarchy of needs. [*Source.* Abraham Maslow, "A Theory of Human Motivation," *Psychological Review*, 50, No. 4. (July–August, 1943), pp. 370–396, and Abraham Maslow, *Motivation and Personality.* (New York: Harper & Row, Publishers, Inc., 1954).]

placing a protective guard over a circular saw, physical working conditions are made more safe for workers. Security needs may be fulfilled through job security that provides the employee with financial security in order to maintain his/her standard of living.

Social Needs

Social needs include the need for belonging, acceptance, giving and receiving friendship and love. Americans are described as a nation of joiners. Most people are members of several groups—social clubs, civic organizations, churches, and, of course, work groups. Group memberships allow individuals to fulfill their belonging and acceptance needs. Employee belonging and acceptance needs are satisfied on the job through their acceptance as an influential member of the work group. According to the need hierarchy, this level of needs does not become important until the first two levels are no longer predominant.

Ego Needs

Ego needs include self-esteem (self-confidence, independence, achievement) and personal reputation (status, recognition, appreciation). Most people need to be independent, both on and off the job as they mature. Employees often express a desire for some degree of freedom from close supervision while performing their work. Ego needs are fulfilled through recognition. Employees

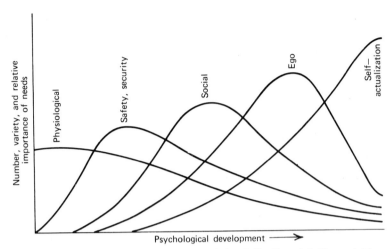

Figure 8-6 [Adapted from David Krech, Richard S. Crutchfield, and Egerton L. Ballachey, *Individual in Society*. (New York: McGraw-Hill Book Company, Inc., 1962), p. 77.]

should be given recognition for their contribution to the company, such as a salesperson of the month or a cash award for a useful suggestion. Recognition also increases one's status. Status is the relative social ranking a person has compared with others in the group. Status may be either formal or informal. "Formal status refers to the rank of people as designated by the authority structure of an organization. Informal status refers to the social rank accorded to people because of feelings toward them. It is the position that one has in an informal social system."[2] Typical status symbols include one's name on the office door, size or color of one's desk, kind of chair, and job title.

Self-Actualization Needs

The highest order need becomes prominent when the other needs have been satisfied. This need refers to a person becoming all he/she is capable of becoming. Maslow suggested that only 10 percent of the population ever achieves this level.

Although it appears that one need level must be completely satisfied before movement to the next level is possible, in reality there is a great deal of overlap between the need levels, as shown in Figure 8-6. By being aware of the hierar-

[2]Keith Davis, *Human Behavior at Work,* Fifth Edition. (New York: McGraw-Hill Book Company, Inc., 1977), p. 31.

chy of needs of the individual, owner-managers will be better equipped to understand the behavior patterns demonstrated by employees. For example, the manager should realize that if a lower order need is threatened, employees will revert back to functioning at the lower need level that is threatened until it is once again reasonably well satisfied. If an employee faces the loss of job, he/she will revert back to the lower survival and job security need level until the threat is removed, such as by getting a new job. He/she can then begin functioning at the higher need levels again.

Owner-managers should develop empathy with their employees. Empathy allows managers to view a situation or a problem through the eyes of another. By empathizing with employees as well as customers, managers will be in a more favorable position to understand employee behavior and needs, which in turn aids them in becoming more effective managers.

ORGANIZATIONAL CHANGE

The importance of understanding employee needs is emphasized because of the interrelationship which exists with the internal organizational environment. Managers should realize that all decisions they make and actions they undertake will affect employee needs. One positive step in building strong employer-employee relations is to assess the impact that proposed actions and decisions will have on employees prior to taking the action and to ascertain what steps should be taken to lessen an adverse impact.

One common problem deals with changes in the company that affect operations and personnel of the firm. Change may be reflected in methods or procedures of work, such as a change to automated facilities, a change in personnel, or a move by the company to a new location. Change has a definite impact on individuals and should be undertaken so as to encounter as few obstacles as possible.

Change is a fact of an organization's life and is desirable if the firm is to remain abreast or move ahead of the competition. Yet, the major barrier to change is resistance. The owner-manager resists change on the grounds that the business has been successful. Therefore, why is there a need to change. Employees resist change because they fear the unknown and desire to maintain the status quo in which they feel secure. Employee relations can be adversely affected if employees feel they are being pressured or manipulated into making changes. Employee resistance to change may be evidenced by more hostility or aggressiveness on the job. They may resort to sabotage in the work area, absenteeism and tardiness may increase, or they may develop apathetic attitudes toward their work.

Resistance to change can be reduced but not totally eliminated. Managers should recognize the importance of communicating clear and complete information about the change. They should also get the employees who will be affected by the change involved by encouraging them to contribute their suggestions on how to implement the change. Participation of employees is the type of constructive action that can aid in reducing their resistance to change.

EMPLOYEE MORALE

The organizational environment can have a major effect on employee morale. Morale is defined as the mental attitude of individuals and work groups toward their work environment (job, company). In this context, employee morale may be described as being either high or low. Since morale is a mental attitude, a feeling that employees have, it is difficult to measure. In fact, morale cannot be measured directly as can the number of dollars profit earned during a business year. Instead a number of different techniques are used to measure the attitudes of employees. These indirect measurements enable the small business owner to obtain a reading of employee morale in the firm.

One technique of measuring employee attitudes is an objective survey. This survey technique asks employees to check how they feel about particular items in the company. Questions may be of the true-false variety, multiple choice, or on a scale ranging from completely satisfied to completely dissatisfied. Figure 8-7 presents one method of collecting data on employee morale.

Descriptive surveys are another method of collecting morale data. Employees are requested to supply written answers to questions. Regardless of the method employed, morale surveys can profitably be used regularly to identify the strengths and weaknesses of the company.

INDICATORS OF EMPLOYEE MORALE

There are some significant indicators, or warning signals, that employee morale is low, which should be recognized by the small businessman. Some of the many indicators that the small businessman should be on the lookout for are shown in Figure 8-8.

Any of these negative morale indicators will adversely affect the small firm. Considerable amounts of time and money, ranging to thousands of dollars, are involved in employee selection and placement. Employees who are properly placed in a job tend to have higher morale. Poor selection and placement procedures lead to frustration and low morale. Eventually, employees will leave the firm or be low producers. Firms that have a high turnover rate of employees experience increased costs of operations. New employees must be

Figure 8-7 Employee morale survey.

Listed below are 20 statements. Please check each of the statements according to how you feel toward them—completely satisfied, moderately satisfied, neither satisfied nor dissatisfied (neutral), moderately dissatisfied, completely dissatisfied—in relation to your present position in this company.

	Completely satisfied	Moderately satisfied	Neither satisfied nor dissatisfied (neutral)	Moderately dissatisfied	Completely dissatisfied
1. Opportunity to have a part in helping to make decisions that affect you.					
2. Communications within the company provide adequate information to employees so that they have information as to what is going on now and also plans for the future.					
3. An absence of excessive or unnecessary pressure exerted by your superiors toward you to meet work deadlines.					
4. Fair and constructive evaluation of how well you are performing your job by your superiors.					
5. Freedom and initiative in the performance of your job allowed and encouraged.					
6. Job security—as long as you perform your job satisfactorily you can be almost certain you will hold your job.					
7. Satisfactory relationships exist between superiors and subordinates.					

Figure 8-7 (Continued)

	Completely satisfied	Moderately satisfied	Neither satisfied nor dissatisfied (neutral)	Moderately dissatisfied	Completely dissatisfied
8. Opportunities available for promotion and advancement to positions of more responsibility and authority.					
9. A salary that is competitive with the salaries of equivalent positions in other companies.					
10. Physical working conditions in the company are satisfactory (i.e., adequate equipment is provided, the work area is clean, safe, and comfortable).					
11. Doing a job that is interesting and challenging to you.					
12. Fair and equal treatment in handling of employees' grievances, gripes, and in disciplining them.					
13. Feeling of mutual trust exists between you and your superiors and you and your subordinates.					
14. Personal satisfaction derived from doing your job well—you have a feeling of pride in the job you are doing.					
15. Recognition given you for doing a good job.					

16. Superiors and subordinates work together as a team—each willingly does his share of the work.					
17. Standards of performance set for your job are realistic and within reach.					
18. Low rate of turnover among employees (excluding those leaving for reasons of promotion or health).					
19. Fringe benefits are at least equal to the benefits offered in other companies.					
20. A satisfactory training program is provided in the company.					

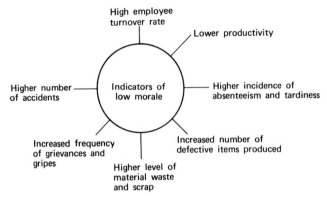

High employee
turnover rate

Lower productivity

Higher number
of accidents

Indicators of
low morale

Higher incidence of
absenteeism and tardiness

Increased frequency
of grievances and
gripes

Increased number of
defective items produced

Higher level of
material waste
and scrap

Figure 8-8 Morale indicators.

selected and placed. While they are being trained, their productivity is low and chances for error or waste of material are greater. Where the firm is experiencing a high turnover rate, the manager's real concern should be to find out the reasons why and take steps to correct them.

If absenteeism increases, the small business will be understaffed. In the retail or service establishment it will be difficult to provide the customer assistance needed, especially during peak business hours. This may result in driving customers away to competitors or at least creating inconvenience for the customers. In the small manufacturing firm, the absence of a machine operator means a machine must be idled, thus reducing the firm's output. Or, if the machine must be operated, it will likely have to be operated by a marginally qualified worker. The result will be lower productivity and increased number of defective products.

If accidents increase, not only must the personal injury be a matter of real concern but also the effect that the accidents have on the company. A valuable worker is lost for a period of time, productivity suffers, and the cost of employee accident insurance increases.

The negative effect of low morale should be an area of major concern for small business managers. Consequently, they should attempt to maintain up-to-date information relating to the state of employee morale and strive to improve the overall state of employee morale in the concern.

If these indicators begin to surface, small business managers should recognize that they are merely *symptoms*. The critical task is to establish the *cause*. Why is turnover increasing? Why is productivity suffering? Why are accidents increasing? Only by ascertaining the *cause* of these problems will it be possible to take constructive steps to correct them.

LEADERSHIP STYLE AND MORALE

The owner-manager's leadership style can be an important factor in determining employee morale. A leadership style that should have a positive impact on employee morale is one that creates a positive environment by providing employees with the opportunity to satisfy their goals and needs while at the same time allowing the firm to realize the attainment of its objectives.

Basically, there are three styles of leadership of which the small business manager should be cognizant. These are the autocratic, free-rein, and participative styles.

AUTOCRATIC LEADERSHIP

Autocratic leaders attempt to assume total control of the firm. They delegate little or no authority and provide few outlets for employee creativity. Close supervision is the practice and pressure is applied to obtain greater employee productivity. Since formal communications flow primarily downward from managers to employees, there is little opportunity for the exchange of information and ideas. Employees are usually reprimanded for mistakes. Autocratic leadership usually has a negative impact on employee morale if employees have strong needs for independence and participation.

FREE-REIN LEADERSHIP

Free-rein managers believe that the best leadership style is one in which there is minimal contact with employees. These managers frequently manage by abdication, not delegation. These managers spend much time away from the business. Instead of delegating authority to employees, however, this manager offers little or no direction for running the company during his or her absence. Employee morale usually declines when managers follow this leadership style.

PARTICIPATIVE LEADERSHIP

These leaders encourage employees to participate in making decisions that affect them. By encouraging participation, the leader desires to get employees ego-involved in their work and in the company. The leader strives to build an organizational environment that recognizes the importance of the individual. The participative leader encourages two-way communication.

Participative leaders also strive to tap the creative talents of their employees. A basic part of the participative leader's philosophy is that employees are more likely to support ideas and actions that they have had a part in creating.

Clearly, small business managers should recognize that no one leadership style is applicable to all situations. Leadership style, of necessity, varies from situation to situation. However, managers who create an organizational environment that encourages employees to participate discover that it can be an important avenue for developing positive employee morale.

EMPLOYEE DISCIPLINE

When employees work together, conflict will occasionally develop. If managers fail to cope with conflict and discipline situations constructively, the result can be a lowering of employee morale. Employees lose respect for managers who cannot tolerate mistakes, who are too lax and apply discipline only under the most severe circumstances, or apply discipline inconsistently.

One suggested way to reduce the number of instances where discipline is required is to inform employees of the company rules and regulations. For example, many firms specify employee actions that are prohibited, and if engaged in will result in termination of the employee. It is important, however, that employees perceive the rules as being fair and related to their job performance. A typical set of guidelines is shown in Figure 8-9.

Some factors involved in discipline or areas where discipline problems arise include (1) absenteeism, (2) tardiness, (3) rule violations, (4) insubordination, (5) failure to carry out orders, (6) errors in work, and (7) deviation from established procedures.

Frequently, these problems arise because of lack of knowledge, poor understanding, poor attitudes, lack of interest, or carelessness.

Progressive discipline is one approach which applies a minimum of discipline to a first offense but which increases the degree of discipline for subsequent

---

Prohibited Acts

1. Disorderly conduct; reporting to work under the influence of liquor or consuming intoxicants on company premises or while on company business.
2. Conclusive evidence of dishonesty.
3. Obtaining employment by using false or misleading information.
4. Continued violation of safety practices.
5. Selling or soliciting in the company.
6. Gambling.
7. Excessive tardiness or absenteeism without reason.
8. Refusal to work as directed (insubordination).
9. Willful destruction of company property.

Figure 8-9 Company guidelines for employees.

violations of rules or policies. Progressive discipline actions may include the following sequence:

Step One: Oral warning.

Step Two: Written warning stating the consequences of future violations.

Step Three: Disciplinary layoff or demotion.

Step Four: Discharge.

The "hot stove rule" has been recommended as a series of steps to make discipline more effective. It uses the analogy of touching the hot stove and administering discipline. The sequence should include:

1. A forewarning—all are warned by the heat generated not to touch the stove.
2. Immediate action—touching the stove results in being immediately burned.
3. A consistent rule—each time the stove is touched, you are burned.
4. Impersonal administration—all who touch the stove are burned.[3]

The most effective type of discipline is positive, that which corrects or strengthens an individual. It is also the most difficult type of discipline to apply. Disciplining should be conducted in private, away from the noise of the job, and certainly not in front of fellow employees. When disciplining, the manager should concentrate on the mistake rather than on the employee himself. It is essential that the manager listen carefully to the employee's view as to what occurred in order to get the full facts. Explain not only that they are doing something incorrect but also explain why they should be doing it another way. A further step is to work out an equitable solution that is fair to both employer and employee.

COMMUNICATION AND EMPLOYEE MORALE

A communication system that allows employees to be informed about company actions is a strong factor in creating high employee morale. An effective two-way communication system provides employees with the opportunity to be involved in company matters. It provides managers with insight into employee attitudes toward the company.

In many small businesses, most communication is exchanged on a face-to-face basis since the manager has direct, personal contact with employees. The manager plans the work, gives instructions and evaluates jobs to see that they

[3] Burt Scanlon and J. Bernard Keys, *Management and Organization Behavior.* (New York: John Wiley & Sons, Inc., 1979), p. 382.

are done properly. Other forms of communication are nonpersonal, such as written or visual (posters, for example).

The manager must realize that effective communication does not just occur. Instead, it involves a conscious effort on the part of the manager to build a communication system. Some specific guides for effective communication are included below.

1. The manager must be a good listener—listening to ideas and suggestions as well as complaints.
2. Employees should be kept informed of matters that affect them, such as changes in policies or procedures.
3. Two-way communication should be encouraged.
4. Subordinates should be allowed to participate in discussions of decisions that will affect them before the final decision is reached.
5. Create a climate of trust and confidence by reporting facts honestly to employees.
6. The communication messages should be accurate, definite, simple, and suitable for the occasion.
7. The communication messages should not contain any hidden messages.

IMPROVING EMPLOYEE RELATIONS

Small business managers should recognize the uniqueness of their firms. However, they can contribute greatly to improving employee relations by being aware of the specific suggestions listed below.

1. Improve your own general understanding of human behavior.
2. Accept the fact that others do not always see things as you do.
3. In any differences of opinion, consider the possibility that you may not have the right answer.
4. Show your employees that you are interested in them and that you want their ideas on how conditions can be improved.
5. Treat your employees as individuals; never deal with them impersonally.
6. Respect differences of opinion.
7. Insofar as possible, give explanations for management actions.
8. Provide information and guidance on matters affecting employees' security.
9. Make reasonable efforts to keep jobs interesting.
10. Encourage promotion from within.
11. Express appreciation publicly for jobs well done.

12. Offer criticism privately, in the form of constructive suggestions for improvement.
13. Train supervisors to be concerned about the people they supervise, the same as they would be about merchandise or materials or equipment.
14. Keep your staff up-to-date on matters that affect them.
15. Quell false rumors and provide correct information.
16. Be fair![4]

DISCUSSION QUESTIONS

1. Identify the functions of the manager.
2. Explain the difference between technical skills and human relations skills.
3. Define the term "employee relations."
4. Explain what is meant by the internal organization environment.
5. What does the "hierarchy of needs" mean?
6. What is the difference between motivation and morale?
7. What is status? A status symbol? Identify different status symbols.
8. How do you measure morale?
9. Name several of the indicators of morale.
10. Why is it difficult to discipline employees? What are some actions that can be taken to make discipline positive?
11. Explain the difference between autocratic, free-rein, and participative leadership styles.
12. What are some suggestions for improving communication?

STUDENT PROJECTS

Interview a small business manager and obtain the following data.

1. What are the objectives of the business? Are the objectives written down?
2. Does the firm have an organization chart? If so, obtain a copy of the chart.
3. Are morale surveys conducted in the firm? If so, how often?
4. Does the firm have written rules and regulations? If it does, what are they?

[4]Martin M. Bruce, *Human Relations in Small Business*. (Washington, D.C.: Small Business Administration).

CASE A

WOOD MANUFACTURING COMPANY

Samuel Jackson is the supervisor of the bending and press department of a small manufacturing company known for its quality products. Forty of the company's 220 employees work in this department. The products of the company include tubular and plate heat exchangers, pressure vessels, absorption towers, and equipment for dairy and chemical plants.

Six months ago, Andrew was hired as a punch press operator. He is 24, single, has received training at a technical training school, and has three years' experience. He is ambitious and plans to work for a higher degree by attending evening classes.

The work of the punch press operators is such that workers must cooperate in performing tasks of similar nature and the contribution of particular members is difficult to measure. The company has a group incentive plan under which production workers are paid a bonus for production above standard. Data of production standards and the bonus rate are arrived at by members of the industrial engineering department with consultation between management and employees. The bonus is available only to direct production workers (machine operators). Tool setters are not eligible and receive a flat, hourly wage. The group of which Andrew is a member usually receives a bonus of between 35 and 40 percent over their basic wage.

Matthew has been with the company seven years and is employed as a die setter in the punch press department. His job is to set dies to the press for stamping or forming metal sheets as required. For each item, different sets of tooling are required. Thus, to change production from one item to another means tools must be set and machines adjusted. This is Matthew's job. He is conscientious, loyal to the company, and particularly methodical in his approach to his task. He is somewhat slow but does his job well. At times the punch press operators became irritated with Matthew because they felt that his slowness kept them from making a bonus.

To speed up the process, Andrew began setting the tools of his machine himself about three months ago. Matthew accused Andrew of trying to take his job away. Andrew assured Matthew that he was only trying to help him. Andrew felt that while they had to wait, the group members were losing money. He did not feel Matthew would mind, since all tool setters were paid a flat hourly wage.

This situation caused resentment to build between Andrew and Matthew. Samuel, the supervisor, was unaware of the conflict between the two. Samuel did notice that Andrew did adjust his machine and set a die occasionally, but he did not object since this helped to get the work out on schedule and Andrew did the work correctly.

One day, near the end of work when both men were tired, Matthew openly accused Andrew of trying to steal his job and a quarrel developed between them. Andrew told Matthew he was too slow and could not do his work properly and that he should be replaced. Matthew became enraged and moved closer to Andrew. Assuming that Matthew was going to strike him, Andrew punched him, knocking him to the floor. A scuffle followed until Samuel came running to the scene and broke it up. He then reported the incident to the personnel manager, Roy.

The company policy prohibits fighting on company premises.

Questions

1. What disciplinary action should be taken by Roy, the personnel manager?
2. What effect will this situation have on employee morale if it is not handled properly?

CASE B

GRAPHICS, INC.

Graphics, Incorporated is a small business that specializes in preparing artwork for training materials, reports, and publications of a number of firms in the area. The nature of the work is such that the company has a history of employee layoffs in the early summer months of June and July.

The organization chart of Graphics is shown below.

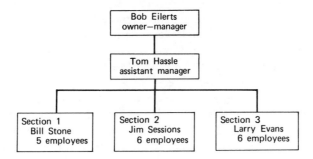

Work has been particularly hectic for Graphics for about two months, as happens every spring, prior to the early summer layoffs. The company has been outbid on two large contracts and will only serve minor functions on them. Mr. Eilerts, the owner-manager, has been particularly busy seeking outside work from the steady clients so that when the current work is completed there will be fewer layoffs.

With the loss of bids, the company is on an economy drive, and several memos have been circulated to that effect. In Graphics, the employees have been instructed to save all potentially useful paper scraps, conserve liquid supplies, only fire-up necessary machines, and become cost conscious. Several phones have been removed, and employees have been asked to minimize outside calls.

A problem has begun to develop. Lately, there has been a high percentage of tardiness in Graphics. Jim Sessions' section has been the leader, but the problem is shared by each section. No particular employees have been repetitious violators, but tardiness has shown a marked increase. Accurate records of who is in violation and when have been kept due to the security procedures necessary in the firm.

If an employee is late, he is not allowed to redeem the lost time during lunch hour or after work. When lunchtime is in effect or at the close of work, all materials are locked in their respective drawers. Therefore, when an employee is late, it is considered a loss.

One morning, without prior knowledge, late employees found themselves greeted at the door by Mr. Eilerts and Mr. Hassle. Neither man made any comments, but made it obvious they were surveying the violators. Later that morning, Mr. Hassle called Jim Sessions' section together and talked for approximately 20 minutes about tardiness and the economy drive. Employees of that section were told that the next person to arrive late would be fired the same day.

Nothing was said to the other sections by Mr. Hassle, but word of mouth spread the information. The other sections did not know whether the ruling pertained to them or not, but after many rumors had circulated, it was finally determined that the ruling covered everyone in Graphics.

A week went by without a tardy entry. The supervisors continued to post watch at the door and to check the register. Meanwhile, the absentee rate went up. Finally, an employee arrived late.

This particular employee, Mr. Lewis, was in Sessions' section. He had been with the company for 8 years and had arrived at national prominence as one of the top illustrators in his field. Liked by most people, he was witty and kept his associates in good spirits. He participated in football, softball, trivia, and had a stock of six foreign cars. Nearly everyone enjoyed him.

As the day wore on, electricity ran through Graphics, with much speculation over the fate of Mr. Lewis. Nothing happened, until two days later, when a younger employee, Miss Right, arrived late and was fired that afternoon.

It suddenly became apparent to the members of Graphics that the issue of tardiness was going to be a convenient tool for the disposal of selected employees. With this realization, the morale of the department caved in, work errors increased, and absenteeism again rose. In the following weeks, four employees quit to go to competitors or to do free-lance artwork. Two of those employees had been at Graphics for 10 years. The others were only new employees. The tension remained high in Graphics.

Questions

1. Why is employee morale low?
2. What type of motivational technique is management using?
3. What leadership style is being used?
4. How should management have handled the situation?

9

PERSONNEL MANAGEMENT IN THE SMALL BUSINESS

PREVIEW OF THIS CHAPTER

1. In this chapter, you will learn the purpose of job analysis, job description, and job specification.

2. You will be able to identify many sources where employees may be recruited.

3. You will understand the various steps involved in the hiring process.

4. You will learn the importance of employee orientation and how the employee manual aids in carrying out effective orientation.

5. You will be aware of the various types of training that employees may receive both within and outside the company.

6. You will understand the important role that counseling plays in the small business.

7. You will be able to identify the various payment plans that the small business manager may use.

8. You will learn of some important federal laws that may affect the small business owner.

9. You will understand what employee benefits are and why they are important.

10. You will be able to discuss why employee safety is so critical to the small business firm.

11. You will be able to explain these key words:

Job description	Counseling
Job analysis	Performance appraisal
Job specification	Fair Labor Standards Act of 1938
Application blank	Civil Rights Act of 1964
Employee orientation	Fringe benefit
On-the-job training	Employee safety
Apprenticeship training	Occupational Safety and Health
Job rotation	Act of 1970
Group training	

In the small business, a key asset is the employees. The level of efficiency achieved in the small firm is significantly influenced by the performance level of the employees.

In larger firms, personnel management specialists are hired and charged with the responsibility for implementing the personnel management functions. However, small business owners, with limited financial resources, do not ordinarily employ a personnel manager. Instead, the owner-manager may take personal charge of the personnel activities or delegate them to an employee who performs them in addition to a regular job assignment.

Although the personnel management function does not have the status of a full-time manager, it by no means detracts from its importance. In fact, it should signal owner-managers that they must devote greater energy if the personnel management function is to be effectively completed.

The purpose of personnel management is to ensure that people are hired and placed in positions that match their qualifications. Specific activities included in the personnel management process are defining the requirements of the job, recruiting employees, establishing the necessary hiring procedures, and providing for employee training.

DEFINE THE REQUIREMENTS OF THE JOB

Small business managers find they can make the process of selecting the right person for each position more efficient by carefully defining the requirements of the tasks that must be performed and the skills and other qualifications that the employee must possess in order to perform them. Defining the requirements of the job encompasses three phases: conducting a job analysis, writing a job description, and preparing a job specification.

JOB ANALYSIS

A job analysis is the foundation for determining job descriptions. The job analysis is a systematic investigation to collect all pertinent job facts. The job analysis identifies the skills, knowledge, and abilities that employees need to perform a task plus the tasks, duties, and responsibilities of the task itself.

The job analysis should provide the following types of information about a task.

1. Job title.
2. Department in which the job is located.
3. Line of supervision.

MEDIA ADVERTISING

Advertising is an often employed technique used to attract potential employees. Job vacancies may be publicized in the local newspaper classified section or broadcast over a local radio station or television station. Newspapers in adjoining cities or counties and trade association magazines are additional possibilities for attracting potential employees.

IN-STORE ADVERTISING

Many owner-managers use in-store advertising to call attention to job openings. Help wanted signs are placed in the store window or the vacancy may be announced on the store's marquee or on a portable sign trailer located in front of the store.

DROP-IN APPLICANTS

On occasion, people will drop in without any vacancy announcement to inquire if jobs are open. Even if a job is not open at the time, the owner-manager should take down some information about the interested party, such as name and phone number and the type of position wanted so they can be contacted if a job opens. Or, they may fill out an application blank. This information may enable the owner-manager to locate an employee to fill a vacancy.

VOCATIONAL-TECHNICAL SCHOOLS

Area schools provide a large pool of potential employees. Many high school students are given excellent training in the necessary vocational or technical skills needed to excel in a job. Junior colleges also have outstanding technical training programs. In addition, private technical training schools, such as business colleges or electronics schools graduate many qualified applicants.

FORMER MILITARY PERSONNEL

Persons retired from military service may be a valuable source of employees to consider. These individuals frequently possess skills and knowledge that can contribute significantly to the small business firm's employment needs.

COLLEGES AND UNIVERSITIES

Placement offices at colleges and universities maintain an active file of candidates who possess a wide range of qualifications. The owner-manager should consider this source, especially if the firm needs an employee who has received specialized training such as in accounting. In addition, the owner-manager should not overlook contacting teachers for recommendations of possible employees.

PUBLIC EMPLOYMENT AGENCIES

Public employment agencies, such as state and federal government agencies, offer their services in helping to locate and place employees. State employment agencies, for example, maintain employment offices at strategic locations throughout the state and each office has direct contact with all other offices. They have on file an up-to-date listing of potential employees who possess a wide range of skills. Unskilled, skilled, technical, and professional employees may be recruited through these agencies. An advantage of public employment agencies is that their services are provided at no cost to users.

PRIVATE EMPLOYMENT AGENCIES

Private employment agencies maintain an extensive listing of applicants who possess skills necessary for performing a variety of tasks. Private employment agencies charge a fee for their placement services which must be paid by either the applicant or the employer.

LABOR UNIONS

Some firms may consider labor unions as possible sources of personnel. Unions can be especially helpful in supplying workers for certain types of occupations, such as carpenters or brickmasons.

FORMER EMPLOYEES

Employees who may have voluntarily quit for personal or health reasons may be rehired at a later date. For example, someone who moved to another city and later returned to the local area may be reemployed.

PART-TIME EMPLOYEES

For many types of business, sales fluctuate sharply upward as a particular holiday season approaches, such as Christmas or Easter. This upturn in business activity often puts pressure on the regular work force to provide all customers with personalized service. Hence, the owner-manager can effectively employ part-time employees to fill in during the rush season. Part-time employees can also work the odd-hour shifts, such as in the evenings or on Saturdays.

Other firms have need of extra help certain times of the day or week, but business activity is not sufficient to justify hiring a full-time employee. For example, a small retail store in a shopping center found its peak business hours were from 2 P.M. to 9 P.M. and its peak days were Friday and Saturday. The manager was able to hire two part-time employees to help meet the needs of the peak hours and days. A small hardware store owner and his wife operate their store by themselves. When peak periods develop or when the owners want to get away for a vacation, they employ their neighbor, a retired military officer, to manage the store.

A plentiful supply of part-time employees is usually available. Possible sources include students, both high school and college, retired persons who desire only a few hours of employment a day or week, or a person whose health permits only a limited amount of work.

THE HIRING PROCESS

The purpose of the hiring process is to obtain as much information about an individual as possible relative to skills, knowledge, and attitudes to determine if that person is suited to the type of work available. Small business managers can prevent unpleasant situations from developing later if they do not attempt to short-circuit the hiring process. In many instances, it is equally as poor a policy to hire someone who is overqualified as one who is underqualified for a position.

What can happen when a highly qualified person is hired and his or her skills are not utilized is shown in the following case example. Jean, an ambitious law school graduate, took a position two years ago as an assistant to the president of a small public relations firm. After a period of job orientation, she was told she would be assigned to handle clients of the firm.

Instead of handling legal matters for the firm, Jean was assigned jobs that amounted to secretarial-receptionist responsibilities. She scheduled the president's luncheons, arranged his tennis matches, and spent much of her time on the job reading novels. As a result of her job skills being underutilized, she became so bored and frustrated that she quit.

The underqualified person will likely become frustrated because of the lack of skill or knowledge, the job performance will probably be inferior, and the person will likely quit or have to be replaced or retrained because he or she is not turning out a satisfactory level of output. Both situations result in an unfortunate loss to both the company and individuals.

The hiring process involves a number of activities all designed to elicit needed data about particular job candidates. These activities include the application blank, interviewing, and testing.

THE APPLICATION BLANK

An application blank, as shown in Figure 9-2, provides managers with a written record of an applicant's qualifications and enables them to compare and evaluate applicants. Generally requested information on the application form is the name, address, telephone number, kind of work desired, social security number, marital status, work experience, education, and job references. The application form is completed by the job candidate. By having the potential employee complete the form, managers can evaluate how well the candidate organizes and presents these data.

The completed application form should be used as a guide by the manager or the person designated by the manager when conducting the employment interview.

PERSONAL INTERVIEWING

An extensively used selection device is the personal interview. During the interview, the manager has the opportunity to learn more about the applicant through face-to-face contact. A prime requirement of any interview is that the prospective employee be made to feel at ease, since the applicant is likely to be a bit edgy. Putting the applicant at ease can often be accomplished by adopting an informal approach at the outset of the interview to help break the tension. After the preliminaries, the interview should be guided but not dominated by the manager. It is especially important to let the candidate speak freely, answering as well as asking questions about areas of concern. By guiding the discussion, using the application blank as a reference, the manager will be able to learn in-depth information about the applicant's background as well as future goals and observe the applicant's personal appearance.

It is usually a good policy for the manager to check the references listed by the applicant. A telephone call to a former employer (immediate supervisor where possible), teacher, or personal reference provides a quick means of validating the accuracy of the data supplied on the application form and in the interview. Another means of obtaining references is by letter, but it takes much longer to get the desired information this way. Some factors to evaluate in checking references are inflated salary figures, incorrect dates of employment, false claims on the amount of education and experience, and claiming a higher level of job responsibility than actually held.

A note of caution is appropriate with regard to reference checks. Some firms do not give information about former employees because of the risk that former

EMPLOYMENT APPLICATION   AN EQUAL OPPORTUNITY EMPLOYER

Date _____

Name _____ Social
                                              Security Number _____
     Last   First   Middle Initial

Address _____ Telephone
                                             Number _____
    Street   City   State   Zip Code

Military Service   Rank
Branch _____ From _____ to _____ Achieved _____

Special Schools or Training in Military _____

_____

If Related to an Employee of This Firm, State Name: _____

Person to Notify in Case of Emergency _____
                              Name   Telephone

List Equipment and Office Machines You Are Qualified to Operate: _____

EMPLOYMENT RECORD
(List most recent employment first)

Name and Address of Company	Position & Duties	Dates Employed	Salary	Reason for Leaving

EDUCATION

Schools Attended	Dates Attended	Major Subject Studied	Degree or Certificate

REFERENCES

Name	Address	Telephone	Occupation

Figure 9-2 Application for employment.

Proper interviewing techniques help in selecting the right employee for the job.

employees may claim an unfavorable reference spoiled their chance for a better position. Such action may result in a former employee bringing legal action against a former employer.

   While most small business managers are busy with the many activities of the firm, they should not neglect spending time on the interview since it is an integral part of the selection process.

TESTS

Some owner-managers may use tests advantageously as part of the selection process. However, it is emphasized that tests are to serve as an aid in making employee selection more efficient, not as the sole basis for selection. Some tests that are used are aptitude, achievement, intelligence, and personality tests.

When the Civil Rights Act of 1964 was enacted, restrictions were placed on the use of tests for hiring and promotion. Specifically, the Act requires that tests must be related to the specific jobs involved and must be designed so as not to discriminate against a specific group on the basis of race, color, religion, sex, or national origin. As a result, many firms no longer use employment tests.

Medical Examination

Some firms require employees to undergo a physical examination as part of the selection process to help determine if they can stand up to the physical requirements of specific tasks. Can they work in dusty or damp areas or do they have the physical strength to lift and move heavy materials? A medical exam requirement is a sound policy for a number of reasons. If the company carries health insurance for employees, the premiums paid for the insurance increase greatly if employees who are hired are in poor health and cannot meet the physical demands of the job. The exam also should reveal any injury the potential employee may have suffered on a previous job. This action protects the current employer from being held liable for injuries suffered elsewhere.

EMPLOYEE ORIENTATION

Once the employment decision has been made, attention should be given to providing the new employee with a thorough orientation into the company and the work area. This procedure helps reduce normal apprehension new employees have, especially during the first few days on the job. New employees should be introduced to the other employees and made to feel welcome, receive an explanation of how his or her job fits into overall company operation, and be informed again of the conditions of employment, method of pay, deductions, and work and break schedules.

EMPLOYEE HANDBOOK

Small business owners should consider the value of an employee handbook as a vehicle for communicating vital information on the company to the employees.

The handbook explains among other things what is expected of employees; what the company expects of employees; policies on pay, working conditions, and benefits; and, company philosophy toward customers.

Handbooks may range from a few typewritten pages to a printed booklet. In addition to being useful for orienting new employees, older employees find it beneficial as a reference. Even though most small businesses do not have an employee handbook, its value should not be overlooked as a means of reinforcing communication and promoting positive employer-employee relations. Figure 9-3, which presents the table of contents of a small manufacturer's employee handbook, illustrates the wide range of topics of interest to employees.

EMPLOYEE TRAINING

New employees may have had prior job experience or this may be their first employment. Regardless, some training must be given. The purposes of employee training is to improve job performance. Furthermore, properly trained employees will likely be more satisfied with their jobs.

Training should not be considered a one-time event but rather a continuous process. Training seeks to improve employee knowledge and skills in order to keep them abreast of the many changes occurring in the competitive business environment. Continuous training means employees will be prepared for advancement to new and more challenging opportunities within the firm. In turn, this should result in higher employee morale and a reduction in employee turnover. The overall effect of a continuous training program is that both employer and employee benefit.

In the small business, the owner-manager has the responsibility for developing and conducting the training program. The kind of training given depends largely on the kind of work being performed. Some types of training available to employees are discussed below.

ON-THE-JOB TRAINING

On-the-job training (OJT) is the most practical and most often used training technique in the small business. Depending on the complexity of the task and experience level of employees, training may vary from a few hours to several full days.

This training is given by the manager or a designated employee and involves three phases. First, the job is demonstrated to the employees and each step of the process is thoroughly explained. The demonstration should be done slowly, instructions should be given clearly, and the trainees should be asked questions

Introduction to Company

Philosophy of the Company

Hours of work

Attendance Incentive Program

Holidays

Insurance
  Employee and Family
  Workmen's Compensation

Jury Duty

Leaves of Absence

Military Obligations

Parking Facilities

Personal Appearance and Work Habits
  Cleanliness
  Dress
  Leaving the Plant Premises During Work Hours
  Personal Debts
  Personal Work
  Phones
  Prohibited Acts

Pay Policies
  Accrued Vacation Pay for Terminated Employees
  Jury Duty
  Loss of Time due to Death in Immediate Family
  Overtime Pay
  Pay Days
  Salaries
  Salary Advances
  Time Cards

Profit-sharing and Retirement Plan

Service Awards—Employee

Termination of Employment
  Discharge
  Layoff
  Reemployed
  Resignation

Vacations
  Permanent Employees
  Terminating Employees

Figure 9-3 Topics covered in employee manual.

to determine if they understand the process. Second, the trainees perform the task by applying what they have learned in step one. In the third step, the work is inspected and immediate feedback of the job performance is given to the trainees. This technique provides for reinforcing correct performance or correcting improper job techniques at the beginning by showing what was wrong.

On-the-job training is used to provide continuous training to employees in order to keep their job skills current or prepare them for a promotion.

Most of the training given salespersons in the small store is on-the-job training given by either the store owner-manager or another experienced salesperson. This training can be supplemented by "role playing," a technique that helps salespersons to identify with customers. In this approach, one person assumes the role of the customer and the other, the salesperson. Role playing permits salespersons to view the sale through the eyes of the customer. After one or more role-playing sessions, the roles may be reversed. This type of training can be conducted on the sales floor during slow times of the business day.

APPRENTICESHIP TRAINING

Apprenticeship training is a formal type of training that combines both formal classroom learning and on-the-job experience. This kind of training program is provided mainly in the skilled trades—plumbers, electricians, meat cutters, bakers. The length of time spent in apprenticeship varies from 2 years to 4 or 5 years, depending on the kind of skill being learned.

JOB ROTATION

Particularly in the small business, it is beneficial if each employee has a good understanding of the different functions performed in the firm. In this way, if one employee is absent, another employee can fill in. One way to accomplish this objective is by rotating employees from job to job for a few hours a day, a few days, or several weeks, depending on the difficulty of the task. Job rotation should best be done during the slack periods of the business day or season.

Job rotation is also one means of combating the problem of monotony and boredom on the job and boosting morale, since a person encounters a variety of work experiences.

GROUP TRAINING

The conference method is one means of achieving group training. A particular advantage of this technique is that each participant in the training session has the opportunity to express his or her viewpoints and share experiences, while listening and learning from the contributions that others make in discussing common problems or expressing opinions.

Some group training aimed at increasing the salespersons' knowledge of merchandise and services may be accomplished in sales meetings. These meetings may focus on a discussion of new products, additional services, a special sale, or a change in store policies. These group meetings can be conducted before the start of the business day or during slow periods during the day. When using group training, care should be taken to see that there are specific goals to be accomplished so that valuable employee time is not wasted.

TRAINING OFF COMPANY PREMISES

Much training can be provided by sources outside the company. Some of these sources are given below.

University and Community College Courses

Some small businesses pay for all or part of the cost for some of their employees to continue their education at the university and community college level. The employee may attend on-campus classes in the evening, early morning, or late afternoon and still be available for employment either all day or a major portion of the work day.

Often this type of training is specialized training such as in engineering, accounting, or computer technology.

Extension Courses and Correspondence Courses

Colleges and universities offer a number of extension courses. Regular faculty members go to a particular locale where there is a demand for a course. They usually teach the course in the evening so it does not interfere with the work schedule of employees.

Correspondence courses enable a person to receive high school or college credit or learn other skills by completing prescribed lessons in his or her own home. A wide range of courses are offered through correspondence, such as accounting or business law.

BUSINESS SUPPLIERS

Business suppliers are often a valuable training resource. For example, suppliers frequently provide specific training in technical operations of new equipment or can instruct employees in the procedures of a new accounting or recordkeeping system.

TRAINING FILMS

Training films are available from private sources, trade associations, and the Small Business Administration. Films are available to serve a variety of training needs, such as group training, job procedures, communication, and leadership.

TRAINING GUIDELINES FOR THE SMALL BUSINESS

In setting criteria for training in the small firm, owner-managers will be aided in determining their training needs by evaluating the following questions.

1. What are the objectives of the training?
2. What do employees need to learn?
3. How much will the training program cost?
4. What type of training should be offered?
5. What method(s) of instruction should be used?
6. What kind of physical facilities will be needed?
7. How long will the training period be?
8. Will training be conducted during or after working hours?
9. Who will conduct the training?
10. Will special equipment be required (such as audiovisual)?
11. Which employees should be selected to attend the training sessions?
12. What type of feedback will be given employees?
13. How will the effectiveness of the program be measured?
14. What is the applicability of the training to the specific needs of the firm?
15. How should the program be publicized?

COUNSELING EMPLOYEES

Counseling, like training, should be a continuous activity, because situations occur daily where owner-managers need to counsel employees. Counseling serves at least four purposes.

1. To give instructions (to explain new job procedures).
2. To gain employee cooperation (to explain changes in company policies, work assignments, and work schedules in order to get employees to support these changes).
3. To obtain information (to deal with employee grievances, information must be gathered as to the nature of the complaints).
4. To give advice (employees may request advice on personal matters). In this

situation, the best posture is for the owner-manager to be a good listener and offer advice sparingly.

It is vital that owner-managers realize that counseling is most effective when it is treated as a two-way relationship. In many instances, the key to good counseling is good listening.

Some specific points about counseling which the owner-manager should find helpful are suggested.

1. Have a purpose for the counseling interview.
2. Counseling should be conducted in private interviews.
3. Use the "we" viewpoint instead of "I" to gain cooperation.
4. Such questions as who, what, where, why, when, and how can be used effectively.
5. Listen without interrupting.
6. Conclude the interview with a positive emphasis.

COUNSELING IN THE PROBATIONARY PERIOD

Many companies have a probationary period for new employees. The length of time for the probationary period varies, depending on the time it takes to learn the task. During the probationary period, employees' performance is observed to determine if they can perform the task, counseling is given, and employees have the opportunity to form their opinion of the company.

At the end of a specified time, preferably at the end of the first week, new employees should be interviewed. This counseling session serves a number of purposes.

1. Employees can raise questions about company rules or policies about which they are not clear.
2. Employees can offer their impressions of the job.
3. Employees can identify types of assistance or instructions they need.

For the remainder of the probationary period, periodic counseling should be conducted to evaluate their progress. The immediate supervisor and fellow employees are also valuable resources for providing data. This procedure makes it possible to determine if new employees, the job, and the company are compatible at the end of the probationary period. If they are, the firm has potentially good employees. If they are not, separation should be as painless as possible.

PERFORMANCE APPRAISAL

Employees are more satisfied if they know how owner-managers view their performance. Owner-managers have the responsibility to know how employees are doing and communicate this information to them. In a real sense, performance is evaluated continuously as the owner-manager works with employees on a daily basis.

It is a matter of sound business policy to have regular, periodic formal employee evaluations. Ordinarily, these are conducted once or twice a year. Where it is possible and company size permits, employees should be rated by the owner-manager and their immediate supervisor.

Employees should be evaluated on factors relating to the type of work performed. Areas commonly evaluated are skill (quality of work), responsibility (judgment, courtesy), effort (quantity of work), and attitude (enthusiasm, loyalty). Periodic evaluations enable the manager to chart the progress of employees and to suggest areas that need improvement.

The success of the performance appraisal and follow-up counseling depends on whether employees recognize its primary purpose—to assist them in im-

Performance appraisal is an important form of communication between owner-managers and employees.

proving their performance. Since most people are apprehensive about any type of evaluation, care should be taken to put employees at ease at the outset of the counseling session. Furthermore, emphasis should not be concentrated on the negative factors of job performance; the positive accomplishments should be stressed as well. Again, the goal of the evaluation is to provide direction for employees to improve their performance.

A sample appraisal form is shown in Figure 9-4 which is suited to the needs of a small business manager. Another rating form, shown in Figure 9-5 enables managers to evaluate employee performance on a simple "yes-no" basis.

WAGES AND SALARIES

An equitable and competitive wage and salary plan is essential in the small business. Paying lower wages or salaries than is paid employees of other companies in the area is certain to increase employee dissatisfaction and increases the chances of losing key employees. Wages are the payments made to workers on an hourly basis while salaries are the specific dollar amount paid weekly, biweekly, or monthly.

Clearly, money is important to employees, and pay should match the requirements of the job. Job descriptions, specifications, and performance appraisals are an aid in designing an equitable wage and salary system. In addition to equity, a compensation plan should be simple to understand and flexible. Compensation plans may also have provisions for merit increases or seniority increases.

EMPLOYEE COMPENSATION PLANS

Pay plans that are easy to understand and to administer are best suited to the small business. Some of the compensation plans commonly used in small businesses are discussed below.

Straight Salary

The most popular payment method in small businesses is salary. Employees receive a fixed amount each pay period, and the plan is quite easy to understand and to administer.

Hourly Wage

Employees may be paid a specific rate for each hour worked. This method of payment can be used to reward employees where it is difficult to measure

Employee Rating Scale

Name _____   Date _____

Dept. _____   Job _____

Rated by _____

Instructions

This Rating Scale is an aid to measuring—with a reasonable degree of accuracy and uniformity—the abilities of one of your employees and his skill in his present job. It will help you to appraise his present performance as compared with previous performance in the same job; and it may indicate promotion possibilities. Because the rating requires your appraisal of the employee's actual performance, snap judgment must be replaced by careful analysis. The following instructions may be helpful.

1. Disregard your general impression and concentrate on a single factor at a time.
2. Read all four specifications for each factor before determining which one most nearly fits the employee.
3. In rating an employee, make your judgment on instances occurring frequently in his daily routine. Don't be swayed by isolated incidents that aren't typical of his work.
4. Don't let personal feelings govern your rating. Make it carefully so that it represents your fair, objective opinion.

Factor	1	2	3	4
a. Quality of work	Poor; often does unacceptable work; is careless, requires constant supervision.	Fair; needs supervision and frequent checking.	Generally good; makes only occasional mistakes; requires little supervision.	Excellent; work is A-1 most of time; makes very few mistakes; needs supervision only very occasionally.
b. Quantity of work	Very slow; almost never does complete job in time assigned for it.	Erratic; sometimes fast and efficient, other times slow and unskillful.	Steady worker, does job consistently, and occasionally does more.	Exceptionally fast; does work quickly and well; does extra work to stay busy.
c. Flexibility	Does not adapt readily to new situations; most of the time, instructions must be repeated frequently.	Adequate; requires thorough, complete instruction before taking on new duties or new type of work.	Quick; learns new assignment in short time if given some instruction.	Very adaptable; fast learner, quickly meeting needs of new situation or assignment.

d. Job knowledge	Limited knowledge of job; shows little desire to improve.	Passable knowledge of job; needs frequent instruction and continuing supervision.	Well informed about job; rarely needs instruction or assistance.	Full knowledge of job; able to proceed alone on almost all work.
e. Responsibility	Irresponsible in attendance; seldom carries out orders without being prodded.	Some absences; occasionally needs reminder to do work assigned.	Attendance record good; reliable in work.	Excellent attendance record; most reliable in doing work assigned; can always be depended on.
f. Housekeeping and safety	Never cleans working area; is reckless in behavior.	From time to time, cleans work area; is occasionally negligent about safety.	Keeps work area clean; is careful about safety.	Keeps work area spotless; is unusually careful about safety.
g. Attitude	Uncooperative; often complains; is a disruptive influence among other employees.	Some cooperation, but is often indifferent both to fellow workers and to quality of own work.	Usually cooperative; attentive to work; gets along well with others.	Exceptionally cooperative; very interested in work; always helpful to others and considerate of them.

Figure 9-4 (*Source.* Small Business Administration, *Personnel Management.* Administrative Management Course Program. Topic 6. Washington D.C.: U.S. Government Printing Office.)

Name _____ Date _____

Position _____

	Yes	No
1. Is prompt in arriving at work	_____	_____
2. Does the required amount of work	_____	_____
3. Does more than required amount of work	_____	_____
4. Works neatly and in an organized way	_____	_____
5. Dresses neatly and appropriately for the job	_____	_____
6. Is not argumentative	_____	_____
7. Assumes responsibility	_____	_____
8. Works well with others	_____	_____
9. Learns quickly	_____	_____
10. Follows instructions	_____	_____
11. Courteous	_____	_____
12. Honest	_____	_____
13. Pleasant and friendly	_____	_____
14. Ambitious	_____	_____
15. Can assume more responsible work	_____	_____

Figure 9-5 Employee rating sheet.

employee output or where the employee has no control over the work output. This plan is also quite easy to understand and to administer.

Piece Rate

This incentive pay plan rewards employees for the number of acceptable units produced. This plan is especially suited to manufacturing operations. Piece rates may be paid on the basis of individual employee output or group output.

Straight Commission

A plan well suited to sales positions provides a built-in incentive since earnings are proportionate to the amount of sales. This method is often used with big ticket merchandise, such as appliances or autos.

Combination Plans

Another plan for rewarding salespersons, this one provides a base salary plus a commission on sales. Advantages of combination plans are that they provide for both economic security and an incentive for greater sales.

Bonus Plan

A bonus plan is suited for managers. This plan compensates managers above their base salary and is tied to company profits. These payments are made to the managers who have a significant effect on profits.

FAIR LABOR STANDARDS ACT OF 1938 AND WAGES

Generally known as the Wage-Hour Law, it applies to most private employers and federal agencies. The basic provision requires employers to pay a minimum wage to employees. For example, on January 1, 1981, the wage increased to $3.35 an hour. The law also set regulations governing the maximum number of hours employees can work (40) without receiving overtime pay. Employees must be paid at least time and one-half their regular rate for all hours of overtime. The law also provides for equal pay to employees doing the same work, regardless of sex. The child-labor provisions stipulate that the minimum legal age is 16 for employing minors, except in agriculture (where the minimum age is generally 14 and hours of employment must not conflict with school).

The wage-hour law applies equally to men and women, homeworkers, factory or office employees, farm workers, and retail and service establishment employees. All employees of businesses are subject to its provisions if they

1. are engaged in interstate commerce.
2. produce goods for interstate commerce.
3. are in an activity closely related or directly essential to interstate commerce.
4. are beyond a certain size (measured by dollar volume of business) and have at least two employees covered under the interstate commerce criteria.

The law has been interpreted liberally and today few small businesses are entirely outside the coverage of the law. However, there are specific exemptions to the law. For example, retail sales and service establishment employees are exempt if the firm has an annual sales volume of $325,000. This increases to $362,000 on January 1, 1982.

There are too many exemptions to be included in our coverage. Small business owners should contact the Wage and Hour Division of the U. S. Department of Labor to determine if the law affects them.

The law also requires employers to maintain specific records covering the following topics, and these required records must be maintained for 3 years.

Name, home address, and birth date if under 19
Sex and occupation

Hour and day when work week begins

Regular hourly pay rate for any week when overtime is worked

Hours worked each workday and total hours worked each work week

Total daily or weekly straight-time earnings

Total overtime pay for the work week

Deductions or additions to wages

Total wages paid each pay period

Date of payment and pay period covered

EMPLOYEE BENEFITS

Employee benefits or fringe benefits have increased considerably in types and cost. For example, the U. S. Chamber of Commerce surveys firms concerning types and extent of fringe benefits provided. Their survey indicates that employee benefits now exceed 37 percent of their payroll, with average benefits costing a firm $4,692 annually.

Wages and salaries are classified as direct compensation while fringe benefits are identified as indirect payments. While fringe benefits are more common in larger firms, many small businesses have added some fringe benefits. An equitable wage and salary plan and a fringe benefit package are an integral part of attracting and holding employees.

Many items may be categorized as fringe benefits. Some are required by law, others are provided as a result of agreement between employer and employee. Benefits vary among firms. Clearly, few small businesses can afford the extensive benefits packages of larger firms. Those small companies that offer benefits provide commonly such fringes as major medical plans, life insurance, and pension plans. A listing of types of fringe benefits provided employees is shown in Figure 9-6.

The company's policy should indicate which days are holidays. Frequently, the days given as paid, regular holidays are New Year's Day, Memorial Day, Independence Day, Labor Day, Thanksgiving Day, and Christmas Day. Vacation time varies, but usually 1 or 2 weeks are given after a year's employment. After 5 or 10 years, vacations may increase to 3 weeks. Sick leave benefits are also important to the employee of the small firm. A policy of many firms is to allow employees to earn one day allowance for sick leave per month.

As with wages, it is a sound policy to observe the pattern in the local community and use them in setting guidelines for your firm relative to employee benefits.

A sound employee benefit plan can be a strong asset for the small business.

Legally required payments (old age, survivors, disability and health insurance)
Pension plan
Insurance plan (life insurance, health insurance, accident insurance)
Discounts on goods and services purchased by employees from the company
Employee meals furnished by company
Paid rest periods, lunch periods, wash-up time, travel time, etc.
Paid vacations
Paid holidays
Payment for jury duty, National Guard, or Military Reserve duty
Profit-sharing payment
Bonuses (Christmas, year end)
Employee education
Worker's compensation
Unemployment compensation

Figure 9-6 Types of fringe benefits.

An outgrowth of a good employee benefit program is that employee morale is improved.

EMPLOYEE SAFETY

Employee safety should be a chief concern of all managers. One key to successful accident prevention in the small firm is employee motivation to observe work rules that make the job as safe as possible. Employee safety is of primary concern because of the costs that both employer and employee incur when a job related injury keeps the employee off the job. For the employee, there is the waste of a productive human asset, the suffering, the medical expense, and the financial loss that may result in the loss of future earnings potential if the employee is unable to return to the same task. For the employer, lost-time accidents result in higher costs of operation. Productivity is lowered if a less qualified employee must be hired to fill in while the injured employee recovers or if the business tries to operate without a replacement during the recovery period.

No business is immune from accidents. In the small business, the best managerial strategy in regard to safety is one that emphasizes accident prevention. Employee safety should be continuously emphasized as part of the company's training program and education process. Reminders in the form of posters or notices of the need for safety should be placed in conspicuous places around the company. Employees should be encouraged to wear protective clothing or goggles, and should be given the reasons why the protection is necessary.

Training films on safety may be beneficial for emphasizing certain aspects of safety. A safety campaign can be used and recognition given to employees or departments that have the longest period without an accident. Periodic checks should be made of employee work habits. When unsafe acts are discovered, they should be explained to the employee so they can be corrected. If unsafe working conditions are discovered, steps should be taken to correct them.

WORKERS' COMPENSATION

Many states require employers, regardless of size of the firm, to provide workers' compensation benefits in the form of insurance. Employers purchase insurance, and the rates they pay are based on the hazards of the industry. Where accident and injury may be expected more often, rates are higher. Hence, by reducing the accident and injury rate, a single firm can reduce its insurance premium costs. Workers' compensation provides for financial reimbursement and/or payment for medical expenses. Payment is made to employees for any physical loss or disease resulting from working conditions.

THE OCCUPATIONAL SAFETY AND HEALTH ACT OF 1970

The federal government is vitally interested in employee safety and health. As a result, one of the most significant pieces of legislation that has been passed in this area is the Occupational Safety and Health Act of 1970 (OSHA).

This law is far-reaching, covering all employers who have one or more employees and who are engaged in a business that in any way affects interstate commerce. Under the original coverage, nearly all firms were covered by the law. However, in 1980, certain exemptions were provided for firms that have 10 or fewer employees and a good safety record. This action allowed 1.5 million small firms to be exempt from OSHA.

The requirements for employers are to provide each employee a place of employment free from recognized hazards that are causing or are likely to cause death or serious harm to employees, and to comply with the occupational standards for health and safety prescribed in the Act.

The requirements for employees are to comply with all occupational safety and health standards, rules, regulations, and orders of the Act that apply to their actions and conduct on the job.

Prior to 1978, federal safety inspectors could enter a firm without advance notice to make safety inspections. However, in 1978, the Supreme Court ruled OSHA inspectors must obtain a warrant to gain entry to a workplace where the owner demands it. In practice, employers should not demand the production of search warrants without good reason.

Firms found in violation of the law may receive stiff fines and penalties, up to $1000 for each violation and up to $1000 a day unless the unsafe conditions are corrected in a specified time period. Under the law, if a particularly dangerous condition exists that could result in serious physical injury or death, the plant or company may be closed down by a federal court order until the situation is corrected.

OSHA may require new methods of operation or new processes to be used on special equipment to comply with the law. It also provides for free medical exams for employees. The small business owner may qualify for a loan under the provisions of the Small Business Act to help cover the cost of complying with the law.

Hence, the impact of the federal law is to focus attention on the significance of health and safety of employees. Many state governments also have state laws regulating health and safety. Small business owners must be aware of the provisions of these federal and state laws as they affect their operations.

THE CIVIL RIGHTS ACT AND THE SMALL BUSINESS

A significant law that may affect the small business owner is the Civil Rights Act of 1964 and its 1972 amendments. The basic coverage of the act extends to employers engaged in an industry affecting commerce who have 15 or more employees for each working day in each of 20 or more calendar weeks in the current or preceding year.

The law stipulates that employers cannot discriminate in employment practice by failing or refusing to hire, discharge, or otherwise segregate on the basis of sex, religion, national origin, race, or color. For example, the small business owner must refrain from using employment application forms which request information that violates either federal or state fair employment practice laws. The Civil Rights Act prohibits discrimination in employee selection except where there is a bona fide occupational qualification (BFOQ). Race and color can never be a BFOQ for any job. Religion, sex, and national origin may be a bona fide qualification but only on rare occasions. Thus, it is unlawful to request personal data from job applicants on the employment form relating to religious affiliation, race, sex, or nationality.

When advertising a job opening, the employer must not place any limitations as to race, color, religion, sex, or national origin unless there is a BFOQ. We have observed that employment tests must not be used to discriminate. Likewise, it is unlawful to advertise jobs separately in ''help wanted-male'' and "help wanted-female" columns. Examples of jobs where sex is a BFOQ are actors and actresses, models, and washroom attendants.

Some state laws conflict with the federal Civil Rights Act. For example, some states have restrictions on the hours women can work or how much weight they are permitted to lift. The federal law prevails, prohibiting such discrimination in those firms subject to the Act. Thus, small business owners must determine if their firm is subject to state or federal law and then abide by the proper regulations.

DISCUSSION QUESTIONS

1. Distinguish between job analysis, job description, and job specification.
2. Identify as many sources of employees as possible. Can you list others not mentioned in the text?
3. Explain the various stages of the hiring process.
4. Why should prospective employees be given a medical examination before they are employed?
5. Why is employee orientation important?
6. How does the employee manual aid in orientation? What kinds of information does it contain?
7. Identify and explain the different types of training programs given within a small business.
8. What sources outside the firm are available to provide employee training?
9. Make a list of the questions a small business owner should ask when planning a training program.
10. What are the purposes of counseling?
11. Explain the difference between the types of payment plans used by the small business owners.
12. What is the significance of the Fair Labor Standards Act of 1938 to the small business owner?
13. Why must the small business owner give special attention to employee safety?
14. What effect does the Civil Rights Act of 1964 have on the hiring practices of the small business owner?

STUDENT PROJECTS

1 Interview one or several business managers and obtain a copy of their job application form.

2. Ask them to discuss their personnel policies.
3. If they have a personnel handbook, examine and make a list of the contents it contains.
4. Ask the small business owner for his or her reactions to the Occupational Safety and Health Act.

CASE A

FRED HOWARD, THE NEW MANAGER

Robert Camp has been the manager of a small coffee-shop for over 2 years. The owner of the shop is satisfied with his performance. However, Robert has found another job and is leaving in 2 weeks.

About a month ago a manager trainee, Fred Howard, was hired to work with Robert and be his replacement. Fred, a conscientious worker, received his BBA degree several months ago. He received excellent performance ratings from Robert.

Fred has observed several situations within the coffee-shop which concern him. He has observed that Robert is very reluctant to exercise authority over employees except when things get completely out of control. This has led to the situation where the head cook has assumed many of Robert's managerial duties and much of his authority. At times this has caused much dissention among the other cooks and the waitresses. The head cook also has considerable influence in other matters such as work schedules, raises, transfers, etc.

The result has been that the head cook is the boss much of the time. Several other cooks have quit or requested transfers because of the head cook's dominance over them. The waitresses have been more successful in resisting the head cook's authority. However, there is considerable conflict between the cooks and waitresses. Many times the two groups have had shouting matches over a mistake on a customer's order. Sometimes the hostility is so apparent that the customers have mentioned it to Robert.

Fred has also noticed the high turnover of dining room attendants. Several times an attendant has quit in the middle of a work day. The attendants perform tasks that are designed to help both the waitresses and the cooks. Sometimes, especially during rush hours, the waitresses and cooks will compete for the services of the dining room attendants. This has furthered the split between the waitresses and cooks and left the attendants in a very undesirable position.

In three days Fred will assume the position of coffee-shop manager.

Questions

1. What should be Fred's first actions?
2. How should the head cook be dealt with?
3. How should Fred attempt to "recapture" Robert's lost authority?
4. What should be the job description of: head cook, waitresses, dining room attendants?

CASE B

TLC INDUSTRIES

TLC Industries is a small manufacturer of cosmetic prosthetic devices employing a total of 50 people in the plant and office. It manufactures very specialized products and orders are received from orthopedic physicians from around the world.

The organizational structure shows that the president, who owns 51 percent of the company stock, also serves as the general manager. The office staff consists of a sales manager, office manager, and one clerical employee.

Edward Green, the sales manager, has a business administration degree and has worked for the firm for 2 years. His job consists of taking orders by phone and by mail, writing specification sheets, routing orders to the plant, and checking on the progress of the orders. Edward has become very knowledgeable of all plant operations and is respected by all employees in the plant. He has been led to believe by the president that he would be promoted to general manager in the near future.

Sally White, the office manager, is the president's stepdaughter and has been with the company 3 years. Sally has a college degree in business. Her job involves serving as personal secretary to the president, maintaining all files, preparing the payroll checks, and other related clerical duties.

The plant supervisor, Tom Brown, has been with the company since it was founded 30 years ago. He knows all aspects of plant operations and is respected by plant employees.

This year, the president reorganized the plant to try to help reduce his own workload. The reorganization made Tom, the plant supervisor, and Sally, the office manager, general managers of the company with sizable salary increases. This change generated resentment among plant workers because they knew Sally had no knowledge or experience in plant operations. Tom resented Sally because she now had equal authority with him in matters of plant operation.

Edward resented the move because he had been overlooked for promotion.

Sally was now his superior and earning much more money than he. In fact, Edward still considered Sally an overpaid secretary.

Questions

1. Identify some of the problems that resulted from the change in the organization structure.
2. What are some factors that caused the resentment toward Sally by Tom and Edward?
3. Promotions in this company appear to be made on what basis?
4. What kinds of problems can this type of promotion policy create?
5. Edward was passed over for promotion. What are his alternatives for actions he can take?
6. Do you think effective communication exists in this company?

CASE C

JOHN'S HOME REMODELING CO.

John Evers began a small business engaged in home remodeling on a contract basis. The company consists of John and four employees.

On one contract job, the work was progressing on schedule. It was late spring and John wanted to enroll in summer school at a state university located in a city 50 miles away. Obviously, this would necessitate John's being absent from the job during the week but he could return to work a half-day on Friday and all day Saturday and Sunday. The four agreed to revise the work schedule and work on Thursday, Friday, Saturday, and Sunday and take off Monday, Tuesday, and Wednesday.

Any materials would be purchased on Friday afternoon by John. Fifty dollars was given to Martin in case an emergency purchase had to be made during the week.

The four employees were expected to keep records of any purchases and the number of hours worked since they were paid on an hourly basis. John explained that anyone abusing the policy would be fired.

After 2 weeks, John realized something must be done. Work was falling behind schedule. John felt that either their work schedule needed to be revised to include more hours, he had to hire another employee, or group members needed to be more productive.

After evaluating the work schedule, it seemed adequate. None of the employees wanted to add another employee. John's conclusion was that the most constructive approach was to try to get employees to be more productive.

Questions

1. Why do you think productivity has declined during John's absence?
2. Should John be concerned about group morale?
3. What should be done to improve this situation?

CASE D

CLIF'S APPAREL SHOP

Clif has decided on his location as well as on the type of physical facility to fit his requirements, as discussed in Chapter 6. Next he directs his attention to determining the number and the type of employees he needs. Clif has decided that at the outset, in addition to his serving as store manager, he will hire an assistant store manager and two part-time salespersons. He plans to hire additional salespersons during the peak seasons. Later, if the business justifies it, he will be able to hire another full-time salesperson.

Clif wants to have two employees in the store at all times for customer service and security purposes. His store will be open 6 days a week, from 10 A.M. to 9 P.M. Either the store manager or the assistant manager must be in the store at all times.

Questions

1. Write a job description for each job: store manager, assistant store manager, salesperson.
2. Where might Clif find an assistant manager? Part-time employees?
3. What kind of training should Clif provide for his employees?
4. Assist Clif by developing the hiring process he should use for his firm.
5. Would an employee manual be useful in Clif's firm?
6. Draw up a list of personnel policies Clif would need for his store.
7. What type of payment plans should Clif use for his employees?
8. What type of fringe benefits should the firm have?
9. Would Clif be concerned about accident prevention in his store? What kind of accidents could happen to employees in his store?

10

FINANCIAL RECORD KEEPING AND CASH CONTROL

PREVIEW OF THIS CHAPTER

1. In this chapter, you will learn that financial record keeping is vital to the successful small business, and it should be custom built for the business.

2. You will understand the accounting equation and how it is the basis for double entry bookkeeping.

3. You will discover how debits and credits are used to record increases and decreases in assets, liabilities, capital, income, and expenses.

4. You will understand the difference between the cash and accrual method of accounting.

5. You will find out how the Sales Journal is a record of daily income to the business.

6. You will understand how the Disbursement Journal is a record of expenditures of funds by the business.

7. You will see how a firm keeps a record of credit purchases by individual customers and how it bills them for the amount they owe.

8. If you ever plan to start a small business, you will be interested to know that your books can be kept by a public accountant, a full-time or part-time employee, a free-lance bookkeeper, or you may keep them yourself.

9. You will discover how a change fund operates for a business that handles many cash transactions.

10. You will learn how a Sales and Cash Receipts form works and why it is important to the small business.

11. You will be able to understand these key words:

Financial control	Assets
Accounting equation	Liabilities

Credit	Expenses
Sales Journal	Debit
Disbursement Journal	Cash accounting
Accounts receivable	Accrual accounting
Public accountant	Free-lance bookkeeper
Capital	Change fund
Income	Sales and Cash Receipts Record

It is not unusual for a small business firm to have adequate sales and still fail because of inadequate financial control. Financial control is vital to the success of a small business firm. Good financial records must be constantly maintained in a business if it is to have effective financial control.

Good record keeping does not mean that a complex accounting system is required for every business. In fact, record keeping should be as simple as possible and still get the accounting job done. To illustrate, a small, one-chair barber shop used an old cash register, a drawer in the cash register stand, a loose-leaf notebook, and a checkbook to maintain its financial records. The owner would "ring-up" each receipt of cash on the cash register during the day. At the end of each day, he would compare his cash register tape against the amount of cash in the register and record it in a loose-leaf notebook. Every time he purchased supplies or paid a bill in cash, he would put the receipt in the drawer. He also kept check stubs of every bill he paid by check in the drawer. At the end of each week, he would add up daily cash sales records, all expense receipts, and all check stubs for the week. He would then subtract the expense items from the cash sales total to determine the amount of his net cash gain for the week. At the end of the year, he divided his expense receipts and cancelled checks into categories of expenses, figured depreciation on his equipment, and totaled his cash sales book. From these records he prepared his income tax return. It was a very simple system, but it fulfilled his accounting needs.

Larger firms, on the other hand, often require rather complex accounting systems with many different types of journals, ledgers, and report forms. However, even for these more complex systems, the accounting system is based on the same general concept—recording changes in the basic accounting equation.

THE ACCOUNTING EQUATION

The basic accounting equation is assets = liabilities + capital (net worth) or assets − liabilities = capital. For a simple illustration of the equation, imagine that all your possessions consisted of the following items:

ITEM	VALUE
Automobile	$ 600
Personal property (clothing, etc.)	800
Cash in the bank	200
	$1600

Your total assets would be $1600. Now imagine your only debt was $400 in payments on your automobile. Using the accounting equation, you would find you were worth $1200.

$$\text{Assets} = \text{Liabilities} + \text{Capital (net worth)}$$
$$\$1600 = \$400 + \$1200$$

If you then earned $100, the accounting equation would change as follows:

Assets	=	Liabilities	+	Capital
$1600	=	$400	+	$1200
+ 100				+ 100
$1700	=	$400	+	$1300

If you made a $75 payment on your automobile, the accounting equation would change as follows:

Assets	=	Liabilities	+	Capital
$1700	=	$400	+	$1300
− 75		− 75		
$1625	=	$325	+	$1300

If you then spent $25 for a night on the town, your equation would be:

Assets	=	Liabilities	+	Capital
$1625	=	$325	+	$1300
− 25				− 25
$1600	=	$325	+	$1275

Recording the effect of every change in the accounting equation is the basis for the foundation of bookkeeping, which is called double entry bookkeeping.

Every financial transaction should leave the accounting equation in balance. Therefore, each time there is a transaction, there must be (1) equal minuses and pluses on one side of the equation or (2) the same amount of minuses and pluses on both sides of the equal sign. For example, purchasing a shirt for $10 gives the results under assets of adding $10 to personal property and reducing cash by the same amount. Also, receiving an asset, such as cash, means increasing an asset on one side of the equal sign and capital on the other side.

The entire process of bookkeeping and accounting, no matter how simple or complex the system, is based on this concept of keeping the accounting equation in balance by the process of double entry bookkeeping.

In order to keep records of what is earned by the business and what is paid out by the business, the categories of "income" and "expenses" are used rather than adjusting the capital section for each transaction. For example, suppose you bought fruit for $20 from a farmer and sold it to customers for $100. The difference between all income and all expenses could then be adjusted to the capital account. This difference would also be equal to the difference in cash.

	INCOME		EXPENSES		CASH
Sale of fruit	$100				+$100
Purchase of fruit			$20		− 20
	$100	−	$20	=	$ 80

The $80 increase in cash would be equal to an $80 increase in capital, when adjusted to the capital account. Your basic accounting equation would then appear as follows:

Assets		Liabilities		Capital
$1600	=	$325	+	$1275
+ 80				+ 80
$1680	=	$325	+	$1355

Accounting language uses the terms "debit" and "credit" to describe increases or decreases in the categories of the accounting equation (assets, liabilities, and capital) and income and expenses. Figure 10-1 shows debits and credits relative to increases and decreases in these categories. Figure 10–1 also shows what type of balance the account usually carries at any given time. Notice that increases in income have the same effect as *increases* in the capital category and that increases of expenses have the same effect as *decreases* in the capital category.

In double entry bookkeeping, for every debit there must be an equal amount of credits and vice versa. For example, imagine you sold your car for $700 cash and paid off the note. The entry in a journal would appear as follows:

		DEBIT	CREDIT
Sale received in cash	(asset)	$700	
Automobile sold	(asset)		$600
Income			$100
Note payable paid off	(liability)	$325	
Paid in cash	(asset)		$325

CATEGORY	A TRANSACTION INCREASING THE AMOUNT	A TRANSACTION DECREASING THE AMOUNT	USUAL BALANCE CARRIED IN THE CATEGORY
Asset	Debit	Credit	Debit
Liability	Credit	Debit	Credit
Capital	Credit	Debit	Credit
Income	Credit	Debit	Credit
Expense	Debit	Credit	Debit

Figure 10-1 Accounting categories and debit and credit entries.

Your income could be transferred into your capital account at a later date by the following entry.

	DEBIT	CREDIT
Income	$100	
Capital		$100

The income account would then have both the same debit and credit entry which would result in a zero balance in the account. Your accounting equation would then appear as follows.

	ASSETS	=	LIABILITIES	+	CAPITAL
	$1680	=	$325	+	$1355
Sold automobile	− 600				
Received cash	+ 700				
Paid note			− 325		
With cash	− 325				
Made profit					+ 100
	$1455	=	0	+	$1455

CASH OR ACCRUAL ACCOUNTING

A small business may use either a cash or an accrual method of accounting. The Internal Revenue Service allows many firms to select either method, but once selected, the firm must stay with the method unless they receive special permission from the IRS.

CASH METHOD

Using the cash method, a business records all monetary transactions, both income and expenses, as they occur. For example, a small business might pay its property taxes for the previous year in January. If January 1 is the start of the firm's fiscal year, then the deduction cannot be counted until the year it is paid, even though the tax expense was incurred during the previous year. (See Figure 10-2.)

The cash method is usually the easiest method in terms of keeping accounting records. However, it sometimes distorts the financial picture of the business when applied to a specific period of time. Because it is easier to use and understand, the cash method is the better method for most small businesses.

ACCRUAL METHOD

The business that uses the accrual method records income and expenses at the time they are earned or incurred regardless of when the monetary transaction occurs. For example, the small business in the previous example would record the property tax expense during the year it was incurred regardless of when it paid the tax. (See Figure 10-2.)

The Internal Revenue Service requires the accrual method in businesses where inventories play an important part in creating income. This means that many retail stores must adopt this method. The accrual method is more complex in terms of accounting records and statements. However, it is usually a

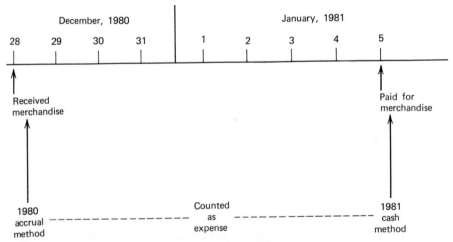

Figure 10-2 Cash versus accrual accounting method.

more accurate picture of the financial state of the firm over a specific period of time.

BASIC BOOKS OF RECORD

While some very small stores can manage to keep adequate accounting records with very few books, such as our barber example, most small stores need at least two basic books of record. These are the (1) Sales Journal and (2) Disbursement Journal.

SALES JOURNAL

Basically, the Sales Journal is a record of daily income to the business. Figure 10-3 presents a simple Sales Journal for a small business which operates on a cash rather than accrual basis. Additional columns may be added to the example when additional information is desired by the small business owner. Many days of income can be shown on very few pages. In the example, the business owner found it desirable to break the sales down by product group. If the owner felt a more extensive breakdown of sales was not needed, all retail sales could have been combined into one column (it is best to have wholesale sales separate for state sales tax information). Having the separate column for sales tax is desirable since all the business owner has to do when it is time to remit sales tax collections to the state is total the column for the period.

Sales information usually comes from sales tickets made out during the day or from cash register tapes.

All income and expenditures should go through the firm's bank account. Consequently, the *Total Cash Received from Sales* column is also the amount that is deposited in the bank each day. This column can be of value when reconciling the bank statement.

Firms that operate on the accrual basis and finance their own accounts must use different columns. Figure 10-4 illustrates a simple Sales Journal for these firms.

The entry for April 30 in Figure 10-4 shows the business had $890 in total sales. Of this amount, $570 ($890 − $320) was in the form of cash sales and $320 was in customer credit sales. The business collected $210 from customer credit accounts, the cash register was short $8 due to change errors, and the business deposited $772 in the bank.

By totaling the separate columns for a specific period of time, the business is able to derive information for their financial statements (financial statements are discussed in Chapter 11). For example, by totaling their sales column, they

Sales Journal

DATE	DESCRIPTION OR ACCOUNT	TOTAL CASH RECEIVED FROM SALES	SALES TAX	RETAIL SALES			COMMERCIAL SALES
				PRODUCT GROUP A	PRODUCT GROUP B	OTHER PRODUCTS	
		Dr.	Cr.	Cr.	Cr.	Cr.	Cr.
Apr. 1	Daily sales	433.50	13.50	100.00	90.00	80.00	150.00
2	Daily sales	455.50	15.50	120.00	100.00	90.00	130.00
3	Daily sales	515.00	15.00	100.00	100.00	100.00	200.00
4	Daily sales	505.50	15.50	120.00	140.00	50.00	180.00
5	Daily sales	547.00	17.00	130.00	150.00	60.00	190.00
	Total for week	2,456.50	76.50	570.00	580.00	380.00	850.00
				(A)*	(B)*	(C)*	(D)*

Figure 10-3 Sales Journal. (*Letters under the totals indicate where they belong in the income statement and will be discussed in Chapter 11.)

Date 19__	Description and/or Account	Total Sales	Credit Sales	Collected on Account	Misc. Income & Expense Items		Cash Deposited In Bank
					Income	Expense	
		(CR)	(DR)	(CR)	(CR)	(DR)	(DR)
4/30	Daily summary	890.00	320.00	210.00			772.00
	Cash short					8.00	
5/1	Daily summary	940.00	290.00	180.00			832.00
	Cash over				2.00		

Figure 10-4 Sales Journal of firm on the accrual basis and financing its own credit.

know the total amount of sales for the period to be used in the income statement.

Errors are easily detected in the Sales and Cash Receipts Journal by adding the total of all credit columns and all debit columns. If the two totals are not the same, then there is an error in the entries. Totaling of debit and credit columns for all daily entries pinpoints the error, since daily entries must also balance.

DISBURSEMENT JOURNAL

The Disbursement Journal is a record of expenditures of funds by the business. (Some small business owners attempt to keep their personal and business funds together but this is a serious error and causes many problems.) With only one exception, all expenditures of the firm should be paid by check. The one exception is the petty cash fund. The petty cash fund is maintained to pay in cash for items of very small value (usually less than one dollar). However, a check should be processed through this journal to establish and replenish the petty cash fund. Records of expenditures from the petty cash fund should also be maintained by the business for tax and control purposes.

Figure 10-5 shows a simple Disbursement Journal. (Additional columns may also be added to the Disbursement Journal if needed by the small business.) Daily entries in the Disbursement Journal must balance in terms of debits and credits. The total of the columns must also balance in terms of debits and credits. Errors are easily recognized by checking debit and credit totals in the columns.

At the end of specific periods of time (the end of every month is recom-

DATE	PAYEE OR ACCOUNT	CHECK NO.	AMOUNT OF CHECK	MERCHANDISE PURCHASED				OFFICE SUPPLIES	GROSS SALARIES AND WAGES	PAYROLL DEDUCTIONS		UTILITIES	OTHER EXPENSES	NONEXPENSE PAYMENTS
				PRODUCT GROUP A	PRODUCT GROUP B	OTHER PRODUCTS	COMMERCIAL PRODUCTS			FICA	INCOME TAX			
			Cr.	Dr.	Dr.	Dr.	Dr.	Dr.	Dr.	Cr.	Cr.	Dr.	Dr.	Dr.
Apr. 1	Smith Wholesale	101	100.00	100.00										
1	Alford Supply	102	120.00		120.00									
2	Jones Supply Co.	103	150.00			150.00								
2	Johnson Products	104	100.00				100.00							
2	Austin Office Sup.	105	30.00					30.00						
2	Austin Utilities	106	200.00									200.00		
3	Trust Insurance Co.	107	50.00										50.00	
3	S.B.A. on note ($20.00 interest)	108	220.00										20.00	200.00
4	Texas International (airline ticket)	109	140.00										140.00	
4	Petty Cash Fund	110	25.00										25.00	
5	Weekly Payroll	111	420.00						500.00	30.00	50.00			
5	States of Texas (sales tax)	112	76.50											76.50
5	Payroll Taxes Paid to IRS	113	60.00										60.00	
5	FICA & Income Tax Deduction paid to IRS	114	80.00											80.00
	Total for week		1,771.50	100.00 (E)*	120.00 (F)*	150.00 (G)*	100.00 (H)*	30.00 (I)*	500.00	30.00	50.00	200.00 (K)*	295.00 (L)*	356.50 (M)*

Figure 10-5 Disbursement Journal. (*Letters below the totals indicate where they belong in the income statement which will be discussed in Chapter 11.)

mended), totals of the columns in the Disbursement Journal may be used to derive various items for accounting statements. Also, combining information from both the Sales Journal and the Disbursement Journal provides valuable information for the business. For example, the total of "Total Cash Received from Sales" or "Cash Deposited in Banks" and the total of the "Amount of Check" column is an excellent device for checking bank statements.

ACCOUNTS RECEIVABLE

Most small businesses no longer carry 30-day charge accounts (discussed in detail in Chapter 20) because of the money required and the cost and time involved in keeping records and collecting accounts. Instead, they accept bank credit cards for sales that are essentially the same as a cash sale. However, some businesses still carry 30-day charge accounts. Those firms that do must keep records of each customer's charges and payments. Figure 10-6 shows a simple card that can be maintained on each customer.

The firms may keep these on cards that are easily reproduced on a copier and put in a window envelope and mailed to the customer on the billing day.

MAINTAINING THE BOOKS

The small business owner can have the books set up to meet his or her specific needs by a public accountant. The accountant will investigate the requirements and build a bookkeeping system that will provide the owner with the financial information needed.

The small business owner may also have the option of using a professional

<table>
<tr><td colspan="5" align="center">Mr. & Mrs. Joe Paul Jackson
3232 Blue Herron Road
Santa Monica, Cal. 90401</td></tr>
<tr><td>Date</td><td>Item</td><td>Charge</td><td>Payment</td><td>Balance</td></tr>
<tr><td>1/20</td><td>Hardware</td><td>$ 28.50</td><td></td><td>$ 28.50</td></tr>
<tr><td>2/5</td><td></td><td></td><td>$ 28.50</td><td>0</td></tr>
<tr><td></td><td></td><td></td><td></td><td></td></tr>
</table>

Figure 10-6 Account Receivable card.

Accountants at work.

accounting service that specializes in his or her type of business. For example, one nationwide firm provides accounting services for gasoline service stations. They provide a complete set of books and forms and train the operator in correct methods of collecting and recording information. This information is then computer processed by the accounting firm and the resulting financial information is provided the service station operator. This firm, because it specializes in gasoline service stations and has records of thousands of stations, is also able to provide the service station with industry percentages against which its own performance may be checked.

Other firms have established general bookkeeping systems and have created copyrighted books and forms for small business owners in many types of businesses to use in maintaining their own financial records. These copyrighted accounting books are meant to make the bookkeeping system as easy and as simple to follow as possible for the small business owner.

Small business owners also have several choices as to how the day-to-day bookkeeping will be performed. They may use (1) a public accountant, (2) a full-time or part-time employee, (3) a free-lance bookkeeper, or (4) they may keep the books themselves.

PUBLIC ACCOUNTANT

Public accountants are available for a wide range of accounting services, such as complete bookkeeping services, auditing, periodic preparation of accounting statements, and preparation of income tax returns.

After the public accountant has set up the books for the small business, the owner can turn over daily sales records, checks for purchases and expenses, and all other financial information to the accountant. The public accountant will then perform the complete bookkeeping function and will also provide periodic financial statements and prepare yearly income tax returns. Some public accountants even make out checks for small businesses based on bills received by the small business and turned over to them.

When the public accountant performs the complete accounting process, he or she must charge for time, expenses, and a profit. This charge may be too expensive for the small business owner. Sometimes, the small business firm keeps many of the daily records and turns them over to the public accountant. From these records, the public accountant prepares financial statements and tax returns for a fee that is much less than when he or she performs the complete accounting function for the small business.

National or regional accounting services that specialize in a specific type of business, such as the gasoline station accounting firm mentioned earlier, often are less expensive than the regular public accountant. Their standardized techniques, volume, and computer application usually allow them to offer complete accounting services at a lower price than the individual public accountant. Even when a public accountant is not used in the small business firm, one should come in at least once a year to audit the books.

EMPLOYEE

The firm may use a full-time employee, who is properly trained, to maintain the books. When the bookkeeping function is not a full-time job, the bookkeeper may be used part of the time for keeping the books and part of the time for other functions, such as selling.

Some firms use part-time people, such as homemakers, who wish to work a few hours a day and have the training to keep a set of books. Retired persons also are sometimes employed on a part-time basis to maintain the books. If a public accountant sets up the books, he or she is usually available to help train a full-time or part-time employee in how to keep the books.

FREE-LANCE BOOKKEEPER

Some people, who are trained in bookkeeping, keep books for several firms on a fee basis. These individuals usually contract with firms that require only a few hours a week of his time to keep their books. Use of these individuals is often less expensive than use of public accountants. Many times, they cost no more than hiring an employee to perform the function and the business is able to avoid the problem of training employees in bookkeeping. The business should still use a public accountant to audit the books once a year even when a free-lance bookkeeper is used.

THE SMALL BUSINESS OWNER

Small business owners may wish to maintain their own books if they have the ability to perform the function or are willing to learn the process. This method of bookkeeping has an advantage in that small business owners are constantly exposed to their financial records. As a result, they are probably more aware of their financial status than if someone else kept the books. However, it also has a disadvantage, in that it takes time, and they may neglect other important functions.

CASH CONTROL

Daily cash control is important to a small business that handles volumes of cash, particularly retail stores. The function of cash control is to compare and balance what is actually received in cash to what should have been received.

Having less cash on hand at the end of the day than should have been received may be the result of (1) recording or ringing up an amount larger than the sale, (2) money taken from the register without being recorded, or (3) giving a customer too much change.

Having more cash on hand at the end of the day than should have been received, may result from (1) not recording or ringing up a sale, (2) not ringing up or recording the full amount of the sale, or (3) not giving a customer enough change.

No matter what the cause of the overage or shortage of cash, it should be detected and steps taken to help prevent any future errors. Of course, any firm

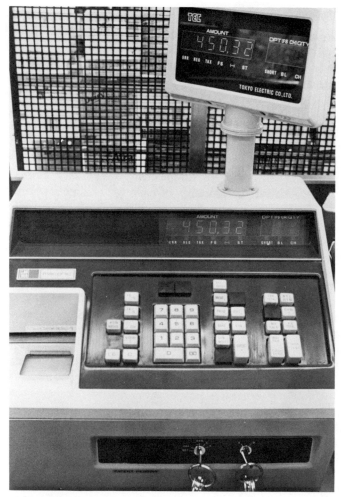

A modern cash register for cash control.

handling large volumes of cash transactions will have some small amount of human error that cannot be totally eliminated.

In addition, cash control is vital to preventing employee theft. No one likes to think that their employees would steal from the business, but the fact is that billions of dollars are lost each year to employee theft. In fact, many authorities feel employee theft exceeds losses from both shoplifting and burglary.

CHANGE FUND

Most retail stores must have currency and coins on hand at the start of business each day in order to make change. A small business should determine what amount of change is needed for each cash register based on past history. This should include a specific number of tens, fives, ones, halves, quarters, nickels, and pennies.

This change should be available in each cash register at the start of the day's business. The same amount should be deducted from the total cash in the register at the end of the day and kept for the next day. All other cash should be placed in the night depository of the bank. The change fund should be left in a safe overnight if possible and, if not, in the cash register itself. Some businesses that handle excessively large amounts of cash for change and open after the

---

Date 5/1/80

Total Sales

1. Cash sales	$ 650.00
2. Credit sales	$ 290.00
3. Total sales	$ 940.00

Cash Receipts

4. Cash sales	$ 650.00
5. Collections on accounts receivable	$ 180.00
6. Total Cash To Be Accounted for	$ 830.00

Cash on Hand

7. Cash in register or till:		
Coins	$ 30.00	
Bills	$ 609.00	
Checks	$ 268.00	
Total Cash in Register or Till		$ 907.00
8. Less change fund		$ 75.00
9. Total Cash Deposit		$ 832.00
10. Cash Short		$
11. Cash Over		$ 2.00

Figure 10-7 Sales and Cash Receipts.

bank opens, place all cash in the bank at night and write a check for the next day's funds, which are obtained before the store opens.

SALES AND CASH RECEIPTS BALANCE

A Sales and Cash Receipts form, as shown in Figure 10-7, should be completed at the end of business each day.

All sales during the day should be recorded on either a cash register, if used, or some other record, such as a sales slip, if a register is not used. There should also be some method of identifying cash and credit sales. Credit tickets, which are posted to customer accounts, are usually used to identify credit sales and then subtracted from total sales on the cash register to arrive at the amount of cash sales.

Cash that is received from customers on their credit accounts should be recorded separately. In addition, any withdrawals from the register should be recorded with full information and placed in the register or cash till.

The small business firm that is able to identify cash sales, credit sales, cash received on customer credit accounts, and cash withdrawals from the business has the information necessary to complete the Sales and Cash Receipt form at the end of the business day. Completion of this form identifies errors and the amount of the error. The Sales and Cash Receipts form may also be combined with inventory control techniques (discussed in Chapter 14) to aid in the control of mistakes, shoplifting, and employee theft.

Financial record keeping, as discussed in this chapter, is vital to the day-to-day operations of the small business firm. It must be performed adequately if the small business is to realize the full benefits of accounting analysis, which is presented in the next chapter.

DISCUSSION QUESTIONS

1. Does every small business firm need the same type of accounting system?
2. What is the relationship between double entry bookkeeping and the accounting equation?
3. What is the relationship between income, expenses, and capital?
4. What is a Sales Journal, and how do you find errors in entries?
5. What is a Disbursement Journal, and how do you find errors in its entries?
6. Which is the lowest cost method of keeping books and give one advantage and disadvantage of this method?
7. Why is cash control important?
8. How does the change fund operate?

9. How does the Sales and Cash Receipts Record function?
10. What is the difference between cash and accrual methods of accounting?

STUDENT PROJECT

Visit a small retail establishment and find out the following information.

1. What type of bookkeeping system does the business use?
2. Who keeps the books and are they audited?
3. What method does the business use for cash control? Do they use a daily Cash and Sales Receipt Form? If so, compare it to the one in the textbook and try to obtain a copy to show the class.
4. Does the business use the cash or the accrual accounting method? What is their reason for using this method?

CASE A

DEBRA LYN DRESS SHOP

The Debra Lyn Dress Shop offers high fashion dresses for women. It is located in a large shopping mall in a city. The prices are higher than average because only high quality dresses of the very latest fashion are offered for sale. There is only one cash register and it contains $50 in change at the start of each day. Debra Lyn works in the store and has one full-time and two part-time employees. Debra Lyn keeps the books herself, but she often has to stay very late to keep them up to date. Debra carries 30-day charge accounts and is on the accrual method of accounting.

On October 30, the store had the following transactions:

1. The cash register tape recorded $765 in sales for the day.
2. Customer charge tickets showed $210 in credit sales for the day (these are rung up on the cash register along with cash sales).
3. Checks totaling $160 were received from customers on their charge accounts.
4. The following checks were issued by the store:
   (a) A $150 check to Ace Corporation for merchandise;
   (b) A $100 check to the Smith Company for a display case;
   (c) A check for $180 was cashed to pay employees their weekly salary in cash. This did not include $30 withheld for income tax and $20 withheld for social security.
5. There was $760 in the cash register in cash at the end of the day.

Questions

1. Set up a Sales Journal similar to Figure 10-4, a Disbursement Journal similar to Figure 10-5, and record the day's transactions in them.
2. Set up and complete a Sales and Cash Receipt form for the day.
3. Do you think Debra Lyn would have been better off to use the cash method rather than the accrual method of accounting?
4. Do you think Debra Lyn should keep her own books?

CASE B

PETE'S PARTS (A)

Peter Wagner worked for a wholesale automobile parts warehouse for 16 years before he decided to open an automobile parts store that would sell retail to individuals and wholesale to service stations, garages, and other businesses that bought automobile parts. Pete found a building for rent on a busy street and remodeled it to fit what he felt was a good layout for a parts store. The store has been open for a week. Business has been good and Pete feels he is making a profit.

All retail sales are for cash only, but he does carry 30-day accounts for his wholesale customers. Pete employs three people—one full-time and two part-time.

Pete's experience with the wholesale automobile parts warehouse did not include an exposure to accounting and Pete feels he does not have the knowledge to set up his books and keep them.

You have been hired to establish Pete's bookkeeping system and train one of the employees to operate it. A study of Pete's records reveals the following transactions for the first week.

Cash Received for the First Week

DAY	TOTAL CASH RECEIVED FROM RETAIL SALES	SALES TAX	TOTAL CASH RECEIVED FROM WHOLESALE SALES*
5/1	$ 126	$ 6	$ 40
5/2	105	5	20
5/3	147	7	50
5/4	126	6	60
5/5	168	8	80
5/6	210	10	20

*Sales tax is not collected in this state on wholesale sales.

Checkbook Entries for the First Week

5/1	U.S. Post Office	(stamps)	$ 15
5/2	Sam's Office Products	(office supplies)	$ 25
5/3	World Parts Suppliers, Inc.	(parts)	$ 200
5/4	Menton Insurance Agency	(insurance payment)	$ 60
5/5	Jones Supply Co.	(parts)	$ 40
5/6	Week's payroll Gross Salaries, $200—FICA withheld, $13—Income Tax withheld $30		$ 157
5/6	First State Bank (payment on loan: Principal $50—interest $2)		$52

After talking to Pete you feel he needs the following columns in his Disbursement Journal: Parts, Utilities, Office Supplies, Gross Salaries, FICA Withheld, Income Tax Withheld, Miscellaneous Expenses, and Nonexpense Items.

Jim's Service Station started trading with Pete the first day he was open. He bought parts on credit the following days: 2/1, $10; 2/2, $15; 2/4, $10. He came in 2/5 and paid his entire bill for the week.

You feel Pete should operate on the cash accounting basis and have his sales broken down only into retail and wholesale sales.

Questions

1. Set up a Sales Journal similar to Figure 10-3 and record the week's sales.
2. Set up a Disbursement Journal similar to Figure 10-5 and record the week's transactions.
3. Set up an accounts receivable card for Jim's Service Station and record the week's charges and payment.

(Save a copy of your journals for use in Chapter 11.)

11

ACCOUNTING STATEMENTS AND ANALYSIS

PREVIEW OF THIS CHAPTER

1. In this chapter, you will learn that a balance sheet is a measure of the basic accounting equation—assets = liabilities + capital.

2. You will understand what items are included under the categories of current assets, fixed assets, intangible assets, current liabilities, long-term liabilities, and capital.

3. You will find out that the balance sheet is an estimate of the value of the business for one moment in time.

4. You will discover the various uses of the balance sheet by small business owners and other groups.

5. You will learn that the income statement measures profit or loss over a period of time by subtracting all expenses from all income of the business.

6. You will be interested in the various uses of the income statement by small business owners, investors, creditors, and governmental agencies.

7. If you ever plan to open a small business, you will be interested in learning that the budget is an estimate of next year's income statement and is a major planning and control device for the small business.

8. You will discover that the budget is comprised of forecasted income, cost of goods sold or manufactured, controllable expenses, and uncontrollable expenses.

9. You will understand how the cash flow statement is comprised of cash receipts and disbursements.

10. You will find out why the cash flow statement is important to the small business owner and the investor.

11. You will learn how to post Sales and Disbursement Journals to a Monthly Income and Cash Flow Statement.

12. You will learn about various accounting ratios and how they act as guidelines to the small business owner.

13. You will be able to understand these key words:

Balance sheet	General expenses
Assets	Profit
Liabilities	Budget
Capital	Controllable expenses
Current assets	Uncontrollable expenses
Fixed assets	Cash flow statement
Intangible assets	Cash receipts
Current liabilities	Cash disbursements
Long-term liabilities	Ratio
Income statement	Current ratio
Income	Acid test ratio
Expenses	Debt to net worth ratio
Cost of goods sold	Rate of return on assets
Cost of goods manufactured	Inventory turnover
Operating expenses	

Accounting statements are very important to the small business firm because they provide a basis for planning and control in the business. The principal accounting statements are the balance sheet, the income statement, the budget, and the cash flow statement.

BALANCE SHEET

The balance sheet provides a measure of the value of the business at one moment in time. Balance sheets should be prepared periodically for the small business firm. Usually, small businesses have accountants prepare a balance sheet at the end of their fiscal year (January 1 and July 1 are the most common). (See Fig. 11-1.)

COMPONENTS OF THE BALANCE SHEET

The balance sheet is a measure of the basic accounting equation:

$$\text{Assets} = \text{Liabilities} + \text{Capital}$$

DOVE WHOLESALE PAINT COMPANY
Balance Sheet
January 1, 1981

Assets

Current Assets:

Cash		$ 9,000	
Accounts receivable	$10,000		
Allowance for bad debts	500	9,500	
Merchandise		24,000	
Supplies		2,000	
General Motors stock		3,500	
Total Current Assets			$ 48,000

Fixed Assets:

Land		$12,000	
Building	130,000		
Depreciation allowance	40,000	90,000	
Equipment	60,000		
Depreciation allowance	15,000	45,000	
Delivery truck	4,000		
Depreciation allowance	1,000	3,000	
Note receivable from Acme Products due 1/1/82		2,000	
Total Fixed Assets			152,000

Intangible Assets:

Organizational costs		$ 1,000	
Total Intangible Assets			1,000
Total Assets			$201,000

Liabilities

Current Liabilities:

Accounts payable		$18,000	
Income tax payable		1,500	
F.I.C.A. tax payable		500	
Total Current Liabilities			$ 20,000

Long-Term Liabilities:

Mortgage payable		$25,000	
Note payable to bank 6/1/88		5,000	
Total Long-Term Liabilities			30,000

Capital

Carl Dove, capital			151,000
Total Liabilities and Capital			$201,000

Figure 11-1 Balance sheet.

Assets

Assets are usually divided into three categories in the balance sheet—current assets, fixed assets, and intangible assets.

Current Assets   Current assets are assets that can be easily and quickly converted into liquid assets (cash). Current assets include such items as cash, accounts receivable, notes receivable that are due in less than a year's time, raw materials inventory, finished goods inventory, supplies, and stocks and bonds of other corporations that are traded regularly on the securities market. Generally, most current assets are used up or change in amounts on hand over relatively short periods of time.

Fixed Assets   Fixed assets are items of property that are not used up over short periods of time. They usually are not easily converted into cash, and they often are depreciated over long periods of time. Fixed assets (sometimes called plant assets) include such items as land, buildings, machinery, equipment, automobiles, trucks, and notes receivable that are due in excess of one year's time.

Intangible Assets   Intangible assets are items that have value to the business but do not exist as tangible property. Some intangible assets that are sometimes listed in the balance sheet are goodwill (the reputation of the business), patents, copyrights, and organizational costs (cost of establishing a form of ownership).

Liabilities

Liabilities are debts of the business. Liabilities are broken down in the balance sheet into current liabilities and long-term liabilities.

Current Liabilities   Current liabilities consist of debts that are due in less than one year's time. Current liabilities include such items of debt as accounts payable, notes payable within a year, and cash that is paid to governmental agencies on a regular basis (e.g., income taxes withheld from employee salaries and paid to the government every 3 months).

Long-Term Liabilities   Long-term liabilities are debts that are due in more than a year's time from the date of the balance sheet. Long-term liabilities include such items as notes payable that are due in excess of one year's time, mortgages, and bonds payable.

Capital

Capital is a measure of the value of the business to the owner or owners. It is a measure of all assets minus all liabilities. The result is the net worth of the business.

CHARACTERISTICS OF THE BALANCE SHEET

The balance sheet is both an estimate of the value of the business and an estimate for only one moment in time.

Estimate

Except for cash, almost all other assets listed in the balance sheet are estimates. All accounts receivable cannot be collected and an estimated amount is subtracted for bad debts. Prices of inventories change from time to time and their value is not always certain. All fixed assets are estimates. Buildings, machinery, equipment, automobiles, and trucks are listed at cost and depreciation is estimated and deducted each year. To illustrate, many firms have depreciated out buildings and machinery over several years and carry them on their books at scrap value; yet, they still have considerable market value. Intangible assets, such as goodwill and patents are very subjective judgments and are extremely difficult to value since they are intangible.

Liabilities are accurate in the balance sheet since they are specific debts the business owes. By subtracting accurate liabilities from estimated assets, one obtains an estimated capital section of the balance sheet. The only real way to determine the exact value of a business would be to sell it.

Moment in Time

Theoretically, the balance sheet measures the value of the business at one moment in time and represents only that moment in time. Assets, such as machinery, are used up a little each day. Consequently, the estimated value of machinery, on the balance sheet, is an estimate for the day the balance sheet is prepared. In addition, raw materials are constantly being used up and regularly being replaced. Therefore, the value of inventory is an estimate only for the day of the balance sheet date. Liabilities are continually being incurred and paid by the business; consequently, liabilities on the balance sheet represent only that day's amount. Since assets and liabilities change from day to day, capital changes from day to day and is estimated for that day only on the balance sheet.

USES OF THE BALANCE SHEET

Since balance sheets are prepared periodically, they present measures of changes in the business. By looking at balance sheets of several years, it is possible to recognize growth or decline in various phases of the company's financial position. The balance sheet also reveals the company's ability to meet both short-term and long-term debt. By computing ratios from balance sheet data, the firm is able to recognize weaknesses or strengths in its financial position. Balance sheets are also important to creditors who make loans to the business because it reveals the firm's potential for repayment of debts.

INCOME STATEMENT

The income statement is a measure of how the business has performed over a specific period of time—usually a year. It measures all income less all expenses to arrive at the amount of profit or loss generated by the business for the period. The income statement is also called the expense and revenue summary, profit and loss statement, and income and expense statement.

COMPONENTS OF THE INCOME STATEMENT

The main components of the income statement are income and expenses.

Income

All income that flows into the firm is listed in this section. There are several items that may come under the heading of income, such as revenue from sales, interest earned, and dividends earned.

Expenses

Expenses in the income statement are usually broken down into Cost of Goods Sold (in retail and wholesale firms), Cost of Goods Manufactured (in manufacturing firms), Operating Expenses, General Expenses, and Other Expenses.

Cost of Goods Sold Cost of Goods Sold in wholesale and retail firms is comprised of the beginning inventory for the period, plus all purchases for the period, minus the inventory at the end of the period (see Fig. 11-2).

Cost of Goods Manufactured Cost of Goods Manufactured in manufacturing operations is comprised of all direct labor, raw materials, and factory over-

Cost of Goods Sold:	
Beginning merchandise inventory 1/1/81	$ 50,000
Purchases for the year	150,000
Merchandise available for sale	200,000
Less:	
Ending inventory 12/31/81	40,000
Total cost of merchandise sold	160,000

Figure 11-2 Cost of Goods Sold section of the income statement for a retail firm.

head (depreciation on building and machinery, supplies, foremen salaries, etc.) that have gone into the manufacturing process during the year (see Fig. 11-3).

Operating Expenses Operating expenses are expenses that contribute directly to the sale of goods. Some of the items commonly included under Operating Expenses are advertising, insurance, truck depreciation, salespersons' salaries and commissions, entertainment, and travel.

General Expenses Items usually presented under General Expenses are those that are indirect costs incurred in the administration of the business. Some of the expenses commonly included under this category are office expenses, postage, telephones, payroll taxes, and utilities.

Other Expenses The category Other Expenses usually contains all other items that do not seem to fit into the other expenses categories, items such as interest expense and bad checks expense.

Cost of Goods Manufactured:	
Direct labor	$120,000
Raw materials	80,000
Factory overhead	90,000
Total cost of goods manufactured	$290,000

Figure 11-3 Cost of Goods Manufactured section of the income statement for a manufacturing company.

CHARACTERISTICS OF THE INCOME STATEMENT

The income statement is an estimate of profit or loss and it measures profit or loss over a period of time.

DOVE WHOLESALE PAINT COMPANY
Income Statement for 1981

Revenue from Sales		$430,000

Cost of Goods Sold:

Beginning inventory 1/1/81	$ 30,000	
Purchases	264,000	
Merchandise available for sale	294,000	
Less ending inventory 12/31/81	24,000	
Total Cost of Goods Sold		270,000

Gross Profit on Sales		$160,000

Operating Expenses

Advertising	$ 20,000	
Insurance	6,000	
Depreciation expenses:		
Building	4,000	
Equipment	6,000	
Truck	1,000	
Sales personnel	35,000	
Entertainment	2,000	
Travel	1,000	
Total Operating Expenses		$75,000

General Expenses:

Office expense	$ 12,000	
Postage	800	
Telephone	1,200	
Payroll taxes	3,000	
Utilities	4,000	
Total General Expenses		21,000

Other Expenses:

Interest expense	$ 3,000	
Bad check expense	1,000	
Total Other Expenses		4,000
Total Expenses		$100,000
Net Income		$ 60,000

Figure 11-4 Income statement.

Estimate

The income statement, shown in Figure 11-4, presents several items of expenses that exist in the form of depreciation. Building, equipment, and truck depreciation for the year appear as operating expenses. If any expense items are an estimate, then the total expenses figure for the firm is an estimate. Income for the firm is accurate, but when the total of all expenses is an estimate, then the profit or loss figure is an estimate.

Firms may manipulate their depreciation in various ways to show different levels of profit. For example, a firm that purchased a building could show the following depreciation expense for the first year.

COST	DEPRECIATION METHOD	YEARS	DEPRECIATION FIRST YEAR
$200,000	Straight line	30	$ 6,667
$200,000	Straight line	20	$10,000
$200,000	Accelerated declining balance	20	$20,000

People investing in or loaning a business money should realize that the income statement is an estimate and check such items as the method of depreciation very carefully.

Measures Profit Over a Period of Time

The income statement deducts all expenses from all income, for a specific period of time, to arrive at the firm's profit or loss for that period. The income statement usually is prepared once a year at the end of the fiscal period; however, it may be prepared for shorter periods. Some business firms feel they gain better control of their business by preparing their income statements monthly.

USES OF THE INCOME STATEMENT

The small business firm uses its income statement to analyze the success of operations of the business over a specific period of time. Investments, purchases of assets, and distribution of profit are just a few of the decisions that rely on the information provided in the income statement.

The income statement is also used by other groups. Federal income tax returns of the business could not be properly prepared without the income statement. Other government agencies, including various state and local taxing agencies, require income statements from the business for their use. Creditors and investors consider the income statement very valuable and few would be willing to loan or invest money without its availability for their analysis.

BUDGET

In reality, the budget is the estimate of next year's income statement. It is a major planning and control device for the small business firm (see Fig. 11-5).

COMPONENTS OF THE BUDGET

The budget is comprised of (1) income, (2) cost of goods sold or cost of goods manufactured, (3) controllable expenses, and (4) uncontrollable expenses.

Income

Expected sales revenue is forecasted by the business and is the basis for almost all the budget. The number of units forecasted to be sold during the next year determines the cost of goods sold or manufactured, controllable expenses, and, to some extent, uncontrollable expenses.

Cost of Goods Sold—Cost of Goods Manufactured

The Cost of Goods Sold section in retail and wholesale firms is estimated usually on the basis of past experiences in markup on the total volume of expected sales. For example, the income statement in Figure 11-4 shows the firm's cost of goods sold are usually about 60 percent of sales. Therefore, with expected sales of $450,000 in its budget, they can expect about 60 percent or $275,000 to be the Cost of Goods Sold figure in the budget.

The Cost of Goods Manufactured section in manufacturing firms is estimated by taking the total number of units estimated to be manufactured for the next year and multiplying by the standard per unit labor and raw material cost. For example, if it requires $1.40 in direct labor and $1.60 of raw materials to produce one unit, it would cost $300,000 of direct labor and raw materials to produce 100,000 units. Factory overhead is usually applied on a past experience basis, usually as a percent of the total direct labor cost. To illustrate, if factory overhead has usually been about 60 percent of direct labor costs, then 60 percent of the forecasted direct labor expense would be used as the forecasted factory overhead expense.

DOVE WHOLESALE PAINT COMPANY
Budgeted Income Statement for 1982

(All figures are estimates)

Expected Sales Revenue		$450,000
Expected Cost of Goods Sold		275,000
Estimated Gross Margin		$175,000
Controllable Expenses:		
Advertising	$25,000	
Sales personnel	37,000	
Entertainment	1,500	
Travel	1,500	
Bad check expense	1,000	
Total Controllable Expenses		66,000
Margin for Uncontrollable Expenses and Income		$109,000
Uncontrollable Expenses:		
Insurance	$ 6,000	
Depreciation expenses:		
Building	4,000	
Equipment	6,000	
Truck	1,000	
Office expense	12,000	
Postage	900	
Telephones	1,300	
Payroll taxes	3,600	
Utilities	4,200	
Interest expense	3,000	
Total Uncontrollable Expenses		42,000
Estimated Net Income Before Federal Income Taxes		$ 67,000

Figure 11-5 Budget.

Controllable and Uncontrollable Expenses

Instead of Operating Expenses, General Expenses, and Other Expenses shown in the income statement, the budget uses controllable and uncontrollable expense categories.

Controllable expenses are those expenses that the firm has some control over. Advertising, number of sales personnel, entertainment, travel, and bad checks (to a lesser degree) may be controlled by the firm.

Uncontrollable expenses are expenses that are relatively fixed if the business is operating in a normal business manner. Insurance, all depreciation, office expenses, postage, telephones, payroll taxes, utilities, and interest are expenses that occur as a result of normal business activity (see Fig. 11-5).

CHARACTERISTICS OF THE BUDGET

The characteristics of the budget are the same as the income statement because it contains the same items and estimates profit or loss over a future period. While the income statement contains many items that are accurate and some that are estimates, all figures in the budget are estimates since they are forecasted amounts for a future period of time. The budget also covers a period of time, usually the coming year. However, some firms do have budgets for shorter periods of time. They forecast the budget for the next year and then break it down into months or quarters.

USES OF THE BUDGET

The budget is one of the most important accounting tools small business owners have at their disposal. It helps control the business, and it aids them in making decisions that concern the business.

The budget is a valuable controlling device, in that it is a standard against which to measure current performance of the business. The business has expenses on a continuing basis, and the manager can compare these against those projected in the budget. If the current expenditures deviate from the budgeted amount, the manager knows something is wrong and may then investigate to discover the problem and correct it.

The budget also tells the manager how much funds are available for different expenditures. The expected profit figure will allow the manager to estimate how much profit can be taken out of the business and how much will be left for purchases of fixed assets, such as machinery.

The budget is also an excellent device for forecasting future financial needs. For example, the manager knows of financial needs months in advance. As a result, he or she is able to arrange for the money in advance, rather than waiting until the need arises.

CASH FLOW STATEMENT

The cash flow statement is a measure of changes in cash the business has on hand from month to month. It records or projects all cash receipts less all cash disbursements. A business may use the cash flow statement as a record of what has occurred to cash and/or as a projection into the future to determine future needs for cash (see Fig. 11-6).

COMPONENTS OF THE CASH FLOW STATEMENT

The cash flow statement takes the amount of cash on hand at the beginning of the month, adds all cash receipts to the balance, and subtracts all cash disbursements to arrive at the amount of cash on hand at the end of the month.

Cash Receipts

Cash receipts includes all funds that are received in the form of cash. It usually includes such items as cash sales and cash received in payment of accounts receivable. It does not include sales in the form of credit.

Cash Disbursements

This category contains all expenses, purchases, and payments made in cash. It does not include depreciation or amounts for any items purchased on credit. The cash disbursement category often includes such items as advertising, payments to vendors for purchases, insurance premiums, salaries, travel, utilities, office expenses, and long-term debt payments. Such items as payroll taxes, which are incurred monthly but are only paid quarterly, are not recorded until they are actually paid.

CHARACTERISTICS OF THE CASH FLOW STATEMENT

The cash flow statement is accurate when it is a record of past receipts and disbursements and an estimate when it is projected for future months. The cash flow statement is usually calculated on a monthly basis for an entire year.

DOVE WHOLESALE PAINT COMPANY Projected Cash Flow			
	January	February	March
Beginning Cash Balance	$ 9,000	$11,850	$19,825
Cash Receipts:			
Cash sales	$22,000	$23,000	$23,000
Cash from accounts receivable	8,000	14,000	16,000
Total Cash Received for Month	$30,000	$37,000	$39,000
Cash Disbursements:			
Cash payments on accounts payable	$18,000	$20,000	$20,000
Advertising	2,500	2,500	2,500
Insurance	500	500	500
Sales salaries and commissions	3,000	3,000	3,000
Entertainment	150	125	125
Travel	200	100	100
Office expenses	1,000	1,000	1,000
Postage	100	100	100
Telephone	100	100	100
Utilities	350	350	350
Interest expense	250	250	250
Payroll taxes	0	0	900
Total Cash Disbursed for Month	$26,150	28,025	28,925
Cash Increase or Decrease from Operations	$ 3,850	$ 8,975	$10,075
Mortgage Payment	$ 1,000	$ 1,000	$ 1,000
Net Change in Cash Position	$ 2,850	$ 7,975	$ 9,075
Cash Balance Carried into Next Month	$11,850	$19,825	$28,900

Figure 11-6 Cash flow statement.

USES OF THE CASH FLOW STATEMENT

The projected cash flow statement is important to small business owners because it identifies future problems with cash. The cash flow statement will warn them months in advance when there will be a cash shortage and tell them how much so that they are able to plan in advance. By knowing in advance, they can often obtain debt funds at the best interest rate available to them. If it shows surplus funds will be available that are not needed in the business, it allows them to make arrangements for use of the funds in other investments.

For an investor, it is one of the most important accounting statements he or she can use. It is possible for a business to show a loss on the income statement and still be an attractive investment. For instance, it is quite common for entrepreneurs to build apartments, take accelerated depreciation on them, show a loss on the income statement for several years, and still have increases in cash each month even after making the mortgage payment. By doing this, the entrepreneur usually keeps the apartments until they are depreciated to the point where he or she is showing a profit. The entrepreneur then sells them and pays only a capital gain tax on the difference between what is received for the apartments and what is shown on the books after depreciation. Since the capital gain tax is paid on only 40 percent of the gain, the entrepreneur has gained considerably in the total profit derived from the apartments.

COMBINED MONTHLY INCOME AND CASH FLOW STATEMENT

The authors recommend to small businesses that they post their Sales and Disbursement Journals to a combined Income and Cash Flow Statement each month. When the columns in their Sales and Disbursement Journals are totaled each month, the business should carry each column total to the statement shown in Figure 11-7. The Sales Journal (Figure 10-3) and the Disbursement Journal (Fig. 10-5) in Chapter 10 are keyed to the various items that appear in Figure 11-7.

By posting to the Income and Cash Flow Statement, the small businesses are able to see how well they are doing each month. They do not have to wait until the end of the year when it may be too late to correct anything that might be going astray.

RATIOS

Accounting ratios are calculated on various items that appear in the accounting statements of a business firm. They are important to the firm in that they provide measures of performance against a guideline to let the business know if it is operating as planned. (All sample calculations shown below are based on data in the accounting statements shown in Figures 11-1 and 11-4.)

CURRENT RATIO

The current ratio is a measure of the firm's ability to meet current debt. It measures the relationship between current assets and current liabilities.

CASH FLOW AND INCOME STATEMENT

Sales:

   Retail:

      (A) Product group A $ 570.00

      (B) Product group B   580.00

      (C) Other products   380.00

          Total Retail Sales   1,530.00

      (D) Commercial   850.00

   Total Sales $ 2,380.00

Cost of Goods Purchased:

   Retail:

      (E) Product group A $ 100.00

      (F) Product group B   120.00

      (G) Other products   150.00

          Total Retail Purchases $ 370.00

      (H) Commercial   100.00

   Total Cost of Goods Purchased   470.00

   Sales Less Cost of Goods Purchased $ 1,910.00

Expenses:

      (I) Office supplies $ 30.00

      (J) Salaries and wages   500.00

      (K) Utilities   200.00

      (L) Insurance   50.00

      (L) Interest on note   20.00

      (L) Travel   140.00

      (L) Payroll taxes   60.00

      (L) Other expenses   25.00

   Total Expenses $ 1,025.00

   Net Cash Increase $ 885.00

Cash Flow		Income	
Net Cash Increase	$ 885.00	Net Cash Increase	$ 885.00
(M) Less Principal Paid on Debt	200.00	Add any decreases in inventory level	160.00
Cash Flow for the Period	$ 685.00	Deduct any increases in inventory level	
		Less depreciation for period	230.00
		Net Taxable Income	$ 815.00

Figure 11-7 Monthly income and cash flow statement. [Letters indicate column totals from the Sales Journal (Fig. 10-3) and the Disbursement Journal (Fig. 10-5).]

$$\frac{\text{Current Assets}}{\text{Current Liabilities}} = \text{Current Ratio}$$

$$\frac{\$48,000}{\$20,000} = 2.4$$

ACID TEST RATIO

This is sometimes called the "quick ratio." It measures the firm's ability to meet current debt by measuring the relationship between its liquid assets (cash plus other current assets that are quickly converted into cash) and current debt. It is a more specific measure of the firm's ability to meet debt than the current ratio.

$$\frac{\text{Cash} + \text{Accounts Receivable} + \text{Marketable Securities}}{\text{Current Liabilities}} = \text{Acid Test Ratio}$$

$$\frac{\$9000 + \$9500 + \$3500}{\$20,000} = 1.1$$

DEBT TO NET WORTH RATIO

The debt to net worth ratio measures creditor contributions relative to owner contributions. It is a measure of the firm's ability to meet creditor and owner obligations in case of liquidation of the firm. It is also a measure of whether the firm is overextended in terms of debt.

$$\frac{\text{Total Liabilities}}{\text{Tangible Net Worth}} = \text{Debt to Net Worth Ratio}$$
(Net Worth − Intangible Assets)

$$\frac{\$\ 20,000 + \$30,000}{\$151,000 - \$\ 1,000} = .33$$

RATE OF RETURN ON ASSETS

The rate of return on assets ratio is a measure of profitability of the firm. It indicates the amount of assets necessary to produce the current level of profit.

$$\frac{\text{Profit}}{\text{Total Tangible Assets}} = \text{Rate of Return on Assets}$$
(Total Assets − Intangible Assets)

$$\frac{\$\ 60,000}{\$201,000 - \$1,000} = .3$$

INVENTORY TURNOVER

This ratio is the measure of how often inventory is sold and replaced. The inventory turnover ratio indicates the adequacy of the amount of inventory on hand relative to the amount of sales. Inventory turnover is usually calculated in terms of how many times it completely turns over each year.

$$\frac{\text{Cost of Goods Sold}}{\text{Average Amount of Inventory for the Year}} = \text{Inventory Turnover}$$
(Beginning Inventory + Ending Inventory divided by Two)

$$\frac{\$270,000}{\dfrac{\$\,30,000 + \$24,000}{2}} = 10$$

A small business firm should strive to maintain each of its ratio measures near some optimum point. To illustrate, if the optimum point for a specific business for its acid test ratio was 1.5, then any figure much below this would indicate the business is not maintaining enough liquid assets in relation to its current debt. The firm could expect to have problems in meeting their debts during the year. On the other hand, if the figure is much above 1.5, the business is maintaining too many liquid assets that could be invested elsewhere for additional profit.

An optimum ratio figure differs not only by type of ratio but also by type of business. For example, one would not expect the same inventory turnover figure for a jewelry store as for a supermarket. Small business owners often establish optimum ratio figures based on experience in their business. Also, they should compare their firm's ratio analysis with industry averages that are published in sources such as the *Almanac of Business and Industrial Financial Ratios*. Many trade organizations also publish financial ratios for their industry.

In conclusion, the authors have found that one of the most common weaknesses of small businesses is their accounting system and analysis. Many activities of the small business firm cannot be fully effective without adequate accounting practices and analysis, for example, inventory control, which is discussed in Chapter 13.

DISCUSSION QUESTIONS

1. What is the balance sheet, and what are some of its components?
2. Why is a balance sheet an estimate for one moment in time?
3. If you were a small business owner, how would you use the balance sheet?
4. What is an income statement, and what items are contained in the income statement?

5. Why is the income statement an estimate, and why does it measure profit or loss over a period of time?
6. Can the small business owner do without some form of income statement? Explain.
7. Why is the budget like the income statement?
8. Why is the budget important to the small business?
9. What is a cash flow statement?
10. Why is a cash flow statement important to the small business and the investor?
11. Why would a small business owner compute ratios?

STUDENT PROJECT

1. Prepare a balance sheet for yourself listing all assets and liabilities to arrive at your net worth.
2. Keep a record of all income and expenditures for a week's period and from this record prepare an income statement and a cash flow statement.
3. Prepare a budget for the next week.

CASE A
LAMSON'S CLOTHING STORE

Leo Lamson owns and operates a clothing store. He has hired you to prepare his accounting statements. From examination of the books and from talking to Leo, you have obtained the following information.

	THIS YEAR	NEXT YEAR
Balance 12/31/End of Current Year		
Cash	$ 12,000	
Accounts receivable	20,000	
Merchandise inventory	100,000	
General Motors stock	2,000	
Land	10,000	
Building	20,000	
Organizational costs	2,000	
Accounts payable	10,000	
Mortgage payable	50,000	
Merchandise Inventory 1/1/Start of Current Year	$ 90,000	

	THIS YEAR	NEXT YEAR
Total for the Year		
Sales	$300,000	$320,000
Purchases of merchandise during the year	190,000	
Cost of goods sold		192,000
Advertising	10,000	12,000
Sales salaries	30,000	34,000
Office expense	20,000	20,000
Interest expense	1,000	1,000
Postage	1,000	1,000
Telephone	1,000	1,000
Utilities	2,000	2,000

All projected figures for next year will be cash transactions. Leo collected all his accounts receivable and changed to "cash only" sales. Leo plans to pay all his accounts payable next year in the form of cash. Leo paid nothing on his mortgage this year, but he expects to pay $10,000 in cash next year. Leo has completely depreciated out his building over past years and the value shown on the books is the scrap value.

Questions

1. Prepare a balance sheet for this year.
2. Prepare an income statement for this year.
3. Prepare a projected budget for next year.
4. Prepare a projected cash flow statement for next year (for the entire year and not by months).
5. Compute the following ratios:
   (a) Current Ratio,
   (b) Acid Test Ratio,
   (c) Debt to Net Worth Ratio,
   (d) Rate of Return on Assets Ratio,
   (e) Inventory Turnover.

CASE B

PETE'S PARTS (B)

See Pete's Parts (A) (Case B in Chapter 10) for background information. After setting up Peter Wagner's Sales and Disbursement Journal, you decided he should have a monthly Income and Cash Flow Statement. To illustrate how it is done you plan to create a sample statement keyed to his journals.

Pete's inventory system involves reordering all items that he sold-from stock each day. He has ordered replacements for everything he sold the first week. However, only $240 worth of parts (at cost) have come in and he still requires $200 worth of parts (at cost) that have not come in to completely restock his inventory. This means he currently has a decrease of $200 in inventory. Depreciation for the first week amounted to $50.

Questions

1. Set up a monthly Income and Cash Flow Statement similar to Figure 11-7.
2. Post the Sales and Disbursement Journals to your Income and Cash Flow Statement. (It will be a weekly statement in this case.)

SECTION
FOUR
MERCHANDISE CONTROL, INSURANCE, AND COMPUTERS

12

PURCHASING IN THE SMALL BUSINESS

PREVIEW OF THIS CHAPTER

1. After studying this chapter, you will understand the role of purchasing in the small firm.

2. You will understand the goals and policies and procedures of purchasing.

3. You will be aware of some of the considerations in the make or buy decision.

4. You will be aware of the activities included in the purchasing process.

5. You will be aware of many of the factors included in vendor analysis.

6. You will understand the importance of time in purchasing decisions.

7. You should be aware of when title to merchandise passes from seller to buyer.

8. You should understand what consignment is and how it affects the small business owner.

9. You should comprehend the value of purchase discounts to the small owner-manager.

10. You will understand these key words:

Purchasing	Consignment
Title	Trade discount
F. O. B. seller	Quantity discount
F. O. B. buyer	Cash discount
Economic Order Quantity	

The purchasing function is a vital cog in the efficient operation of all small business establishments. Small manufacturers plan for the purchase of raw materials that can be converted into goods for sale. Small wholesalers make purchase decisions that will enable them to have merchandise available for resale. Small retailers analyze customer buying habits and plan their purchases in order to have goods available that will satisfy their needs. Service firm managers plan their buying in order to have materials available which they use in performing their service functions. Purchasing decisions must be coordinated with all other management decisions with the objective being to improve total company performance. In the small firm, the owner-manager or an assistant designated as the purchasing manager has the responsibility for initiating and carrying the purchasing activity through to completion.

GOALS OF PURCHASING

Frequently it appears that some small firms are consistently ahead of their competitors. Ordinarily, this competitive edge is not accidental but is achieved in part by the quality of purchasing decisions made by the firm's owner-manager or purchasing manager. Effective purchasing represents one of the factors that contributes to making the goal of growth of the small firm a reality.

Small business owners realize that the purchasing process involves a series of interdependent activities. Purchasing is the process of buying the right quality of materials, products, and supplies in the appropriate quantity at the best available price at the proper time from the right vendor (see Fig. 12-1).

QUALITY

Purchasing the right quality relates to the suitability of the product for the intended purpose. For a manufacturer, the raw material must be of a high enough quality to meet the manufacturing specifications but not too high quality so that the cost is too high.

QUANTITY

Together with quality, an objective of purchasing is to buy the proper quantity. For example, if a small retailer purchases too large a quantity of merchandise, it may result in an unusually high proportion of company funds being tied up in inventory. There is the added possibility of spoilage or obsolescence of goods. Obsolescence is one of the most serious problems associated with merchandise in inventory. On the other hand, purchasing in too small quantities means that frequent reorders will be necessary. In addition, there is the added likelihood of

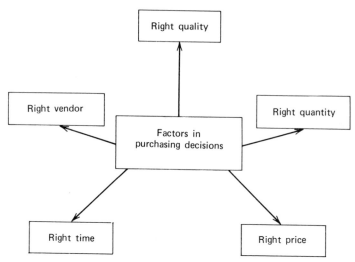

Figure 12-1 Factors in purchasing decisions.

being out of a product when it is needed. Furthermore, frequent reordering of small quantities may result in higher cost for each unit purchased, whereas substantial cost savings may result if a few orders of greater size are placed with vendors.

PRICE

For the owner-manager, purchase price is always a significant factor. However, this does not necessarily imply that the lowest priced merchandise should be purchased. Instead, the best purchase price is the lowest price at which merchandise can be obtained that is consistent with the quality needed. Consequently, the aim is to locate the highest value that meets the specific requirements at the lowest cost.

TIME

An essential component of effective purchasing is buying at the right time. Goods should be purchased so that they are available when needed. However, the small owner-manager must exercise care so as not to be overstocked. Procedures for controlling merchandise inventory are discussed in the following chapter.

VENDOR

To complete the purchasing activity, care must be taken to ensure that merchandise is purchased from the right vendor. Factors to be evaluated in selecting a supplier are discussed later.

PURCHASING POLICY AND PROCEDURE

In order for purchasing goals to be realized, purchasing policies and procedures must be set which provide guidance for achieving the objectives. The following are examples of purchasing policies and procedures suitable to the small business.

1. Requisitions which supervisors and other operating people submit should clearly define specifications and date delivery is required.
2. Purchasing should make every effort to locate two or more sources of supply.
3. All requests for samples should be routed through purchasing.
4. Purchasing should initiate, conduct, and conclude all negotiations for materials and services.
5. Contacts with suppliers by others in the company should be conducted with the knowledge and prior approval of purchasing.
6. Purchasing has full authority to question the quality and type of materials requested for the purpose of protecting the best interests of the company.[1]

MAKE OR BUY POLICY

A policy that must be set by some small manufacturers is whether to make or buy needed product components or entire products. In the small firm, the owner-manager should seek advice of others rather than relying solely on his or her own judgment on this decision. The factors of quality, quantity, vendor, price, and time enter into this decision also.

The small manufacturer evaluates three possibilities: purchase the complete product or component, purchase some parts and manufacture some, or manufacture all components. Usually, growth companies should buy parts because they can more profitably spend funds to expand product lines. A company with highly competitive product lines may make its parts as one method of reducing costs.

---

[1]Floyd D. Hedrick, *Purchasing for Owners of Small Plants,* Small Business Bibliography No. 85 (Washington, D.C.: Small Business Administration, 1976), p. 3.

There are many factors that enter into the make or buy decision. Some specific considerations for determining make or buy decisions are included below.

The buy decision:

1. What is the seasonal demand for the product?
2. Can the vendor produce the quality product needed?
3. What is the vendor's performance in regard to delivery?
4. What will be the cost per unit of buying versus making?

The make decision:

1. What are the quality limitations of the vendors?
2. What is the type of demand (how much is demanded and when)?
3. How many vendors are available? If there are too few, extra risks are involved.
4. Does the firm have the necessary skilled personnel?
5. Can present equipment be used or must new equipment be purchased?[2]

THE PURCHASING PROCESS

The purchasing process describes the activities that must be performed to complete the purchase transaction. These activities are shown in Figure 12-2.

RECOGNITION OF NEED

The need for an item is recognized in the department where the material is to be used.

DESCRIPTION OF NEED

To purchase the correct materials, the needed items must be accurately described. Poorly described items can be costly since the wrong materials may be ordered.

SELECTION OF SOURCES

Decisions concerning source selection is the next stage in the purchasing process. Factors to consider when selecting vendors are examined in a later section of this chapter.

[2]Lawrence C. Hackamack, *Should You Make or Buy Components?* Management Aid No. 189 (Washington, D.C.: Small Business Administration, January 1977), p. 3.

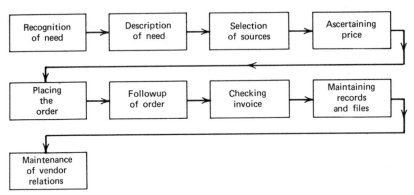

Figure 12-2 The purchasing process. (Adapted from J. H. Westing, I. V. Fine, and Gary J. Zenz, *Purchasing Management*, 3rd ed. New York: Wiley, 1969, pp. 10–16.)

ASCERTAINING THE PRICE

Prices may be determined for materials from several sources. One method is from current catalogs of manufacturers containing price quotations. A second method is through negotiation between buyer and seller. A third method is through competitive bidding. This latter method involves considerable time to secure price quotations and usually is not used by the purchasing manager of the small business.

PLACING THE ORDER

If the groundwork has been properly done as identified in the preceding stage, the order placement should be a fairly routine matter. The order should be placed on the buyer's purchase order form and should be signed only by the authorized company officials.

FOLLOW UP OF THE ORDER

An effective purchase control technique is to follow up on the purchase order with the vendor. This ensures that the order has been received and that the vendor will be able to meet the delivery date. Follow up also serves to improve communication between the buyer and the vendors.

CHECKING INVOICES

When invoices are received, they should be checked promptly to determine that merchandise meets specifications and to make certain that payments are made to take advantage of any purchase discounts.

MAINTENANCE OF RECORDS AND FILES

Proper records should be maintained for legal purposes as well as for effective control over the purchasing activity. Purchasing records can be checked regularly to evaluate how effective vendors have been in filling orders.

MAINTENANCE OF VENDOR RELATIONS

Goodwill between vendor and the small business owner aids in ensuring future success of the purchasing activity to reach its goals of quality, quantity, price, time, and place.

VENDOR ANALYSIS

Small business managers find that the analysis of vendors is one of their most important tasks. They attempt to select the vendors best suited to furnish them with merchandise that meets their demands for quality, service, and price. Evaluation of vendors requires an analysis of a variety of factors.

DEPENDABILITY

Clearly important is the dependability and reliability of the vendor. Is the vendor capable of supplying the merchandise requirements as often as needed?

SERVICES OF THE VENDOR

Another relevant criterion for owner-managers to judge is the type of service the vendor is capable of performing. For example, if technical equipment is purchased by the small manufacturer, what services does the vendor provide in relation to installation and service of the equipment after installation?

THE NUMBER OF VENDORS

In the evaluation process, the managers are confronted with determining if a single vendor can best meet their needs or should several vendors be considered? Owner-managers should be aware of the possible problems that may develop if their firm becomes overly dependent on a single vendor. The vendor may encounter financial difficulties or encounter unforeseen events such as a fire or labor problem, making it impossible for delivery dates to be met. Another consideration is that a single vendor may not be able to adequately supply the firm's needs at peak sales periods. Ordinarily, the small business owners will find that it is to their advantage to concentrate purchases with a few selected vendors and develop a close, harmonious working relationship with them. This policy offers the best assurance of a regular supply of merchandise. Figure 12-3 relates the advantages of purchasing from a small group of selected vendors.

LOCATION

The geographical location of suppliers is important for a variety of reasons. First, transportation costs can substantially increase the cost of merchandise if the supplier is located some distance from the buyer. Correlated with this is the time involved in shipping goods and getting them to the point where they are needed. Small business managers may find that a local supplier may adequately serve their needs, since they are usually able to supply merchandise quickly. Where possible, purchasing from local suppliers enables small business managers to demonstrate their support for the community as well, since purchases from local vendors mean that dollars will stay in the community. An added benefit is that buying locally creates goodwill toward the small business owner by area residents.

TERMS OF SALE

Small business owners should analyze the terms of sale offered by vendors since they may vary considerably. For example, one vendor offers cash discounts if payments are made within the regular credit period, while another vendor makes no such allowance. Cash discounts make a significant difference in costs of goods. Another criterion in vendor selection is the length of the credit period offered by the vendor. One vendor may offer a 30-day credit period while another may extend credit for 60 or even 90 days.

---

1. Receive more individualized attention and assistance from suppliers who know you are giving them most of your business.
2. Maintain a smaller inventory investment.
3. Purchases of larger quantities that may result in larger purchase discounts.
4. Simplifies credit problems.
5. Become known in local community as seller of certain brand or line of merchandise, if buying for resale.
6. Maintain a fixed standard for products, if buying materials to be used in making other goods.

Figure 12-3 Advantages of concentrating purchases with a limited number of suppliers. [*Source.* Wendel O. Metcalf, *Starting and Managing a Small Business of Your Own* (Washington, D.C.: Small Business Administration).]

VENDOR'S SALES REPRESENTATIVES

An additional factor to evaluate is the quality of the sales representatives of the vendor. Small business managers frequently rely on the vendor's sales representatives to provide them with prompt and accurate price quotations, to follow through on their orders, to expedite delivery, and to handle complaints in a satisfactory manner. Small business managers also expect sales representatives to be knowledgeable about the company and the products they are selling as well as to make regular sales calls.

Vendor representatives also perform an inventory function for many small retail stores. In cases when the vendor's representatives visit regularly and are considered dependable, the owner will use them to check inventory items and recommend how much stock should be purchased.

While the above listing is not exhaustive, it is suggestive of many of the major components that small business owners should incorporate into their evaluation of possible vendors.

PURCHASING AT THE RIGHT TIME

The question of when to purchase merchandise or materials requires skillful planning in anticipation of what the firm's needs will be at some future time.

A sales representative helps a store owner determine what merchandise to purchase.

Delivery of merchandise on time is an essential consideration in choosing suppliers.

Strong interrelationships exist between the vendors and buyers with regard to the timing of purchase orders and the capability to deliver them when needed.

Manufacturers should plan their purchase of raw materials so that these materials are available at the time they are needed in the manufacturing process in order to convert raw materials into finished goods. Manufacturers produce goods for stock in anticipation of ultimate demand for them. Or, they manufacture them to specific customer requirements. Whichever situation exists, they must be able to deliver according to date promised. Wholesalers should plan their merchandise needs to allow sufficient lead time to ensure delivery of goods when they are needed. By planning purchases with sufficient lead time, the wholesaler will be able to make delivery of merchandise to retailers or operators of service firms as the need arises. In turn, retailers or service establishment operators then have merchandise available when consumers demand it.

When planning a purchase, the amount of lead time necessary to have merchandise delivered on the date needed must be determined. For example, the small retailer who purchases merchandise too far in advance of the selling season ties up operating capital in merchandise inventory. Items purchased after the selling season has peaked will result in having large quantities of unsold merchandise in inventory. Consequently, these goods will have to be disposed of at cost or at a loss.

While orders may be placed to allow sufficient time for delivery, the merchandise must actually be delivered by the supplier. Small business owners will be able to reduce problems caused by late delivery of merchandise by ordering from reliable suppliers. Likewise, the small business owners should maintain a close check on promised delivery dates. Orders outstanding should be followed up in order to ensure that no problems have developed in either manufacturing or shipping. Orders that are delivered late will likely result in lost sales. Equally as important, late delivery usually results in ill will being generated toward the store by customers and affecting future sales.

ECONOMIC ORDER QUANTITY (EOQ)

Economic Order Quantity or EOQ is a method for arriving at the right quantity to order which results in the lowest annual cost and inventory.

Assume a firm has an annual requirement (R) of inventory of 2400 units or an average of 200 units per month.[3] What is the correct amount to order? The formula for EOQ is

$$EOQ = \sqrt{\frac{2RS}{C}}$$

where R equals the yearly requirement, S equals the procurement or setup costs, and C equals carrying costs per order.

Therefore, in the example, if we know that S is $20 and C is $0.60 per unit, we can compute the EOQ.

$$EOQ = \sqrt{\frac{2 \times 2400 \times 20}{0.60}} = \sqrt{160,000} = 400 \text{ units}$$

Thus, the EOQ is 400 units.

TRANSFER OF TITLE

When the small business manager makes a purchase, the ownership (title) of merchandise passes from the seller to the buyer. It is essential to establish the time and place where title actually passes in order to determine legal ownership of the merchandise.

While some sales transactions may be very simple, such as in a face-to-face situation where money is exchanged for goods, the usual purchase transaction is somewhat more complicated. Ordinarily, the matter of when title to goods passes in a sale is answered by a designation of "f.o.b." (free on board) to either seller or buyer.

[3]This example is adapted from: Burt Scanlan and J. Bernard Keys, *Management and Organizational Behavior*, 2nd ed. (New York: Wiley, 1979), pp. 561–562.

"F.O.B." SELLER'S LOCATION

The designation "f.o.b." seller's location means that title to goods passes as soon as the seller delivers the merchandise to the shipper (airline, truckline, bus, or railway system). Under the terms of this arrangement, the buyer pays for the shipping costs and is responsible for all activities relating to the movement of goods, such as providing insurance protection against damage or loss during shipment. Figure 12-4 depicts when title passes under "f.o.b." seller's location.

Figure 12-4   "F. O. B." seller's location.

"F.O.B." BUYER'S LOCATION

Transactions designated as "f.o.b." buyer's location indicate that the title of goods does not pass until the merchandise is delivered to the buyer's place of business. Under the terms of this arrangement, the seller pays for shipping charges to the buyer's firm. In addition, the responsibility for insurance protection of goods in transit remains with the seller. Figure 12-5 illustrates when title passes under the "f.o.b." buyer's location agreement.

By mutual agreement, the buyer and seller may select any other intermediate point for delivery of goods where title would then pass.

Figure 12-5   "F. O. B." buyer's location.

CONSIGNMENT

Under a consignment agreement, vendor merchandise is displayed in the small business owner's establishment and the vendor is ordinarily responsible for maintaining the merchandise display. The vendor retains ownership of the merchandise. Consignment may be advantageous to the small business owner. While there is merchandise displayed on the premises, the owner's funds are not tied up in merchandise inventory. If the merchandise does not sell, the vendor reclaims it. Consigned goods may attract customers to the store and while there they may also make additional purchases, resulting in increased sales.

For example, a rack jobber often consigns merchandise to retail firms. They place their own display rack of merchandise in the store. Rack jobbers regularly check the merchandise rack to see that there is an adequate stock of goods and that they are priced and displayed properly. Title does not pass and payment for the merchandise is not made until the products are sold or are used by the small business manager.

The small business owner must have a complete understanding with the vendor regarding the status of the consigned goods. The following factors should normally be included in the written consignment agreement.

1. Listing of items to be consigned, prices, quantities, and maximum and minimum levels.
2. Duration of consignment agreement, which should not exceed a year's period.
3. Title of consigned inventory remains with the vendor until withdrawn from stock.
4. Designation of insurance responsibility.
5. Policy on rejects—seller responsible for defects, buyer to be responsible for any missing or damaged materials resulting from buyer's negligence.
6. Termination provisions.
7. Provisions for disposition of any unused consigned inventory at end of consignment agreement.[4]

PURCHASE DISCOUNTS

Small business owners should take advantage of all opportunities to reduce the cost of operation and improve the firm's profit position. One such avenue is to take advantage of purchase discounts available from vendors. Types of discounts available are trade discounts, quantity discounts, and cash discounts, shown in Figure 12-6.

TRADE DISCOUNTS

Suppliers may establish a pricing system that allows discounts to small business owners on the basis of their classification as a manufacturer, wholesaler, or

---

[4]Scott W. Tyree, "The Right Quantity Through Inventory Management," in *Purchasing Handbook,* 3rd ed., edited by George W. Alijian (New York: McGraw-Hill, 1973), pp. 13–31.

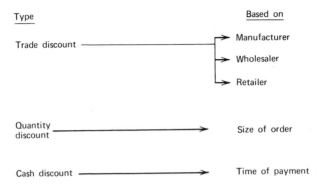

Figure 12-6 Types of discounts.

retailer. Trade discounts are usually set up on a graduated scale and are made available to purchasers, regardless of the size of the order.

Small manufacturers selling both to wholesalers and retailers may allow different percentage discounts to each because each performs a different type of selling function. For example, the manufacturer may grant a 40 percent discount to the wholesaler and a 25 percent discount to the retailer.

At other times, the supplier may provide for a string of chain discounts. A wholesaler might be offered a chain of discounts of 30, 20, 10. Thus, a wholesaler would receive a discount off the manufacturer's list price of 30 percent, less an additional 20 percent, less an additional 10 percent. The discount allowed would be calculated in the following manner.

Manufacturer's list price	$100
Less 30%	$ 30
	$ 70
Less 20%	$ 14
	$ 56
Less 10%	$ 5.60
Net price paid by wholesaler	$ 50.40

It is helpful to point out that trade discounts are often tied to catalog or price lists. Many suppliers publish comprehensive and costly catalogs at infrequent time periods. The wholesaler or manufacturer can use the same catalog or price list for different types of customers. For example, a manufacturer might publish a list price of a specific item at $10, then allow the wholesaler to take a 30 percent discount, the retailer a 20 percent ·discount, and the consumer a 10 percent discount. The discounts are often used to allow a business to adjust prices in a catalog or price list without having to reprint the entire catalog or price list. For example, an item might sell to wholesalers for $10 with a 20 percent discount. If the firm wishes to reduce the price for clearance, it may offer a 20 percent, 10 percent chain discount. Or, if the firm wishes to increase the price, it may only offer a 10 percent discount on the item.

QUANTITY DISCOUNTS

Quantity discounts are used by vendors in order to encourage small business owners to purchase larger orders. Two types of quantity discounts are found in business practice. One plan is the noncumulative quantity discount. Under the terms of this plan, quantity discounts are granted if a larger volume of merchandise is purchased in a single order. To illustrate, a supplier may put forward the following schedule.

SIZE OF ORDER	PERCENT DISCOUNT ON ORDER
Under a dozen	0
1–2 dozen	2
3–4 dozen	4
5–6 dozen	6

The second plan is a cumulative quantity discount. This discount plan calls for the supplier to allow the purchaser a discount if purchases exceed a specified quantity or dollar amount over a predetermined time period. The time span may be a month, but a yearly basis is more common. For example, a manufacturer may permit a 3 percent discount if a small business firm's purchases total $5000 for a year.

Quantity discounts are justified on the basis that it is more economical to process and ship fewer orders of greater size rather than many smaller orders.

CASH DISCOUNTS

Cash discounts are offered as an incentive to small business owners to pay for merchandise promptly. The small business owner should recognize that cash discounts make it possible for the purchase price of merchandise to be reduced, thus making cash available for other purposes. Commonly used types of cash discounts include the following.

1/10, net 30	2/10, net 60
2/10, net 30	2/10, EOM

These cash discount terms are important to the owner-manager. The "2/10, net 30" means the vendor extends credit to the small business owner for the amount of the purchase for a period of 30 days. The total bill is payable at the end of 30 days. However, if the bill is paid within 10 days of the invoice date, the small business owner will receive a 2 percent discount on the purchase price. Depending on the size of the purchase order, this can result in a sizable cash saving. Funds saved by taking advantage of the cash discounts thus become available for other uses in the firm.

The "2/10, EOM" means that a 2 percent discount can be taken if the small business managers pay the bill by the tenth of the month following the purchase. For merchandise purchased in September, the owner-manager would be able to take the 2 percent discount if the bill were paid by October 10.

Another way to further demonstrate the value of cash discounts to the small business owner is to figure them on the basis of annual interest rates. To illustrate, the "2/10, net 30" cash discount gives the buyer 36 percent annually, since there are 18 periods of 20 days each that can be expected if the small business owner receives merchandise shipments regularly throughout the year. Other examples of the range of cash discounts available on an annual basis are shown below.

> 1% 10 days—net 30 days = 18% per annum
> 2% 10 days—net 60 days = 14% per annum
> 2% 30 days—net 60 days = 24% per annum
> 3% 10 days—net 30 days = 54% per annum

Clearly, the small business owner should recognize the various types of discounts, and make every effort to take advantage of them in the business operations.

DISCUSSION QUESTIONS

1. Identify the goals of purchasing.
2. What are some purchasing policies and procedures suitable for a small business?
3. What activities comprise the purchasing process?
4. List the factors that an owner-manager should include when selecting a vendor.
5. Explain the importance of time in the purchase decision.
6. What is EOQ and what is its relationship to purchasing?
7. Discuss the difference between "f.o.b. seller's location" and "f.o.b. buyer's location."
8. What is meant by consignment of goods?
9. Distinguish between a trade discount and a quantity discount.
10. Explain what the term "1/10, net 30" means.

STUDENT PROJECTS

Interview one or several small business owners and seek to obtain the following information.

1. What factors do they consider most important in choosing vendors?
2. Do they handle goods on consignment? If so, what kind of goods are kept on consignment?
3. What types of discounts, if any, do they receive from suppliers?
4. What kinds of services do service representatives provide?

CASE A

ARDEN'S GIFT SHOPS (A)

Mrs. Jean White is the manager of Arden's Gift Shops. Arden's Shops consist of the main gift shop and three smaller gift shops plus a warehouse which are located in a tourist attraction complex owned by Philip Arden. The nature of the business is highly seasonal.

Not all shops carry the same merchandise. Anywhere from 6000 to 10,000 items may be carried in stock. The items range in price from less than $1 to higher prices for turquoise jewelry.

In addition to being the manager for 18 years, Mrs. White has also been the buyer for merchandise for all the shops for 16 years. She has been assisted in managing and purchasing for the last 2 years by Mrs. Barbara Adams. Mr. Arden oversees the operation of the tourist operation but leaves managing the shops and warehouse to Mrs. White. Mrs. White and Mrs. Adams maintain close control over the operation and both are very competent personnel.

In the firm, there is no standard inventory level set. For example, there is no determination of the number of different items to be stocked nor of the quantity levels for the particular items which are stocked. Consequently, there is no set time to order or reorder. All inventory and purchasing inventory is kept in the heads of the two buyers rather than being put into formalized policies and procedures. Purchasing decisions are based on the buyers' intuition.

It should be noted that the gift shop has always managed to show a profit.

Question

What problems are indicated in the gift shop operation with regard to purchasing procedures?

CASE B
MELBA'S APPAREL BOUTIQUE

For several years, Melba has looked forward to the day when she would be able to realize a long-held ambition of becoming the owner of her own women's and girls' retail apparel shop. In one month, her dream will become a reality when she opens her shop in the new North Star Shopping Center. She intends to carry a wide range of apparel and accessories in the store. Melba has attempted to equip herself with as much knowledge as possible about small business operations in order to increase her chances of success in a very competitive field of business.

She realizes that women's and girls' fashions change rapidly. Consequently, she has attempted to become as knowledgeable as possible about purchasing of merchandise. As she evaluates the purchasing activity for her type of store, she is thinking of several pertinent issues.

Questions

1. What factors need to be included in purchasing decisions?
2. What should I consider in trying to evaluate suppliers?
3. Should I consider accepting merchandise on a consignment basis?
4. How important will purchase discounts be?

13

INVENTORY CONTROL

PREVIEW OF THIS CHAPTER

1. In this chapter, you will learn that inventory control is important to small business because it reduces costs while aiding customer relations.

2. You will understand how keeping a record of customer requests for items not in stock aids in inventory control.

3. You will discover how the basic perpetual inventory system works and how some firms use specialized forms of perpetual inventory control.

4. You will understand how visual, periodic, and partial inventory control systems operate.

5. You will find out the importance of the two basic methods of physical inventory counts.

6. You will learn how to identify and clear slow moving items in inventory.

7. If you ever plan to enter small business, you will be interested in learning the value of shelf space analysis and how it is performed.

8. You will be able to understand these key words:

Storage	Partial control system
Spoilage	Bin tags
Obsolescence	Sales ticket control
Turnover	Stub control
Inventory	Floor sample control
Perpetual inventory system	Punched card control
Visual inventory system	Physical inventory count
Periodic inventory system	Shelf space analysis

Retail and wholesale firms carry merchandise for resale, manufacturing firms carry raw materials and finished goods inventories, and service firms carry parts and supplies. All of these firms incur expenses that are a result of their inventory. How much inventory they carry and how well they control it is very important to their business.

IMPORTANCE OF INVENTORY CONTROL

The size of the inventory determines several costs associated with inventory. The size of the inventory may also have an effect on customer relations.

COST OF INVENTORY

The major costs of inventory are from (1) storage facilities, (2) spoilage and obsolescence, (3) insurance, (4) handling, and (5) interest.

Storage Facilities

The larger the size of the inventory, the larger storage facilities must be to accommodate the merchandise. Land, building, and/or rental costs are major expenditures for the small business. The requirements of storage also may vary in cost. For example, construction and maintenance of a sheet metal shed is much less expensive than construction and maintenance of cold storage facilities.

Spoilage and Obsolescence

Some inventories are perishable and larger inventories of these items usually result in some losses from spoilage. Other goods are subject to obsolescence due to fashion changes, for instance, clothing. Inventory items may also suffer from obsolescence because better products are introduced on the market and the greater the amount of the item in stock, the greater the loss.

Insurance

Various types of insurance should be carried to provide coverage on the inventory, primarily fire and theft. Larger amounts of inventory mean higher insurance costs, since premiums are based, in part, on the dollar value of the inventory.

This seafood store is selling highly perishable products.

Handling

Generally, the more inventory a small business carries, the more often it must be handled. This handling is an expense to the business in terms of costs of manpower, equipment, and damaged goods.

Interest

Inventory also requires an investment of funds. If the firm borrows money to maintain an inventory, it must pay interest on the borrowed funds. Even if the business does not borrow funds, it is still considered an expense since it would be able to use the funds it has invested in inventory for other uses. Even putting the funds into a savings account would earn the firm money that it will not receive if it is tied up in inventory.

All these are costs that the business firm must sustain in order to maintain an adequate inventory. However, if the firm carries too much inventory, it will significantly increase these costs. In addition, if the firm does not perform good inventory control, it can sustain additional losses to these costs. For instance, one small retail appliance store discovered that it had several thousand dollars worth of appliances that had been covered with other merchandise in a crowded storeroom for several years. The appliances were out of style and had to be sold at a large loss.

Poor inventory control encourages employee theft and prevents the business from recognizing shoplifting problems or even knowing how much is being lost to theft. Inadequate records of inventory cause problems in insurance claims in losses resulting from burglary. The small business that does not practice good inventory control may lose money it does not even know it is losing.

One example of how much a firm can lose without knowing about it is the case of a large store handling hardware and do-it-yourself items. The firm did not have an adequate inventory control system in their three stores in one city. They were notified by the police that three of their employees were caught in a police fencing operation run to trap thieves. The employees, it was later discovered, had stolen more than $100,000 of merchandise during the past year. The store had no idea it had lost any merchandise until the police uncovered the loss.

INVENTORY AND CUSTOMER RELATIONS

A small business must carry sufficient amounts of inventory in order to maintain good customer relations. A customer that goes into a retail store several times and is told they are out of a product soon develops a feeling that he won't be able to find what he wants if he returns. He will soon trade elsewhere. The service firm that makes customers wait for service while the business obtains parts or supplies will suffer the same fate from its customers. The wholesaler that is often out of products retailers order will find that these merchants will soon patronize other wholesalers. Customers of manufacturers who experience too many delayed delivery dates will also shift purchases to other manufacturers.

The idea, then, is to balance inventory costs and customer relations. The firm must maintain as small an inventory as possible to reduce costs, yet maintain an inventory that is adequate to satisfy customer needs. Good inventory control is the key.

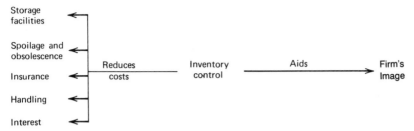

Figure 13-1 Good inventory control reduces costs and aids customer relations.

REQUESTS FOR NOT IN STOCK ITEMS

As a part of their inventory control system, small business firms should keep a record of all requests for merchandise that they do have in stock. Inadequate reorder points can be easily spotted through this type of record. If a specific item that is regularly carried in inventory appears more than once over a reasonable period of time on the report, the firm should consider setting the reorder point higher. If an item that the firm does not stock appears more than once over a reasonable period of time, the business should consider adding the item to their inventory.

INVENTORY CONTROL SYSTEMS

A business firm may utilize three basic types of inventory control systems: (1) perpetual inventory systems, (2) visual systems, and (3) periodic and partial control systems.

PERPETUAL INVENTORY SYSTEMS

A basic perpetual inventory system is used by many types of small business firms, including manufacturers, wholesalers, retailers, and service establishments. In addition, specialized perpetual inventory systems are used by different types of businesses, particularly retail operations.

Basic Perpetual Inventory System

A basic perpetual inventory card is shown in Figure 13-2. Variations of this basic card are used by many small businesses. Some manufacturers, wholesalers, and service firms use bin tags that carry the same information as this card

Item Green Giant English Peas - 303 Can				
Reorder Point 100 cs		Order Amount 400 cs		Stock Control # CV-1604

In		Out		Balance
Date	Amount	Date	Amount	
				80
3/21	400			480
		4/1	60	420
		4/4	40	380

Figure 13-2 Perpetual inventory card (grocery wholesaler).

but are in the form of a tag. These tags are attached to the storage bin or shelf, and receipts and withdrawals of the item are noted on the tags when they are made. Retailers use several variations of the basic perpetual inventory system, which will be discussed later in this chapter.

The perpetual inventory card carries such general information as the name of the item, stock number, and reorder point. Every time additions to the inventory of this item are received from vendors, the number is recorded and added to the balance. Every time some of the items are issued or sold, the withdrawal is recorded and subtracted from the balance.

Using the perpetual inventory method, a look at the balance at any time will reveal the amount of inventory on hand for this item. According to need, other information may be recorded on the card, such as price, amount ordered but not received, specifications, location in stock room, and what department uses the inventory item.

Firms that have a relatively small number of items and a small number of transactions per day are ideal for perpetual inventory systems using these in-out-balance cards. It does not take a person too long to record about 50 purchases a day. However, in small stores that have a large variety of items and/or a large number of purchases each day, it takes a considerable amount of time to post the daily purchases to perpetual inventory cards. For example, the small drive-in grocery would find it very time consuming to make a record of each item purchased and post them to perpetual inventory cards.

Medium and large firms with a wide range of inventory items and many additions and withdrawals each day have generally gone to computer based inventory control. The same basic system is used in computer systems as is used in a manual operation. Instead of using perpetual inventory cards, data on receipts and withdrawals of specific items are fed into the computer and a balance is retained in its memory banks.

The price of small computers has dropped during the past few years to such an extent that it is now feasible for most small businesses to perform their inventory control function on a computer.

Specialized Perpetual Inventory Systems in Retail Stores

Retail stores often use specialized systems for collecting and transferring information into their perpetual inventory systems. Some of the more common methods are (1) sales ticket control, (2) stub control, (3) floor sample control, and (4) punched card control.

Sales Ticket Control   Sales tickets are one method of collecting perpetual inventory sales information. Sales tickets are completed each time merchandise is sold, listing such information as department, number of items sold, type of item sold, unit price, tax, and total price. This ticket is then used for posting to the perpetual inventory system. The sales ticket is also useful in accounting control, such as cash control and sales taxes payable (see Fig. 13-3).

A good method for using sales tickets is to have a locked box with a slit in the top and each time a sales is made the clerk puts the ticket in the box. At the end of the day, the box is opened and the total of the sales tickets is used as a check against the amount of cash in the register and the cash register tape. The sales tickets are then posted individually on perpetual inventory cards. When the inventory is checked against the perpetual inventory cards, any shortages are identified and the manager immediately knows he or she has a theft problem.

Another method of using sales tickets for perpetual inventory control is common in some retail firms, such as automobile parts stores. A basic inventory is established on a yearly basis and all items of the desired inventory are placed in stock. When a sale is made, a sales ticket is completed listing the part, its code number, and the number of units sold. Each day, all items that appear on sales tickets are reordered to bring the inventory back to its original level. If the inventory on hand plus all items on order differs from the basic inventory, it is a warning signal to the manager that he or she has a theft or recording problem.

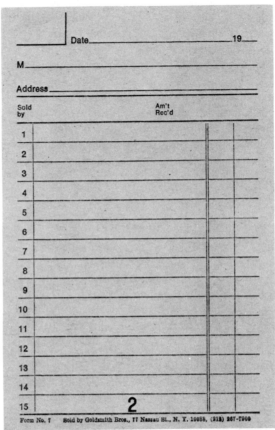

Figure 13-3   A very simple sales ticket sold by most office supply firms.

Stub Control   Stub control of perpetual inventory consists of attaching a two or more part stub to each item that is offered for sale. All of the stub parts have such information as the department number, vendor code, types of merchandise, and any other coded information of value to the inventory and accounting systems of the store. When the merchandise is sold, one part of the stub is removed and placed in a collection container. The removed stub is then used to post to the perpetual inventory system and in accounting control procedures. If the customer returns the merchandise, the stub remaining on the merchandise is used to restock the merchandise and correct accounting records.

Floor Sample Control   Floor sample control is common to appliance and furniture type operations that use floor samples to sell merchandise in stock.

Figure 13-4   Sales stub inventory control.

One method is to have small pads with consecutive numbers printed on each page. The pads may be numbered from 1 to 100 and the total number of merchandise items that are received in stock are attached to the floor sample. For example, an appliance store may receive 25 units of a specific model of refrigerator. Numbers 26 through 100 are removed from a printed pad and the numbers 1 through 25 are attached to the floor sample. Each time a clerk completes a sale, he or she removes a number. Consequently, sales personnel are able to look at the remaining numbers on the pad and know immediately how many are left in stock.

Punched Card Control

A punched card control system uses two or more part tags or standard computer punched cards attached to the merchandise for sale. When an item of merchandise is sold, a part of the tag or punched card is removed from the item and placed in a collection container. The tags or standard computer cards are fed into a special ticket-converting machine or automatic card sorter for sorting into categories. The cards are then fed into specialized tabulating equipment or a computer to record inventory and accounting control information.

VISUAL CONTROL SYSTEMS

Many small firms feel they are unable to maintain a perpetual inventory system for various reasons—high volume of small value items, large stock of small value items, or lack of funds to pay personnel to maintain a perpetual system.

The small business manager often is very familiar with inventory and knows approximately how much should be on hand at any given time. A daily visual examination allows the manager to estimate how much should be ordered.

Visual control is probably the most common method of stock control in small business firms and is the least effective. Visual control works better for firms that have stable sales, large numbers of each item in stock, merchandise that can be obtained quickly from vendors, and merchandise that is segregated on shelves or in bins. Inability to determine shortages of items is a major disadvantage of the visual control system.

For example, one small business located near a school was losing several thousand dollars each year due to shoplifting and never realized the extent of the problem until one of the authors set up an inventory control system for the business. Shortages in inventory revealed by the inventory control system indicated the extent of the problem. By installing several shoplifting prevention techniques, the firm was able to significantly increase its profit level.

PERIODIC AND PARTIAL CONTROL SYSTEMS

Small business firms that feel they are unable to maintain perpetual systems because of inventory volume, size, and/or cost may elect a periodic or partial system in conjunction with the visual system.

The periodic control system involves recording purchases and inventory levels at reorder times. For example, a sporting goods merchant would record the amount of baseballs on hand. When he or she feels it is time to reorder, the number purchased and the number remaining in stock are recorded. This record tells the merchant what normal turnover period is for each item and gives the merchant some approximation of how many items are on hand based on this normal turnover. It also has a major weakness of not identifying shortages.

A closely related system involves taking a complete inventory count of the business and then at the end of some period (such as 3 months) taking the entire physical inventory count again. The difference between the first and the second inventory count is computed and all purchases for the period are added to the balance. All items that have the same percentage markup are then put in a category (such as 20 percent markup items into one group and 30 percent markup items into another group). By taking the cost of all the items and applying the markup for each group, the firm can come somewhat close to what their sales should have been for the period. If the sales total for the period differs significantly from the projected sales figure, the firm then knows it probably has a theft problem.

In order to help identify shortages, but still not use a perpetual inventory system for all merchandise, some small business managers use a partial perpetual inventory system. They may keep perpetual inventory records on more expensive items or items of merchandise more prone to theft. Other low value merchandise is maintained by visual or periodic inventory control.

Some small business managers attempt to identify shortages by keeping a perpetual inventory on part of their merchandise on a rotating basis. For example, one drug retailer takes a physical inventory count on one part of total stock, such as gift items. He or she then keeps record of all gift item sales and purchases for a month's period. At the end of the month, the drug retailer then takes another physical inventory count. By adding purchases to starting inventory and deducting the ending inventory, he or she knows how many gifts should have been sold during the month. By applying markup on gifts and comparing the total to sale of gifts, he or she is able to identify shortages from employee or shoplifting theft. The revolving perpetual inventory also allows the drug retailer to (1) more accurately identify reorder points, (2) more accurately establish optimum order size, (3) spot slow moving items, (4) institute greater control over items more susceptible to theft, and (5) identify sections of the store that have greatest losses of merchandise.

PHYSICAL INVENTORY COUNT

Every small business should perform a periodic inventory count. Even if the firm has a perpetual inventory system which is designed to provide inventory information on a continuous basis, it should still perform a physical inventory count to identify mistakes and shortages. There are two basic methods of performing inventory counts.

One method is to perform it on all inventory at regular intervals, at least once a year. Retailers often run special sales to reduce their inventory just before inventory time. They then bring employees in on an overtime basis when the store is normally closed to perform the inventory count. This method provides the most accurate income statement if prepared at the same time as the inventory count. The count is also checked against the perpetual inventory at this time.

Another method is to perform a count of a few items each week on a continuous basis. These continuous inventory counts provide an on-going check against the perpetual inventory system. This method sometimes allows the identification of mistakes and shortages sooner than the periodic count.

SLOW-MOVING ITEMS

Items in inventory tend to turn over at widely different rates, whether they are raw materials or finished goods inventory of manufacturers, merchandise of wholesalers, parts and supplies of service establishments, or goods of the retailer. The slower the turnover of items in inventory, generally, the greater the chance of loss due to spoilage or obsolescence. A good inventory system is necessary to keep this loss at a minimum by identifying slow-moving items. Once the slow-moving items are identified, there are various means that a small business manager may employ to deal with them.

One possibility is to eliminate the item from inventory. An analysis should be made to determine the amount that this item contributes to profit each year, relative to the cost of keeping it in stock. Many items that are slow movers cannot be eliminated from stock. The firm's customers may expect them to carry the item, and it may effect customer relations and patronage if eliminated.

The most common method of dealing with slow-moving items is markdown. Markdown of merchandise is not only a method of clearing slow-moving merchandise but is also a good promotional technique. In fact, many retail stores offer markdowns on a wide range of merchandise at one time in order to maximize the promotional effect. Almost all retail stores engage in markdown sales, which are attempts to build customer patronage and store image, as well as clearing slow-moving items from inventory.

Markdowns may be the result of various factors. The firm may buy too many of the item in expectation of greater sales volume than is actually realized. They may price the item too high in relation to competitors. They may order too many as a result of poor inventory control. The sales personnel may be pushing the sale of another similar item and cause the other item to be slow in sales. Even the weather may have an effect on how fast a product sells, such as an unusually dry season's effect on umbrella sales.

Many times it is advisable to sell a particularly slow item below cost in order to clear it out of inventory. The cost of storage plus lost sales from not having a faster moving item in its place may make sale of the item at a price below cost desirable. For example, one men's clothing store kept a style of men's sports shirts in stock for 3 years after they had gone out of style. Even reducing the shirts to one-fifth their original cost would not move them. The owner finally gave them to a charity in order to clear them from the shelf to have the space for more fashionable shirts.

SHELF SPACE ANALYSIS

Up to now, we have talked in terms of slow-moving items and have generally ignored profitability of products. As a simple illustration, a firm may sell 10

The large number of products and brands carried by this drugstore make perpetual inventory control possible only with a computer. The number also makes shelf-space analysis very desirable.

watches in a month at a gross profit of $2 each and still make more money on them than by selling 100 toys at a 10¢ gross profit per unit. Another factor that has not been taken into consideration is the amount of store space required to sell a specific item. The store mentioned above might be able to sell watches and rings in the same space it would require just to sell the toy.

A retail store has just so much space it may use to sell products. The firm must also pay for its selling area in the form of rent, depreciation, utilities, and so forth. Consequently, maintaining every square inch of selling space is a cost to the firm.

A technique called "shelf space analysis" is a means of measuring the profitability of each item in terms of turnover, profit per item, and amount of selling space required to sell the product.

To perform shelf space analysis, the firm must first measure each item it sells in terms of the amount of shelf space (in square inches) it occupies in the selling area. The average number of items it sells per month is then computed using beginning inventory plus all purchases for the year minus ending inventory and dividing by 12. Seasonal goods should be computed over the number of months they are actually carried in the selling area. Other seasonal goods may be carried in the same space during the other seasons. For example, the following two items:

	WATCHES	BEACH BALLS
Beginning inventory	30	100
Purchases for year	50	1150
	80	1250
Less ending inventory	20	50
Total sold for year	60	1200
Divided by months in stock	5 (12 months)	300 (4 months)

The average cost of a unit plus markup is then computed to determine the average gross profit per unit sold. The average number of items sold per month times the per unit gross profit gives the gross profit per month.

	WATCHES	BEACH BALLS
Cost per unit	$ 20	$0.50
Times markup percentage	× 50%	× 40%
Equals gross profit per unit	$ 10	$0.20
Times units sold per month	× 5	×300
Equals gross profit per month	$ 50	$ 60

The amount of shelf space required for each item is then computed and divided into the average monthly gross profit to determine the amount of gross profit per square inch of shelf space each item produces. The linear inches of the front of the shelf space can be used in place of square inches when it produces just as good an analysis, such as when the depth of all shelves are the same.

	WATCHES	BEACH BALLS
Shelf space occupied	15 by 20 inches	40 by 60 inches
Total shelf space occupied	300 square inches	2400 square inches
Gross profit per square inch of shelf space per month	$50 ÷ 300 = $.167	$60 ÷ 2400 = $.025
	or 16.7¢	2.5¢

It is obvious in our example that watches are more profitable in terms of gross profit produced relative to selling area required.

Cost of item per unit	×	Percentage markup	=	Gross profit per unit
Gross profit per unit	×	Number of units sold during period	=	Total gross profit for period
Total gross profit	÷	Shelf space occupied in square inches	=	Gross profit per square inch for the period

Figure 13-5 Shelf space analysis.

This is a fairly simple process, but a more complex formula may be used that includes such items as storage cost, investment cost, spoilage and obsolescence costs, and frequency of stocking the items on the shelves.

It would appear that shelf space analysis would be a large undertaking for a store with a large number of inventory items, such as a drug or grocery retailer. The best method of achieving shelf space analysis in this type of store is to take a few items each week until the entire inventory analysis is completed. After the initial analysis is completed, it is necessary to perform the analysis on items that are added or on items that have undergone some drastic change in price, volume, or shelf space required.

Retailers are able to carry just so many goods on their shelves; however, at the same time, they are continually offered new products to stock and sell. In this case, shelf space analysis is a method of measuring the profitability of different products and knowing which to eliminate. New products can be analyzed on the basis of cost, markup, shelf space required, and estimated volume of sales. As pointed out before, there are some items that a merchant is not able to eliminate because the customer expects the merchant to carry them. For example, a drugstore manager would probably carry tobacco products even if they were among the lowest gross profit items per square inch of shelf space. Walk-in trade for tobacco products increases other sales, and customers expect the store to stock them.

From this chapter, it should be obvious that the small business manager must maintain good inventory control techniques in order to maximize profit.

DISCUSSION QUESTIONS

1. Why is inventory control important from the standpoint of costs? From the standpoint of customer relations?
2. Why is the basic perpetual inventory control system called perpetual?
3. Which inventory control system is the most efficient? Why?

4. Briefly explain how the following work:
   (a) Sales ticket control,
   (b) Stub control,
   (c) Floor sample control,
   (d) Punched card control.
5. Which types of inventory control systems have failure to identify shortages as their major weakness?
6. What are the two basic methods of physical inventory counts?
7. What are some of the reasons for having markdowns of items in inventory?
8. Is there a good side to markdowns? Explain.
9. Why is shelf space analysis valuable?
10. What does shelf space analysis attempt to discover?

STUDENT PROJECT

Visit an area with a high concentration of retail stores such as a shopping center or mall. Select three small retail stores and attempt to discover what types of inventory control system they use.

STORE 1

STORE 2

STORE 3

CASE A

KAREN KAY PERFUMES

Karen Kay last year leased space in a new shopping mall and opened a shop named "Karen Kay Perfumes." She stocked her store with several brands of perfume, one top line of cosmetics, and a limited line of higher priced toiletries. The shop has a total of 60 different items offered for sale.

Sales have been good since she opened her shop, but she does not seem to be making as much profit as she feels she should considering her volume of sales. In addition, she has had some complaints because a few customers were unable to purchase a particular item they wanted. Most of the time it was because

Karen was out of the item in stock, and a few times because it was in stock but she overlooked it and thought she was out.

Karen has exclusive distributorships for two brands of very expensive perfume. She wants to get rid of one brand so that she will have room to add another perfume that she feels has a very high profit potential. However, she is not sure which is the more profitable of the two brands she now carries. The following is some information she has gathered about the two brands:

	BRAND X	BRAND Y
Total yearly bottle sales	144	420
Cost per bottle	$15	$10
Markup percentage	100%	100%
Shelf space occupied	15 by 10 inches	20 by 10 inches

The difference in shelf space used for the two perfumes is the result of Brand Y requiring Karen to exhibit their perfume in a special display device on the shelf.

Questions

1. Does Karen need some type of inventory control? Explain.
2. What type of inventory control system would you suggest?
3. If she uses a perpetual inventory system, what kind would you suggest?
4. Would you suggest a physical inventory count and, if so, what type?
5. Perform a shelf space analysis on Brands X and Y. Which should Karen eliminate?
6. How would you suggest she dispose of current stock of the brand you have chosen to eliminate?

CASE B

QUALITY ELECTRONICS

Quality Electronics is owned and operated by Ruby Jackson. The store sells equipment and parts to people using citizen band and short wave radios. Quality Electronics has always been profitable and the inventory in the store has grown considerably over the past 10 years the business has been in operation.

Ruby suspects she may have a theft problem, but is not sure. An expensive short wave radio recently disappeared and no one remembers selling it. Ruby does not know if this is an isolated incident or if it happens regularly. Ruby has considered a perpetual inventory system for her inventory but it seems out of the question since she carries about 650 items in stock. About 600 of these items are small parts with most having a value of less than $2. The store averages about 50 customer purchases a day.

Ruby has noticed that about three customers each day do not obtain what they come to purchase. She estimates that one-third of these requests are for items the store is out of and two-thirds are for items she does not carry.

Since you are known to have considerable knowledge about the operation of small businesses, Ruby has come to you for help.

Questions

1. What kind of inventory control system will you recommend to Ruby?
2. What would lead you to believe that she has an inventory problem?
3. What other recommendation might you make to Ruby?
4. Do you think shelf space analysis would be beneficial to Ruby? Explain.

14

RISK, INSURANCE, AND THEFT

PREVIEW OF THIS CHAPTER

1. In this chapter you will learn that all small businesses face risks on a daily basis.

2. You will discover that small businesses control risk by (1) avoiding the risk, (2) reducing the risk, (3) assuming the risk, and (4) shifting the risk.

3. You will be interested to find out that small businesses often need fire, theft, liability, loss of earning power, surety, automobile, and life insurance.

4. You will understand the difference between the three basic types of life insurance—whole life, endowment, and term.

5. You will discover the various benefits a business may derive from life insurance and the relative cost of each type.

6. You will find out that there are different types of people who are shoplifters—juveniles, housewives, psychologically sick persons, vagrants, addicts, and professionals.

7. If you ever plan to go into a small business, you will be interested in discovering different methods you may use to discourage shoplifting.

8. You will learn that employee theft is a major problem in business. You will discover different methods employees use to steal from small businesses and how to discourage employee theft.

9. You will be interested in finding out how to discourage burglary.

10. You will be able to understand these key words:

Risk	Term insurance
Subcontracting	Loan value
Hedging	Premium
Insurance	Loss of earning power
Fire insurance	Shoplifting
Theft insurance	Surety insurance
Liability insurance	Automobile insurance

Life insurance	Ticket switching
Whole life insurance	Employee theft
Endowment insurance	Burglary

Small business owners face risk on a continuing basis. Risk to small business owners exists in many forms. Every time they purchase merchandise they take a risk that it will not sell. They face a risk every time the delivery man drives the company truck. This list is almost endless. Many of the risks, to which the small business is exposed, are major risks that could result in failure of the business.

RISK CONTROL

Small business owners must control risks if their businesses are to survive and prosper. There are four basic methods with which they are able to deal with

Earthquakes are an unusual and unexpected business risk.

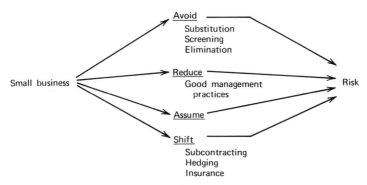

Figure 14-1   Risk control in small businesses.

risks: (1) avoid the risk, (2) reduce the risk, (3) assume the risk, and (4) shift the risk (see Fig. 14-1).

AVOID THE RISK

Sometimes it is possible for a small business to avoid risks, particularly high level risks. A small business owner may avoid risks by substitution, screening, and/or elimination.

Substitution

A small business may avoid risk by substituting high risk materials and processes with low risk materials and processes. For example, a manufacturer using a highly explosive chemical in the manufacturing process may find it is possible to substitute a chemical that is safer and achieves the same results.

Screening

The small business owner may avoid risk by screening out high risk items. To illustrate, a small business should not extend credit to everyone; rather, they should screen out high risk individuals to aid in helping reduce bad debt losses.

Elimination

Sometimes the small business is able to avoid risk by elimination of high level risks. The firm that requires employees to wear eye goggles when operating a grinder is eliminating one chance of injury to the employee.

REDUCE THE RISK

Many risks the small business faces may be greatly reduced with good management practices. To illustrate, periodic inspections and training often contribute greatly to reducing risk of injury to customers and employees. Good hiring procedures help reduce the risk of employee theft.

Even when risks are shifted to others, such as in the case of insurance, good management practices can still reduce the risks and lower the cost of insurance to the business.

ASSUME THE RISK

Some small businesses assume certain risks because it is either impossible to avoid the risk or too costly to shift the risk to someone else. There are many risks that the small business must face on a continuing basis. Often, the only thing the business can do is practice good management in order to reduce the risk as much as possible.

To illustrate, a small women's clothing store must purchase clothing several months in advance of its being sold. It is often very difficult to determine what fashions will be so far in advance. If the store purchases the wrong style of clothing, it may lose a considerable amount of money. To reduce the risk they must take, they need to continually evaluate their customers' tastes, study the market, and find out what authorities in the fashion field are predicting.

SHIFT THE RISK

The small business owner may shift many risks to other persons by subcontracting, hedging, and insurance.

Subcontracting

A small business may be willing to perform certain functions, but feel other functions are too high a risk for the capabilities of the business. To illustrate, a small contracting firm may feel that it has the ability to adequately perform all construction activities on a new building except the electrical work. To avoid the risk of failure on electrical work and still get the contract, the small business may bid on the contract and subcontract the electrical work to another firm for a specified price.

Hedging

Small business firms that deal in goods traded on the commodity market often shift the risk of price fluctuations by hedging. For example, a cattle feed lot may buy and sell cattle futures in the commodity market in order to avoid price fluctuations that could ruin the company.

Insurance

The most common method of shifting risk in small businesses is by purchasing insurance. For premium payments, insurance companies are willing to insure a business against a wide range of risks.

The small business may shift the entire risk or a part of the risk. It usually depends on the probability of the risk occurring and the cost of shifting the risk.

TYPES OF INSURANCE FOR SMALL BUSINESS

The principal types of insurance used by small businesses are fire, theft, liability, loss of earning power, surety, automobile, and life (see Fig. 14-2).

FIRE

Fire insurance policies insure the small business from loss due to fire and lightning. Both the building and its contents may be insured in a policy. In addition, a small business may obtain insurance against all the loss or part of the loss. Most small businesses carry fire insurance against part of the loss due to the difference in cost. For example, a small business may have 90 percent coverage, in which case, the insurance company pays for 90 percent of the loss and the small business pays for the other 10 percent of the loss.

Additional riders may be purchased to accompany the fire insurance policy. For an additional premium, the small business firm may purchase insurance against explosion, riot, windstorm, hail, aircraft and vehicle-caused damage, and smoke damage.

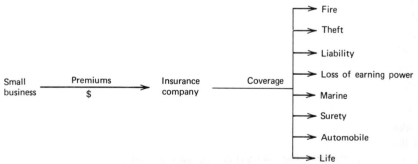

Figure 14-2 Types of risks shifted to insurance companies.

There is a growing concern among fire fighters in the United States over the rapidly increasing number of arson fires. Mentally ill persons who set fires have always been a problem; however, most of the increase is believed to be due to property owners themselves. For example, the owner of one small store who was floundering financially was sentenced by a jury to 2 years in prison when firemen discovered the fire in his store was due to a cup full of gasoline with a candle in it. In addition to accidental fires, the small business person may face a risk of having the firm's property damaged by the acts of adjoining property owners. Also, the fire insurance premium of the small business is determined by the statistics of fires in its city which may result in higher premiums.

THEFT

The small business firm may purchase insurance for all types of thefts. They may be protected against loss from theft by persons outside (burglary and robbery) and inside (employee theft) the business. Small businesses with employees who handle money often insure against embezzlement of funds by bonding these employees.

LIABILITY

Owners of small business firms may be liable for (1) their own acts, (2) acts of their employees while at work, or (3) conditions within the business. If an individual is injured while on the firm's premises, the business is liable for damages if the injury is the result of neglect. For example, if a customer fell and was seriously injured because of a broken step, the business would be liable. Also, the business would be liable for damages if an employee, driving the delivery truck, ran a stop light and injured the occupant of another automobile.

Liability insurance is one of the most important forms of insurance for the small business to carry. Injuries to individuals often result in very large damages being awarded by the courts against the business. To illustrate, an accident that caused the death of a person, such as the delivery employee running the red light, would usually amount to very large sums, often in excess of $100,000. Very few small businesses are able to sustain this type of loss. In addition, unlimited liability for the general partner and the sole proprietor may not only result in business failure but may also put them personally in debt for long periods of time.

There are many types of coverage by liability insurance. Some of the forms of liability coverage are damages resulting from elevator operations, druggists' mistakes, physicians' malpractice, and contractor accidents.

It is also important that the small business purchase sufficient amounts of liability insurance. The small business may have a $50,000 liability policy against losses, but this does not limit the amount of the judgment that may be obtained against the business in court. If the same business were to sustain a $100,000 judgment, then the insurance company would pay only $50,000, and the small business would be required to pay the rest.

LOSS OF EARNING POWER

The small business firm may sustain losses not only to physical aspects of the business but also to its ability to earn income. Loss of income may be very damaging and can result in failure of the business in some cases. For example, a fire might cause the business to cease operations for several months, but the need for income to the owner still exists and may not be covered by the fire insurance policy. Also, the owner of a business might sustain an injury that would prevent him or her from working in the business, resulting in the loss of income.

Insurance covering loss of earning power may be purchased for many different occurrences. The owner may purchase disability insurance which provides against loss from disability. He or she may also purchase insurance against loss of income due to the business not operating as a result of property damages. Loss of income may prevent the owner from meeting debt payments.

SURETY INSURANCE

Some types of small business firms obtain bonding to assure their customers of their ability to complete contracts. To illustrate, a small business contracting company may bond itself against losses to customers arising from its failure to complete contracts. If it fails to complete a contract, the bonding company will hire some other business to complete the terms of the contract. It is common, in some industries, that a business must bond itself or the business finds it very difficult to obtain business, such as in the construction industry.

AUTOMOBILE INSURANCE

Automobile insurance is in reality another form of property and liability insurance. There are several types of property insurance available covering the automobile, such as collision, theft, fire, glass breakage, and damages from malicious mischief. Automobile liability insurance covers other peoples' property, other automobiles, persons in other vehicles, and persons in the insured automobile.

Property type automobile insurance often has a deductible clause. For example, a small business may carry $100 deductible on collision. If the car is damaged in an accident, the owner must pay the first $100 and the insurance company pays anything above $100 of the damages.

Small businesses may feel that it is not economical to carry property type insurance on their automobiles and trucks after they are several years old. However, a small business should carry liability on their vehicles regardless of age. Liability claims may be so expensive that they ruin a business. In fact, many states require businesses and individuals to carry liability insurance to protect other people.

COST OF PROTECTION

Insurance premiums differ by coverage, type of business, and location. However, adequate coverage is a significant expense for most small businesses. One small fast food hamburger restaurant currently spends $2700 in premiums each year just for property and liability insurance (including $300,000 personal injury liability). A feed and seed ranch store is spending $3500 a year in premiums. To most small businesses this is a major expense; however, when you consider the protection it provides against loss, it is well worth the cost. Businesses face many losses which could easily bankrupt them.

LIFE INSURANCE

Many people feel that life insurance is for individuals and is not important to business firms. This is not true, particularly in the case of small business firms. If a general partner or sole proprietor dies, the form of ownership ceases to exist and the sale or transition usually results in some loss. Even if it is a corporation, the death of a principal officer often creates some problems and losses. In many partnerships, the firm may carry life insurance on the partners as a means of the other partners having the funds with which to buy out the partner in order to create a new partnership.

Some of the benefits derived from life insurance by a small business are:

1. Assures that immediate funds are available to meet taxes, debts, and other expenses.
2. Provides an income for the heirs of the small business person and not drain cash from the business.
3. Allows for a more equitable distribution of the property values to the heirs.
4. Enables the executor, administrator, or trustee to dispose of the business to best advantage if the family is not taking over.
5. Puts the heirs on a sound financial footing if they are assuming direction of the business.
6. Stabilizes the credit of the business.

7. Helps maintain good employee relations by removing uncertainties and hazards.[1]

It is not at all unusual for a person to build a very profitable business and then have it sold at less than it is worth at his or her death. When the business person dies, the estate must pay estate taxes. Often, the business person has considerable assets but not large sums of cash. In order to pay the estate taxes, the heirs often must sell the business to raise the cash. The time that is allowed to raise the cash is often not sufficient to get the best price for the business. Rush sales usually result in a low price.

There are all types of attachments that can be added to life insurance policies, such as a rider that provides for insurance premiums to be waived in case of disability of the person paying the premium. However, there are only three basic categories of life insurance policies: whole life, endowment, and term.

Whole Life

Whole life insurance insures an individual for the remainder of his or her life as long as premium payments are maintained. Usually, premium payments continue until the person dies or reaches 100 years of age. However, there are exceptions in that the person may pay the entire premium at one time or compact them into a limited time, such as 20 years. The amount of the premiums are based on the age when the policy is first taken out. An individual, at 25 years of age, would expect to pay premiums for many more years than a person 50 years of age. The younger the individual, the lower the cost of premiums. When the insured dies, the heirs are paid the face value of the policy.

Whole life insurance also has a cash or loan value. The policy holder may obtain cash or a loan on the policy after it has been in effect for a specified length of time, usually 3 years. The longer premiums are paid, the greater the cash or loan value. If the policy holder takes out a loan, the amount of the loan is subtracted from the face value if he or she dies before it is repaid. Often interest rates on policy loans are lower than the market rate. Many owners of small businesses have found insurance policy loans to be a cheap source of debt capital.

Endowment

Endowment insurance policies insure the individual for a specific period of time. If he or she dies during that period of time, the heirs are paid the face value of the policy. However, if the individual does not die, he or she is paid the

[1]*Business Life Insurance,* Small Business Administration, Management Aid No. 222, 1975.

face value of the policy, at the end of the specified period. Premiums are usually paid for the entire period of coverage. Although it is not common, the insured may also elect to pay one lump sum payment, or compact the premiums into a shorter period of time than the coverage.

Endowment insurance premiums are also based on the age of the insured when the policy is purchased and the time period of the policy. Endowment insurance also has a cash or loan value.

Term

Term life insurance insures an individual for a specific period of time and then terminates. The term policy may be for any length of time, but the most common period is 5 years. The insured pays premiums on a regular basis for 5 years and if he or she dies within the 5-year period, the insurance company pays the full face amount to the heirs. The cost of premiums are based on life expectancy for the individual's age during the 5-year period. Term life insurance does not have a cash or loan value.

Another type of term life insurance is decreasing term. This type of insurance is popular with homeowners. If they borrow a specific amount of money to purchase a home, say $30,000 for 25 years, then they take out a decreasing term insurance policy on the life of the main provider in the family. The term policy would be valued at $30,000 and decrease in the same proportion as the home loan over the 25-year period. Small business owners sometimes find decreasing term insurance very attractive to protect payment of their loans on land and buildings.

Term insurance is very attractive in terms of cost to young people since it is for a specific period of time, and cost is based on their age during this period. Young people who start a small business may find it appealing because it holds their cost of insurance down while they are getting started. Of course, term becomes less attractive as a person gets older.

COST OF LIFE INSURANCE

The cost of life insurance varies by type of insurance, company, age, and riders added to the policy. To illustrate the differences between types of insurance, one large insurance company charges the yearly premiums shown in Figure 14-3 for each $1000 of the face value of the policy for a person 25 years of age.

ADJUSTABLE LIFE

Adjustable life is a new type of policy that can vary between whole life and term. It allows the insured to (1) raise or lower the amount, (2) increase or decrease the premium, (3) lengthen or shorten the protection period, and (4)

TYPE OF INSURANCE (NO SPECIAL RIDERS)	YEARLY PREMIUM PER $1000 AT AGE 25
Whole life	$11.44
Endowment with maturity at age 65	20.00
5 year term	3.49
25 year decreasing term	2.51

Figure 14-3 Annual premiums for various types of insurance.

lengthen or shorten the premium payment period. For example, a higher face value could be put in when the insured is born and then changed to a lower amount when the insured graduates from college. It can be changed from whole life to cheaper term when the insured cannot afford the higher premiums but needs more coverage, and then switch back to whole life again while the insured is still young but can afford the higher premiums. If the insured were to get into a financial bind, the policy could be changed to the shortest term possible (which would mean the cheapest premium) and then changed back when the financial problems disappear. The insured avoids the cost of having several policies issued during his or her lifetime.

SHOPLIFTING

Authorities report that business crime in the United States is currently amounting to more than $40 billion each year. This amounts to about $175 for each man, woman, and child in the United States. Shoplifting accounts for a large part of this loss. Shoplifting is a major problem for retail stores. Department stores continually try to control shoplifting and still estimate they lose between 1 and 2 percent of their total sales to shoplifting. Small business retail firms that do not make a continuing effort to control shoplifting undoubtedly lose much more to shoplifters.

Shoplifting is not only a burden to the business firm but it is also a cost to every consumer. Losses due to shoplifting are a cost of business, and retail stores pass this cost on to their customers in the form of higher prices. In addition, they must pass on to the consumer the more than $10 billion per year they spend trying to control various types of theft. Many small businesses who close their doors each year report they were forced to do so as a result of employee and customer theft.

TYPES OF SHOPLIFTERS

There are several different types of shoplifters; in fact, most are amateurs rather than professionals. Some of the types of shoplifters are (1) juveniles, (2)

A gift shop in a museum store is taking steps to reduce a shoplifting problem.

housewives, (3) psychologically sick persons, (4) vagrants, (5) addicts, and (6) professionals.

Juveniles

Juveniles account for more than half of all shoplifting. Almost all juvenile shoplifting occurs, not because of need of the goods, but from dares or for "kicks." The problem has become so bad around large high schools that some merchants will not allow more than a few students in their store at a time.

Often, merchants are unsure about juvenile shoplifters. They know in order to reduce shoplifting, they must prosecute on a regular basis. Many are hesitant to prosecute youngsters. In addition, the small theft of a child may result in the loss of a good customer, the parent.

Housewives

Women comprise the largest number of adult shoplifters. Most of the women who are caught shoplifting are housewives. Most housewives shoplift on impulse and if caught early will stop before it becomes a regular pattern of behavior.

Psychologically Sick Persons

Some individuals shoplift for psychological reasons. The more common name for this group is "kleptomaniacs." The value of the goods is seldom any motivation for this group. Their motivation is the act of stealing. These individuals are in dire need of psychological therapy. If being caught results in their receiving psychiatric attention, the merchant has done them a service.

Vagrants

Vagrants and habitual drunkards shoplift because of a real need. They usually steal for food, drink, and clothing. This group is usually the easiest to detect because of appearance and clumsiness.

Drug Addicts

Narcotic addicts must have large sums of money daily to support their habit. Some of these individuals obtain money by shoplifting items and selling them for money. Of all the shoplifters, this group is usually the most dangerous for the merchant to apprehend.

Professionals

The professional engages in shoplifting strictly for the money obtained by "fencing" stolen goods. This individual is also the most adept at shoplifting and is usually difficult to detect. The professional shoplifter is also adept at picking the easiest stores from which to steal. As a result, the store owner who does not practice good shoplifting prevention techniques is more likely to be the target of the professional shoplifter than the store owner who does practice good prevention techniques.

The professional shoplifter may also be a member of a crime organization.

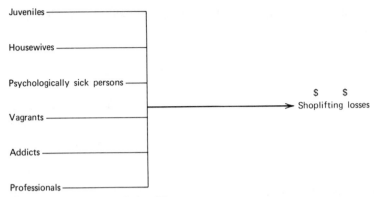

Figure 14-4   Types of shoplifters.

These shoplifters usually have a ready market for their stolen goods and, often, an organization that helps them out with bail and attorneys when they are arrested.

PREVENTION OF SHOPLIFTING

Often, merchants may have a serious shoplifting problem and not even know the problem exists. Consequently, one of the most important aspects of shoplifting control is to recognize it as a problem and also know the extent of the problem. This can best be achieved by adequate records and a good inventory control system. The merchant who keeps good records of sales, purchases, and inventory will recognize if merchandise is getting out of the store without anyone paying for it. By this method, the merchant is able to determine the extent of losses to shoplifting and employee theft.

There are many things a merchant can do to help prevent shoplifting, but the most effective is a sales force trained in shoplifting detection. Another major weapon for discouraging shoplifting is a consistent policy of prosecuting all shoplifters. Persons caught shoplifting usually have some type of "heart wrenching story" and claim it is their first time. Most of the time it is not true, and even if it is, letting them get by with it usually encourages them to do it again. Stores that have a reputation for apprehending and prosecuting shoplifters are usually shunned by professionals and, to some extent, by many amateurs.

Some other practices that can help reduce shoplifting losses are:

1. Post signs around the store saying that shoplifters are prosecuted by the store. One store posted the number of shoplifters it had caught and prosecuted as of that date and found it to be very effective.

2. Keep small expensive items in an enclosed display case and near where a clerk can see it at all times.
3. Have clerks keep a watchful eye on rest rooms and fitting rooms.
4. Keep unused checkout lanes closed.
5. If possible, post a guard at the exit door. Keep the number of exits as few as possible.
6. Have an adequate number of salespeople at all times. Part-time help can be valuable in rush periods.
7. Large convex mirrors placed around the store and two-way mirrors are good devices for reducing shoplifting.
8. Large stores often find that two-way radios, closed circuit television, and store detectives are helpful.

To inhibit the amateur shoplifter, a store owner may find that simple devices and techniques may be of help in reducing shoplifting. To illustrate, one of the authors assisted a small store that had an extremely bad shoplifting and employee theft problem. The store was in such bad shape financially that the author obtained an old home movie camera, installed a small red bulb in the front of it, wired the bulb so that it could be plugged into an electrical socket, mounted the camera in a prominent place, and placed a sign below it that said the store was electronically surveyed to prevent shoplifting. This simple device proved to be so effective in frightening amateur shoplifters that the night after the second day it was installed, someone fired a rifle shot through a door window into the camera.

One of the more effective means of preventing shoplifting is being used by many clothing stores. A 1 by 3 inch tag imbedded with a simple microwave transmitter the size of a pencil point is attached to the items of clothing. The tag can only be removed by the cashier with special shears. Anyone leaving the store without having the tag removed sets off an alarm from a hidden receiver. Cashiers must be very conscientious in removing the tags. One woman sued a clothing store when the clerk forgot to remove a tag and the alarm sounded as she left the store. She was detained by store personnel until the mistake was discovered.

One form of shoplifting is what is called "ticket switching." Some shoplifters change price tags or exchange them with a cheaper item. Some methods of preventing ticket switching are as follows:

1. Hide an extra price tag on the merchandise.
2. Place hard-to-break strings on tags.
3. Use gummed labels that tear apart when removed.
4. Use rubber stamps or machines to mark tags, do not use pencils.
5. Use special type staples when attaching price tags so clerks will know if a tag has been removed and restapled.

Merchants must be very careful in apprehending shoplifters so that they do not leave themselves open to lawsuits for false arrest. In some states they must wait until the shoplifter is out of the store to detain and have him or her arrested. The shoplifter may claim that he or she intended to pay for the merchandise and it is up to the merchant to prove otherwise. There have been cases where the item was concealed under the person's clothing and the individual maintained successfully in court that he or she was still going to pay for the item before leaving. Also, sometimes a shoplifter will have a confederate and pass the merchandise on to the other person before leaving the store. Fortunately, many states have adopted new legislation aimed at protecting the merchant from so much risk of suits for false arrest. These new laws often have "willful concealment" clauses which permits the merchant to move on the shoplifter before the shoplifter leaves the premises. Every small business person should check the law in his or her state. In addition, local police departments are usually able to provide valuable advice on shoplifting prevention and prosecution.

EMPLOYEE THEFT AND BURGLARY

Employee theft and burglary are major problems to most small businesses and are increasing each year.

EMPLOYEE THEFT

Everyone likes to think their employees are honest, particularly small business owners, because they are usually close to their employees. Unfortunately, employee theft is widespread and accounts for business losses in the billions of dollars each year. Most authorities claim that employee theft accounts for more losses than either shoplifting or burglary.

As was the case with shoplifting, many small business owners don't even know they have a problem with employee theft. For example, one small grocery store recorded an almost unbelievable theft record by having $59,000 cost of goods sold and sales of only $56,000 for one year. The owner was convinced employee theft was not a factor. It turned out that two nephews had pocketed several thousand dollars while working the cash registers during the year. In another case, an employer found that his trusted employee had been systematically pocketing $100 a week for several years. One of the most important factors in stopping employee theft is keeping adequate records of sales, purchases, and inventory to determine if a problem exists and, if it does, the extent of the problem.

Employee thefts may occur by several different methods. Many times employees will carry merchandise out of the business in pockets, in lunch boxes, or hidden somewhere on their person. Employees sometimes leave merchandise in trash boxes carried out of the business. They return at night and recover the merchandise.

One person found 14 watches in a box behind a large discount house when he was collecting boxes to store some of his personal belongings. When he returned them to the store they were completely unaware they were missing any watches. A restaurant owner found several top quality steaks wrapped in a plastic bag when searching the garbage for knives, forks, and spoons. Employee theft may also take the form of salespeople charging friends or accomplices lower prices or not charging for all the goods they purchase.

Some stores sell damaged goods to employees. Employees have been known to remove a part from a piece of merchandise, buy it at a greatly reduced price, and then restore the part when they get it home.

Cash thefts by employees also may occur in different ways. Clerks may not register all sales and pocket the cash. Some short-change customers and pocket the extra cash. This practice is particularly bad in that the business may also lose customers. Some employee theft occurs in the form of embezzlement through manipulation of accounting books and checks.

Most employee theft is done by people who would never think of committing any other type of crime and do not consider themselves to be dishonest. They rationalize their theft in various ways with the most common being the business is not paying them what they are really worth and it is a way of supplementing their salary. This is why some small business persons are completely taken by surprise when they discover an employee, who they thought was incapable of stealing, stealing from the business.

The best way to prevent employee theft is be aware that a problem exists. Good accounting records, good cash control procedures, and having a good inventory control system are the keys to controlling theft. Without these a small business can go bankrupt and never even know the primary reason was theft.

The following is a list of things a business should do to help prevent employee theft:

1. Let your employees know you expect honesty and will not tolerate thefts.
2. Inspect all employee packages leaving the premises.
3. Keep all doors, except customer exit doors, locked and make someone responsible for the key.
4. Keep trash from accumulating in the store and inspect it at *irregular* intervals to make sure no merchandise is going out of the store in this way.
5. Watch the loading-unloading area. Collusion between drivers and employees sometimes occurs. Spot check incoming merchandise to make sure you receive all of it. Do not let drivers load their own trucks from stock.

6. If at all possible, assign clerks to one register only. Check the register tape against the amount of cash at the end of the employee's time on the register. If trading stamps are given, check these against the tape and cash to spot missing stamps or cash.
7. Have your books audited regularly by a competent accountant.
8. Watch cashiers to make sure they are ringing up all sales and ringing them up at the correct price.
9. Above all, check out each employee hired in an attempt to determine his or her honesty and character.
10. Many of the devices used to detect shoplifting may also be used to identify employee theft, such as two-way mirrors, closed circuit television, and convex mirrors.
11. Have persons not known to the employees periodically buy an item in the business and have them watch to make sure the correct amount is rung up on the cash register.

Some firms use lie detectors and voice analyzers in order to attempt to spot and stop employee theft. Some persons question the use of these devices. They point out that they are not 100 percent accurate, are sometimes run by incompetent operators, have been used by unethical persons to learn personal matters such as sex habits, and are a crutch for the business that does not have adequate financial and inventory control systems. Others feel if they are used correctly, it is ethical to use them, and that they are an effective and valuable aid in controlling a serious problem, employee theft.

BURGLARY

Burglary is also a problem for small businesses. More than 80 percent of all burglaries are never solved. This is a crime that is committed mostly at night. Apprehension of burglars should be left to the police because the thief often can be a very dangerous person.

Although small business owners should never try to apprehend a burglar, they can perform many functions that will lessen the likelihood of loss due to a burglary. The following are some of the things they may do.

1. Install good locks and sturdy doors.
2. Install a burglar alarm system. Silent alarms direct to the police are very effective.
3. Maintain adequate indoor and outdoor lighting.
4. Use steel gratings over windows when possible.
5. Keep show window advertising in a manner where the inside of the store can still be seen from the outside.

6. Don't leave more cash than is absolutely necessary for starting the next day's business in the store. Take all other funds to bank night depositories.
7. Have a good safe, if change must be kept overnight in the store.
8. Change the locks on your doors on a periodic basis. Control the keys with records of what employees have what keys. If keys are lost, have the lock changed immediately.
9. Ask the local police to inspect your store to point out things you might change to protect your store from burglary.
10. Post signs that state that no money is kept on the premises overnight.
11. Check the possibility of an armored car service if large amounts of funds are used in the business.
12. Check the feasibility of using a guard dog. Even a pet dog that barks can often scare off a would-be burglar.

Burglar Alarm Systems

There are about eight basic systems used in burglar alarm systems. These are:

Electromechanical Electromechanical devices are simple alarm systems that rely on something activating an electrical circuit. For example, window and doors can be equipped so that a spring and plunger will function to make contact if they are opened, thereby setting off the alarm.

Pressure Pressure devices are often used under mats and carpeting. Any pressure on them closes the circuit and the alarm sounds.

Taut Wire These detectors consist of wire strung along a fence or wall so that anyone climbing them will disturb them. They are often used on roofs. Any change in the tension of the wire will set off the alarm.

Photoelectric Photoelectric devices use a beam of light that is transmitted for a distance to a receiver. If the beam is broken, the alarm is sounded. For best protection infrared or ultraviolet light is used.

Motion Detection Motion detection alarms may be either radio frequency or ultrasonic wave transmissions. The first method uses a set radio frequency which is transmitted to a receiver. Any disturbance in the wave patterns sets off the alarm.

Ultrasonic involves transmitting specific ultrasonic waves to a receiver. The alarm sounds when the waves are disturbed.

Capacitance Alarms These alarms are proximity alarms used to protect metal containers such as safes. They may also be used on door knobs. An electromagnetic field is set up on an ungrounded metal object by using two oscillator circuits which are set in balance. Whenever these circuits are disturbed, the alarm sounds.

Sonic Systems These alarms consist of microphones connected to a receiver which sets off the alarm when noise is detected in the area. They are usually set above normal noise to avoid false alarms.

Vibration Detectors Vibration alarms consist of special type microphones attached to an object. If the object is disturbed, the vibrations are picked up by the microphone and sent to the receiver which sounds the alarm.

Cost of System

Burglar alarm systems range from simple systems to very sophisticated systems. They may be alarms that are sounded at the business or they may be silent alarms that are activated only at a police station. Their cost may range from a few hundred dollars to several thousand dollars. Most small businesses should have some form of burglar alarm system. It can save them in insurance premiums and losses from burglary. The firm's resources and individual situation determine which system is best for them.

This chapter discussed many risks the small business firm faces in its operations; however, these risks should not discourage the prospective small business entrepreneur. Good management practices allow the small business owner to control these risks and operate a profitable business.

DISCUSSION QUESTIONS

1. Give an example of each of the following methods of controlling risk in a small business:
   (a) Avoid the risk,
   (b) Reduce the risk,
   (c) Assume the risk,
   (d) Shift the risk.
2. Why is liability insurance so important to small businesses, and what types of liability may a small business be protected against.

3. If a small business burns to the ground and the owner has 100 percent fire insurance coverage, is he completely covered against all types of loss? Explain.
4. What is surety insurance?
5. What is the basic difference between coverage of whole life, endowment, and term insurance?
6. What is the difference between cash and loan value of the three basic types of life insurance?
7. Identify the following shoplifters:
   (a) The most common,
   (b) The most common of adult women,
   (c) The one who needs therapy,
   (d) The easiest to detect,
   (e) The hardest to detect,
   (f) Usually, the most dangerous.
8. Give three ways that a drugstore could help prevent shoplifting.
9. What is ticket switching and how can it be discouraged?
10. Why is employee theft a problem in small businesses?

STUDENT PROJECT

Visit a small business that is a retail store and find out the following information:

1. What types of insurance does the business carry? Do you personally feel the insurance coverage is sufficient? Explain.
2. Is shoplifting a problem for the store?
3. What methods of shoplifting prevention does the store use?
4. Is employee theft and burglary a problem for the store?
5. Does the store do anything to prevent employee theft and burglary?
6. Could you make recommendations that would help the business prevent the different types of theft?

CASE A

THE PHARMACIST

Oscar Mulkey has just graduated from pharmacy school and he plans to open a neighborhood drugstore. His father is giving him a lot about a block from the local high school that he has owned for years. His uncle is loaning Oscar the money to open the business on a 15-year, no interest loan.

Oscar plans to operate the pharmacy department by himself and hire one full-time and two part-time clerks to wait on customers in the rest of the drugstore. He plans to carry the usual merchandise found in a drugstore, such as gifts, some photography equipment, toiletries for men and women, small appliances, tobacco products, and various drug items. He plans on offering credit and making deliveries to offset discount house competition.

Since you had a course in small business management in college, Oscar has asked you to help him plan certain phases of his business.

Questions

1. Give Oscar one example each of the four ways to control risk in his drugstore.
2. Should Oscar carry life insurance and what type would you recommend?
3. What other types of insurance, if any, should Oscar carry?
4. Do you feel shoplifting could be a problem for the new drugstore? If so, draw up a plan helping Oscar prevent shoplifting.
5. While he is still having his building designed, help Oscar prevent other types of theft.

CASE B

PRETTY PETS

Eric Oram is getting ready to open his new pet store which he has named Pretty Pets. The building is completed and all shelves, equipment, fish tanks, furniture, and inventory are being installed and stocked and the store should be ready for opening in about 10 days. Eric owns the store building and everything inside it. However, he does have a $75,000 Small Business Administration loan which has a first lien against his store and everything in it. Eric has hired one full-time employee and one part-time employee. Eric has been so busy he has not thought about insurance or theft until today.

He is stocking a wide range of tropical fish, some birds, hamsters, white mice, fish and pet medicine, pet toys, grooming products, fish and pet foods, and other miscellaneous products normally associated with a pet store. The building has a front and back door with large windows in the front.

The store will have a panel truck that will be used to pick up tropical fish at the local airport when they arrive and to pick up and deliver pets the store grooms. The part-time employee will drive the truck most of the time.

The layout of the store is shown below.

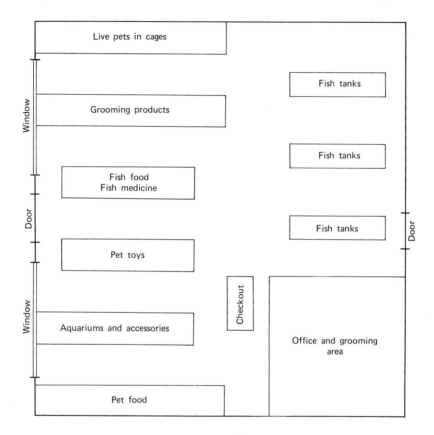

Questions

1. What kinds of insurance does Eric need? Explain.
2. Do you think Eric should expect shoplifting problems? Explain.
3. What can Eric do to minimize shoplifting?
4. What can Eric do to minimize employee theft?
5. What can Eric do to minimize the chances of burglary?

15

COMPUTERS IN THE SMALL BUSINESS

PREVIEW OF THIS CHAPTER

1. After reading this chapter, you will be aware of some of the advantages derived from utilization of a computer system.
2. You will be able to distinguish between a computer service center and a time-sharing center.
3. You should recognize some of the factors to be considered in making a feasibility study of computer usage in the small business.
4. You will be aware of some of the advantages and disadvantages of buying, leasing, or renting a computer.
5. You should be able to identify the components of the computer system.
6. After studying this chapter, you will have knowledge of the functions performed by the computer.
7. You will be aware that minicomputers and microcomputers can be used in a small business.
8. You will be aware of some of the many applications of computers in the small business.
9. You should be able to identify these key words:

Computer service center	Output
Time-sharing center	Flowchart
Turnaround time	Program
Feasibility study	Minicomputer
Input	Microcomputer
Processing Unit	

Small business owners may feel that computers are not feasible for their size of operation because of cost. In many instances, this analysis is correct. However, there are many applications of computer technology which are well within the scope of a small business. The use of computers in small business should not be categorically written off as too costly or inappropriate without first examining the potential of a computer for the firm.

New developments in computer technology are occurring almost daily. In fact, it could almost be said without exaggeration that changes are occurring so rapidly that what is new today is out of date tomorrow in computer technology. Small businesses are the beneficiaries of many of these computer technological advances. These new dimensions have resulted in smaller sized computers and computer applications which are feasible for the small business at an acceptable cost level.

ADVANTAGES OF COMPUTERS

In the small business, as with all businesses, all types of detailed information is essential for continuous monitoring of the company's performance. We have observed earlier that a common problem which may contribute to business failure is nonavailability of vital information, such as inadequate recordkeeping in the areas of inventory control and credit control. A specific purpose of electronic data processing (EDP) is to provide owner-managers with detailed, accurate information which will aid them in more efficiently managing their business.

Small businesses are deriving observable benefits from using small computers. Small computers provide them with the same type of operating and accounting information formerly available only to large computer users. Some illustrations are noted below.

1. A small automotive parts warehouse installed a computer system to handle inventory. In 6 months, the inventory was reduced by $30,000 with no loss in effective delivery of auto parts to dealers.
2. An accountant who prepares about 1500 tax returns annually switched from a computer service center costing $18,000 annually to his own microcomputer for a one-time cost of $11,000. The system paid for itself in one year.
3. A small marine construction company owner purchased a microcomputer. The first application of the system was to handle cash disbursements. He was able to complete one week's clerical work in one day.[1]

---

[1]Bill Langenes, "Personal Computers in Business: An Emerging Competitive Edge," *Apple* **1**, no. 2 (undated), pp. 4 and 5.

Some distinct advantages which may be anticipated as a result of computer usage normally include some or all of the following.

1. New types of information can be made available.
2. Accuracy of information is increased through reduction of processing errors.
3. Fewer employees are engaged in clerical operations.
4. Speed of processing data is increased which allows information to be made available on a more timely basis.
5. Internal control over the firm's operations are improved.
6. Customer service and customer relations are improved as a result of the ability to handle more customers with existing facilities.
7. Production is better scheduled.
8. There are less inventory requirements through more efficient purchasing procedures.
9. Preparation of required reports, such as those mandated by governmental agencies, is facilitated.
10. Overall efficiency of the firm's operations is increased.

DATA PROCESSING IN THE SMALL BUSINESS

In the small firm that does not have its own computer facility, information may be processed in a variety of ways. The most commonly used are manual methods or electronic accounting machines. The advantages of computers may be employed through computer service centers or time-sharing centers.

If the small business owner desires computer capability but cannot afford the cost of ownership or rent and the payroll cost of one or several computer personnel, a computer service center or a time-sharing center may prove to be a feasible alternative.

The small business manager may justify employing one of these alternatives on the basis of the increase in overall operational efficiency of the firm.

COMPUTER SERVICE CENTERS

Computer service centers may be particularly suited to the requirements of small businesses. Computer service centers are computer organizations whose main purpose is to computerize a part or all of a company's operations for a stated fee. Computer centers will analyze the information needs of the user and prepare computer programs needed to perform the information processing. Computer service centers convert the user's input data into computer accept-

Computer service centers process data of small businesses and provide owner-managers with current information on company operations.

able form, process the data, and generate output which is returned in the form of various reports needed by the owner. The computer center may supply the owner-manager with reports designed specifically for the business, such as processing information related to a single report of payroll or inventory control. Or, computer centers may provide more complete service by processing all paperwork included in specific phases of the business operation. In a small manufacturing plant, the entire processing of data from receiving the customer order to shipment and invoicing of the merchandise and updating accounts receivable may be handled by the computer center.

Some types of information that computer centers may process include cash receipts journals, check registers, payroll registers, sales journals, general ledgers, accounts receivable and accounts payable ledgers, income statements, balance sheets, inventory status reports, and aged-accounts receivables.

Fees charged by computer centers include the cost for designing a specific program for processing the firm's data and the charge for information processing. If the firm can use one of the standard or "canned" data processing programs, the costs are substantially less than for a custom designed program package. If a canned program is used, recordkeeping and reporting systems of the small business must be designed to conform to the standardized programming package. The cost for using a standardized package is based on the computer time required to generate the necessary reports.

Each firm must justify the use of computer centers according to the cost-benefit relationship. Rapidly growing companies may find it more economically efficient to use a computer center than to add more clerical personnel. Relatively stable companies may find that greater operations efficiency can be achieved through computer service centers.

TIME-SHARING CENTERS

Many small businesses can effectively use computer services for a specified number of hours a week or have specific operations that should be computerized. A method whereby small firms can utilize computers for a few hours each week is through a time-sharing center. Through time sharing, computer time is leased or rented from a computer firm, enabling the small company to use another firm's computer and pay for the time used.

Computer terminals, the input/output equipment, are placed in the user's company. Data are transmitted via the terminal to the central computer where information is processed and returned. "Turnaround time" refers to the time it takes for the data to be processed and returned to the user. Costs of time sharing include the rental fee for the computer terminal and the charges for the amount of computer time used.

The use of time sharing is justified on the basis of increased operating efficiency. Time sharing may be productive because current employees can be freed from routine tasks to concentrate their energies and time on more demanding activities. Some applications of time sharing are preparing payroll checks, sales analysis by line of merchandise, sales analysis of salespersons showing the percent of sales quotas reached, many types of cost analysis reports, purchase order preparation, accounts receivable followup letters, and inventory analysis.

The following checklist shown in Figure 15-1 offers some guidelines in the decision-making process of whether or not to use the services of the computer service center or a time-sharing arrangement in the small business.

If your total comes to 100 or more, you would probably benefit from using a computer service center or time-sharing center. Even if your total is less than 100, you might be able to benefit. But no simple test such as this can make the decision for you. Look into it carefully.

How many of these do you have each month?		Give yourself these points	Your points
Number of checks written	_____	10 points for each 100	_____
Number of employees (including salesmen)	_____	1 point per employee	_____
Number of customers' accounts receivable	_____	10 points for each 100	_____
Number of invoices you prepare	_____	10 points for each 100	_____
Number of purchases or purchase orders	_____	10 points for each 100	_____
Number of different items you carry in inventory	_____	10 points for each 1,000	_____
Do you have very large items in inventory, such as trucks?	_____	10 points if answer is yes	_____
Do you need help in keeping track of your inventory?	_____	10 points if answer is yes	_____
Total points for your business			_____

Figure 15-1 Do you need EDP? *Source*. John D. Caley, *Computers for Small Business*. Small Marketers Aid no. 149 (Washington, D.C.: Small Business Administration, 1977), p. 4.

Some factors to be considered in evaluating a computer center and a time-sharing center are listed below.

1. Type of service offered. Is turnaround time satisfactory for your needs?
2. Cost of services. Are rates competitive?
3. Experience of the personnel.
4. Type of equipment available.
5. Reputation.
6. Reliability.

IMPACT OF COMPUTER SERVICE CENTER AND TIME-SHARING CENTER ON PERSONNEL

The utilization of a computer service center or a time-sharing center should be evaluated also in terms of the impact on company personnel. As stressed in

Chapter 8, the introduction of any type of change should be considered with respect to its impact on the employees. Positive steps, noted earlier, should be taken to introduce the change to the new system in an orderly, well-planned approach to lessen the impact on employee morale and reduce the resistance to the new system.

FEASIBILITY OF COMPUTERS IN SMALL BUSINESS

Before a decision is reached to use or not use a computer in the small business, a comprehensive evaluation should be undertaken to include the overall objectives and the specific information requirements of the firm. The benefits to be derived from using the computer must be weighed against the costs of the system. A feasibility study is a survey of the current information requirements of the firm, what areas of the company would benefit the most from a computerized system, an evaluation of the possible computer systems that would meet the firm's requirements, the anticipated costs savings of the system, and a recommendation of the preferred system. Some specific concerns to be studied in the feasibility analysis would include the following:

1. Analysis of the current operations of the company, its goals, and objectives.
2. Determination of the desirability of using a computer to achieve information processing goals. Current operations may be revised which may eliminate the need for the computer.
3. Determination of the cost-benefit relationship of the computer. Will the costs be offset by the benefits?
4. Evaluation of the rental, purchase, and lease costs of the computer.
5. Determination of the effects of the system on the personnel.
6. Determination of the costs of training personnel to use the computer.
7. Determination of the specific output needs of the firm.
8. Determination of the weaknesses or inadequacies of the current information processing method.
9. Study of the desired overall information flow in the company.

METHODS OF COMPUTER ACQUISITION

From the foregoing, it is apparent that an essential aspect of the feasibility study involves determining the relative advantages and disadvantages of purchasing, leasing, or renting the computer system or some combination plan of the three.[2] Some factors used to evaluate the appropriate method of acquisition for the specific business are mentioned below.

RENTING

The most common method of computer acquisition is by renting from the computer manufacturer. This method does not require a large initial investment but is the most expensive if the equipment is needed for a period of 5 years or longer.

PURCHASING

This method is less expensive if the computer is to be kept for a longer period of time.

LEASING

When equipment is leased, the user and supplier determine the type of computer service needed. The supplier leases the equipment to the user for a stated time period.

COMBINATION

On some occasions, a combination plan involving the methods listed above may be used. It is a flexible plan but involves more recordkeeping.

The advantages and the disadvantages of each of the methods is summarized in Figure 15-2.

COMPONENTS OF THE COMPUTER

Data processing systems consist of two chief elements: computer hardware and computer software. Computer hardware consists of the physical computer equipment and any related devices, such as input terminals. Computer software is all the programs and routines used by the computer.

[2]John G. Burch, Felix R. Strater, and Gary Grudnitski, *Information Systems: Theory and Practice,* 2nd ed. (New York: Wiley, 1979), p. 322.

Figure 15-2 Advantages and disadvantages of the four methods of equipment acquisition. [*Source.* John G. Burch, Felix R. Strater, and Gary Grudnitski, *Information Systems: Theory and Practice,* 2nd ed. (New York: Wiley, 1979), p. 322.)]

METHODS	ADVANTAGES	DISADVANTAGES
Rent	1. Helpful to user who is uncertain as to proper equipment application. 2. Normally psychologically more acceptable to management. 3. High flexibility. 4. If an organization does not have past experience with computers, this may be the safest method. 5. Maintenance charges included in rental payments. 6. Allows a favorable working relationship with the vendor. 7. No long-term commitment. 8. Avoids technological obsolescence.	1. Over approximately five years, this is the most expensive method. 2. Rental payments increase by some factor less than one if usage exceeds a specified number of hours per month, assuming prime shift contract.
Purchase	1. The more mature users no longer need to depend on the security of renting. 2. Stabilization of computer industry means that changes in technology are not as disruptive as they once were. 3. Lower costs for an organization with a fairly stable growth pattern that will keep the equipment relatively longer than a growth company (i.e., not subject to operational obsolescence). 4. Investment credit offers certain tax advantages. 5. All other advantages accruing to ownership.	1. Organization has all the responsibilities and risk of ownership. 2. Usually if equipment is purchased, separate arrangements must be made for maintenance. 3. In a growth company there is a high probability of being locked into a computer configuration that fails to meet the changing requirements of the system. 4. Must pay taxes and insurance on equipment. 5. If the organization has better alternative investment opportunities, it would be more profitable for it to use the funds for these alternatives. 6. Ties up capital, thereby impinging upon cash flow. 7. Increased risk of technological obsolescence. 8. Low resale value.
Lease	1. In long run, can save 10–20 percent over the rental method. 2. Tax benefits. 3. Conservation of working capital because of low monthly payments. 4. Allows users to select their equipment, have it purchased, and then have it leased to them.	1. Lessee is obligated to pay a contracted charge if lease is terminated before end of lease period. 2. Little support and consulting service. 3. Lessee loses a great deal of negotiating leverage. 4. For maintenance, the lessee must depend upon a service contract from the vendor, not from the leasing company.
Combination	1. Optimizes the best advantages of other methods. 2. Flexible.	1. More recordkeeping. 2. Might have to deal with several vendors in case of breakdown.

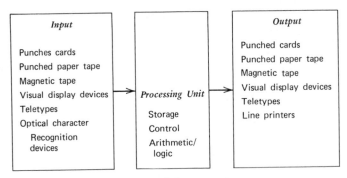

Figure 15-3 Components of the computer.

The major components of the computer hardware system include (1) input, (2) processing unit, and (3) output (see Fig. 15-3).

INPUT

Input refers to the data that are put into the computer to be processed. Input also refers to the various devices used to bring the data to be processed into a computer. The various input devices are shown in Figure 15-3.

PROCESSING UNIT

Input is transmitted to the central processing unit. The processing unit contains the storage, control, and arithmetic/logic sections of the computer. The computer processes the data according to the computer program which is the detailed set of instructions that outlines the specific operations the computer is to complete.

Batch processing is a widely used technique. Data are accumulated for a specific period of time and at the end of the time period are processed by data processing. Payroll data and inventory data are two examples where batch processing is commonly used.

On-line processing makes it possible to process data as they are collected through direct access to a central computer. This processing system is used when output is needed continuously, such as in a manufacturing operation.

Storage

The storage unit, the computer's filing system, holds data for current or future use. Computer programs are stored in the computer's memory bank in an orderly manner. This information can be rapidly retrieved when needed. It is necessary to store those data that contain information pertaining to the regular reports of the firm that must be compiled, such as the annual balance sheet and income statements.

Control

The control unit oversees all operations of the computer. It coordinates and controls the operations to ensure that the instructions contained in the computer program are properly carried out. The control unit gives the computer the capability to execute in an orderly manner the instructions contained in the program and to direct and coordinate the entering and removing of data from storage. The control unit also directs the arithmetic calculations of the computer and controls both the input and output of data.

Arithmetic/Logic Unit

The arithmetic/logic unit performs the arithmetic and logic function contained in the program at high rates of speed. The arithmetic section performs the basic math functions of addition, subtraction, multiplication, and division. The logic unit performs the decision-making function by making simple arithmetic comparisons of data.

OUTPUT

The final product is the data that have been processed, the computer output. Output must be processed and presented to the owner in an understandable and usable format. Output provides the computer user with the information needed for decision-making and action-taking. Output may be produced in many forms as shown in Figure 15-3.

COMPUTER OPERATIONS INVOLVED IN PRODUCING INFORMATION

While there are many sophisticated applications of the computer, the primary purpose in the small business is to increase the efficiency and effectiveness of recordkeeping and improve overall control of operations. The computer processes data through a step-by-step sequence of specific operations. This principle is the same as processing data manually; however, computers are capable of processing the data at much faster rates.

For example, when the payroll clerk manually prepares a payroll check, the clerk identifies the employee and determines how many hours the employee has worked during the pay period from a time card or sheet. Then the payroll clerk determines the employee's hourly wage, multiplies the number of hours worked by the hourly wage, and records the gross wage information in the company records. Any deductions, such as for withholding tax, social security, or insurance, are made from the gross wage. A check is then prepared for the net amount. This process is repeated for each employee check.

The computer performs the same sequence of activities according to the instructions it is given. To provide the computer with the necessary instructions of the specific activities to perform, a flowchart may be prepared. The flowchart is a pictorial or symbolic representation outlining the detailed sequence of steps necessary to complete a transaction.

From the flowchart, the computer program is written. The program contains the detailed instructions and the sequence of activities the computer is to perform to solve a problem. Specific operations performed by the computer which facilitate processing of raw data into usable information are briefly discussed below.

ORIGINATING

All information for data processing systems originate by being recorded on various business forms, called source documents. Source documents include sales orders, payroll time cards, and purchase order orders. These data must be recorded clearly in order to facilitate the recording step.

RECORDING AND VERIFYING

At this step, data are converted into a usable form for processing, such as being put on punched cards or tape or on magnetized tapes or disks. Accuracy of the data must be verified. A part of the recording process includes checking data to ensure correctness. One way of verifying data is for one person to check another's work.

CLASSIFYING AND CODING

After data are recorded in usable form and verified for accuracy, they have to be classified in specific categories which are meaningful to the user. Common forms of classification are grouping merchandise according to product line, sales data according to geographical territory, sales by type of customers, or sales by size of orders. Data must also be coded. Coding refers to the process of converting data to some symbolic form such as numeric, alphabetic, or number-alphabet (alphanumeric) combination.

SORTING

Sorting arranges data in a desired order oɪ logical sequence to facilitate information processing. For example, all transactions may be sorted into an account-number sequence, such as the sorting of all check transactions numerically. Inventory may be arranged by product code.

CALCULATING

The process of performing the arithmetic and/or logic operations is calculating. For example, computations may be performed to derive a customer's bill or an employee's pay. Calculating converts data into final form so that data may be summarized.

SUMMARIZING AND PREPARING REPORTS

Data are summarized to emphasize main points of interest. Summarizing presents the processed data in usable form for decision making by the owner.

COMMUNICATING

If an owner-manager is to be able to use the information, it must be presented clearly, concisely, and promptly either in report form or on a visual display device, such as a cathode ray tube (CRT). This enables the owner to use data effectively for decision making.

STORAGE AND RETRIEVAL

Data are stored so that retrieval is expedited. Retrieval is the operation of searching out and gaining access to the specific data desired. The computer makes rapid retrieval possible from the computer's memory bank.

MINICOMPUTERS AND MICROCOMPUTERS IN THE SMALL BUSINESS

Small scale computers that have application in the small business are minicomputers and microcomputers.

MINICOMPUTERS

Minicomputers are very small computer systems designed to handle general data processing functions. These computers perform the same arithmetic and logic functions and use a number of the same programs as larger computer systems. Their cost is low and they have many data processing applications, such as financial planning, accounts receivable, and accounts payable.

Potential users of minicomputers include small firms that process their data manually, use the services of an accounting firm, or use electromechanical posting and billing equipment.

MICROCOMPUTERS

One significant accomplishment in computers has been the advancing technology of integrated circuitry which has led to the development of microcomputers. Microcomputers are often referred to as a "computer on a chip." The miniature integrated circuitry containing the central processing of the microcomputer, called the microprocessor, is printed on a silicon chip. Microcomputers can be programmed to perform many of the functions of much larger systems, such as word processing, type setting, writing purchase orders, locating slow-moving inventory items, and alphabetically sorting a mailing list.

The development of microcomputers (also called personal computers) has reduced the size and cost of computers. Today, a small business owner can buy a microcomputer for a few hundred dollars that several years ago would have cost many thousands of dollars. These systems permit the small business owner to design a system according to the specific needs of the business. More dramatic changes are forecast for microcomputers as they become more powerful and less expensive.

COMPUTER APPLICATIONS IN THE SMALL FIRM

A wide range of basic computer applications exists for a small business. A problem or operation to which a computer system can be applied is a computer application. Four representative computer applications are described in the following paragraphs.

PAYROLL

Payroll preparation is one of the basic uses of the computer. It is frequently the first computer application because of the amount of computation required. Input data are time cards and output is the payroll check and the earnings statement which shows the amount of taxes and other deductions withheld.

ACCOUNTS RECEIVABLE

Accounts receivable is the amount owed the company by its customers. The computer application of accounts receivable is to provide current information to the owner to help keep the amount owed the company under control. Typical input data are invoices, payment vouchers, and credit memos indicating adjustments in customer accounts. Output data are individual customer records, monthly statements, and management reports, such as showing delinquent accounts and the length of time amounts have been owed by customers.

Accurate processing of accounts receivable is important because they represent money to the firm. Additionally, accuracy is important to keep customer goodwill since inaccurate records are a source of irritation to customers.

ACCOUNTS PAYABLE

Accounts payable is the amount owed other companies. Input data include the accounts payable records of the charges and payments and accounts payable checks. This application assists the owner-manager in determining correct charges before payment is authorized by comparing the purchase order and invoice. The accounts payable application aids the owner by being able to take advantage of any cash discounts. Additionally, the information provided helps to keep costs under control.

INVENTORY CONTROL

A large share of the firm's assets are tied up in inventory. Control over inventory enables the small business owner to protect the business against two key problems: not enough inventory resulting in lost sales or too much inventory resulting in excessive carrying costs and possibly spoilage and loss due to theft. Many types of computer technology, including punched cards, are available for use in inventory control which monitors changes made in inventory.

For example, a manufacturer using punched cards could follow this procedure. Items issued from inventory for use in production have punched cards attached which contain information relating to the individual items. These cards are removed when the parts are taken out of inventory by the inventory clerk who records the date and number of the project on which the part is to be used.

All cards are collected at the end of the workday and taken to data processing where they are keypunched and batch processed perhaps once a week. The output is an inventory control report showing all parts used listed by part number. This management report provided inventory control information such as which items need to be reordered and which are moving rapidly.

Many additional basic computer applications are possible, including those shown in the following listing.

Financial statement preparation
Monthly sales analysis
Credit screening
Cash reconciliation
Ratio analysis
Scheduling loan payments
Financial statement analysis
Lease or buy analysis
Lead time for purchasing
Make or buy decision
Quality control
Writing sales orders
Billing of customers
Production scheduling

When evaluating a computer system, the business user must recognize the specific needs of the firm. In a system, the user must determine what software is available as well as the expandability of the hardware system as the needs of the business justify additional operations.

DISCUSSION QUESTIONS

1. What is a computer service center?
2. Explain how a small business owner could use time sharing.
3. Why should the small business owner conduct a feasibility study before deciding whether to use a computer?
4. What are some advantages of leasing a computer?
5. What are the components of the hardware system?
6. Identify some of the functions performed by a computer.
7. What is a microcomputer?

STUDENT PROJECT

1. Read and summarize an article from a magazine or newspaper which describes how a computer is used in small business.
2. Interview a small business owner who uses a computer in the firm's operations and have him or her explain the reasons used to justify the computer in the firm.

CASE A
EDWARD'S AUTO PARTS

Edward's Auto Parts was founded 25 years ago by Edward Franks. From one building housing the warehouse and all sales operations, the firm has grown to a central warehouse and six sales outlets all located at strategic locations in the same city. Edward's Auto Parts carries an inventory of 30,000 different items and sells both wholesale and retail.

While the firm has grown, competition has also increased. More "do-it-yourself" mechanics account for a substantial part of the increased business.

Edward feels that to remain competitive he must continually search for more efficient methods of operation and provide better customer service.

One source of data Edward feels is essential is to maintain better recordkeeping. Specifically, Edward wants a record of each transaction affecting the 30,000 different items as it occurs. He feels this is mandated if the firm is to maintain its competitive stature.

Questions

1. What considerations should Edward analyze in respect to a computer system for the firm?
2. Would you recommend a computer system for the firm?

CASE B
ARDEN'S GIFT SHOPS (B)

Arden's Gift Shops (Part A, Chapter 12) maintains an extensive variety of gift item merchandise sold through a larger main gift shop and three smaller gift shops. Each retail gift shop sells a differing and wide range of products, typical of the souvenirs found at tourist attractions.

One of the main problems that the operation has encountered has been in control of inventory. All purchases of the thousands of items bought are recorded manually as are all withdrawals from inventory. This recording process is extremely time consuming.

Another problem has developed around the fact that the managers of the individual gift shops do not have formal, continuous means for providing input to the buyers concerning sales and inventory levels of specific merchandise. Neither is there a standard inventory as to the number of items or the quantity of a particular item to be stocked.

There is a warehouse in which inventory is stored. However, all purchases and disbursements are made through the main gift shop account rather than through a warehouse account.

A physical inventory is taken at the end of the firm's fiscal year, September 30. This inventory is completely manual and requires many hours to accomplish. Even though the firm is profitable, Mr. Arden is considering the feasibility of installing a computerized system to improve overall operational control and efficiency.

Questions

1. What are some points to consider in determining the feasibility of the computer for the firm?
2. What types of computer applications would be appropriate in this business?
3. Would you recommend a computer system for this gift shop operation?

SECTION
FIVE
MARKETING THE PRODUCT
OR SERVICE

16

MARKETING FOR THE SMALL BUSINESS

PREVIEW OF THIS CHAPTER

1. After reading this chapter, you will understand what the term "marketing" means.

2. You will be able to identify the eight functions of marketing.

3. You will understand what the marketing concept is.

4. You will be able to explain what is meant by the "marketing mix" of a firm.

5. You will understand why marketing policies are essential for a small firm.

6. You will comprehend the role and scope of marketing research for the small business.

7. You will be cognizant of the sequence of activities in the marketing research process.

8. You will be aware of the various sources of marketing research data available to the small businessman.

9. You will be able to distinguish between the observation, interview, and experimentation methods of collecting data.

10. You will understand the relationship of sampling to marketing research and learn a technique for conducting a sample survey.

11. You will be aware of the role of small business in international markets.

12. You will be able to explain these key words:

Marketing	Customer buying profile
Functions of marketing	Internal records
Marketing concept	External records
Marketing mix	Observation method
Marketing policies	Interview method
Marketing research	Experimentation method
Sample	Universe

For all small businesses, one of the major needs is to identify and develop the marketing strategy for its product lines or services. Unfortunately, many small business owner-managers believe that the only requirement for business success is to open the doors for business; then customers will flock in to buy their goods and services. However, the astute small business owner–manager realizes that marketing products or services in the dynamic, competitive business world is a very complex undertaking. In this chapter, we will explore some of the important components of the firm's marketing strategy that are beneficial to small business owners.

WHAT IS MARKETING

A strong marketing program is a fundamental requirement for the small business. Marketing refers to "the performance of business activities that direct the flow of goods and services from the producer to the consumer or user."[1] We see then that marketing is a process that encompasses a variety of business activities. To develop a vigorous marketing program for the small business requires that a number of marketing functions be performed. These marketing functions are described below.

SELLING

In addition to making sales, the selling activity includes determining who are potential customers of the firm and using a variety of sales promotion techniques to stimulate demands for goods and services.

BUYING

Success in selling is directly related to the buying function. Small business owners must anticipate the demands of customers. They must have the merchandise in stock or be able to secure it in a reasonable time.

TRANSPORTATION

Today's modern transportation systems make it possible for goods to be manufactured long distances from where they are finally sold. The small manufacturer may locate a factory in an area, taking advantage of any special attributes

[1]Committee on Definitions, *Marketing Definitions* (Chicago: American Marketing Association, 1960), p. 15.

of that area, and then ship goods to distant markets. Small retailers or wholesalers rely on transportation systems to make delivery of goods and services necessary for their business operations or to their customers.

STORAGE

Obviously, not all goods are sold at the time they are produced. To provide for customer convenience and to meet their demands, storage must be provided. Storage also makes many seasonal products available year round.

RISK BEARING

In storage, risk is involved. For example, producing too large a stock of goods may mean a manufacturer will end up with large quantities that cannot be sold. Natural disasters, fire, theft, and a change in customer preferences are all risks that must be borne. Some risks can be shifted through insurance coverage. The small business owner should realize that the only effective means of dealing with risk is sound judgment in making decisions.

STANDARDIZATION AND GRADING

Standardization sets the specifications of the manufactured product, such as quality or size in clothing. Grading is used to classify products that cannot be produced uniformly in color, weight, or size, such as oranges or eggs. Standardization and grading are important in that they facilitate the buying and selling functions and make it possible for the consumer to make comparisons.

FINANCING

Credit is an essential marketing function. The small retailer ordinarily does not have sufficient funds to pay cash for his merchandise shipments, so the wholesaler may grant him credit for a period of time until he has the funds. Likewise, the small businessman may grant credit to his customers, usually the 30-day charge account or a revolving charge plan.

MARKET INFORMATION

Up-to-date information about customers or trends in styles is mandatory if the goods or services that customers demand are to be available. More coverage will be given this topic later when we discuss "marketing research" (see Fig. 16-1).

Figure 16-1   The functions of marketing.

THE MARKETING CONCEPT

Currently, marketing programs in the small business embody the philosophy of the "marketing concept." The marketing concept stresses that the purposes of the business are first to identify the needs of potential customers and then to use all the resources of the firm to provide the goods and services that will satisfy the consumers' needs while producing a profit for the firm. To ensure that the small business stays on track to reach its goals, it is important to establish marketing policies. Policies represent the guidelines that provide the basis for decision making relative to the marketing programs. Decision making should be guided by policies as to how best to maximize customer satisfaction while earning a profit. Small businesses should incorporate these basic guidelines in planning their marketing program.

1. Identify potential changes taking place in the firm's market that could materially affect the business.
2. Identify the firm's target customers.
3. Maintain an inventory of merchandise that appeals to the customers' needs in terms of price, quality, and selection.
4. Integrate all marketing functions and related activities to maintain the company's profit position.

THE MARKETING MIX

To properly implement the firm's marketing program, the owner–manager must decide on the proper combination of marketing activities if the goals of consumer satisfaction and company profitability are to be realized. The four areas in the marketing program about which decisions must be made include (1) products and services, (2) promotion, (3) distribution, and (4) pricing. These four marketing areas are referred to as the firm's "marketing mix." The marketing mix is used to determine the emphasis the firm places on each of the four areas as it develops its overall marketing program to reach its target market. Each area of the marketing mix is briefly discussed below.

PRODUCTS AND SERVICES

The policy on products and services sets the product lines to be sold or manufactured (quality, style, variety, etc.) and the customer services to be offered to penetrate the market segment. The policy includes guidelines for determining whether to add or delete products or a service or complete services. The policy should also provide the guidelines for simplifying the product lines so that costs can be kept competitive.

The sale of products and services is facilitated when customers are aware of products and ask for them by name. Brand names of products or services make this possible.

A brand is "a name, term, sign, symbol, or design, or combination of them which is intended to identify the goods or services of one seller or group of sellers and to differentiate them from those of competitors."[2]

In establishing a product line, the small business owner should have a brand policy to determine if national brands or distributors' brands will be sold.

A manufacturer's brand, or national brand, is owned by a manufacturer and is advertised and sold in all, or nearly all, sections of the country. Private

[2]Committee on Definitions, *Marketing Definitions* (Chicago: American Marketing Association, 1960), pp. 9–10.

brands, or distributor's brands, are owned by a wholesaler or a retailer and are usually advertised and sold on a more limited geographical basis, such as regionally. However, the private brands of Sears, A&P, and Montgomery Ward are also sold nationwide. The primary advantage of selling private brands is that their selling price is lower than the national brands.

The decision of whether to stock and sell national or private brands is important for the owner, since brand names of products sold by small retailers are directly linked to the demand for the product. For the owner, the general guideline to follow should be to stock and sell the better-known national brands promoted by national firms that have a good reputation for the quality of their products. The small business owner should find that the well-known national brands offer several advantages. They usually sell faster, and the owner is able to capitalize on the popular brand names when advertising.

PROMOTION

Promotional strategy informs customers about the firm's products and services by means of advertising, personal selling, and sales promotion. Promotional policies set the guidelines for the advertising program: what types of media to use, how often to advertise, how much to spend.

Promotional strategy policies also should set guidelines for special sales or promotional events. (See Chapter 19.)

DISTRIBUTION

Manufacturers and wholesalers must decide how to distribute their products. The proper channel of distribution for their products must be identified and used. The channel of distribution is determined by whether the goods are consumer goods or industrial goods. Consumer goods are products that are bought by the ultimate consumer for personal or household use whereas industrial goods are goods used in making other products.

Figure 16-2 illustrates the alternate channels that the small manufacturer of consumer goods may use for the distribution of products. The channels available are:

1. Manufacturer—Consumer.
2. Manufacturer—Retailer—Consumer.
3. Manufacturer—Agents or Brokers—Retailer—Consumer.
4. Manufacturer—Wholesaler—Retailer—Consumer.
5. Manufacturer—Agents or Brokers—Wholesaler—Retailer—Consumer.

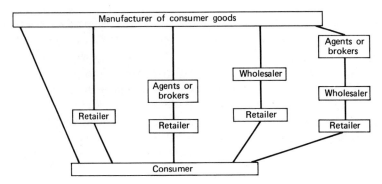

Figure 16-2 Channels of distribution for consumer goods.

Manufacturers of industrial goods have available four basic channels for distributing their products, as shown in Figure 16-3.

These four channels are:

1. Manufacturer—Industrial Users.
2. Manufacturer—Agent or Broker—Industrial Users.
3. Manufacturer—Industrial Distributor—Industrial Users.
4. Manufacturer—Agents or Brokers—Industrial Distributor—Industrial Users.

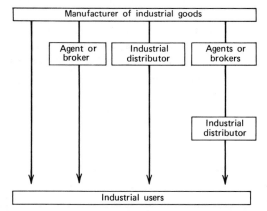

Figure 16-3 Channels of distribution of industrial goods.

PRICING

Customers must be charged a fair price for the products or services which will also produce a fair profit for the company. Pricing policies should give guidance in several areas. They must be set in accordance with the potential market to which the firm seeks to cater. Pricing should also reflect the pricing strategy of competitors. Other pricing decisions must include consideration of whether to adopt specific prices such as odd-even and whether to use varying prices or a one-price policy as well as quantity discounts.

MARKETING RESEARCH

One of the important requirements of small business owners is to have sufficient, accurate, and up-to-date information on which they can base their decisions concerning the firm's marketing program. For years, marketing research has been recognized by managers of large- and medium-sized firms as the basic tool for collecting the information needed for decision making. Small business owner-managers, however, have almost completely neglected the practical application of marketing research for their firms.

Because of limited financial resources and expertise, some small businessmen have relied on "hunch" or intuition rather than marketing research techniques in their efforts to maximize customer satisfaction. Managers offer products and services they "feel" will satisfy customers. Seldom do they receive feedback from customers as to the success of their efforts. As a result, many small business owners have instituted practices that are objectionable to customers. However, the small business owner may never realize that a problem exists.

Many small business owners feel they are doing an outstanding job. However, they are unaware of serious problems confronting them in the area of customer relations. To illustrate, an owner-manager of an automobile dealership in a relatively small community had a stated policy toward customers "to present a high-volume, low-price dealership that has a reputation for good service." However, a random survey of customers reported they felt his prices were too high. Two-thirds of the customers who had used his service department were dissatisfied with the service and indicated they would no longer do business with him.

It is also possible for the small firm to be located in an area where a large part of the population is unaware of its existence. For example, one small appliance store had been in business for six months in a town of 12,000 population. A random survey of people in the community indicated that 55 percent had never heard of the firm.

Cases such as these are common and stress the use and value that marketing research can have for the small firm. For example, in the second illustration above, the appliance store manager was able to use the information to advantage. By changing its advertising policy and installing adequate store signs, the firm was able to make people aware of its location and its products and services. As a result, its sales were substantially increased.

PURPOSES OF MARKETING RESEARCH

Marketing research is the process of collecting, recording, and analyzing data pertaining to the specific market to which the firm caters. These data include identifying (1) the market potential, such as size and income level of possible customers; (2) changes in consumer interests, tastes, and habits; (3) competitor's practices; and (4) economic trends in the market area.

Small business owners can benefit greatly by using marketing research techniques to survey customers' attitudes and opinions. Specifically, this marketing research survey can provide the small business owner with the means to accomplish the following.

1. To determine if the firm is obtaining a reasonable share of the market.
2. To decide if it is carrying a product brand best suited to the demands of its specific market.
3. To determine if the price range of the firm's merchandise is compatible with the demands of the market.
4. To uncover facets of the business that customers find objectionable.
5. To identify what customers like about the business so these features may be continued and reinforced.

Marketing research, then, enables the small business owner to base many decisions on facts, instead of relying on hunches.

THE MARKETING RESEARCH PROCESS

In order to make the marketing research survey more meaningful, the entire marketing research process should be carefully thought through. The framework of the marketing research process involves a sequence of activities as shown in Figure 16-4.

Defining the Problem

The initial step in the process is to determine if a problem exists. If a problem exists that requires the use of marketing research techniques, it is important

Figure 16-4   The marketing research process.

that it be correctly defined. Correct identification of the problem makes it possible to determine what issues are involved in the research, what type of information needs to be collected, and what types of alternative solutions are needed. This first step is especially critical, since the amount of time, effort, and money spent initially diagnosing the problem frequently results in substantial savings of time and money on the overall project.

Determining Relevant Information

Once the types of information that are needed are identified, it is possible to determine what data are already available from both internal company records and external sources. If the available information does not appear to be sufficient to provide answers to the problem, then the decision must be made as to what additional information must be collected.

Planning the Research Design

After identifying the additional information needed, we develop a research design in which the market researchers set out the plan that will enable them to gather the needed data. For example, if data are to be collected from interviews with customers, then a survey questionnaire must be designed and the number of people to be interviewed must be decided. In preparing the questionnaire, one must take care to see that it does not contain biased or prejudicial questions.

Conducting the Research

The first three steps in the marketing research process involve a considerable amount of planning. However, a properly planned marketing research project expedites the data collection. A number of methods may be used to collect the data, such as interviews, observations, or experimentation. The methods used are determined by the research design and the information already available.

Analysis of the Data

After the data are collected, it is helpful to present the information in a format that allows one to more easily analyze the results. For example, data can be tabulated and presented in table, chart, graphical or map format. From this analysis, the data should lead to the most constructive solution to the problem at hand.

After the marketing research process is completed and the data are available, the small business manager can take action. The quality of the decision should be strengthened since the manager now has much more support on which to base a decision than mere intuition or hunch or rule of thumb.

SOURCES OF ASSISTANCE FOR MARKETING RESEARCH

Small business owners will find that there are several sources of assistance available for collecting market research data. One possibility is to organize a marketing research effort using the firm's own personnel resources. However, for many small businesses, this alternative is not practical since they do not have personnel who possess these specialized skills. Another source of assistance may be provided by various trade associations and business suppliers. A third alternative is through Small Business Institute programs at colleges and universities, sponsored jointly by the Small Business Administration and the participating colleges and universities. In this program, college students undertake research projects in coordination with small business owners. A fourth alternative consists of hiring a professional marketing research consulting firm.

In deciding which alternative to choose, the small business owner-manager should weigh such factors as the following.

1. The availability in the firm of personnel with research expertise.
2. The availability of the required data.
3. The cost of the project and funds available in the firm.
4. The complexity and size of the problem to be studied.
5. The importance of the problem to the firm's survival and growth.

SOURCES OF MARKETING RESEARCH INFORMATION

Sources of marketing information may be collected from the internal records of the firm or from sources outside the firm.

Internal Records

The firm's own records are a valuable resource. For example, by analyzing the firm's sales records, it is possible to determine how many units of a product were sold, which units were the best sellers, whether the best sellers were in the high-priced lines or lower-priced lines, whether sales increased or decreased, the amount of the average purchase for which sales personnel had the best sales performance, what percentage of customers were drawn from different areas of the town or city, and which were the best sales months. Other valuable data that may be ascertained from the firm's own records include how much credit was granted, how much merchandise was returned, number and ages of employees, and other information.

External Sources

An extensive array of external sources is available to provide marketing research information. Much of this information is already in published form. It is feasible to identify only a small portion of the data sources available.

Government Sources   Federal, state, and local government agencies publish numerous resource materials that contain marketing information.

The federal government publications include those published by the U. S. Bureau of the Census. These census publications contain data on population, housing, agriculture, business manufacturers, and so forth.

Other government agencies, including the Small Business Administration, Departments of Labor and Commerce, and the Federal Reserve Board, publish reports and pamphlets covering many subject areas, many specifically directed to the small business. Government agencies also publish special reports relating to specific industries, trades, geographic areas, and marketing operations. Retail trade and wholesale trade are examples of subjects of these publications.

State and local governments also publish vast quantities of data pertaining to specific geographic areas, such as industrial growth.

Trade Associations   Trade associations often develop statistical and marketing research programs to assist their members. The Retail Merchants Association, the Automobile Dealers Association, and the National Association of Manufacturers are just three of the many trade associations that can supply data to members.

Local Business Sources   The chamber of commerce is often able to provide information on local business conditions at no cost to the firm. Likewise, the telephone company, utility companies, banks, and local newspapers can provide market research information.

Bureaus of Business Research at colleges or universities provide data covering a wide range of topics, such as employment, market surveys, and economic conditions of the area.

Other Sources Trade journals offer market research data. Such journals include *Chain Store Age, Oil and Gas Journal, Printer's Ink,* and *Advertising Age.*

Business magazines, such as *Business Week, U. S. News & World Report,* and *Fortune,* are also useful to the small business owner's market research program.

Business newspapers, such as the *Wall Street Journal,* are invaluable sources of marketing information and current business trends.

METHODS OF COLLECTING MARKET RESEARCH DATA

A number of methods can be employed to gather desired information. These include the observation, interview, and experimentation methods.

Observation Method

This technique involves direct observation for collecting marketing data. For example, observers may count the number of pedestrians or autos passing a site in order to determine if there is enough traffic to locate a store in that location. Automatic counting machines are also used for making traffic studies. An observer, perhaps posing as a customer or a store employee, may record the comments of customers regarding the store, layout, or service. In this way, positive steps could be taken to improve service or rearrange displays or add signs to make it easier for customers to complete their shopping.

The major disadvantage of the observation method is that only a limited number of observations are possible because of time and cost factors. Thus, this method is not feasible for collecting much of the information needed for decision making by the owner-manager.

Interview Method

The interview method is most widely used for gathering external information. A number of techniques are employed in asking for the desired information. Interviewers should be trained in order to handle the questioning skillfully.

Personal Interviews A major advantage of using personal interviews is the likelihood of getting a higher percentage of responses if individuals are asked face to face for their opinions. The disadvantage of this method is the high cost involved in collecting the data.

Store Interviews Customers may be asked a limited number of questions as they leave the store or at the point of sale, such as how often they shop in the

Interviewing shoppers is an important way of collecting market research data.

store, why they buy at this store, or why they purchased a specific product. While this is the simplest interview technique, questions must be short and data must be recorded easily so as not to irritate the customer.

Home Interviews   Although this method is most useful, it is also the most expensive. Interviews in the home make it possible to collect a broad range of data: consumer attitudes, socioeconomic status, size of family, size of home, and other personal data. The personal nature of the interview is a positive feature. However, the success of the method depends largely on the effectiveness of the interviewers. If they lack motivation or are not properly trained, they may record incorrect data, ask the wrong questions, or offend the consumer. There is also the disadvantage that some prospective interviewees may refuse to participate in the survey.

For the results of home interviews to provide valid information, a representative number of homes must be included since it is impossible to survey every home in an area. Marketing research depends, then, on "sampling." A sampling technique will be discussed later in this chapter that is practical for use by the small business owner.

Mail Surveys   Questionnaires mailed, along with a stamped return envelope, to consumers are another method of collecting information. Mail surveys are an inexpensive method of data collection but must be prepared carefully.

A low return rate has been a significant problem in the use of mail questionnaires. Frequently the percentage of return had been as low as 25 percent. However, most well-run surveys today get over 50 percent return and some get as much as 80 percent.[3]

To encourage responses, a premium may be offered the respondent who completes the questionnaire. Mail questionnaires should be easy to fill out with clear directions and they should be attractively designed.

Telephone Surveys   Telephone surveys are an inexpensive means for collecting data as compared to personal interviews since one interviewer can interview many respondents without having to travel. This technique requires interviewees to answer questions at once, thus providing faster feedback of results than does a mail questionnaire.

Among the disadvantages of telephone surveys are that interviewees can easily terminate the interview by merely hanging up. Furthermore, not all homes have telephones or listed numbers.

[3]Harper Boyd, Ralph Westfall, and Stanley Stasch, *Marketing Research,* 3rd ed. (Homewood, Ill.: Richard D. Irwin, Inc., 1977), pp. 127–128.

A Telephone Survey Technique   A practical method of conducting a telephone survey is outlined. This procedure has been used extensively by the authors, and the results have been very satisfactory.

Step 1.   The first stage is to determine the number of telephone exchanges in the trading area served by the firm.

Step 2.   The second step is to determine the total number of telephones in each exchange of the trade area. Information for steps 1 and 2 can be obtained with the assistance of telephone company personnel.

Step 3.   The third step involves selecting the telephone directory page numbers to be used to locate the actual telephone numbers to be dialed. If 100 telephone contacts are desired, and if there are four telephone exchanges in the firm's trading area, then 25 pages must be selected. Random numbers selected must fall within the maximum number of pages in the directory. To illustrate, the Austin, Texas, telephone directory has 547 pages of listing of residential phones. Random numbers must be between 1 and 547. A table of random numbers was used to generate the following 25 random numbers. These numbers specify the page numbers to be used for the telephone survey.

1. 345	6. 199	11. 117	16. 354	21. 514
2. 423	7. 048	12. 435	17. 139	22. 163
3. 062	8. 164	13. 322	18. 341	23. 481
4. 356	9. 174	14. 046	19. 014	24. 167
5. 279	10. 136	15. 202	20. 004	25. 085

Step 4.   On the pages selected, the first telephone number for each exchange prefix previously identified should be dialed. Thus, from each page, four numbers (one from each exchange) should be contacted. No business firms should be included in this survey. If a number is dialed and there is no answer, the next number with the same exchange prefix should be called until there is an answer for that prefix. If a selected page does not have any or all of the telephone exchanges, then either the next page can be used or the random numbers table can be used to select another page.

If there is more than one telephone exchange in the trade area, calls should be allocated according to the percentage of telephones in each exchange. This should account for the population density in the trade area. For example, suppose 100 people are to be called and there are two exchanges in the trade area and one exchange has 60 percent of the phones. Then, 60 percent of the calls should be made to that exchange and the remaining 40 percent to the second exchange.

Based on actual usage of this sampling technique, we find that the number of calls necessary to provide satisfactory results will range from 60 to 100, with 100 calls preferred.

Experimentation Method

The small business owner can use experimentation to gather some types of important market research data. Experimentation may take different forms. For example, the retailer may use different promotional strategies to determine which is more effective. Or, the store may experiment staying open longer hours to ascertain if sales sufficiently increase to justify the longer hours of operation. Another possibility for experimenting is the handling of different lines of merchandise to discover which has the greatest customer appeal. This method usually has limited application for gathering specific marketing data, and it can be costly and time consuming.

The small business owner-manager may use one or a combination of the above methods to collect data to fit his specific requirements.

SAMPLING

The total of every person or every household in a city or trade area that is to be surveyed is called the *universe*. However, it is not feasible, both in terms of time and money, to make a complete survey. Instead, marketing researchers rely on sampling. A sample is the part of the total population (the universe) that is included in the survey. If the sample is to provide valid data, it is mandatory that the people who are included in the sample be representative of the universe. The reason for this is that the results that are obtained from the sample are used to make generalizations about the total population.

A representative sample can be obtained by use of random sampling. A random sample is designed so that every person in the universe has an equal and known chance of being selected. To illustrate, if there are 2000 people living in the market area and a random sample of 100 is to be taken, then the chances of being included in the survey are 100 in 2000. Since the sampling process is random, with each person having an equal chance of being selected, those surveyed should be representative of a cross section of the area's total population. The sample results can then be used to draw conclusions about the characteristics of the total population.

Sampling Technique

The survey technique outlined below presents a method of obtaining as random a sample as possible within practical limitations. This technique has been designed to meet the specific needs of the small business owner.

1. Draw equally spaced horizontal and vertical lines on a map of the market area. Spacing of the lines should usually range from 1/4 to 1 inch depending on the size of the map. Usually more than 100 squares should result from the intersections of the lines. These resulting squares should then be numbered consecutively, eliminating all squares that are business districts and unoccupied land areas.
2. Determine the percentage of the market to be surveyed. While statistical methods may be used, a more realistic approach for small business firms is to take into consideration cost, time, and size of the market to arrive at a sample size on a judgment basis. For this type of sample, 100 households is often an optimum size sample. It is usually a large enough sample to provide sufficiently accurate data while not being too expensive and time consuming.
3. On small pieces of paper place numbers from one to the largest number appearing on the consecutively numbered map. From a table of random numbers or the slips of paper, select the numbered squares that are to be used in the sample, in a quantity equal to the size of the sample. Mark these areas on the numbered map.
4. The members of the research team should be "clean-cut" and courteous. The team should inform customers interviewed that the survey is being performed to measure customer opinion as part of the firm's continuing efforts to better serve the community.
5. A standardized pattern for selecting households to survey should be established—such as the first house in the selected area or the most northeastern house. If an interview cannot be conducted at this house—no one at home, refusal to answer the questions, and so on—the interviewer should then proceed to the next house until a survey has been performed in the randomly selected area.

Survey Questionnaire

The sample survey questionnaire shown in Figure 16-5 has been used successfully in making surveys of men's clothing stores. However, it can easily be modified to meet the survey requirements for a wide range of business firms.

Analysis of the Survey Data

From the data collected, it is possible to develop a "Customer Buying Profile," which measures the firm's potential share of the market, suitability of brands to the market, and acceptability of product prices.

To determine the firm's potential share of the market, each individual survey must be analyzed on a judgment basis to measure what part of the customer's

Customer Buying Profile

Age of all males in household over 16 years _____

Answer the following for all purchases of apparel made by this household for males over 16 years of age in the *average year*. FILL IN THE NUMBER bought in each price range.

1. Suits $50-80 ___, $80-100 ___, $100-120 ___, $120-150 ____, Other ____,
                                 None ___.
   Where purchased? _____
   Why there? _____
   What brand? _____

2. Sport Coats $20-30 ___, $30-40 ___, $40-50 ___, $50-60 ___,
                 $60-70 ___, $70-80 ___, Other ___, None ___.
   Where purchased? _____
   Why there? _____
   What brand? _____

3. Slacks $5-10 ___, $10-15 ___, $15-20 ___, $20-25 ___, $25-30 ___,
                 $30-35 ___, $35-40 ___, Other ___, None ___.
   Where purchased? _____
   Why there? _____
   What brand? _____

4. Shirts $5-7 ___, $7-10 ___, $10-12 ___, $12-15 ___, $15-20 ___, Other ___, None ___.
   Where purchased? _____
   Why there? _____
   What brand? _____

5. Shoes $10-20 ___, $20-25 ___, $25-30 ___, $30-35 ___, $35-40 ___,
                 $40-50 ___, Other ___, None ___.
   Where purchased? _____
   Why there? _____
   What brand? _____

6. How much do you spend on socks, undergarments, ties, belts, and hats?
   $1-10 ___, $10-20 ___, $30-40 ___, $40-50 ___, Other ___.

Check the three most important reasons in order of importance for your selection of a clothing store.

Size of store: large _____   Quality _____   Convenience _____
                small _____   (time factor)

                                              Merchandise
Price _____   Parking space _____   selection _____

Other _____(fill in)

Figure 16-5 Customer survey.

total yearly expenditure for each item the firm should be receiving. The total of all item expenditure estimates is a measure of how much the customer would be expected to spend in the store after considering his brand preference, price preference, and reason for purchasing at different stores. A total of all dollar estimates on all the surveys divided by the total number of surveys yields an average per household expenditure the firm should expect to receive. This average expenditure per household multiplied by the total number of households in the market area will produce the total amount of sales potential for the firm. This figure should then be compared to total yearly sales to determine if there is an excessive deviation. If the difference is large, the causes should be uncovered.

The profile also measures the distribution of consumer preference for different product brands and price ranges in the firm's market area. An analysis of the firm's competition and market helps determine which brands and price lines offer the greatest sales potential for the store.

INTERNATIONAL MARKETING AND THE SMALL BUSINESS FIRM

The growth of worldwide markets has given rise to opportunities for the small business owner to expand operations into international markets. While exporting is the major area open to the small business owner, there are opportunities available in foreign countries to establish a small business. If a small business venture is planned in a foreign country, it must conform to the laws and the special regulations of the host country as well as its social customs.

Of course, many small businesses sell imported merchandise. Usually, the small business owner purchases imported merchandise through an importer or a wholesaler. Novelty items, electronic equipment, and specialty foods are representative of imported merchandise. Some owner-managers who live close to the Mexican or Canadian border travel to that country, buy merchandise, and transport it back for sale in their businesses.

Exporting represents an important source for business expansion since developing international markets show much economic potential. Exporters, usually producers of raw materials or manufacturers of finished goods, ordinarily choose indirect exporters to distribute their goods. Indirect export firms or agencies are professional export companies who distribute goods in foreign markets. Export firms buy the merchandise from the small business and sell it in the foreign markets. Export agencies, however, act as middlemen. They represent the small business owner in the foreign market and charge a commission for their selling efforts.

It has frequently been assumed that a firm must be large to export its goods.

However, a recent survey of manufacturers revealed that small firms (those with 250 or fewer employees) had greater export sales than did firms with over 250 employees. Exporting has distinct advantages. One, the firm can increase its profits by expanding its sales territory. Two, the diversity of markets served may help to reduce the impact of an economic downturn in one country if the economy is on the upswing in other markets. Three, there is a favorable tax advantage allowed exporters by the U. S. government. Four, since many products have a seasonal domestic market, it may be possible to sell merchandise to other countries in the off-season.

Some small business owners have been reluctant to enter world markets. Reasons for this are complications that are encountered in international markets, such as:

1. Different market requirements that may require different product design, dimensions, packaging, or other standards.
2. Uncertainties and differences in laws, regulations, and business practices.
3. Differences in marketing distribution methods.
4. Unfamiliarity with local competition.
5. Difficulties and cost of maintaining effective communication, especially in foreign languages.
6. Special considerations governing payments, credit, currency relationships, duties, product warranties, and so on.
7. Physical and procedural problems and costs associated with export handling, such as packing and traffic.[4]

When evaluating the export market, the small business owner should conduct market research. This research will suggest the potential demand for the goods and also the potential market share. In effect, this market research provides basically the same data as does market research conducted in domestic markets.

Specifically, the small business owner will need to obtain data on the following types of questions.

1. How large is the market for my type of product?
2. What types of customers are in the market?
3. Where are the customers located? (urban or rural)
4. How much of my type of product is being sold in the foreign market?
5. What share of this market is each of my competitors getting?
6. What are the selling prices for my competitors' merchandise?
7. What kind and how much advertising do my competitors offer?

[4]Eugene Lang, "Venturing Into the World," *Enterprise*, September 1978, p. 13.

8. How do my products compare with competitors in terms of style, price, advertising, and services?
9. Is the country an agricultural or an industrial nation?
10. What is the income level of the population?
11. What is the educational level of the population?
12. Are products made in the United States allowed in the country?

In evaluating the export decision, the small business manager should consider the "levels of exporting" to determine the firm's export plan. The characteristics of the four levels of exporting are outlined below.

Levels of Exporting

Level 1: Export of surplus

The firm is interested only in overseas sales of surplus products or is without resources to fill overseas orders for most products on an ongoing basis.
An Observation: If you have some available resources to devote to exporting, there is much to gain by selling in an area similar to your domestic market.

Level 2: Export marketing

The firm actively solicits overseas sales of existing products and is willing to make limited modifications in its products and marketing procedures to accommodate the requirements of overseas buyers.
Recommendation for Management Action: If you can see overseas sales as a regular part of your future, move to this level as quickly as possible.

Level 3: Overseas market development

The firm makes major modifications in products for export and in marketing practices in order to be better able to reach buyers in other countries.
An Observation: One-half of exported products require little modification; about one out of three requires moderate modification; and a few, major changes.

Level 4: Technology development   The firm develops new products for
                                   existing or new overseas markets.[5]

   The checklist provided below should enable you to evaluate the potential of
exporting for your company.

Checklist for Evaluating Exporting

1. What domestic forces are likely to make exporting more attractive in the
   future?
2. At what level of commitment can the company most profitably enter exporting?
3. If exporting is undertaken, what strains would be created on the company,
   and how can they be met?
4. What domestic sales and profit opportunities exist? What costs, risks, and
   returns can be expected?
5. What features of the product currently being sold in the United States
   provide a competitive edge in overseas markets?
6. Is the market being sought likely to be a country or a group of buyers?
7. What kind of buyers is this product likely to appeal to? How can they be
   identified?
8. What are the consequences of product modification for the company?[6]

SOURCES OF ASSISTANCE FOR THE SMALL EXPORTER

Assistance is available from the major export service organizations discussed
below.

Bureau of International Commerce, U. S. Department of Commerce

The Bureau of International Commerce, which is specifically responsible for
promoting overseas trade, helps small businesses to:

1. Find overseas buyers and learn about specific, current opportunities for
   selling, exhibiting, and promoting their products abroad.

[5]*Export Marketing for Smaller Firms*, 4th ed. (Washington, D.C.: Small Business Administration,
1979), p. 8.
[6]*Export Marketing for Smaller Firms*, 4th ed. (Washington, D.C.: Small Business Administration
1979), p. 9.

2. Keep abreast of important marketing, economic, government, and other developments abroad.
3. Exhibit their products overseas and meet foreign buyers through sponsorship of trade missions, trade exhibitions, trade fair exhibits, and other specialized events.

Bureau of East-West Trade

Organized in 1972, the Bureau of East-West Trade assists businesspersons who are doing or desire to do business with Eastern European countries or the People's Republic of China. This agency provides information on contracts, negotiating tactics likely to be used, possible contract clauses, and alternate financing arrangements.

Department of Commerce

The Department of Commerce in Washington, D.C., or any of its 43 field offices provide personal counseling services. The department's personnel can help the owner-manager plan a business trip abroad if he or she wishes to evaluate an overseas market personally or can give him or her specific data about a country's market potential for the products of his or her firm.

International Banks

Banks with international operations can provide valuable services to exporters, such as to:

- Assist in locating new offshore markets.
- Develop data on the business climate in particular countries.
- Match sellers with overseas buyers.
- Introduce clients to overseas banking and trade contacts.
- Advise on current developments, new regulations, or changing restrictions that might affect trading relationships.
- Investigate credit backgrounds of foreign companies.
- Provide advice on financial aspects of export transactions.
- Offer export-import financing.
- Furnish assistance with documents, letters of credit, draft collections, and foreign exchange.
- Arrange for export sales insurance.[7]

[7]"Exporting," *Small Business Reporter*, Bank of America, 1974, p. 7.

Foreign Freight Forwarder

Foreign freight forwarders provide services to exporters of moving goods into overseas markets. Some specific functions of the freight forwarders are to:

- Provide routing and scheduling information.
- Book ocean cargo or air freight space.
- Quote rates and related charges in advance.
- Advise on consular and licensing requirements.
- Prepare all necessary shipping documentation.
- Handle shipping insurance.
- Assure suitable packing of products.
- Provide information on marking and labeling requirements.
- Arrange for warehouse storage.
- Make complete arrangements for smooth, safe delivery of goods to overseas buyer.[8]

Additional Sources of Assistance

Some additional sources of assistance for the exporter are available from the following sources.

Research facilities, such as the World Trade Library in San Francisco, are a source of wide-ranging material on all aspects of exporting and provide an excellent point of departure for initial research.

Industry trade organizations to which a firm belongs may provide valuable information about existing and potential overseas markets for the specific type of product handled. Trade associations sometimes sponsor export expansion drives, and **trade publications** keep abreast of changing world trade conditions affecting their particular commodity.

Local chambers of commerce occasionally sponsor export seminars, trade shows, and other special programs. The **U.S. Chamber of Commerce** and many

foreign chambers of commerce provide services and marketing information designed to promote two-way trade.

Some exporters have found valuable export data through their **state departments of commerce and economic development, large port authorities,** and other active **official trade development agencies.**

Foreign consulates can often provide helpful information on receptive market areas.

International **shippers** and world **air freight carriers** can also furnish excellent assistance.

Export management companies who specialize in specified products and overseas markets can be located through the assistance of the Department of Com-

[8]"Exporting," *Small Business Reporter,* Bank of America, 1974, p. 7.

merce. The EMC specialist can provide information regarding the product's overseas market potential.

International consulting firms or **international marketing research specialists** may be retained to determine the exact potential for a product. Although the costs for their services may run high, they supply unbiased assessments of both markets and products.

Source: "Exporting," *Small Business Reporter*, Bank of America, 1974, p. 8.

DISCUSSION QUESTIONS

1. What is the correct definition of marketing for the small business owner?
2. Briefly explain each of the functions of marketing.
3. What is the "marketing concept"?
4. What is the "marketing mix"? What are the elements that make up the marketing mix?
5. Why should a firm have marketing policies? What are some examples of marketing policies?
6. What is marketing research?
7. What are the purposes of marketing research?
8. List the steps in the marketing research process.
9. Identify three sources of aid for the small business owner in conducting marketing research.
10. List different sources where the small business owner can obtain marketing research information.
11. What is the difference between the observation method and experimentation method of collecting marketing research data?
12. Identify the different types of interviews that may be used to collect marketing research information.
13. What is the difference between a sample and a universe?
14. Discuss the role of the small business in international marketing.

STUDENT PROJECT

Use the customer survey in Figure 16-5 and interview several people. Develop a "Customer Buying Profile" for a store.

CASE A

HOUSE'S JEWELRY STORE (B)

One of the concerns of Mr. House was to determine the image his store projected in the community as well as the share of the market he obtained.

In order to accomplish this task, he employed two students from the state university in the city to design and conduct a market survey.

A questionnaire was designed and a telephone survey of 100 people was conducted. Every twentieth name in the local phone book was called, and, if there was no answer, the next number was called.

The questionnaire followed the pattern of questions below.

1. My name is (interviewer's name) . We are conducting a survey on jewelry stores. Will you please tell me which store you would go to in order to buy jewelry? (name of store)
2. Why do you prefer (name of store) ?
3. On a scale of one to five (with one the most important and five the least important) how would you rate these items for (name of store) ?

   1. Convenience (2.7).
   2. Extra services provided (gift wrapping, layaway, credit) (2.9).
   3. Quality of merchandise (1.5).
   4. Price (1.8).
   5. Selection (1.9).
   6. Expertise of sales staff (1.8).
   7. Watch repair work (1.9).

Seventy-six percent of those surveyed were women and 24 percent men. Of those responding, 41 percent shopped at House's Jewelry, 31 percent shopped at the other local jewelry store, and 28 percent shopped out of town.

The numbers in parentheses above are the average score for the responses to each question. The lower the average, the more important the item.

Questions

1. Evaluate this market research technique (telephone interview).
2. Are there additional questions that should be asked to assist Mr. House in obtaining the information he needs?
3. What are some other techniques that might have been used to develop the same or additional information?
4. Do you see any errors in the research method used?

CASE C

CLIF'S APPAREL SHOP (C)

Clif's clothing store has become very popular and one of the leading stores in the community. However, Clif recognizes that it is dangerous to become too complacent in the highly competitive business that he is in. He wants to retain his competitive position and also maintain growth and profits. As a result, Clif reads a great deal about ways to improve his business. Recently, he attended a one-day workshop presented by representatives of the Small Business Administration. A part of the afternoon session, which lasted from 1 to 2 P.M., centered on the topic of *Marketing Research for the Small Business*. Clif was particularly enthusiastic about the ideas presented in this session. After returning to his shop, he wondered if it would be beneficial to his firm to conduct a survey of his customers.

Place yourself in the role of an adviser to Clif and assist him in making a decision.

Questions

1. What would be the purposes of a marketing research survey for his firm?
2. What steps would be involved in making a survey?
3. What possible sources may Clif use to collect data?
4. What internal and external sources of information are available to Clif?
5. What methods could Clif use to collect data?
6. Explain the sampling technique that Clif could use to conduct the customer survey.
7. What use could Clif make of the "Customer Buying Profile"?

17

PRICING

PREVIEW OF THIS CHAPTER

1. In this chapter, you will learn why and how a small business promotes a price image to customers.

2. You will discover the relationship between price and volume of business.

3. You will find that there are other factors that can offset price.

4. You will learn that retail establishments use one or more of these methods of setting price—markup on cost, markup as a percentage of selling price, suggested retail price, follow-the-market pricing, competitive pricing, and pricing for clearance.

5. You will understand how manufacturers set their price using direct labor, raw materials, manufacturing overhead, and nonmanufacturing overhead costs, plus a margin for profit.

6. You will discover that wholesalers add all their costs to their cost of goods plus a profit to set their price.

7. If you ever thought of starting a service firm, you will be interested to know that they usually set their price by charging an hourly fee plus list price for parts.

8. You will understand why bidding is a difficult pricing activity for small business firms.

9. You will discover how a small business can use a bid, cost, variance system to measure profit on each job, set bidding prices, and see how far from the estimates its actual costs are.

10. You will be able to understand these key words:

Price	Convenience
Price image	Markup
Discount prices	Standard markup
Volume of business	Flexible markup
Customer services	Suggested retail price
Selection	Follow-the-market pricing

Competitive pricing   Bidding
Pricing for clearance   Bid, cost, variance system

Pricing of products and services is one of the more important decisions a small business owner-manager must make. Prices that are established set the firm's price image to the consuming public and to a large extent determine the volume of business the firm receives. Various types of small business firms have different pricing practices.

PRICE IMAGE

Any small business firm must determine what segment of the market the business is going to operate in. It must then determine who its customers are (demographics, etc. that describe customers) and what they want. This establishes the image the firm must present to its customers. The firm should never do anything to damage this image. Its advertising, pricing, and so on, should always be pointed toward maintaining this image.

To a great extent, what the customer perceives as reality is more important to the small business than what reality is. Most customers are unable to judge accurately the quality of most products they purchase. Consequently, what they perceive as quality in products is what is important to the small business. For example, aspirin is a chemical compound that must be marketed in a certain state of purity to meet federal government standards. Consequently, all brands of aspirin tablets are, for all purposes, the same. If customers realized this, they would probably purchase the lowest priced aspirin they could find. However, the largest selling aspirin for many years is also one of the highest priced aspirins. It would seem customers of this product perceive the brand to have a higher quality, which is not a reality. Advertising tends to continue this false perception of the product.

It is possible for a small business to build in its customers' minds a perception that may or may not be reality. For example, a small drive-in grocery must maintain higher prices than the supermarket. It is impossible for it to be price competitive. By offering items whose price the customer is familiar with (bread, milk, etc.) at competitive prices it can somewhat build an image in many customers' minds that its prices are not as high as they really are. The customer still realizes there is some difference but thinks there is a narrower gap than there really is. An automobile parts house can do the same thing. It can offer items that the customers buy more often (spark plugs, oil filters, oil, etc.) at cost or slightly above cost. When customers see that prices on these items are competitive or below the discount house price, they tend to perceive the price image of the firm in the same light. The firm can have the same price markup or slightly higher on other products and the customer will tend to see them as low prices. For instance, do you know, even within 50 cents, the price of a master cylinder repair kit for your car? This image building may not work for all customers, but it does for a large part of them.

Some of the images a small business actively tries to promote with prices are discount prices, high quality products, or exclusiveness.

DISCOUNT PRICES

It would be rare, if at all possible, to find a business that intentionally attempts to represent to the public that it handles low-quality goods. However, many firms attempt to convey to the public the idea that they offer quality products at discount prices. The discount house is an outstanding example. Discount houses attempt to maintain a pricing policy that holds prices at a low level in order to create an image of offering discount prices to the consumer. Most

A store that promotes a discount price image.

small businesses that stress discount prices are attempting to offer a low markup in order to build their volume of business.

Many manufacturers also attempt to build a price image on their products. Often, they strive to convince the consumer that their product is of good quality and offered at "popular" prices. For instance, Black and Decker, a manufacturer of tools, has long maintained a reputation of quality for its line of tools. In recent years, it has used this image, along with low price, to achieve an image of good quality at low prices. By creating this image, the company is obviously attempting to use price as a means of increasing sales of its products.

HIGH QUALITY

In direct contrast to the discount image is the firm that attempts to create an image of high quality and uses pricing decisions to reinforce this image. These small business retailers, manufacturers, and service firms are relying more on higher per-unit profit than on volume. In fact, some firms use price to establish an image of high quality even when the quality is not high. In addition, some

This store portrays the same image as the products it sells: top-quality antiques.

firms achieve high volume because of their higher price (this is the exception rather than the rule). To illustrate, the manufacturer of a perfumed shaving lotion had the option of offering its product at a low price because of the basic cost of producing the product. The final decision involved a choice between \$.50 a bottle and over \$3.00 a bottle. They selected the higher price in an attempt to establish a high quality image. A large part of the per-unit cost of the aftershave was added on in the form of expensive packaging and advertising. This firm enjoyed a large volume of sales, probably many times higher than if they had decided on the lower selling price.

EXCLUSIVENESS

Exclusive stores often try to maintain a high price image to promote the idea of exclusiveness (high quality usually accompanies the exclusive image in the mind of the customer). These firms are attempting to stress per-unit profit rather than volume of sales. To illustrate, high fashion designers often price their creations in terms of hundreds and thousands of dollars. Their customers buy their creations because of the image of exclusiveness. Even though other firms copy their designs and reproduce it in the same, equal, or even better cloth, the customer of the high-fashion designer will still pay many times more for the original. Another example is Neiman-Marcus (a Dallas-based exclusive retail store), which uses its annual catalog offering expensive items such as his-and-her airplanes to build its image of exclusiveness.

PRICE VERSUS VOLUME

As a general principle, price does not move with volume. Most often, as price increases on a product, volume tends to decrease. Conversely, as price decreases, volume tends to increase. The shaving lotion example, mentioned earlier, is one of the rare exceptions. (See Fig. 17-1).

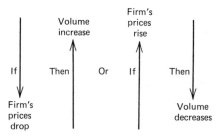

Figure 17-1 Inverse changes in price and volume of goods sold.

As a result, most small business firms are faced with the decision to (1) offer low prices and strive to obtain volume, (2) offer high prices and make more per-unit profit on fewer sales, or (3) set prices somewhere in between and obtain volume somewhere in between. It is often a difficult decision and usually a qualified guess as to which is the more profitable. To illustrate, suppose a manufacturer is considering three different prices for his product and each price will produce the following amount of sales:

Price	$ 15.00 each	$ 16.00 each	$ 17.00 each
Volume	40,000 units	35,000 units	25,000 units
Total sales	$600,000	$560,000	$425,000
Cost $13 each	520,000	455,000	325,000
Profit	$ 80,000	$105,000	$100,000

It might appear that a small business would be able to experiment with price in order to determine its most profitable selling price. However, there are some problems with experimenting with prices. First, the firm may not have the financial ability to sustain fluctuations in business. Also, the firm presents one price image with one price and another price image with another price. This changing of price and price image will damage customer relations to some extent, possibly enough to ruin the firm. Consequently, the small businessman must perform an analysis of his market and make an estimate of the effect on profit of various pricing policies. He should then stay with this pricing decision until he finds evidence that another pricing policy is more profitable.

OTHER FACTORS THAT OFFSET PRICE

Price is important to most customers, but it is not the only thing that is important to them. As previously discussed, high quality and exclusiveness are able to offset and even negate price considerations. In addition, service, selection, and convenience are factors that offset price considerations to some extent.

SERVICE

Many customers find different types of customer services important and are willing to pay higher prices, within reason, for these extra services. Some customers want credit and purchase from stores that offer credit even though the price they pay is usually higher. Customers of some small businesses, for example, drugstores, often pay higher prices in order to have merchandise delivered to them. In addition, some customers are willing to pay a slightly higher price for products such as appliances in order to be sure of after-purchase repair and service.

SELECTION

Being sure of finding what they want at a specific store is important enough for some customers that they are willing to pay slightly higher prices. For example, an individual may want a specific piece of merchandise and feel he could pay a little less for it at a discount house. However, he may go to another store because he is not certain if the discount store sells it, and he is sure the higher priced store will have the product. One store has built its patronage on this concept. One large do-it-yourself and building materials store has such a large selection of merchandise that a person is almost sure of finding what he needs at this store. The prices are a little higher on most products than at many other stores that do not have the same degree of selection. Many people patronize this store for the extensive selection of merchandise. They may be justified in their patronage because, if they have to go to several stores to find what they want, the cost of transportation can more than make up for the difference in price.

CONVENIENCE

Many people are willing to pay higher prices for goods and services because of convenience. For example, the small drive-in grocery almost always charges higher prices than the supermarket, but it is able to stay in business because of the convenience it offers customers on small purchases. Convenience is particularly important to consumers when small amounts of money are involved and becomes less important as the money amount of the purchase increases.

PRICING PRACTICES OF RETAILERS, MANUFACTURERS, WHOLESALERS, AND SERVICE FIRMS

Retailers, manufacturers, wholesalers, and service firms use various methods of pricing their products and services. However, while some have similar basic methods of pricing, each category of business has its own pricing practices.

RETAIL PRICING PRACTICES

Retail firms use several methods in pricing their merchandise. Each firm may use one method or a combination of more than one method. The most common methods of pricing in retail establishments are (1) markup on cost, (2) markup as a percentage of selling price, (3) suggested retail price, (4) follow-the-market pricing, (5) competitive pricing, and (6) pricing for clearance.

Markup on Cost

Markup on cost by retailers is achieved by taking the cost of the merchandise (which includes incoming freight) from the vendor and adding a percentage of the cost to the amount.

Cost	$4.00		Cost	$4.00
Markup percentage	40%		Markup amount	1.60
Markup amount	$1.60		Selling price	$5.60

In our example, the 40 percent markup of $1.60 is designed to cover all selling costs (sales personnel salaries, advertising, etc.) and overhead costs (rent, utilities, etc.), and provide a profit. For instance, the retail store may figure 20 percent for selling costs, 14 percent for overhead costs, and 6 percent for profit.

The small business owner should be careful in determining what markup to add to the cost of goods. If the store has been in business for a time, then the firm's records will reveal how much selling and overhead costs have been, historically, in proportion to the cost of goods. If it is a new business, the small business owner should attempt to identify and estimate as accurately as possible every cost he or she expects to incur. Mistakes or overlooking a cost can be very costly to the firm because any increases will reduce profit. Good financial records are very valuable to the small business firm.

Markup on cost of goods can be used by the small business as a standard markup or as a flexible markup.

Standard Markup   A small business firm may elect to mark up all merchandise on one standard markup percentage. This policy usually is adopted by retail stores that have products that are alike or closely related. Many retail stores that are franchised operations, handle products in the same price range, or have little competition often are able to use a standard markup.

The standard markup is easy to administer in daily operations; however, a retail store may find it difficult to maintain in the face of varying degrees of competition on different merchandise.

Flexible Markup   Flexible markup is used to adjust price when there is a change in competition or market demand. Increases in competition or decreases in market demand usually require a retail firm to lower its markup in order to maintain a satisfactory volume of sales.

Flexible markup is also used when there is wide variation in types and prices of products. For example, a department store may vary its markup from department to department in order to allow for the vast difference in products handled. If the department store were to attempt to adopt a standard markup for all products in the store, it would find that its volume of sales of some products would be very low.

Markup as a Percentage of Selling Price

Some small businesses like to tie their markup to their expenses by taking expenses as a percentage of their total sales. For example, a small business might take all its expenses (other than cost of the goods sold) from last year's income statement and find it was $50,000. It could then derive its total sales for the same period and find it was $200,000. Its expenses as a percentage of sales then would be calculated as follows:

$$\frac{\text{Expenses}}{\text{Sales}} \quad \frac{\$\ 50,000}{200,000} = 25\%$$

After analyzing its market and competition, the firm might feel 10 percent of sales would be a reasonable profit. This would mean that 35 percent of each item's selling price would be markup. Knowing the cost of each item sold ($8 in this example), it would then be able to compute its selling price on each item as follows:

$$
\begin{array}{ll}
\text{Selling price} & 100\% \\
\text{Markup} & -35\% \text{ of selling price} \\
\text{Cost of item} & \overline{\quad 65\%} \text{ of selling price} \\
\end{array}
$$

$$\frac{\text{Cost of item in dollars}}{\text{Cost of item as a \% of selling price}} \quad \frac{\$8.00}{65\%} = \$12.30$$

Using this method, the firm can easily derive expenses and total sales from its income statement each year and compute the ratio of expenses to total sales. Its profit markup can be adjusted as the business desires after taking into consideration competition and the market. If its volume of sales increases faster than its expenses, it may want to pass on the savings to customers in an attempt to capture more of the market or it may want to increase its advertising for the same purpose. Its profit as a percent of sales would remain the same; however, it would increase its total income because sales volume would increase.

Suggested Retail Price

Many manufacturers print suggested retail prices on their products, supply catalogs with suggested retail prices, or give suggested retail prices on invoices.

Some wholesalers also provide suggested retail prices to retail stores. For example, some wholesale grocers provide inventory lists to their customers that have both the wholesale price and a suggested retail price.

It is very common for small business firms to follow these suggested retail prices. It allows the small business owner to avoid the pricing decision. Many small business owners feel uncertain about the adequacy of their pricing decisions or do not want to go to the trouble of checking prices of other merchants.

The suggested retail price is easy to use. However, it may create a price image the small businessman does not want. In addition, it does not take into consideration competition, which varies to some degree by locale and type of business.

Some stores, such as retail automobile parts stores, use the manufacturer's suggested retail price as a base and then sell to the customer at a lower price, which is often the manufacturer's suggested wholesale price. Often, the retailer lists both prices on the sales ticket to build an image in the customer's mind that he or she is getting a very good price on his or her purchase.

Follow-the-Market Pricing

Some small business firms do not attempt to lead in competitive pricing and simply follow the usual or average price of other firms. They attempt to stay close in price to other firms. In fact, in small towns, it is not unusual for the owners of the same types of stores to agree to prices (this is actually a violation of antitrust legislation, which is not usually enforced in the case of small businesses because of the large number of them). For example, in the past, it had been standard practice in many small towns for the owners of gasoline service stations to meet and determine what prices will be in their stations. They often set categories of prices for major brands located on highways, major brands located in residential areas, and independents.

Competitive Pricing

Some firms strive to set prices on part or all of their products that are lower than most other firms. These stores often run competitive shopping lists on their competition. For example, a supermarket sends an employee to other supermarkets to record prices on various items of merchandise. From these lists, the supermarket then adjusts its prices in order to be highly competitive.

Many retail stores adopt one of the previous pricing methods discussed, but, in addition, are often forced to adjust prices on some products to a more competitive price.

Pricing for Clearance

A large number of retail firms regularly reduce prices, sometimes below cost, to clear slow-moving items from their stock. In addition, many retail stores have loss leaders in which they sell merchandise at cost or below cost in order to attract customers for other products (this is a common practice of supermarkets). (A discussion of reduced pricing in order to clear slow-moving stock is contained in Chapter 13.)

MANUFACTURERS' PRICING PRACTICES

Manufacturers usually base their product prices on cost plus profit. The specific categories they use are direct labor, raw materials, manufacturing overhead, nonmanufacturing overhead (selling and administrative costs), and profit. (See Fig. 17-3.)

Some manufacturers take one additional step. They use the previously mentioned categories to determine their cost and then add on their profit plus the usual markup added on by the retailer. This then becomes their suggested retail price. They then sell the merchandise to retailers at a discount from suggested retail price. For example, it is common practice for textbook publishers to sell books to bookstores for 80 percent of suggested retail price. This 80 percent covers their cost and profit markup. If the bookstore uses the sug-

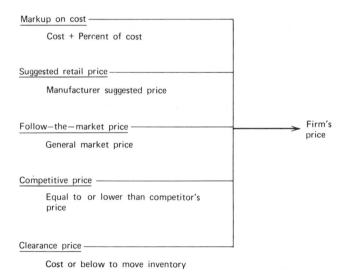

Figure 17-2 Retail pricing practices.

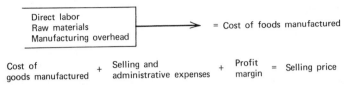

Figure 17-3 Formula for manufacturers' pricing.

gested retail price, 80 percent of sales price covers the cost of the book and 20 percent of sales price must cover all other expenses plus a profit for the store.

As in other types of businesses, the manufacturer must take competition into consideration when pricing his product. He also must make a decision about volume relative to price. In order to obtain sufficient volume, he must balance price, advertising, and quality of the product in terms of market conditions, which include competition.

The manufacturer who has produced his product over a period of time is able to determine his labor costs by the number of products each work station is able to complete in a day's time. The number of products divided into the labor cost for each work station and totaled for the entire process provides per-unit labor costs. The total of all raw materials used in the production of one unit of product plus waste allowances provides per-unit raw material costs. Past records of expenditures for supervisor salaries, plant depreciation, machinery depreciation, supplies, plant utilities, and other factory-related costs provide a basis for arriving at manufacturing overhead. Office salaries, sales salaries, advertising, travel, office depreciation, office utilities, and administrative salaries are among the items that comprise nonmanufacturing overhead. All these costs plus a margin for profit, adjusted for market conditions and competition, provide the necessary information for the manufacturer to set his price.

The manufacturer who is producing a new product does not have historical records to provide this information. Consequently, he must estimate these costs and data in order to arrive at a price for his product. The manufacturer of a new type of product also faces an important question about price. Should he price the product high until competition arises to recover as much development cost as fast as possible, or should he set the price low to discourage competition from entering the field as long as possible?

WHOLESALER PRICING PRACTICES

Wholesalers generally base their price on cost of goods (which includes freight required to bring the product from the manufacturer to the wholesaler) plus a markup, which covers all other costs plus a profit. The wholesaler must take into consideration all his costs when arriving at a markup, including such items as building rent or depreciation, warehouse salaries, office salaries, administrative salaries, selling salaries, delivery costs, utilities, and equipment depreciation.

Cost of goods from manufacturer	+	All costs	+	Profit	=	Price

Figure 17-4 Wholesaler pricing practices.

The wholesaler must also pay close attention to competition and market conditions when setting his price.

Many wholesalers print catalogs that contain both product listings and prices and provide them to retail customers. From time to time, they issue loose-leaf pages that notify the retailer of changes in price. However, the price they charge the retailer for products is, to some degree, inflexible for a period of time because it requires some time before they are able to notify customers of changes. This inflexibility means the price decisions must be sufficient to provide a profit while maintaining an effective competitive position.

SERVICE FIRMS' PRICING PRACTICES

Service firms generally charge an hourly fee for the number of hours spent in providing service. Some even charge one amount for the main service man and another rate for a helper. This is common practice in the plumbing trade. This hourly fee includes not only service salaries but also overhead, all other costs (except parts), and a margin for profit.

Some firms charge by the actual number of hours spent in repair. Others charge a standard number of hours the job should have required regardless of the time spent. For example, most automobile repair shops usually charge the customer so much per hour of labor. For example, they may charge $18 per hour. However, they do not charge for the actual time spent in repair but, rather, consult a standard rate manual for how long it should take to complete the job. For example, the rate manual may list replacing a water pump at 2 hours. In this case, the customer would be charged for 2 hours times $18 or $36 in labor costs. In addition, parts are charged to the customer at list. As a general rule of thumb, list is roughly twice the cost of the part to the automobile repair shop.

Actual time or standard time	×	Hourly rate	+	List price of parts	=	Price

Figure 17-5 Service firms' pricing practices.

The automobile repair shop usually pays the mechanic a fee that is a part of the total labor cost. In our example, the automobile repair shop might pay the mechanic 50 percent of all labor costs or $18 of the labor costs on the water pump repair job. The owner of the shop then keeps $18 for the labor costs plus the markup on the parts to cover his overhead (equipment, building, utilities, office expenses, supplies, etc.).

When price is based on a standard rate manual, the efficient mechanic that can complete the work in less time receives more per hour than the mechanic who is not as efficient and takes as much or more time than the manual allows. In this way, the customer is neither rewarded nor penalized for the speed of the mechanic.

Service firms that use actual hours or standard rate manuals usually adapt their price to meet competition by adjusting the dollar amount charged per actual or standard hour. To illustrate, using our automobile repair shop example, the shop might drop its labor cost from $18 to $16 per hour to meet new competition that is reducing its volume.

BIDDING

Bidding is probably one of the most difficult pricing activities in which a business can engage. Many times, the firm has not produced a specific product or service exactly like the one on which it is bidding. For example, a construction firm may bid on construction of an apartment complex. Even though it has constructed other apartment complexes, there are usually problems unique to each job, such as site preparations, foundations, or new construction designed by the architect. It is often very difficult to figure the exact cost of each problem and technique before it is performed.

On the other hand, the firm that is bidding a job must be fairly accurate in its bidding. If the job costs more than expected, the firm sustains the loss. Conversely, if the firm bids too high, it probably will not get the job.

Another aspect of bidding is the costs to bid on a contract, which may range from a few hours of one person's time to the million or more dollars it sometimes costs aircraft manufacturers to design and build a mockup for a bid to the government. Consequently, a firm must be efficient enough in bidding to be assured that it has a reasonable chance to obtain contracts.

Another problem a firm faces in bidding on contracts that extend over long periods of time, sometimes in terms of several years, is continuing inflation of costs. Bidding usually requires a specific price. The firm that bids may find that costs have increased because of inflation to the point that fulfilling the contract costs more than the price it is receiving. However, it is becoming increasingly common to find contracts that contain some form of escalator clause as a hedge against inflation.

BID, COST, VARIANCE SYSTEM

Any job order shop (one that does not produce to stock but only to customer orders) that bids or prices based on estimated costs should maintain a simple cost system as shown in Figure 17-6. It allows the firm to learn just exactly how much it is making on each job. In addition, it allows the firm to see how accurate its bids are and over a period of time makes the bidding of the firm much more accurate by showing how much variance there is from bid price to actual cost for direct labor, raw materials, manufacturing overhead, selling and administrative overhead, and profit.

Direct Labor

The amount of time each operation should take to complete the work is estimated and multiplied by the hourly rate paid the workers at each work station. For example, Figure 17-6 shows it is estimated that it will take the welder 2.4 hours to complete the task, Since the welder is paid $6.00 per hour, it is estimated that it will cost $14.40 to weld the job. However, it only took the welder 2 hours to complete the job and the actual cost was only $12.00. Thus, the business saved $2.40 on this job.

Raw Materials

All raw materials that are needed to finish this job are estimated. Some firms call suppliers to check current prices at this point. Some items that are used in the job are difficult to assign to any one job, such as nuts and bolts. The welding rods used in Figure 17-6 are considered a supply rather than a raw material. These items are taken into account in manufacturing overhead.

In Figure 17-6 the cost of strip steel is estimated to be $210 but the firm was only charged $205, giving a savings of $5. On the other hand, angle steel had gone up and it cost the firm $20 more than the estimate.

Manufacturing Overhead

A common shortfall of small business is to fail to apply overhead on a realistic basis in pricing. To illustrate, one small business bid $6800 on a city government job. Later it found city engineers had estimated the job at $8200 and the second lowest bid was $10,200. The owner of the business had been estimating

JOB # 106		BID		ACTUAL COST			VARIANCE
Direct labor	Hours	Rate	Amount	Hours	Rate	Amount	Amount
Cleaning	.5	$4.50	$2.25	.5	$4.50	$2.25	$ 0
Cutting	.8	5.00	4.00	.6	5.00	3.00	−1.00
Welding	2.4	6.00	14.40	2.0	6.00	12.00	−2.40
Painting	1.1	4.50	4.95	1.0	4.50	4.50	− .45
Total direct labor			$25.60			$21.75	−$3.85
Raw materials							
Steel ¼ × 2 × 8 ft. strip			$210.00			$205.00	$−5.00
¼ × 4 × 8 ft. angle			300.00			320.00	+20.00
Paint 4 gal.			30.00			30.00	0
Total raw materials			$540.00			$555.00	+$15.00
Manufacturing overhead							
Direct labor × overhead ratio							
× .55			$14.08			$11.96	$2.12
Total manufacturing cost			$579.68			$588.71	+$9.03
Selling & administrative							
overhead							
Total mfg. × Total S&A							
cost overhead ratio							
× .20			$115.94			$117.74	+$1.80
Total cost of goods							
manufactured			$695.62			$706.45	$10.83
Profit markup 10%			$69.56			Price $765.18	
						Cost $706.45	
Bid price			$765.18			Profit $ 58.73	−$10.83

Figure 17-6 Bid, cost, variance sheet.

his cost of direct labor and raw materials and then applying a 60 percent markup to cover overhead and profit. An analysis of past income statements showed that overhead costs were running 120 percent of each dollar spent in direct labor. The entire markup of 60 percent did not even cover his overhead much less profit. Needless to say, he lost money on the job.

Manufacturing overhead is computed by taking the total direct labor cost and multiplying it times the manufacturing overhead ratio. The manufacturing overhead ratio is determined by taking the manufacturing overhead cost from the income statement for the last year and dividing it by the total direct labor costs for the same period. Manufacturing overhead is comprised of such items as foremen salaries, machinery depreciation, supplies, utilities assigned to the factory, cost of the factory space in rent or depreciation, and insurance for the factory space and equipment.

In our example, the total of last year's manufacturing overhead was $264,000, while the total direct labor expense for the same period was $480,000. The calculation of the manufacturing overhead ratio would be:

$$\frac{\text{Manufacturing Overhead Cost}}{\text{Total Direct Labor Cost}} \quad \frac{\$264,000}{\$480,000} = .55$$

Multiplying the job labor cost in Figure 17-6 of $25.60 by the overhead ratio gives $14.08 for estimated manufacturing overhead. Notice that the actual direct labor hours are also multiplied by the manufacturing overhead ratio. The labor cost savings are also reflected in a manufacturing overhead savings of $2.12.

Selling and Administrative Overhead

The selling and administrative overhead cost is calculated by multiplying total manufacturing cost by the S&A overhead ratio. The S&A overhead ratio is calculated by taking all selling expenses and administrative expenses from the income statement and dividing them by the total cost of goods manufactured for the same period. Selling and administrative overhead is comprised of all expenses other than direct labor, raw materials, and manufacturing overhead. In Figure 17-6, the total selling and administrative expenses for the year were $280,000. The S&A overhead ratio should be:

$$\frac{\text{Selling and Administrative Costs}}{\text{Total Cost of Goods Manufactured}} \quad \frac{\$\ 280,000}{\$1,400,000} = .2$$

In Figure 17-6, multiplying the estimated total manufacturing cost of $579.68 by the selling and administrative overhead ratio of 0.2 gives an estimated S&A overhead of $115.94. The actual manufacturing cost is also multiplied by this ratio to give the actual S&A overhead cost.

Profit Markup

The profit markup is a somewhat arbitrary percentage assigned by the small business. Of course, competition must often be a prime factor in setting the profit markup percentage. Our example in Figure 17-6 shows the firm wants to have a profit equal to 10 percent of total costs. Unfortunately, the small business missed its projected profit by $10.83 primarily due to estimating the angle steel price too low.

As with other forms of pricing, effective bidding is dependent on good records and careful analysis of costs. The small business firm that approaches pricing on a hunch or halfway basis usually doesn't stay in business very long.

DISCUSSION QUESTIONS

1. Name one type of small business that would use price to promote the following images—discount prices, high quality, and exclusiveness.
2. Explain the relationship between price and volume of business.
3. Is price the only factor that causes patronage of small business firms?
4. If you were to establish a neighborhood drugstore with delivery service, what type of pricing policy would you use? Explain your reasons.
5. What are some of the factors involved in the method manufacturers use to price their products?
6. What method of pricing is used by most wholesalers to set their prices?
7. If you set up an automobile repair shop, how would you set your prices?
8. Why is bidding one of the most difficult pricing activities in which a small business can engage?
9. If you owned a job shop manufacturing operation, would you use the bid, cost, variance system for bidding and recording actual costs? Explain how you would use it.

STUDENT PROJECTS

1. Attempt to identify retail stores (one each) that use price to create:
   (a) A discount image
   (b) A high quality image
   (c) An exclusive image
2. Identify a retail store that attempts to offset price considerations by using either service, selection, or convenience.

3. Attempt to identify a retail store (one each) that you feel uses the following pricing methods:
   (a) Markup on cost
   (b) Suggested retail prices on some items
   (c) Follow-the-market pricing.
   (d) Competitive pricing
   (e) Pricing for clearance
4. Identify a service firm that uses a standard rate manual.
5. Identify a business that bids for jobs.

CASE A

THE BAT AND BALL

The Bat and Ball is a sporting goods store owned by Jim Matson. The store is located in a town of 50,000 population and has only one competitor, which is a smaller store. The Bat and Ball offers a complete line of sporting goods and also has a gun repair shop that does enough business to keep a skilled repairman busy on a full-time basis.

In addition to its regular retail sales, the Bat and Ball bids on athletic equipment purchased by the local college. Jim Matson computes all the bids the store makes to the college. Jim includes the cost of the merchandise plus his usual markup in figuring the bids. Jim is concerned because the other sporting goods store usually gets the college purchase by bidding lower than he does.

Jim has decided that he is going to review all his policies and practices and revise any that need changing. Since you have completed a course in small business management, he has asked for your help, particularly with his pricing policies.

Questions

1. What method or methods would you advise Jim to use on pricing his merchandise for regular retail sales?
2. What method of pricing would you establish for Jim in regards to the gun repair shop?
3. Would you advise any changes in his method of bidding on the college purchases?
4. What pricing image would you attempt to establish with your pricing recommendations?

CASE B

THE ELECTRO SPLICER COMPANY

The Electro Splicer Company manufactures wiring connectors. The manufacturing process consists of cutting cable that contains several wires, sometimes as many as 14, and soldering special attaching devices on each end. These wiring harnesses are built to customers' specifications and are used in computers and other special electronic equipment. The company contracts separately with its customers for each job and it must keep its price in line with what its competitors charge since it secures the work by bids.

Electro Splicer has just received a request for a bid from a customer for 50 wiring harnesses, each of which will contain eight wires and two special connectors. The firm estimates it will require the following time at each work station:

	Man-hours	**Wage Rate per Hour**
Cutting	2 hours	$5.00
Soldering	6 hours	6.00
Testing	2 hours	6.00

The job will require 500 feet of wire at a cost of 25 cents per foot and 100 connectors at a price of 50 cents each.

The company has been very happy with its profit and it would like to continue making the same amount of money on the amount of work it is doing. Its most recent income statement for last year's operations is shown below.

ELECTRO SPLICER
Income Statement
For the period ending July 1, 1981

Sales		$600,000
Cost of Goods Manufactured:		
Direct labor	$100,000	
Raw materials	180,000	
Manufacturing overhead	80,000	
Total Cost of Goods Manufactured		360,000
Gross Profit from Operations		$240,000
Selling Expenses:		
Sales commissions	$35,000	
Advertising	10,000	
Travel	5,000	
Total Selling Expenses		$ 50,000

Administrative Expenses:

Office rent ....$ 6,000

Administrative salaries 76,000

Office utilities 4,000

Office supplies 2,000

Depreciation of office equipment 2,000

    Total Administrative Expenses 90,000

Total Selling and Administrative Expenses $140,000

Net Profit $100,000

Question:

Construct a bid, cost, variance sheet for this job using a format similar to that of Figure 17-6.

18

CONSUMER BEHAVIOR AND PERSONAL SELLING

PREVIEW OF THIS CHAPTER

1. When you complete this chapter, you will be aware of the importance of consumer buying behavior to the small business.
2. You will have an understanding of why people want products or services.
3. You will be cognizant of the role of motivation research in studying buyer behavior.
4. You will be aware of the buying motives that influence customers.
5. You will be aware of the importance of the business image of the firm.
6. You will understand what patronage motives are.
7. You will understand why good customer relations are critical for the small business.
8. You will understand the importance of personal selling activities to the success of the small business.
9. You will be able to explain these key words:

Motivation research
Conscious motive
Subconscious motive
Unconscious motive
Buying motives
Primary buying motive
Selective buying motive

Rational buying motive
Emotional buying motive
Patronage motives
Customer relations
Service selling
Creative selling

An area of special concern for the small business owner is the problem of finding answers to such questions as, Why do customers buy certain products or prefer certain brands or services over others? and, Why do people patronize one store and not another?

It is essential for firms that sell consumer goods or services to be sensitive to the reasons underlying consumer buying behavior. This knowledge enables small business managers to plan more effectively for the types of goods and services consumers want as well as have them available at the time and place they are demanded. In today's highly competitive marketplace, small business owners who can anticipate customer demands have a distinct competitive edge. Likewise, as the standard of living of our population changes, buying patterns of people will change as their wants and needs change. Thus, consumer buying behavior is a dynamic process that demands the full attention of small business owners.

WHY PEOPLE WANT PRODUCTS OR SERVICES

Perhaps the most fundamental answer to the question Why do people buy? is that they want a particular good or service. Consumers are motivated to make a purchase, and the small business owner's concern is to analyze and identify these motivating forces. The following discussion identifies some of the motivational drives of consumer buying behavior.

SATISFACTION OF PHYSICAL NEEDS AND SAFETY AND SECURITY NEEDS

In an earlier chapter, we stated that motivation is the force that drives people toward the satisfaction of needs. Thus, one apparent answer is that people want a product to satisfy a specific need. In order to survive, people need food, so they purchase food. They need shelter, so they purchase a home; they need clothing, so they buy clothes. Although we recognize that these purchases are made to satisfy needs, these needs do not explain why some products are selected over others. For example, when an individual needs clothing, why does he/she purchase one style of apparel and not another? Hence, small business owners must try to show consumers how their products will satisfy the consumers' needs.

Customers also buy to fulfill their safety needs. Safety features may be added to a home, such as replacing a slippery tile flooring with carpeting. The need for security may influence a consumer to have a burglar alarm and burglar bars installed in the home. These purchases are motivated by the desire to satisfy a basic physical need of safety or security.

SATISFACTION OF HIGHER ORDER NEEDS

However, we realize there are higher order, or secondary, needs that individuals have that must be satisfied. Hence, a major influence underlying buyer behavior is his or her desire to make purchases that will satisfy both higher order needs as recognition, peer approval, and status and lower order needs. The purchase of a home satisfies the need for shelter and safety. But the type of home (price, style, size) and its location satisfy higher order needs as well. The purchase of the home in a particular neighborhood in order to be near friends satisfies the needs of belonging and acceptance. The size or style of home or furnishings satisfies the need for recognition and status. Thus, consumer buying behavior is motivated by the desire to satisfy a combination of both the lower order and higher order needs. Briefly stated, there is no single, simple answer to why people buy what they do.

MOTIVATION RESEARCH

Motivation research, a technique designed to discover the underlying motives of consumer behavior—to answer "why" they buy rather than "what" they buy, draws heavily from the fields of psychology and sociology. Motivation research has two basic purposes—first, the identification of the needs and wants that motivate people; second, the explanation of why people behave the way they do.

There are three basic kinds of motives that influence people to act the way they do. These are conscious motives, subconscious motives, and unconscious motives.

CONSCIOUS MOTIVES

Conscious motives are those of which people are aware (or think they are aware). People can explain why they like one product and dislike another. However, these may or may not be the real reasons people behave the way they do or buy the products they do.

SUBCONSCIOUS MOTIVES

Frequently, people know what motivates them but are hesitant to admit it or do not care to think about it. For example, an individual may purchase an expensive wristwatch giving as the reason for the purchase the need for a timepiece.

However, the reason often not admitted, a subconscious motive, is to gain recognition from peers through the purchase of an expensive watch.

UNCONSCIOUS (DORMANT) MOTIVES

Unconscious or dormant motives influence behavior of people, but the people are not aware of the reasons why they act the way they do.

An early in-depth study of the meaning of automobiles illustrates how motivation research can be used to identify consumer needs and wants and then explain why people behave as they do. This study found that the automobile has practical, social, and personal meanings for the individual. The meanings can be grouped around five main points.

1. The car is a mechanical object that serves practical uses (transportation). This represents the sensible reason why people buy cars.
2. The car represents a sizable investment, second only to the home—economic motive.
3. The car has social meaning. It provides a means for togetherness—family vacations, people carpooling to work. The car is also a status symbol.
4. The car represents a symbol of self-control. The driver controls the vehicle.
5. The car is an important avenue of self-expression. The type of car purchased suggests what an individual wants to be (or what he thinks he is) as a person.[1]

Ordinarily, the small business owner does not have the financial resources to conduct costly research projects. But by keeping abreast of changes and new findings (through reading and other means), the owner can reap some of the benefits gained through greater awareness of consumer buying behavior.

BUYING MOTIVES

We recognize that consumer purchases are ordinarily influenced by a combination of buying motives rather than a single motive. However, in order to more fully understand the purchase process, we will identify some of the basic motives that are a part of the decision to buy.

---

[1]Pierre Martineau, "What Automobiles Mean to Americans," in *Motivation and Market Behavior,* edited by Robert Ferber and Hugh Wales (Homewood, Ill.: Richard D. Irwin, Inc., 1958), pp. 39–42.

PRIMARY BUYING MOTIVE

Sam enjoys working in his yard. In fact, he takes great pride in the appearance of his lawn. On several occasions he has received the "yard of the month" citation by the neighborhood garden club. While mowing his lawn last week, however, Sam did not see a large rock that had been thrown into his yard. His mower hit the rock, breaking the blade and the drive shaft. His repairman told Sam it was not feasible to have it repaired. Thus, Sam recognizes that he needs a new lawn mower. Whatever the item, consumers initially must be aware that they have a need for a product. The need may be to replace a broken product, such as the lawn mower. Or, it may be that they want to purchase additional products, such as new clothing or a new radio or television set.

SELECTIVE BUYING MOTIVE

Sam realizes he needs a new lawn mower (a primary buying motive). The task facing Sam now is to "select" the type of lawn mower to replace the old one. The selective buying motive involves answering many questions, such as

1. What size cutting mower do I want (19 in., 20 in., 21 in., 22in., or larger)?
2. What type of mower do I want (rotary or reel type)?
3. What brand of mower do I want?
4. Do I want a push-type, self-propelled, or riding mower?
5. Do I want a grass catcher?
6. Do I want a mower that has an electric starter or a pull-type starter?
7. Do I want an electric or gas-powered mower?
8. Will the place where I buy the mower service it also?
9. What price range can I consider?

These are a few of the alternatives Sam has to consider as he selects his new lawn mower. The motives that influence the final decision of which mower to buy are the selective buying motives.

RATIONAL BUYING MOTIVES

Rational purchases involve conscious thought and deliberation. Before making the purchase, the consumer tries to consider all its positive and negative aspects. A number of factors influence a rational decision to buy.

Economy

Sam may purchase a new mower on the basis that it is relatively inexpensive compared to other makes and models, both in terms of initial cost and maintenance. The popularity of compact and subcompact cars is largely attributed to their economy of operation, especially since the energy shortages have occurred.

Dependability

Sam wants a mower that will provide dependable service. For example, he wants a mower that starts easily. Manufacturers may stress that consumers can depend on their mower's starting on the first pull almost every time. Hence, his purchase decision may be justified on the basis of the reliability of the product.

Convenience

Sam may consider in his purchase decision some of the convenience features that a mower has. For example, he may choose a mower with an electric starter over one with a pull-type starter because it is easier to operate. He may choose a mower that has a mechanism for adjusting the cutting height on each wheel, which enables the mower to be raised or lowered in a matter of seconds with little effort. Hence, many consumers are influenced to purchase products because they offer many convenience features. Electric grass clippers, electric can openers, electric dishwashers, electric drills, and electric saws are but a few of the many products that emphasize convenience characteristics.

EMOTIONAL BUYING MOTIVES

Unlike rational motives, emotional motives involve little or no thought prior to purchasing a product. As we noted earlier, these motives may be prompted by unconscious motives so that consumers are not aware of what influences them. Or, they may be influenced by subconscious motives, and they are not willing to admit the true reason for their purchase. This broad class of motives is designated as emotional buying motives. Some of the underlying emotional buying motives influencing a purchase are discussed below.

Social Acceptance

For many, the desire to be accepted and to belong is a strong motive. As a result, many purchases are influenced by this desire. One avenue of gaining social acceptance is through conformity. Some purchase decisions of which products to buy are influenced by the desire to conform to the accepted standard of those around us and be accepted as a part of the group.

Emulation

The desire to imitate or be equal to individuals who use a product is a strong emotional motive. Famous personalities from the sports world or entertainment field are shown in advertisements using a product. By buying and using the products shown in commercials, the consumer is fulfilling the desire to be like or to identify with a well-known personality.

Esteem

By purchasing a unique or distinctive article, consumers hope to gain recognition from their friends or fellow workers. The purchase of a television set with remote control unit or clothing from an exclusive apparel shop are examples of purchases that may satisfy the consumer's desire for recognition.

BUSINESS IMAGE

Small business owners strive to establish a distinct image for their firm. The manager may choose to establish a store that projects an image of an exclusive atmosphere by selling fashion merchandise, for example. Another store builds an image emphasizing economy. In developing the business image, almost everything the manager does reflects the image. For example, the reputation of the owner plays an important role in the store image. Customers have confidence in owners who have built a reputation for quality and service through the years. Store managers attempt to enhance their reputation by recognizing that customer satisfaction is paramount. The following statement of a small retail store emphasizes this point.

THANK YOU

The merchandise purchased by you from this store was selected because of its unusual Quality and Style—we hope it will live up to your expectations. If for any reason it does not you will confer a favor upon us by reporting same to the Management so that we may serve you BETTER.

The store image is in part created by the physical appearance of the store as well as the attitudes and appearance of employees. Advertising (discussed in the next chapter) is an essential link in building the store image. Stressing patronage motives and customer relations are two major components in building a store's image.

PATRONAGE MOTIVES

Patronage motives are the factors that influence customers to return time and again to a particular store to make purchases. Small business owners should be aware of the acute need of identifying these factors. In this way, they will be able to stress their strong points and correct any weak points. Again, there is no single or simple answer to why customers prefer one store over another. Some of the representative patronage motives are discussed below.

Sales Personnel

One factor that influences consumer opinion, especially about retail or service establishments, is the quality of the salespersons. Salespersons who are courteous and friendly and who volunteer assistance to customers do much to help create a positive store image. Customers frequently remark that they

Courteous, helpful salespersons help create a positive image for the small business.

patronize a particular store because they enjoy the kind of service accorded them by the salespersons. Conversely, indifferent or discourteous salespersons are often the reasons many customers begin patronizing the firm's competitors. The importance of building and maintaining positive customer relationships should be constantly emphasized in the sales training program.

Customer Service

Customers may be attracted to a store because of the product-related services it provides. Service after the sale is especially important as products become more complex. Often, shoppers are willing to pay more for an item because of the quality service that the store provides. Consumer-oriented services are frequently cited as significant patronage motives also. These may include layaway, delivery, product return policies, check cashing, receiving of payment for utility bills, selling of car license plates, or serving as a postal substation.

Convenience of Location

Convenience of location has been a prime reason for the growth of shopping centers and drive-in type stores. Customers seek to avoid the traffic congestion and shop at stores where parking is accessible. As previously noted, some downtown merchants have banded together and provided parking facilities for shoppers to make their store locations more convenient to customers.

Merchandise Selection

The variety as well as the breadth of assortment of merchandise is cited as a patronage motive. This makes it possible for consumers to find the merchandise they want at one place.

Price and Quality

Customers expect to receive a dollar's worth of value for each dollar they spend. A policy that will help build repeat purchases is to charge a fair price for the quality of merchandise offered for sale.

FACTORS THAT DISCOURAGE BUYING

A practical way of identifying factors that discourage patronage of a store is to take the opposite views expressed above. If customers consider service important, and they perceive the store does not offer product-related and customer-related services, they will be discouraged from shopping there.

Likewise, poor attitudes on the part of the salespeople discourage buying. It is very frustrating to ask a salesperson for assistance and be treated with apathy. Or, a customer asks for a particular item and the salesperson makes no effort to help find it or explain how it works.

Another factor that irritates many customers is high-pressure selling. Salespeople may attempt to hurry the customer into making a decision. Others even go so far as to insult the intelligence of the consumer by their remarks and actions.

CUSTOMER RELATIONS

The following short, direct statement of business philosophy underscores the value placed on developing positive customer relations for the small firm. This statement is taken from the back of a sales ticket of a small grocery store.

> We are your friends and neighbors. The money you spend in our store stays in our town and helps support your schools, roads, churches, and other local enterprises. This is our way of saying THANK YOU—CALL AGAIN.

The small business owner should recognize that positive customer relations are built by the roles that the owner plays in the store as well as in outside community activities.

Outside Activities

The small business owner can make substantial progress toward the goal of building a positive image for the business by wisely investing a part of his/her time in community activities.

Investment of time usually is more productive if the small business owner is an active participant in and supporter of a few community activities and does not spread himself or herself too thin in many activities, thus failing to participate effectively in any. Furthermore, it is advisable that the small business owner establish a priority list of community involvement and recognize that the business comes first.

There are many worthwhile avenues for expressing community involvement. Examples are shown below.

1. Membership in civic club (Lions, Rotarians, Kiwanis, etc.).
2. Membership in local chamber of commerce.

3. Supporting of town activities, such as July 4 parade, or special events, such as water shows or art festivals, by contributing time and/or money.
4. Sponsorship of a Little League team (buying uniforms or equipment) or coaching a team.
5. Contributing use of equipment, such as a truck, during town's annual cleanup day.
6. Selling tickets to local events.
7. Supporting programs that will promote civic progress, such as bond elections, for new schools or utility improvements.

In-Store Activities

The most important point to remember in building positive in-store customer relations is that the customer comes first. Store owners must demonstrate through their actions and attitudes that they believe the customer is right and that they need the customer more than the customer needs the store. Stated simply, if customers stop buying at your store, you will not have a business.

The wise store owner will attempt to empathize with customers. Try to look at your store objectively, as the customers see it. Do you like what you see? Would you feel comfortable if you were a customer in your own store?

Positive customer relations are built on fair and honest treatment of customers. Some stores state their policy as "We treat all customers the same." This policy recognizes that the company's integrity is the basis for building consumer confidence.

Customers should be treated courteously and attentively. Salespersons should be alert to the customer's presence in the store and assist them in finding what they want or answering their questions quickly and courteously.

The advertising in the store should be believable. False, misleading, or exaggerated statements should be avoided. Advertising should be clean and simple.

Good customer relations are built if the store has merchandise in stock. If the store is consistently "out" of merchandise, this represents a lost sale as well as inconvenience to the customer. It may even result in losing a good customer permanently.

The proper handling of customer complaints is another means of enhancing customer relations. The store owner should make every effort to rectify a mistake in favor of the customer rather than to view the customer with an accusative eye.

A clean physical environment is also beneficial in establishing sound customer relations. A store that has a poor physical appearance may discourage shoppers from even entering the premises.

Once again, it is emphasized that customer relations must be considered in the total context of the store. This means that a firm develops a definite program for strengthening customer relations both inside and outside the store. It does not happen accidentally.

CUSTOMER STORE EVALUATION

In addition to using the Customer Buying Profile discussed in Chapter 16, the small business owner should attempt to learn as much as possible about the opinions that customers have of the store. These data can be collected by using the Customer Store Evaluation questionnaire shown in Figure 18-1.

This questionnaire is designed to identify customer attitudes toward the store. The small business owner can measure the total responses to each question individually in order to arrive at a pattern of responses. Visual observation of the completed questionnaire serves to identify favorable and unfavorable attitudes toward the firm.

As we have noted, the identification of the strong points enables the company to adopt policies that will make it possible to retain them. Steps can be taken to correct the weak areas of customer relations. In turn, this will result in increased customer goodwill and enhance the image of the store.

PERSONAL SELLING

Considerable attention has been devoted to the importance of sales personnel's role in developing positive patronage motives and enhancing the store's customer relations.

Personal selling is especially important for small retailing firms. Since many large retail stores have gone to more self-service, the small retailer has the opportunity to provide a valuable service and perhaps even gain a competitive advantage by emphasizing personal selling.

Effective personal selling involves matching customers' needs to the retail firm's merchandise and services. When this goal in selling is reached, the result is a satisfied customer, and there is a strong possibility that a long-term relationship between the store and the customer will be established.

TYPES OF PERSONAL SELLING

Most types of personal selling in the small firm can be distinguished as either service selling or creative selling.

Customer Store Evaluation

Name of firm: _____ Town: _____

1. Have you ever traded with this firm?___ Yes___ No. If your answer is no,
   please state why _____

2. If your answer is yes, do you still trade with this firm?___ Yes___ No. If your answer is no,
   please state your reason for no longer trading with this firm _____

3. If you have ever traded with this firm, please rank the firm in comparison to other men's clothing
   firms by placing an X in the appropriate column.

	Very high	Above average	Average	Below average	Very low
Convenience of location					
Quality of goods or service					
Variety of choice of goods or services					
Quantity of goods or services					
Appearance of establishment:					
Neatness					
Cleanliness					
Spaciousness					
Uniformity of appearance					
Number of hours a day the business is open					
Number of days in week the business is open					
Management's knowledge of product or service					
Availability of latest fashion or style					
Speed of service					
Prestige of business					
Adequacy of displaying merchandise					
Customer services:					
Liberal credit policy					
Layaway					
Delivery					
Product guaranty					
After guaranty repairs					
Product return policies					
Purchase bonuses (trading stamps, etc.)					
Satisfies customer complaints					
Parking facilities available					
Quality of advertising					
Dependability of business					
Employees:					
Knowledge of product or service					
Attitude: (1) friendly					
(2) helpful					
Appearance					
Adequacy of price of goods or service					
Acceptability of sales pressure					
Adequacy of traffic congestion:					
Street					
Sidewalk in front of store					
Inside store					

Figure 18-1 Customer store evaluation.

Service Selling

Service selling involves completing a sale to a customer who has already made up his/her mind to buy and has a good idea of what he/she wants. The salesperson provides the customer with the information needed to make the buying decision. For example, if a customer wants to buy new clothing, the salesperson's service selling activities center around showing the customer various styles, fabrics, colors; providing assistance in measuring for size; making arrangements for alterations if necessary; writing up the sales ticket; and informing the customer when the purchase can be picked up or delivered.

Creative Selling

Creative selling is more challenging. The salesperson tries to arouse demand for merchandise when the potential customer's attitude is either neutral or negative toward making a purchase. Salespersons try to redirect these attitudes to a positive desire. In effect, the customer is influenced to make a purchase, something he/she had not intended to do. The salesperson accomplishes this creative sale by arousing desires in the customer that can only be satisfied by buying the product.

MANAGING SALES PERSONNEL

One of the most effective means for achieving success in small business is effective personal selling. The owner-manager or some designated individual has the authority and responsibility for selecting, training, compensating, and motivating the sales personnel. In developing the sales staff, one should recognize that salespeople need at least three basic skills to make personal selling effective.

1. Salespeople must be skilled at learning the needs of the customer.
2. They must have a thorough knowledge of the merchandise and service offered by the retailer.
3. They must have the ability to convince customers that the merchandise and services offered by their store can satisfy the customer's needs better than that of their competitors.[2]

---

[2]Bert Rosenbloom, "Improving Personal Selling," *Small Marketers Aids, No. 159* (Washington, D.C.: Small Business Administration, November 1976).

SELECTING SALES PERSONNEL

In selecting among applicants to staff the personal selling positions of the firm, the small business owner must define clearly what the jobs involve. As shown in the personnel management chapter, job descriptions are a valuable aid in selecting the right person for the job by identifying the qualities desired in salespeople. The *Dictionary of Occupational Titles* suggests some of the duties of a general sales position.[3] This information can serve as a guide for small business managers as they develop the specific job requirements in order to match people and jobs.

The *Dictionary of Occupational Titles* job description for a retail and wholesale salesperson is as follows.

SALESPERSON (ret. tr.; whole. tr.)
Sells merchandise to individuals in store or showroom, utilizing knowledge of products sold: Greets customer on sales floor and ascertains make, type, and quality of merchandise desired. Displays merchandise, suggests selections that meet customer's needs, and emphasizes selling points of article, such as quality and utility. Prepares sales slip or sales contract. Receives payment or obtains credit authorization. Places new merchandise on display. May wrap merchandise for customer. May take inventory of stock. May requisition merchandise from stockroom. May visit customer's home by appointment to sell merchandise on shop-at-home basis. Classifications are made according to products sold as SALESPERSON, AUTOMOBILE ACCESSORIES (ret. tr.; whole. tr.); SALESPERSON, BOOKS (ret. tr.); SALESPERSON, SURGICAL APPLIANCES (ret. tr.).

Additional steps in the selection process for salespeople are the same as those in the selection process outlined in the chapter on personnel management. Briefly, the small business owner-manager must

1. Identify the sources of potential salespeople.
2. Evaluate the prospects. The application form is a helpful aid.
3. Conduct personal interviews.
4. Test candidates, if applicable.
5. Select the best candidate.
6. Orient the new salespeople to the job.

[3]*Dictionary of Occupational Titles,* 4th ed. (Washington, D.C.: U.S. Department of Labor, 1977), p. 215.

Employees are slow in greeting customers.
Employees appear indifferent and make customers wait unneccessarily.
Personal appearance of employees is not neat.
Salespeople lack knowledge of the store's merchandise.
Customers complain of employees' lack of interest in their problems.
Mistakes that employees make are increasing.
Qualified employees leave for jobs with the store's competitors.

Figure 18-2 Ways to drive customers away. [*Source.* Bruce Goodpasture, "Danger Signals in Small Store," *Small Marketers Aids, No. 141* (Washington, D.C.: Small Business Administration, 1978).]

SALES TRAINING

A strong training program in sales reinforces the selection process. Even though the small firm has only a few salespeople, the owner-manager needs to recognize the contribution that sales training offers to the success of the firm.

Quite often, one area of employee performance that is weak is personal selling. For example, the owner manager should be concerned about the warning signals noted in Figure 18-2 that reflect employee attitudes and actions that threaten to drive customers away.

Thus, one of the concrete steps that can be taken to prevent poor attitudes from developing is to provide proper sales training. And training is a continuous process. The underlying theme of all selling activities should be one of customer satisfaction. This objective can be reached by stressing four areas of knowledge important to the salesperson: know yourself, know your company, know your product or merchandise, and know your customer.[4] (See Figure 18-3.)

KNOW YOURSELF

Salespersons must be aware of the type of image they project to others. In knowing themselves, they must be conscious of such attributes as physical appearance, personality, tact, intelligence, and integrity. Training provides the opportunity for each person to assess himself or herself and to seek improvement in each of these fields.

KNOW YOUR COMPANY

A part of the training program should make the employees familiar with the company so that they can effectively represent the company to the public as

[4]Small Business Administration, *Managing to Sell,* Administrative Management Course Program, Topic 13 (Washington, D.C.: U.S. Govt. Printing Office, 1964).

Figure 18-3 Salesperson's knowledge.

well as understand their own position. Information provided employees about the company should include general information: history of the company; objectives; organizational framework; departmental structure; policies on customer service, sales, advertising, and personnel; and rules and regulations on work schedules, uniforms, use of equipment, and credit and collections. Much of this information is also contained in the employee manual discussed in Chapter 9.

KNOW YOUR PRODUCTS AND SERVICES

Knowledge of the products and/or services one is selling is essential. It is frustrating to both the customer and the employee when salespersons attempt to sell merchandise or service when they obviously know little or nothing about them. The type of product and service knowledge needed by salespersons may be either general or specific. General knowledge may be adequate if salespersons sell a wide range of merchandise, such as in a variety store. Specific product knowledge is required when salespersons are selling technical products.

Salespersons should be knowledgeable in such areas as:

Uses of the product or service.
Quality of merchandise.
Performance of the product.
Special features.
Warranties of the product.

A salesperson must know the company products and services in order to provide the best assistance to customers.

Sales training should provide the employees with pertinent information about the company's products and services so that salespeople can relate them to the needs of their customers.

KNOW YOUR CUSTOMER

The first part of this chapter is devoted to studying consumer buying behavior. We have stated that, to satisfy consumers, salespeople must know something of their needs, interests, characteristics, and buying motives.

One of the important qualities of all salespersons is empathy, the ability to look at a situation from the other person's perspective. Empathy permits the salesperson to closely identify with and more fully understand the customer and provide more personal attention, which helps build customer loyalty to the store. A great deal of knowledge about customers can be gained if the salesperson learns to listen to the customer.

THE PERSONAL SELLING PROCESS

Personal selling is the most widely used technique in marketing goods and services. Consequently, salespersons must have a thorough understanding of the selling process. The owner-manager of the small firm must be familiar with the personal selling process and see to it that this information is presented in the sales training program. The personal selling process includes these stages (Fig. 18-4).

1. Prospecting and preapproach.
2. Sales approach.
3. Sales presentation.
4. Handling objections.
5. Closing the sale.
6. Follow-up after the sale.

The personal selling process in retail firms usually emphasizes the last five steps. Prospecting and preapproach may be of minor importance except for big-ticket items.

PROSPECTING AND PREAPPROACH

In this stage, the salesperson tries to identify potential customers and then accumulate as much information about them as possible in order to make an effective sales approach.

SALES APPROACH

A proper approach to the customer involves the salesperson's making a favorable impression on the customer. When a warm and friendly relationship exists, the customer will be more likely to be receptive to the sales presentation. In the small firm, it is frequently possible for the salesperson to greet the customers by name and demonstrate that they really want to help the customer and are

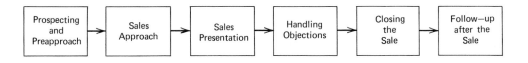

glad to have them in the store. Care must be taken not to neglect customers, a point that should be stressed during the sales training sessions.

SALES PRESENTATION

The salesperson must identify the customers' needs and then make an effective presentation of the merchandise. The sales presentation is enhanced by demonstrating the product or explaining the service. The customer may be permitted to handle the product in order to fully appreciate it. These procedures may serve to increase the customers' desire for the product or service. Some fundamental procedures that should be included in the sales presentation are listed below.

1. Make strong, persuasive points about merchandise or service early in the presentation—there may be no second chance.
2. Work on "selling benefits"—the value should be established before discussing price.
3. Give the customer complete attention.
4. Never confuse the customer with too wide an assortment.
5. Whenever possible try to show the item in use.
6. Whenever possible, involve the customer.
7. As a sales presentation progresses, be more specific and more emphatic.
8. Listen to make the customer feel important.
9. Look for polite ways to make the customer feel at ease.
10. Demonstrate enthusiasm and a sense of satisfaction about your job.[5]

HANDLING OBJECTIONS

Handling objections in a satisfactory manner is probably the most difficult step in the selling process. Salespersons should anticipate some objections. Customers' objections may include: the price is too high; the merchandise is the wrong color; it is not the kind of material I want; or, I have an older model with which I am satisfied.

Some common methods of handling objections are shown below.

1. Use the "yes-but" technique. (Turn the customer attention to other factors. The key here is not to contradict.)
2. Ask questions of the customer.

[5]C. Winston Borgen, *Learning Experiences in Retailing* (Pacific Palisades, Cal.: Goodyear Publishing Company, 1976), pp. 296–298.

3. Use the turn-it-around principle. (Give the customer confidence in his/her own thinking and a feeling the observation is his/her own.
4. Select another feature for emphasis. (Turn customer attention from the objection point to another point with more appeal.)
5. Direct denial. (Handle very carefully so no offense is taken by the customer.)[6]

CLOSING THE SALE

Salespersons should be prepared to close a sale at any time during the presentation or handling objections. In closing the sale, the salesperson tries to find the appropriate time to get the customer to act—to buy the product or service. Among the reasons a salesperson fails to close a sale is that they push the customer to make a decision before he/she is ready or that they demonstrate a feeling of superiority over the customer.

A number of closing techniques are offered below.

1. Use the principle of positive suggestion and assume the sale is made. If the customer does not stop the salesperson, the sale has been completed.
2. Offering an added incentive may help in prompting customer action. If the customer appears to be hesitant about the purchase, the salesperson may offer an extra incentive to buy, such as a cash discount or free delivery.
3. A good closing technique is to summarize the main benefits of the product or service. Emphasize those benefits that match the customer's buying motives.
4. Asking for the order is an obvious but often overlooked closing technique. Many customers respond favorably to this sales technique.

FOLLOW-UP AFTER THE SALE

A supportive step that aids in developing goodwill and repeat sales is a follow-up after the sale by the salesperson. This may be accomplished by a telephone call or by a short, courteous personal note thanking the customer for the purchase and offering to be of assistance to the customer any time in the future. Follow-ups are usually provided on larger purchases, such as freezers or television sets.

[6]Ibid., p. 299.

1. Greeting:
   Be friendly, courteous, prompt, businesslike.
   Learn consumer's name and use it.
   Make customer feel important.
   Talk favorably about merchandise.
2. Presentation:
   Ask questions, listen, learn what he wants.
   Place customer's interest first.
   Suggest merchandise that best fits his need.
   Demonstrate as in actual use.
   Give at least three benefits for each item.
   Let customer handle the merchandise.
   Don't talk too much.
3. Close:
   Help customer decide.
   Ask which item customer prefers.
   Remove unwanted merchandise from sight.
   Use utmost tact.
   Assume sale has been made.
   Write all details on the order.
4. Pleasing:
   Assure satisfaction.
   Show a related item.
   Show it is a pleasure to serve him.
   Keep all promises to customers.
   Be cheerful whether you make the sale or not.
   When a customer returns, he has been well served.

Figure 18-5 How to Sell. [*Source*. L. T. White, *Strengthening Small Business Management* (Washington, D.C.: Small Business Administration, 1971).]

In summary, Figure 18-5 presents some specific suggestions that will contribute to making a sale.

SALES PERSONNEL EVALUATION

Salespersons' performance should be evaluated with the goal being to help them improve their job performance. Performance evaluation should be applied in a systematic manner in order to benefit employer and employee. Performance can be evaluated by using a rating scale similar to the one presented in Chapter 9. The guide shown below can be used in counseling the salesperson in the areas of planning, measuring, and correcting performance.

GUIDE FOR IMPROVING A SALESPERSON'S PERFORMANCE

One goal of measuring a salesperson's performance is to help him/her improve. The three steps in bringing about improvement, when, and if, it is needed are: planning, measuring, and correcting.

PLANNING

- Get the salesperson's agreement about what he/she is to attain or exceed for the next year.
  (1) Total profit contribution in dollars.
  (2) Profit contribution in dollars for:
      Each major product line.
      Each major market (by industry or geographical area).
      Each of 10–20 target accounts (for significant new and additional business).
- Get the salesperson's agreement about expenses within which he/she is to stay for the next year:
  (1) Total sales expense budget in dollars.
  (2) Budget in dollars for: travel, customer entertainment, telephone, and other expenses.
- Have the salesperson plan the number of calls he/she will make to accounts and prospects during the next year.

MEASURING

- Review at least monthly the salesperson's record for:
  (1) Year-to-date progress toward 12-month profit contribution goals.
  (2) Year-to-date budget compliance.

CORRECTING

Meet with salesperson if his/her record shows that he/she is 10 percent or more off target. Review with him/her the number of calls he/she has made on each significant account plus what he/she feels are his/her accomplishments and problems. In addition, you may need to do some of the following to help him/her improve performance:

- Give salesperson more day-to-day help and direction.
- Accompany salesperson on calls to provide coaching.
- Conduct regular sales meetings on subjects which salespersons want covered.
- Increase sales promotion activities.
- Transfer accounts to other salespersons if there is insufficient effort or progress.
- Establish tighter control over price variances allowed.
- Increase or reduce selling prices.
- Add new products or services.
- Increase salesperson's financial incentive.
- Transfer, replace, or discharge salesperson.

Source: Raymond Loen, *"Measuring the Performance of Salesmen," Small Business Administration Aid No. 190* (Washington, D.C.: Small Business Administration, 1977) p. 7.

DISCUSSION QUESTIONS

1. Why do small business managers try to analyze consumer behavior?
2. What reasons are given for people's wanting products?
3. What is motivation research?
4. Distinguish between conscious, subconscious, and unconscious motives.
5. Explain the difference between a primary and selective buying motive.
6. Identify several rational buying motives and emotional buying motives.
7. What are patronage motives?
8. Identify some of the factors that discourage buying in a particular store.
9. Why is personal selling so important, especially to the small retailer?
10. What areas of knowledge should be stressed in a sales training program?
11. Identify the steps in making a sale.

STUDENT PROJECT

Use the "Customer Store Evaluation" of Figure 18-1 for evaluating one or two stores where you do your shopping.

CASE A

JOE'S AUTO REPAIR

Joe Black is the owner of Joe's Auto Repair. Some 30 complaints have been filed with the state attorney general alleging violations of the state's Deceptive Trade Practices.

The complaints allege that Joe would quote one price for the repair work and then charge a substantially higher price, that it took longer to repair the autos than he had promised, and that he charged customers for new parts when rebuilt parts were actually installed.

An example of one customer's complaint is typical of the allegations.

Jerry Carothers had his 1964-model car towed to Joe's Auto Repair. Jerry was told he needed new battery cables and the car's front end needed to be reworked. The cost was estimated at $125.

Jerry was told the car would be repaired in a few days but a week later was told that Joe was having trouble finding parts for that model car. After that conversation, Jerry even helped to find most of the parts and brought them to the shop.

When Joe got the parts, he told Jerry the cost would be $100 more than estimated. Jerry didn't have that much money but obtained a bank loan and instructed Joe to repair the car.

When Joe took the car apart, he didn't have the proper tools to put it back together. The price for repairs also kept increasing. By the time the auto was repaired, the price had increased to $350 but Jerry paid anyway just to get his car.

After Jerry left the garage and drove about two blocks, the transmission burned up. This happened because all the transmission fluid had been drained during repair and not replaced.

Questions

1. Comment on Joe's business practices.
2. What effect does this type of business practice have on the image of the business in the community?

CASE B

A TO Z FABRIC SHOP

A to Z Fabric Shop is a small retailing firm specializing in the sale of fabrics, sewing notions (thread, zippers, tape, machine accessories, buttons), and patterns. In addition to the manager, there are two salespersons. Unfortunately, the store does not have a very positive image in the community. Many people feel the lack of concern for the customer is due primarily to the fact that this is the only fabric shop in town. The nearest competitor is located in a larger city 45 miles away. As a result, when shoppers go to the larger city, they try to complete a number of shopping activities in one trip. However, for small items or a small amount of material, it is not practical to drive out of town. For the sake of convenience, customers buy only what is absolutely necessary in the A to Z Shop.

Mrs. Whyte wanted to sew a new dress for herself to wear to the company Christmas party. However, she did not have the material, and she did not have time to go to the larger city. Instead, she elected to go to the local store. When she arrived, she tried to find a salesperson but could not. Finally, she found the material herself and at last was able to locate a salesperson, who completed the sale. However, when she got home and was getting ready to cut out her pattern, she noticed a flaw in the material. Consequently, she decided to return the material and ask for a refund.

Mrs. Whyte showed the material to one of the salespersons. She informed Mrs. Whyte that she could not make an adjustment, but she would have to see the manager. When Mrs. Whyte began to explain her problem, the manager's face became flushed. Mrs. Whyte showed the imperfect material, and the manager became more irritated. Finally, when Mrs. Whyte said she wanted a refund, the manager lost his temper. He dashed over to the cash register, jerked out the cash for the refund, and rudely pushed it into Mrs. Whyte's hand. As Mrs. Whyte was leaving, the store manager shouted at her, "Don't ever come back to my store again!"

Questions

1. Evaluate the personal selling in this fabric shop.
2. Place youself in the role of the customer. What are your reactions?
3. Evaluate the store manager's actions.
4. Use role playing to find the correct method of handling this situation.

CASE C
NOTHING BUT LOOKERS*

Stan Clark and Wilbur Fiddler, two shoe clerks in the National Shoe Store in the Plaza Shopping Center, were totaling up their sales for the day. As usual Stan had had a pretty good day compared to Wilbur's mediocre one.

"Stan, you must be made of luck. I just can't understand it," said Wilbur. "You get all the customers and all I get is 'lookers.' "

"Do you really think it's luck, Wilbur?" asked Stan.

"What else would it be? It isn't as if I bit off customers' heads or something," replied Wilbur firmly.

"Oh, I think you are very courteous and helpful to customers," said Stan tactfully.

"Well, then, what is the matter?" implored Wilbur.

Stan hesitated, then said, "I'm not sure I can answer that, Wilbur. But maybe you don't help potential sales along as well as you could."

"Help them along? What more can I do than show them the shoes, tell them about the quality, and see that they fit?" asked Wilbur.

"Oh, there's a good deal more than that," suggested Stan. "You have to work to find out what they really want, then help them satisfy those wants."

*Source. *Why Customers Buy, Instructor's Manual, Management Development Program,* (Washington D.C.: Small Business Administration, 1967).

"I guess I'm going to have to study your methods. I sure would like to improve my sales volume," Wilbur said sincerely.

"I'll be glad to help any way I can," Stan replied.

That night Wilbur thought things over. Maybe there was something he was doing wrong. He would listen when Stan approached prospects and see what he said in answer to their questions. Then Wilbur had an idea. Maybe Stan would also listen to his sales technique when Stan wasn't busy with customers himself and help Wilbur locate anything he was doing wrong.

When Wilbur presented the idea to Stan next morning, he said he'd do his best to help. The first time that Wilbur had a customer, Stan took his dusting cloth to the display behind the fitting lounge so he could hear Wilbur.

Wilbur began, "Good morning! May I help you?"

The lady customer returned his smile and said, "Why yes, do you have those smart little 'T' strap pumps in anything but black? And in size 6 double 'A'?"

Wilbur shook his head and said, "I'm awfully sorry but we're all out of those in other colors. That was last season's fashion, you know. But we have lots of the blacks in your size. Would you like to try them on?"

Rather regretfully the lady said, "No, I guess not."

"Can't I show you something else?" Wilbur put in eagerly.

Thoughtfully the lady said, "Well, I guess if you have something in beige, something like that only in the newer style. What I wanted was something to wear . . . ."

Happily, Wilbur interrupted, "Beige. Yes, we've got something in beige. Just came in. Let me get your size and please have a seat over there."

Thinking he was on the way to the sale, Wilbur dashed off for the shoes. The lady started for the seat, saw a display, and stopped to examine a dressy pair of black pumps.

Wilbur came back hurriedly with the shoes and the box. He pulled one shoe out of the box and held it up proudly. "How about this one?"

The lady reached for the shoe and said, "Well, I don't know. I had thought something a little dressier."

"These are very practical and comfortable." said Wilbur. "Let's try them for size."

"It looks so big!" the lady said as soon as one was on.

Wilbur laughed good-naturedly, then said, "Oh, come on now, they're only size 6. This one probably just looks big next to the black one you're wearing."

"No, these won't do at all. I'm sorry." she said firmly.

"We've got a dressy little linen shoe in beige trimmed with black," said Wilbur hopefully.

"Wouldn't linen be hard to keep clean?" asked the lady.

"Gosh, I don't know," said Wilbur. "Maybe not."

"No, I wouldn't want linen," said the lady. "I was just looking, anyway."

Questions

1. If you were Stan what would you tell Wilbur he could do to improve his sales technique?
2. What questions might Wilbur have asked the customer to develop what she wanted more fully?
3. How do you think Stan would have handled the same customer?

19

ADVERTISING AND SALES PROMOTION IN THE SMALL BUSINESS

PREVIEW OF THIS CHAPTER

1. After studying this chapter, you should be aware of the purposes of advertising.

2. You will understand some of the limitations of advertising.

3. You will be familiar with the advertising media used by the small business manager.

4. You will understand the overall ingredients that go into the advertising program of the small business.

5. You will understand the difference between advertising and sales promotion.

6. You will learn some of the commonly used sales promotion techniques employed by the small business manager.

7. You should understand these key words:

Advertising	Institutional advertising
Advertising copy	Sales promotion
Advertising medium	Point-of-purchase display
Advertising media	Impulse buying
Publicity	Specialty advertising

Billions of dollars are spent annually by firms to advertise their goods and services. By far the greatest portion of these advertising dollars is spent by the very large firms.

In typical small businesses, financial resources are limited. Consequently, many small business owner-managers feel they cannot afford the added expense of advertising their products or services. Sound business practice suggests that this attitude will greatly reduce the small firm's chance for success. Instead, the small business owner should recognize the value of advertising to the firm and the fact that advertising on a regular basis will greatly enhance the possibility for continued existence and growth of the firm.

Sales are the lifeblood of the small business, since they are the means by which income is generated. In a competitive business environment, advertising is one of the most effective methods of increasing sales. Through a well-planned advertising program, consumers can be made aware of the existence of the firm and encouraged to buy its products and services.

PURPOSES OF ADVERTISING

Personal selling was described in the previous chapter as face-to-face contact between the customer and the salesperson. On the other hand, advertising is any type of sales presentation that is nonpersonal and is paid for by an identified sponsor. The advertising message, called the advertising copy, contains the written and/or spoken words of the ad. The small business manager may choose to place advertising messages in a single source (i.e., advertising medium such as newspapers) or in more than one source (i.e., advertising media such as newspapers and radios). Ordinarily, the small business manager should use several sources for advertising messages.

Advertising can have many purposes, depending on the nature of the business and the products and services promoted. For example, a manufacturer's advertising is intended to stimulate interest and increase sales in the line of merchandise. A retailer's advertising seeks to stimulate consumer awareness and build sales for the store. Within the general objectives of advertising, small business managers can identify numerous specific objectives for a particular type of business.

In this chapter, we examine the role and the purposes of advertising as they relate primarily to small retail stores and small service establishments. However, other firms such as wholesalers and manufacturers can adapt these goals to meet their specific requirements.

For the small retailer and service establishment, advertising has two general goals. One objective is promotional advertising, that is, to promote the goods and services of the firm. The second objective, to build the image of the firm, is called institutional advertising.

PROMOTIONAL ADVERTISING

The discussion that follows suggests some of the specific purposes of promotional advertising.

Increasing Sales

One strategic purpose of promotional advertising is to bring about direct action on the part of the customer to buy a product or use a service, thus increasing sales. In the attempt to realize this goal, the small business firm's advertising may emphasize certain appeals, as shown below.

1. Encourage potential purchasers to visit the store.
2. Prompt immediate purchases through the announcement of special sales or contests.[1]

Creating Awareness of a Company's Products or Services

The advertising of the small firm can be directed to create customer awareness or interest in the firm's products or services, thus motivating purchases. This advertising tries to provide potential customers with such information as follows.

1. The types of products or services sold.
2. The benefits to be gained from the use of company products or services.
3. How products can be used.
4. The prices of products or services.
5. Where company products or services may be obtained.[2]

Attracting New Customers

Small business managers should not be complacent with their current volume of business and patronage. They may feel they have all the customers they can adequately serve and consequently see no purpose in advertising to attract new customers. However, the National Retail Merchants Association estimates that the small business would have to close its doors at the end of 3 or 4 years if it stopped advertising. This association reports that a store annually loses between 20 and 25 percent of its customers. Each year the market composition

---

[1] Adapted from Harry D. Wolfe, *Measuring Advertising Results,* Studies in Business Policy, No. 102 (National Industrial Conference Board, Inc., 1962), p. 10.
[2] Ibid., pp. 10–11.

changes as people move in and out of the trading area. For example, the Bureau of the Census estimates that about 18 percent of the nation's population changes its place of residence annually. Other customers change their shopping habits and buy from competitors. The younger generation has different demands from the older generation it replaces. As a result, in order to maintain the status quo, small business owners must use some advertising to keep the firm's name before the public in the attempt to attract new customers to replace the lost customers.

To maintain or increase the number of customers the small firm should identify its market segment and then develop and direct its advertising to this market. Markets may be segmented in a number of different ways, such as age grouping, ethnic grouping, or geographical grouping. Thus, if the target market is teenagers, then the small business manager should find out such characteristics as where they live and which radio and televisions they listen to or view. In this way, advertising can be more closely directed to the specific market.

Promotion of a Special Offer or Special Sale

Advertising may be planned for the purpose of promoting a special event or a special sale. To illustrate, a pizza parlor advertises a special price on its pizzas to help celebrate the pizza parlor's birthday. By purchasing one size of pizza (such as giant size) at the regular price, the customer will receive the next smaller size (such as regular size) of the same kind of pizza free. The ad also specifies how long the special price is good. Ads can be used to promote special sales, such as the 1-cent sale. Buy one item at the regular price and get a second for only 1-cent more. A men's store ad promotes a "1-day-only" sale of its famous name brand suits at a specially reduced price.

Promoting Greater Use of Products

Through advertising, consumers may be informed of additional uses for products. Baking soda is shown as an ingredient used in baking but also as a deodorizer for the refrigerator. Some ads may attempt to stretch the length of the buying season for a product. Antifreeze is advertised for its use as an engine coolant for summer driving as well as a protection against radiator freeze-up in the winter. This type of advertising may also suggest increasing the number of items purchased at one time or replacing the products more frequently.

Introducing New Products or Services

Not only do customers change but so do the products or services that a store offers for sale. Many old products are replaced by new ones. Advertising helps

Advertising and personal selling aid in introducing new products and services.

to inform customers of the availability of new merchandise when it is introduced. In addition the small business may also begin offering new services that are announced in the firm's advertising.

INSTITUTIONAL ADVERTISING

Institutional advertising is directed toward providing the general public with information about the company. Institutional advertising's purposes are to create goodwill toward the company, to build consumer confidence in the company, and to create or strengthen the image of the firm in the community. Through institutional advertising, the small business manager seeks to improve the firm's public relations stature by demonstrating that the owner is a concerned, active, socially responsible member of the community. For example, with the energy shortage one firm advertised in a local newspaper a message reminding consumers and business firms alike of the critical need to employ energy conservation measures. The ad also contained suggestions on how energy might be conserved.

The small firm may also direct some of its advertising emphasis toward public service announcements. For example, announcements may be made informing the public of activities that are going to take place in the community. Announcements about special community events, such as an arts and crafts show or activities of local civic organizations, may be sponsored by a particular firm. This type of advertising aids in fostering good public relations and strengthening the ties of the business to the community.

The company may also benefit from the publicity it receives. Publicity is not the same as advertising, however. Publicity is a news item about a company reported by the media because the information has some apparent news value. A firm may donate time, money, or merchandise to a civic project that is reported by the various media. Unlike advertising, publicity is not paid for by the firm.

LIMITATIONS OF ADVERTISING

Although advertising is a powerful tool to aid the small business owner, its limitations must also be recognized. For example, advertising cannot force people to buy things they do not want. Another limitation of advertising is that, if a firm advertises extensively but offers poor service or inferior products, no amount of advertising will overcome these deficiencies. Many customers visit a store in response to an ad. However, if they are ignored or treated discourteously by sales personnel during their visit, the outcome will be dissatisfied customers who are unlikely to return to the store. If the small business manager charges higher prices than competitors for similar merchandise, advertising will not aid in selling the overpriced merchandise indefinitely. A further limitation of advertising is that it usually does not produce dramatic results immediately. Rather, the manager should follow an advertising strategy of advertising consistently in at least one medium. Furthermore, advertising effectiveness will be severely reduced if it contains false or misleading statements. Not only is this illegal but it also seriously harms the firm's image in the community. Additionally, advertising's value will be diminished if it is poorly timed or improperly prepared.

In summary, the owner-manager should recognize the advertising limitations.

1. Advertising will not overcome discourteous treatment of customers by salespersons.
2. Advertising will not sell inferior products or services more than once.
3. Misleading or untruthful advertising will result in a loss of customer confidence in the firm.

4. A single advertisement will not bring about a sustained increase in sales and store traffic.

ADVERTISING MEDIA

One of the many decisions facing small business managers is deciding which advertising medium or media best serves their type of business. No one formula is available to provide the answer. Advertising media that are appropriate for the needs of the small business are discussed below.

NEWSPAPERS

Newspapers are the single most important advertising medium for the small business manager. Nationwide, about 30 percent of all advertising dollars is spent for newspaper ads. An advantage of newspapers is that circulation covers a selected geographical territory (a section of a city, a single town, a number of adjoining towns, or a number of adjacent counties). In addition, newspaper advertising provides broad coverage in the trade area. Ads reach people in all economic classes. Newspaper ads are flexible and timely since they can be changed frequently if there are morning and evening editions. Newspapers have short closing times. "Closing times" refers to the deadlines prior to publication by which advertising copy must be submitted. For daily newspapers, this period seldom exceeds 24 hours, thus giving the advertiser the opportunity to make last-minute changes. Closing dates for Sunday supplements, however, are generally much longer, usually ranging from 4 to 6 weeks.[3] When compared with other media, advertising costs in newspapers are relatively low. This is significant for the small business manager who has a limited budget for advertising. Newspapers serve as a guide for shoppers who are looking for information about products or services. The ads inform them what is available, where it is being sold, when, and at what price. Managers should study the feasibility of using the newspaper coverage that matches their goals. If they are concentrating on a trading area of a specific section of town, they may advertise in a newspaper that has a circulation limited to one section of town, such as the "Southside News."

A disadvantage of newspaper advertising is that its coverage is not selective. If the firm caters to a specific market segment, much of the newspaper ad coverage will be wasted. Another disadvantage to consider is that many ads are presented together in one newspaper and a single ad may be missed. Most

---

[3]James Engel, Martin Warshaw, and Thomas Kinnear, *Promotional Strategy,* 4th ed. (Homewood, Ill.: Richard D. Irwin, Inc., 1979), p. 273.

newspapers are read or scanned hurriedly and are not kept long in the home. Hence, the life of the ad is of extremely short duration. The small business manager should analyze what the target market is in order to determine whether newspaper advertising should extend to a larger audience or be limited to a smaller audience.

Newspaper ads must meet certain criteria if they are to be effective. One set of guidelines for newspaper ads is the "AIDCA Principle." This principle outlines the basic requirements of a good newspaper ad.

1. Attention—causes the customer to stop and read the copy.
2. Interest—brings about a sense of curiosity.
3. Desire—increases the urge to acquire.
4. Conviction—substantiates that a decision to buy would be a good judgment.
5. Action—actually moves the consumer to going out to buy.[4]

Figure 19-1 presents a checklist for a promotional ad in a newspaper.

RADIO

Nationwide, 99.9 percent of all households have radios and most autos also have radios. Thus, radio provides the small business owner a medium for reaching nearly all listeners in the local trade area as often as necessary. Radio advertising is advantageous in that it makes it possible for advertisers to select the market they wish to receive their message. Radio ads can be aired to a particular market segment in a trade area since radio stations plan their programming to appeal to specific groups of listeners, such as listeners of certain types of music or talk shows. Other advantages of radio advertising are its flexibility and timeliness. Commercials can be prepared in the morning and aired the same afternoon. Certain times are better for reaching a large market, such as before, during, or after sporting events. Radio ads can also be presented frequently and at different times of the day or night if the small business manager chooses.

Radio ads are sold in 10-, 30-, and 60-second spot announcements. Ad costs vary according to the time of day and size of the listening audience. Most expensive rates are usually for the prime time periods from 6 A.M. to 10 A.M. and 3 P.M. to 7 P.M. on weekdays.

Other factors influencing cost are (1) how often the business advertises in a given week, (2) how many consecutive weeks the ads run, (3) whether spots are scheduled on a run-of-the-station basis, that is, aired at times the station

---

[4]C. Winston Borgen, *Learning Experiences in Retailing* (Pacific Palisades, Cal.: Goodyear Publishing Company, Inc., 1976), p. 259.

*Merchandise	Does the ad offer merchandise having wide appeal, special features, price appeal, and timeliness?
Medium	Is a newspaper the best medium for the ad, or would another—direct mail, radio, television, or other—be more appropriate?
Location	Is the ad situated in the best spot (in both section and page location)?
Size	Is the ad large enough to do the job expected of it? Does it omit important details, or is it overcrowded with nonessential information?
*Headline	Does the headline express the major single idea about the merchandise advertised? The headline should usually be an informative statement and not simply a label.
Illustration	Does the illustration (if one is used) express the idea the headline conveys?
*Merchandise information	Does the copy give the basic facts about the goods, or does it leave out information that would be important to the reader? ("The more you tell, the more you sell.")
Layout	Does the arrangement of the parts of the ad and the use of white space make the ad easy to read? Does it stimulate the reader to look at all the contents of the ad?
Human interest	Does the ad—through illustration, headline, and copy—appeal to customers' wants and wishes?
*"You" attitude	Is the ad written and presented from the customer's point of view (with the customer's interests clearly in mind), or from the store's?
*Believeability	To the objective, nonpartisan reader, does the ad ring true, or does it perhaps sound exaggerated or somewhat phony?
Typeface	Does the ad use a distinctive typeface—different from those of competitors?
*Spur to action	Does the ad stimulate prompt action through devices such as use of a coupon, statement of limited quantities, announcement of a specific time period for the promotion or impending event?
*Sponsor identification	Does the ad use a specially prepared signature cut that is always associated with the store and that identifies it at a glance? Also, does it always include the following institutional details: Store location, hours open, telephone number, location of advertised goods, and whether phone and mail orders are accepted?

*The seven items starred are of chief importance to the smaller store.

Figure 19-1 Checklist for promotional advertising in a newspaper. [*Source:* John W. Wingate and Seymour Helfant, *Small Planning for Growth,* 2nd ed. (Washington, D.C.: Small Business Administration, 1977), p. 69.]

selects, or in more costly fixed time slots, and (4) any combination packages of time amounts, slots, and frequencies.

Rates for a station are available from the station itself and are also quoted in the *Standard Rate and Data Service,* an industry survey of the costs of various media. For example, a spot announcement rate taken from this publication for a station is shown below along with its time rates.

TIME RATES

AAA: Monday through Saturday   5:30 to 10 A.M. and 3 to 7 P.M.
  AA: Monday through Saturday   10 A.M. to 3 P.M.
    A: Monday through Saturday   7 P.M. to midnight
       Sunday   6 A.M. to midnight

COST FOR EACH SPOT ANNOUNCEMENT, 1 MINUTE*

	6 TIMES PER WEEK	12 TIMES PER WEEK	18 TIMES PER WEEK
AAA	$80	$75	$70
AA	70	65	60
A	55	50	45

---

*20- and 30-second ads cost 80 percent of 1 minute.
Source. Spot Radio Rates and Data, Standard Rate and Data Services, Inc., Skokie, Ill., Vol. 62, no. 6, p. 780, June 1, 1980.

There are some disadvantages to radio advertising that should be recognized. Obviously, radio advertising will not reach a person who is not listening. Frequently, radios are turned on while people are busily engaged in other activities and they may not be paying attention to the advertising message. In addition, radio permits only a spoken message to describe a product or service, radio ads must be brief because of the time limit, and radio ads must be broadcast repeatedly in order to reach the target market.

TELEVISION

Television is being used with increased frequency by small business managers. One reason for the growth is that costs have been lowered, enabling more small business managers to fit this medium into their advertising budget. Television is an important medium for reaching large markets. Census data indicate that nationwide there are television sets in 96 percent of the households; and in the average home a television set is turned on over 6 hours a day. Consequently, in a local market area, the likelihood of a firm's ad being seen and heard is quite high. Television ads offer a threefold advantage: (1) products or services can be advertised, (2) they can be demonstrated, and (3) the advertising message can be presented simultaneously with the demonstration.

Television time is sold in 10-, 20-, 30-, and 60-second spots. The 30-second spot is most popular with small business owners. Spot announcements enable the advertiser to select the time, audience, and program for the commercial ad. The ad message can vary since it can be presented over different stations. As with radio advertising, the time and makeup of the viewing audience should be considered for the television ad. For example, a toy store can effectively present its ad during the Saturday morning time period when cartoons are to be televised and there is a large children's viewing audience.

There are some disadvantages to television ads.

Television ads are projected onto the screen for a short time and may be missed by the prospective customer. Also, most trade areas are exposed to more than a single TV station, meaning only a part of the total viewing audience will be exposed to the ad. And the viewing audience usually does something else during commercials, especially when they are aired during station breaks.

In evaluating radio and television station advertising, the small business manager should consider using small stations or stations in small towns. Advertising rates on these stations are lower and frequently are more effective in reaching a particular market segment.

HANDBILLS

Handbills are one of the most inexpensive methods of advertising if properly managed. The cost of producing handbills is low. They are usually reproduced by either mimeograph or multilith methods. The small business manager is able to control the distribution of the handbills since they are distributed by store employees or others (school children) in a small selected area. Handbills may be distributed door to door in selected neighborhoods, placed under the windshield wiper blade of cars parked in a shopping center lot, handed out to customers in the store, inserted in their shopping bag by cashier as they check out, or laid out on store counter where they can be picked up by the customers. (See Fig. 19-2.)

A disadvantage is that many customers consider handbills a nuisance and react negatively when they find handbills on their car or at their front door and many are thrown away without ever being read. In addition, individuals who distribute the handbills should be reliable.

DIRECT MAIL ADVERTISING

Circulars, letters, folders, postcards, and leaflets stuffed into monthly bills are types of direct mail advertising. An advantage of direct mail advertising is that

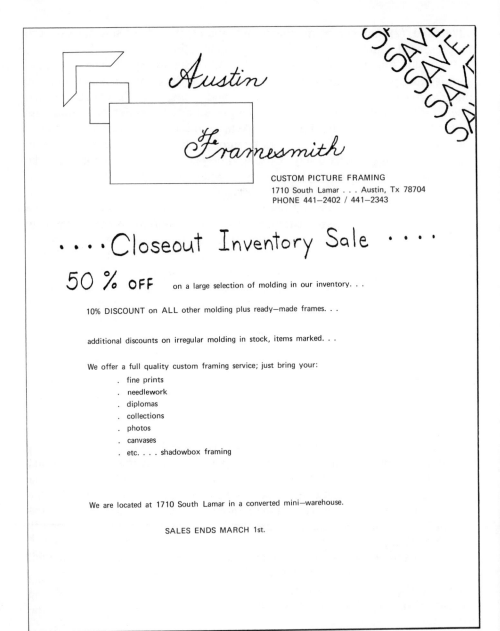

Figure 19-2 A handbill placed on autos at an arts and crafts show.

Dear Preferred Customer,
    Naomi's south Austin store in Cherry Creek
Plaza is having a SMOKE DAMAGE SALE –
–30% + OFF – THURSDAY MAY 29 starting at
    10 a.m. General public sale starts Friday.
This is your card to TREMENDOUS savings.
Please bring it with you.

                                    Naomi's Dress Shop
Phone: 447-9292   5732 Manchaca Road

Figure 19-3 Direct mail ads enable the small business to direct its advertising message to a specific group.

advertisers can select the specific audience whom they wish to receive their message. The tone of the message should be personal. (See Fig. 19-3.)

One main consideration for direct mailing is that the mailing list be accurate and current. Usually the small business manager can compile an effective mailing list from charge account records and sales slips. Lists can also be compiled from city directories, obtained from government agencies such as licensing bureaus, or bought or rented from firms that specialize in compiling and selling or renting mailing lists. Fees are charged for each name or for each thousand names.

Mailings may be made on a regular basis, such as a weekly mailing of a grocery store circular. Or, they may be used for a one-time announcement, such as a change in store name, hours, personnel, or ownership. Also, a series of mailings may be sent to promote the sale of a single offer. Other uses of direct mail ads are shown in Figure 19-4.

STORE SIGNS

Store signs and other outdoor signs such as billboards and portable trailers are one of the most useful direct forms of visual advertising available to the small business owner.

Store signs are street advertising. Effective signs must be noticeable and readable. They are important because they provide in an easily recognizable

To solicit mail-order or phone-order business.

To presell prospects before a salesperson's call—to soften up the buyer by acquainting him or her with your company and your products.

To announce new models, new designs, new lines, new items, or changes in your products, services, or equipment.

To notify your customers of price increases or decreases.

To substitute for a salesperson's call on a regular customer.

To follow up on salespersons' calls to prospects.

To welcome new customers.

To help regain lost customers.

To increase the full-line selling of your salespeople.

To thank all customers for their business at least once a year.

To create an image for your business.

To remind customers and prospects of seasonal or periodic needs.

To make the most of special events such as feature sales.

To take advantage of printed advertising materials supplied by manufacturers.

Figure 19-4 Uses of direct mail advertising for manufacturers, retailers, and service businesses. [*Source.* Harvey R. Cook, *Selecting Advertising Media* (Washington, D.C.: Small Business Administration, 1969).]

form information about the business and its products and services, give directions to the business, and help build the image of the business. Specific advantages of store signs are:

1. Signs are oriented to your trade area.
2. Signs are always on the job repeating your message to potential customers.
3. Nearly everyone reads signs.
4. Signs are inexpensive.
5. Signs are available to every shop owner.
6. Signs are easy to use.[5]

TRANSPORTATION ADVERTISING

The company name may be painted and displayed on the sides of the firm's delivery vehicle. Another form of transportation advertising is to display an advertising message on a mode of public transportation—taxicabs, buses,

[5]Karen Claus and R. J. Klaus, "Signs and Your Business," *Small Marketers Aids No. 161* (Washington, D.C.: Small Business Administration, 1977).

Store signs should clearly identify the store.

commuter trains. Posters may be displayed on the sides of buses or on the backs of taxicabs, or rotating signs may be displayed on top of taxis. This type of advertising is relatively inexpensive and the advertising area to be covered can be controlled.

MAGAZINES

Magazine advertising can be used by the small business owner if it is used selectively. National magazines, which have high circulation and charge advertising rates that far exceed the advertising budget of the small firm, are impractical. However, magazines published in the local area, which have smaller circulation and lower advertising rates, permit the small business owner to consider them as a medium for ads. There are a variety of types of local magazines that can adequately serve the needs of the small business manager.

This shoe repair shop advertises fast service.

City and Community Magazines

These magazines do not differ greatly from national magazines. The content of these magazines relates to the local area. Some of them are privately owned; others are sponsored and published by local groups, such as the chamber of commerce.

Visitor Magazines

These magazines emphasize places to go and things to do in the local area. Ordinarily, these magazines are placed in hotels and motels and are directed toward the tourist or convention visitor.

Publications of Special Interest Groups

Each locality has specific groups, such as women's clubs and fraternal orders. Frequently, these associations publish a magazine, either on a regular basis throughout the year or annually. If magazines are sent to a specific segment of the market to which the firm caters, the small business owner may wisely use this source as an effective vehicle for conveying advertising messages.

The advantage of advertising in a magazine is that the ads have a longer life expectancy than newspaper ads since magazines are kept longer and read in a more leisurely fashion. A disadvantage of magazine advertising is that the ads must be placed well in advance of the time of actual publication of the magazine as well as at a higher cost for ad space.

SPECIALTY ADVERTISING

Advertisers may get their advertising message into the consumer's hands and keep their advertising message before the consumer by use of specialty advertising. Specialty advertising means merchants print their name and message on a wide range of useful items and distribute them free to their customers. They use these tokens to say thank you to their customers for their patronage. Ball-point pens, pencils, rulers, key rings, coin purses, book matches, calendars, thermometers, and ashtrays are just a few examples of items that are distributed each year to customers.

DIRECTORIES

Small business owners commonly use the "Yellow Pages" of the local telephone directory for their ads. These ads have long life, usually a year, as well as wide circulation. Another benefit is that the telephone company extensively advertises the Yellow Pages, making potential customers aware of the value of looking in the Yellow Pages for specific firms. In addition to the Yellow Pages, other industry and trade groups frequently publish directories identifying their membership and their business products or services.

THE ADVERTISING PROGRAM OF THE SMALL FIRM

It is necessary for the owner to realize that an advertising program requires systematic planning. Decisions must be made regarding the purposes of the advertising campaign. Media to be used must be determined, and advertising copy must be developed. The small business manager faces many decisions in regard to the advertising program. (See Fig. 19-5.) Since each business firm is unique, these decisions must be based on meeting the requirements of the specific firm. Several guidelines are offered that should prove beneficial for the owner in planning the firm's advertising program.

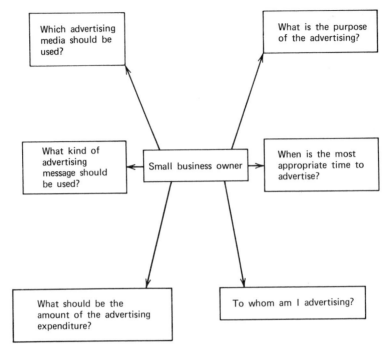

Figure 19-5   Some advertising decisions of the small business owner.

ANALYSIS OF FIRM AND CUSTOMERS

An initial concern of small business owners should be to analyze their own strengths and weaknesses as well as identify their potential market. In this way, a coordinated advertising program can be developed and implemented.

The evaluation of the firm should reveal how well it compares to competitors—what unique services or products are offered that are not provided by competitors. Another facet is the quality of merchandise carried in the store. Other factors include identifying customer services offered, location of store, and selling techniques used.

An effective advertising program necessitates the identification of the market segment the firm is attempting to reach. Examples of specific markets that have been cited earlier include age groups, income levels, educational levels, geographic location, occupation, and home ownership. Another significant need relating to the composition of the customer market is to forecast changes that are anticipated. Especially pertinent is the determination of whether the market size is expected to increase or decrease, whether incomes continue upward, and so forth.

SALES OBJECTIVE

The purpose of planning has been stated to attempt to project the short-term and long-term growth of the firm. To illustrate, the small business manager may establish a goal to increase sales by 6 percent a year over the next five years. Advertising must be planned and coordinated to aid in achieving this goal. In setting the projected goal, the owner must evaluate the trading area to establish the feasibility of the sales objective. As noted previously, if the objective is to attract 10 percent more customers but the market potential is not there, no amount of advertising will make the goal attainable. The small business owner should plan the sales objectives for the year on a month-by-month basis. As each month passes, the manager will be able to gauge the sales performance and compare the sales forecast with actual results. The manager will be able to evaluate how well the advertising program is progressing.

SCHEDULING OF ADVERTISING

Deciding when and what is the appropriate time to advertise in order to reach the desired audience is necessary to maximize the advertising dollar expenditure. For a small retailer, advertising can be planned to coincide with days when shopping is heaviest. Friday and Saturday are traditionally heavy shopping days for grocery stores. Consequently, many grocery store owners plan their food ads to appear in Thursday papers. Other advertising should be scheduled to coincide with payroll days in the trading area. The small business owner must also consider what is to be advertised—new merchandise, closeout items.

THE ADVERTISEMENT

The small business owner should realize there are a number of desirable qualities in an ad that assist in making it more effective in achieving the intended results.

1. *Make your ads easily recognizable.* Try to give your own copy a consistent personality and style.
2. *Use a simple layout.* In printed media, your layout should carry the eye through the message easily and in proper sequence, from art and headline to copy and price and to signature.
3. *Use dominant illustrations.* Featured merchandise should be shown in the dominant illustrations. Pictures emphasizing the product in use are good.
4. *Get the main benefit to the reader or viewer.* Prospective customers want to know, "What's in it for me?" Emphasize the main reason why readers or listeners should buy the advertised item.

5. *Give complete information.* Give all essential information about the item such as: the manufacturer, model, various sizes, and colors. Your description should have a warm, sincere, and enthusiastic tone.
6. *State price or range of prices.* Don't be afraid to quote a high price. If the price is low, support it with statements that create belief, such as clearances or special purchases.
7. *Specify branded merchandise.* If the advertised merchandise is a known brand, say so. Take advantage of advertising allowances and the preselling that the manufacturer has done. As one small marketer says, "Cooperative advertising is one of the most valuable types of programs available to me from my suppliers."
8. *Be sure to include store name and address.* Check every ad or commercial to be certain you have included store name, address, telephone number, and store hours.[6]

THE ADVERTISING BUDGET FOR THE SMALL BUSINESS

The small business owner wants to get maximum return of sales for each dollar of advertising. How much should be budgeted for advertising depends on a number of factors.

1. Stores in less favorable locations or managers opening a new store or expanding a present store may require more advertising.
2. The intensity of competition increases advertising requirements.
3. The greater the number of special sale dates, the greater the need for an increased advertising budget.
4. The larger the competing firm or the more it spends for advertising, the more you may need to spend for advertising.

In preparing an advertising budget, small business managers most commonly use the "percent of sales approach." National averages of advertising as a percentage of sales for your type of business can be used as guidelines (see table), but specific ad budgets must be adjusted for local conditions by considering such factors as those listed above.

One means for the small business owner to get more results for each advertising dollar spent is to feature nationally advertised products in the ads. Millions of dollars are spent each year by manufacturers to advertise their products and services nationwide. By incorporating these brand names and symbols into

[6]Charles T. Lipscomb, Jr., "Checklist for Successful Retail Advertising," *Small Marketers Aids* (Washington, D.C.: Small Business Administration, 1973).

advertising, small business owners are able to take advantage of the pulling power that these products and services, which are household names, have. Small business owners' advertising can emphasize that their stores are places where nationally known merchandise or services can be purchased.

COOPERATIVE ADVERTISING

Another way of getting more for each advertising dollar is through "cooperative advertising." Cooperative advertising is a plan in which the cost of advertising is shared by manufacturers of nationally known brand name products and the retailer who advertises and sells the product at the local level. The advantage of this type of advertising is that it permits the retailer to reduce advertising cost. This is the result of the typical cooperative advertising agreement, which calls for the manufacturer to pay for 50 percent of the cost of advertising, but percentages vary. National manufacturers also supply the retailer with materials to be used in the advertisements. The small firm with a limited advertising budget can greatly benefit from this type of advertising arrangement.

SALES PROMOTION

Sales promotion includes "those marketing activities other than personal selling and advertising, and publicity, that stimulate consumer purchasing and dealer effectiveness, such as displays, shows and expositions, demonstrations, and various nonrecurrent selling efforts not in the ordinary routine."[7]

Sales promotion techniques are designed to give added sales push for products. These promotional events take place within the store as well as outside. A number of sales promotion techniques suitable to the needs of the small businessman are discussed below.

POINT-OF-PURCHASE DISPLAYS

The small businessman, in planning his interior store layout, should definitely consider how best to encourage "impulse buying." Impulse buying refers to purchases made by customers that are not planned beforehand.

Point-of-purchase advertising displays, strategically placed throughout the store, represent one of the most effective means of stimulating impulse purchasing. Usually, these displays are prepared by the manufacturer or distributor of products and are made available to the small businessman. Typical

---

[7]Committee on Definitions, *Marketing Definitions: A Glossary of Marketing Terms* (Chicago: American Marketing Association, 1960), p. 20.

Advertising as Practiced

TYPE OF BUSINESS	AVERAGE AD BUDGET (% OF SALES)[a]	FAVORITE MEDIA	OTHER MEDIA USED
Bars and cocktail lounges	1.0 to 1.2%	Newspapers (entertainment section), local magazines, tourist bulletins	Specialties
Bicycle shops	1.5 to 2.0%	Newspapers (sports section)	Fliers, Yellow Pages, cycling magazines, direct mail
Book stores	1.5 to 1.6%	Newspapers, shoppers, Yellow Pages	Direct mail
Building maintenance services	1.0 to 1.5%	Direct mail, door-to-door, Yellow Pages	Signs on company vehicles and equipment
Camera shops (independent)	2.0 to 3.5%	Direct mail, handouts, Yellow Pages	Newspapers (*except* large urban)
Drug stores (independent)	1.5 to 3.0%	Local newspapers, shoppers	Direct mail (list from prescription files)
Dry cleaning plants	0.9 to 2.0%	Local newspapers, shoppers, Yellow Pages	Storefront ads, pamphlets on clothes care
Equipment rental services	1.7 to 4.7%	Yellow Pages	
Gift stores	2.2%	Weekly newspapers	Yellow Pages, radio, direct mail, magazines
Hairdressing shops	2.0 to 5.0%	Yellow Pages	Newspapers (for special events), word of mouth

[a]*Slightly higher in new establishments. Source.* Small Business Reporter, Bank of America, San Francisco, 1978.

forms of display are wall or shelf displays, interior or overhead signs, and counter displays.

While shopping, the consumers' attention may be attracted by a point-of-purchase display sign that describes the merits of a product. After reading the sign and examining the product, customers frequently decide to try the product. Consequently, a sale is made.

Point-of-purchase displays may be used effectively to remind customers of a product they need but had forgotten to include on their shopping lists. Another

by Selected Small Businesses

TYPE OF BUSINESS	AVERAGE AD BUDGET (% OF SALES)*	FAVORITE MEDIA	OTHER MEDIA USED
Home furnishing stores	5.0 to 6.0%	Newspapers	Direct mail, radio
Liquor stores (independent)	0.2 to 0.6%	Point-of-purchase displays	Newspapers, Yellow Pages
Mail order firms	15.0 to 25.0%	Newspapers, magazines	Direct mail
Pet shops	2.0 to 5.0%	Yellow Pages	Window displays, shoppers, direct mail
Plant shops	1.3 to 1.5%	Local newspapers, word of mouth	
Recreational vehicle and mobile home dealers	0.5 to 1.0%	Local newspapers, radio, Yellow Pages	Direct mail, television for multi-lot dealers
Repair services	1.0 to 1.6%	Yellow Pages	Signs on vehicles, direct mail, shoppers
Restaurants and food services	4.0%	Newspapers, radio, Yellow Pages, transit, outdoor	Television for chain or franchise restaurants
Shoe stores	3.0%	Newspapers, direct mail, radio	Yellow Pages (especially for specialty shoe vendors)
Small job printers	0.5 to 1.0%	Salespeople in the field	Direct mail

Slightly higher in new establishments. Source: Small Business Reporter, Bank of America, San Francisco, 1978.

purpose of these displays is to suggest additional uses of a product. This technique is often successful in influencing a customer to buy a product.

A point-of-purchase display sign on a bargain table full of hardware items (hammers, pliers, wrenches, screwdrivers, etc.) may remind the customer of the need for another hammer for use outside in the garage. And the display sign stresses the items on sale now at a special low price. Another point-of-purchase display suggests the usefulness of an electric grass trimmer with a long handle, which eliminates the need for bending over to trim around trees or fences. Placing umbrellas or other rain apparel near the checkout counter of the store during a rainstorm is an excellent merchandising plan for stimulating impulse purchases. Many point-of-purchase displays are strategically located at the store's checkout counter. For example, razor blades, chewing gum, and flashlight batteries are just a few of the convenience goods displayed where consumers can pick them up on impulse and buy them.

SHOW WINDOWS

Merchandise displays or signs in the show window should be appealing to the customer as well as attention getters. Show window displays should be designed for the purpose of presenting merchandise in such a way that the passerby stops, looks, enters the store to find out more about the merchandise, and is encouraged to make a purchase. Show windows can be effectively used to stimulate impulse buying. Show window displays should be changed regularly to make them most effective. If the same people pass your store daily, window displays should be changed more frequently.

SAMPLES

One sales promotion technique is to distribute free samples of a product to customers. In this way, the small business puts the product in the hands of the customers for the purpose of getting them to try it. The expectation is that they will like it and become regular users. A sample tube of a new toothpaste, a sample box of a new detergent, or a sample jar of a new brand of freeze-dried coffee is given to customers to try. When a new food item is to be introduced, such as a new breakfast sausage, samples may be prepared in a grocery store. Customers are offered a sample and its unique characteristics are explained. Customers who like the item then are encouraged to buy the product. An advantage of this sales promotion technique is that consumer acceptance or nonacceptance of the product is known as soon as it is tried.

TRADING STAMPS

Trading stamps offer the customer an extra value for each purchase in that the stamps can be redeemed for cash or merchandise. By offering stamps as a sales promotion technique, store owner-managers attempt to provide customers with an additional incentive to patronize their store. Or they may give stamps to gain a competitive edge over stores not offering stamps. By getting customers to save stamps, store owner-managers hope to build repeat patronage of the store.

PREMIUMS

Premiums are products that are offered free or at minimal cost to the customer. Consumers may receive a dish, glass, or other merchandise free if they purchase another product or make a purchase in excess of a stated dollar amount, such as over $10.00. A retailer may offer one pair of shoes at the regular price and the second for 1 cent more.

COUPONS

A frequently used sales promotion technique is coupons. Coupons are intended to stimulate sales by offering the consumer a discount on purchases. For example, a retailer may offer a series of coupons that are redeemable during a specified week. Or, a service firm may offer a coupon that provides a discount for carpet cleaning.

SPECIAL SALES

Store owner-managers may have a special sales promotion that features low prices. These may be clearance sales at the end of the year or end of a season. Or special sales may be held in conjunction with special observances, such as Labor Day or George Washington's Birthday.

CONTESTS

Some contests are intended to attract new customers to use a product already in existence or to introduce a new product. Other contests attempt to get customers into the store to register for a cash prize or merchandise to be presented at a drawing held in the store. For example, a small grocery store may have a contest or a drawing for a free turkey to be given away at Thanksgiving.

DISCUSSION QUESTIONS

1. What is the difference between advertising and sales promotion?
2. Explain some of the basic purposes of promotional advertising.
3. Discuss the difference between publicity and institutional advertising.
4. Identify some of the limitations of advertising.
5. Identify the advertising media that may be suitable to the needs of the small business manager.
6. Outline the procedure for designing an effective advertising program for the small business.
7. Explain the role of point-of-purchase displays in sales promotion.
8. Identify several sales promotion techniques.

STUDENT PROJECTS

View local television programming, listen to local radio stations, observe transportation ads and outside signs, read newspaper and magazine ads, and if possible, collect direct mail ads and handbills of local small business firms. Make notes of the advertising messages and types of stores using the various advertising media. Also note how many different advertising media are used by the same stores.

CASE A

SMITH LUMBER COMPANY

Smith Lumber Company was formed in 1947 by Mr. and Mrs. J. T. Smith. They sold only one grade of lumber (#1) and a limited line of high-quality building accessories. Their main customers were building contractors and a group of customers who preferred quality and service over price. The Smiths carried on this tradition for 30 years until 1977 when Mr. Smith suffered a heart attack and they were forced to sell the business.

The new owner, Mack Walls, purchased the physical plant, the inventory, and the company name. Shortly after the purchase, the business was relocated in a new, modern "Home Center" facility.

A chief objective of the new owner was to expand the offerings of products and services of the lumber company so as to serve building contractors as well as the "do-it-yourself" customers. Walls observed that there was a real need for this type of business in the area since none existed in the city. Walls also increased selling emphasis on hardware business, which he believed would aid in increasing sales and profits without sacrificing the personal touch of customer service Smith Lumber had become known for.

All nine employees of the company were retained. Mr. Walls felt their knowledge and experience could help in the operations and decision making of the business. The former owner also agreed to serve as an adviser to the company, which aided the smooth transition of ownership.

A concern of Walls was the best type of advertising strategy to use to achieve the growth objective. Walls was undecided which combination of advertising media to use and their relative effectiveness in order to reach the "do-it-yourself" customer in the trade area and to maintain the image of service and quality.

Walls has considered the following alternatives.

1. Radio advertising—the town has one radio station.

2. Television advertising—television stations from two large metropolitan areas cover the city trade area.
3. Newspaper—two local biweekly papers are published on Thursday and Sunday. Both newspapers provided duplicate coverage of the trade area.
4. Circulars—direct mail circulars sent to all residents cost 11.7 cents per copy or newspaper inserts were available.
5. Miscellaneous sources—Yellow Pages, school programs, and so on.
6. No advertising.

Question

What advertising strategy would you recommend for Mr. Walls in order for him to reach his objectives?

CASE B
JOEY'S PIZZA PALACE

Joey's Pizza Palace has just recently opened its doors for business. Naturally, Joey is anxious to have his eating establishment become a popular spot for dining out in the community. However, he realizes this is not going to be an easy task because of strong competition not only from other pizza establishments in the city but also from all other types of food operations. Joey realizes he has spent a lot of money getting his pizza palace off the ground and operating. He would like to think that he could rely on word-of-mouth advertising from satisfied customers instead of having to advertise in the various media. However, he recognizes that this type of advertising is not totally satisfactory, although he prides himself on the quality of his foods and services, and his customers have expressed much satisfaction with his pizzas. Thus, Joey is concerned about getting the most for the dollars he is going to spend for advertising. And he also wonders about the feasibility of special sales promotion events for his pizza palace.

Questions

1. Outline a positive program of advertising for Joey's Pizza Palace.
2. Which advertising medium or media would you recommend he use?
3. What sales promotion techniques, if any, could you recommend for Joey to use in his pizza palace?

20

CONSUMER CREDIT

PREVIEW OF THIS CHAPTER

1. In this chapter, you will discover how important retail credit is to most small business firms.

2. You will learn how the traditional 30-day charge account operates.

3. You will understand how the revolving charge account functions and how small business firms use credit card companies to finance this credit.

4. You will learn how important bank credit cards are to small businesses and what functions they perform for them.

5. If you ever bought a car or appliance on credit, you will be interested to know how installment credit functions.

6. You will learn how small business firms obtain credit information.

7. You will be interested in finding out how the truth-in-lending law attempts to put credit on a more competitive basis and what information it requires business to disclose to customers.

8. You will learn the importance of the bad debt ratio and the system for collection of overdue accounts.

9. You will be able to understand these key words:

Credit	Credit cards
Consumer credit	Retail credit bureaus
Retail credit	Mortgage credit
Charge account credit	Nonmortgage credit
Thirty-day accounts	Truth-in-lending
Revolving charge accounts	Bad debts
Installment credit	Collections
Interest	Bank credit cards

Many small business firms extend either trade credit or retail credit. Manufacturers and wholesalers often extend trade credit to their customers. This trade credit usually exists in the form of supplying products to their customers on 30-, 60-, or 90-day accounts. Various forms of trade credit were discussed in Chapter 7.

Some sources consider credit extended to retail stores to be retail credit and credit extended by service firms to be service credit. However, for our purposes, retail credit will consist of credit extended to customers by both retail stores and service firms, that is, firms that conduct business directly with the ultimate consumer. This chapter is devoted to a discussion of various aspects of this retail credit.

IMPORTANCE OF RETAIL CREDIT

Retail credit has increased at a phenomenal rate since World War II. Today personal income has multiplied over 9 times what it was in 1945. Mortgage credit (credit that has a specific item mortgaged as security for the loan) has kept pace by multiplying 10 times what it was in 1945. However, during the same period, nonmortgage credit (credit that does not have any specific asset mortgaged as security against the loan) has multiplied to 63 times its original 1945 amount. For the same period, the population only increased by a little over 1½ times.

To further illustrate the importance of retail credit, Figure 20-1 shows the rapid growth of various types of consumer credit from 1950 to 1979.

TYPE OF CREDIT	AMOUNT (in billions of dollars)			
	1950	1960	1970	1979
Total consumer credit outstanding	25.6	65.1	143.1	355.0
Installment	15.5	45.1	105.5	287.6
Automobiles	6.0	18.1	36.3	109.2
Revolving	NA	NA	5.1	46.5
Mobile homes	NA	NA	2.5	16.5
All other loans	9.5	27.0	61.6	115.5
Noninstallment	10.1	20.0	37.6	67.4
Single payment loans	3.6	9.1	19.3	38.1
Charge accounts	4.9	7.2	9.2	11.7
Service credit	1.6	3.7	9.1	17.6

Figure 20-1 Consumer credit: selected years. (*Source: Statistical Abstract of the United States,* 1979.)

This vast amount of credit existing in the United States indicates the importance of consumer credit to most small business concerns. Many small business firms do not extend credit for various reasons, such as offering lower prices in place of customer services. However, most small business firms offer credit, and many of them could not obtain sufficient volume of sales to stay in business if they did not.

Considering the amazing increase of credit, it would appear that providing customer credit will become increasingly important to small business.

TYPES OF RETAIL CREDIT

Although there are many deviations in retail credit offered by firms to their customers, there are only two basic categories of retail credit—charge account credit and installment credit.

CHARGE ACCOUNT CREDIT

The two primary types of charge account credit are the traditional 30-day charge accounts and the more modern revolving charge accounts. Neither type of charge account credit holds a chattel mortgage against a specific item purchased, as does installment credit.

Thirty-Day Accounts

The traditional 30-day charge account extends credit to customers by allowing them to purchase merchandise on credit during the month and then pay the entire balance of the account at the end of the month. For example, a customer's record of charges and payments for three months might appear as follows.

	CREDIT PURCHASES DURING THE MONTH	PAYMENTS AT THE END OF THE MONTH
September	$30	$30
October	44	44
November	68	68

While it traditionally has been the practice of charge account creditors, both 30-day and revolving, to issue statements at the end of the month, many firms with large numbers of credit accounts have gone to cycle billing. Cycle billing is used in order to reduce the pressure of billing at the end of the month and to better utilize billing personnel by spreading the billing process over the entire month. Every two or three days, a different part of the accounts is billed, usually in alphabetical order of the customers' last names. Instead of the account's being due at the end of the month, it is due in a specific number of days after the billing date shown on the statement (usually in 10 days).

The customer is usually not required to pay any interest on his credit if he pays it off by the due date. Some stores give their customers credit cards as a means of identifying them as credit customers. However, this is not the most common practice. Most stores offering traditional 30-day charge accounts use some form of credit slip, which lists purchases and dollar amounts and is signed by the customer.

Retail stores that use 30-day charge accounts usually carry the credit accounts themselves. These stores sometimes borrow money against their charge accounts from banks or factors as a means of financing them (a discussion of factoring is contained in Chapter 7).

Revolving Charge Accounts

The revolving charge account method is similar to the traditional 30-day charge account in that the customer may purchase merchandise on credit and pay it off at the end of the monthly billing period. However, it differs from the traditional 30-day charge account in that the customer is not required to pay off all credit purchases on a monthly basis. The revolving charge account method only requires the customer to pay a part of the total amount owed. The minimum amount he is required to pay is based on the total amount that he owes. Usually, if the customer uses his revolving charge account as a traditional 30-day charge account and pays off the entire amount at the end of the billing period, he is not charged interest. However, if he uses it as a revolving charge account and does not pay the total amount owed, he is charged interest on the amount that is carried over to the next period. A customer's revolving charge account for three months might appear as follows.

	PURCHASES DURING THE PERIOD	INTEREST CHARGED	PAYMENT	BALANCE AFTER PAYMENT
January				$368.28
February	$54.60	$5.11	$50.00	377.99
March	0	5.27	50.00	333.26
April	35.38	4.81	20.00	353.45

Firms that issue credit cards place a maximum amount that may be purchased using the card. The most common limit of credit cards is one that does not allow the card holder to exceed a balance of $500. If requested, higher credit card limits may be established for the individual, depending primarily on his record and income.

Most retail firms charge interest based on the average daily balance. The average daily balance is calculated by totaling the balance outstanding for each day of the month and dividing by the number of days in the billing period. Historically the most common rate of interest charged on revolving charge accounts has been 1.5 percent per month, which amounts to an annual percentage of 18 percent.

Almost all revolving charge accounts are set up to use credit cards. Firms sometimes carry their own accounts, but most small businesses accept credit cards issued by other companies. Some of the credit cards they accept may be from firms who produce a product and whose primary function is acting as something other than a financial institution. For example, many petroleum firms have their own credit cards and allow motels and other selected types of business to accept their credit cards for a fee.

Financial institutions also issue credit cards that may be used to purchase a wide range of merchandise and services. Visa and MasterCard are the principal bank-issued credit cards. In addition, Diners Club and American Express are two firms that specialize in consumer credit for many products and services. In 1979, debt on credit cards issued by banks totaled $24 billion.[1]

Bank-issued credit cards have been a real boon to small businesses. Several years ago it was common for the authors to hear a small business owner say the firm's biggest problem was credit and collections. Many small businesses have gone out of business in the past due to improper control of credit and inability to collect customer credit accounts. The bank credit cards have largely eliminated this problem for most small businesses. The cards have become so common that most small businesses do not offer credit except on the credit cards.

The small business does have to pay a percentage of all charges to the bank. The percentage ranges from 2 percent to 6 percent of the amount charged. The percentage charged each small business is determined primarily by the average amount of sales charged on each ticket. For example, the small business that usually turns in charge tickets that only amount to a few dollars is charged a much higher percentage than the firm that turns in charge tickets amounting to several hundred dollars each.

While the small business does have to pay a fee for the service, they have usually found it well worth the cost. Every charge ticket they receive they enter on their bank deposit slip and the amount is immediately added to their account. The bank then bills them for the cost of their tickets. The small business, in a sense, can count bank credit charges as cash to their business. In general,

[1]*Statistical Abstract of the United States*, 1979.

they run no risk of bad debts. The cards also allow them to function on much less working capital, which is a cost to them. They do not have to process credit applications and maintain no credit or collection records.

One risk the firm runs is to fail to check the card against the invalid card list issued by the credit card company or to fail to telephone about all purchases over a specific amount. The small business must sustain the loss in these cases. Usually, credit card companies will pay a reward, usually about $25, to a clerk who calls the credit card company and takes up a card that appears on their invalid lists. This helps the small business by motivating clerks to be more diligent in checking the list in hopes of receiving a reward. Another risk is that the clerk does not properly imprint the charge ticket with the card machine. If the credit card company can not trace the customer, they will not accept the credit ticket.

When using bank credit cards, customers may avoid interest payments if they pay the full amount of their bill within 30 days. If they do not pay the bill in full, they are charged a percentage of the average monthly balance. This percentage has usually been 1½ percent per month. Some firms, such as Diners Club and American Express, not only charge the customer interest and the business a percentage fee but they also charge the credit card holder an additional yearly fee to receive the card.

The United States government has passed several laws concerning credit cards. One requires that no one can be sent a credit card unless he or she has requested the card. Another limits the liability of the card holder to $50 if the card is lost or stolen provided the customer notifies the credit card company as soon as possible. A court decision also allows the small business to offer the customer a discount for cash without the danger of losing the bank credit card service. A law passed in 1975 prohibits discrimination in credit due to sex or marital status and another passed in 1977 prohibits discrimination in credit due

 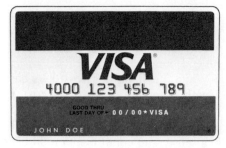

Credit cards of financial institutions can be used in many stores.

to race, national origin, religion, age, or receipt of public assistance. The Fair Credit Billing Law allows customers to withhold payment to the credit card company if the merchant refuses to help with defective products. Also, in this law the customer may refuse to pay the first $50 of a disputed bill if his or her written complaint is not responded to within 30 days and/or ruled on within 90 days, regardless of who wins the billing argument.

Credit cards are important to some customers not only because of the deferred payment but also because it provides information for their income tax returns. For example, some salesmen use credit cards as a record and means of proof of travel and customer entertainment expenses.

The small business can also use bank credit cards to allow employees away from the business to purchase needed items, such as gasoline, meals, and lodging for salesmen and truck drivers.

INSTALLMENT CREDIT

Installment credit is primarily used when customers purchase items of merchandise that costs several hundred or thousands of dollars, such as appliances, automobiles, boats, and homes. Interest is calculated on the amount that is financed after the down payment, if there is a down payment. The balance due plus the interest charge is then divided by the total number of months over which the purchase is to be financed to determine monthly payments.

The number of years allowed for the installment purchase to be repaid varies by item and financial firm. Some of the more common lengths of financing periods are: large appliances, 1 to 3 years; automobiles, 3 to 4 years; boats, 1 to 4 years; and homes, 20 to 30 years.

Customers who obtain merchandise by installment purchases usually are required to sign an installment sales contract. This contract contains such information as total amount to be financed, interest rate, interest amount, repayment period, and an agreement in which the purchaser pledges the item purchased as security against repayment of the loan (installment credit is mortgage credit; legal aspects of different types of installment contracts are discussed in Chapter 21).

Some firms finance their own installment credit; however, most small businesses use financial institutions to carry their installment credit. They usually sign customers to installment sales contracts and then sell or discount the contracts to banks or sales finance companies. (Banks and sales finance company credit operations are discussed in Chapter 7.)

See Figure 20-2 for a comparison of the characteristics of charge accounts and installment credit.

CHARGE ACCOUNT CREDIT		
TRADITIONAL 30-DAY ACCOUNTS	REVOLVING CHARGE ACCOUNTS	INSTALLMENT CREDIT

1. Nonmortgage credit
2. Store financed (may factor)
3. No interest charged
4. Paid off in full each month
5. May or may not use credit card
	1. Nonmortgage credit
	2. May be financed by:
	    store
	    other producing com-
	    panies (such as oil com-
	    pany credit cards)
	    financial institutions
	    (such as bank credit
	    cards)
	3. No interest if paid in 30 days
	    Interest charged on balance past 30 days
	4. Only a minimum amount must be paid each month and balance carried forward
	5. Usually involves credit card
		1. Mortgage credit (chattel mortgage)
		2. May be financed by:
		    store
		    bank
		    sales finance company
		3. Interest added to amount financed
		4. Monthly payments for several months or years
		5. Sometimes requires down payment

Figure 20-2 Characteristics of charge account and installment credit.

SOURCES OF CREDIT INFORMATION

Small business firms that carry their own customer credit have two basic sources of credit information about their customers: (1) credit application forms and (2) retail credit bureau reports.

The small business firm that does carry its own credit should require all credit customers to complete a credit application form. The small business may create its own application form or use a standardized application form.

Most cities have a local retail credit bureau to which the small business firm may belong to aid in credit decisions. These local credit bureaus are usually cooperatives owned by the local merchants. All local members supply the credit bureau with copies of all their credit applications. In addition, each month each member also supplies the local credit bureau with information on customer purchases, payments, and delinquencies. By collecting this information, the bureaus are able to obtain extensive credit files on large numbers of people in the community. Members of the local credit bureau are then able to telephone the bureau about new credit applicants and obtain credit ratings in a matter of two or three minutes. The bureau will also provide the small business with a more detailed report by mail, if requested. In addition, if a small business has a delinquent account, he is able to obtain a "trade clearance" report, which summarizes the customer's more recent credit purchases and payments to other stores.

Most local credit bureaus also belong to Associated Credit Bureaus, which is a national organization. Thus the small business can obtain information on a nationwide basis.

Although local credit bureaus provide a valuable service to small businesses that grant credit, there have been some abuses. In some cases, information that was wrong or biased inadvertently found its way into the files of a few customers and created unwarranted problems for them. Federal law has been enacted that allows a customer to see his or her file on request and makes provisions for having the file corrected.

Although this chapter is devoted primarily to retail credit, another source of credit information is used to such an extent by businesses that it seems practical to mention it at this time. Dun and Bradstreet sells to subscribers a publication that contains credit ratings of several million business firms in the United States and Canada. Dun and Bradstreet also prepares detailed reports on many of the companies listed in its reference publications.

THE "TRUTH-IN-LENDING" LAW

In 1969, the United States Congress passed the Consumer Credit Protection Act, which is popularly called the "truth-in-lending law." This law was intended to put credit on a more competitive basis by helping the consumer more easily know what credit costs him. Small businesses that offer credit must be familiar with the law in order to comply with its provisions.

The most important of the disclosure items are the finance charge and the annual percentage rate. The business firm must advise the customer of these two credit expenses in writing that is the equivalent of 10-point type, 0.075 inch computer type, or elite-size typewritten numerals. The finance charge is the total of all costs paid by the consumer for credit. It includes all interest, carrying charges, cost of insurance premiums if required for credit protection, and credit investigation costs. The annual percentage rate is the percentage interest rate charge on a yearly basis. This annual percentage rate must be reported to the nearest quarter of 1 percent.[2]

The truth-in-lending law requires specific information be disclosed for re-

---

[2]Computations on installment sales can be complex for most people. To assist you, *Annual Percentage Rate Tables* is available from the Federal Reserve System in Washington, D.C., for $1.00.

volving charge accounts (called open-end transactions in the law) and installment contracts (called closed-end transactions).

REVOLVING CHARGE ACCOUNTS

The following information must be disclosed before the account is opened.

1. Conditions under which a finance charge may be made and the period within
   which, if payment is made, there is no finance charge (such as "30 days
   without interest").
2. The method of determining the balance upon which a finance charge may be
   imposed.
3. How the actual finance charge is calculated.
4. The periodic rates used and the range of balances to which each applies as
   well as the corresponding Annual Percentage Rate—for instance, a monthly
   rate of 1½ percent (APR, 18 percent) on the first $500, and 1 percent (APR,
   12 percent) on amounts over $500.
5. Conditions under which additional charges may be made, along with details
   of how they are calculated. (This applies to new purchases, when charges
   are added to the account.)
6. A description of any lien (secured interest) you may acquire on the customer's property—for instance, rights to repossession of a household
   appliance.
7. Minimum periodic payment required.[3]

The following information must be included on each and every monthly
statement sent to the customer in the correct terminology which is indicated in
boldface type in the quoted material below.

1. The unpaid balance at the beginning of the billing period (**previous balance**).
2. The amount and date of each purchase or credit extension and a brief description of each item bought if not previously given to the customer.
3. Customer payments (**payments**), and other credits, including those for re-
   bates, adjustments, and returns (**credits**).
4. The finance charge expressed in dollars and cents (**finance charge**).
5. The rates used in calculating the finance charge, and the range of balances, if
   any, to which they apply (**periodic rate**).
6. The annual percentage rate, which must be expressed as a percentage after
   January 1, 1971 (**annual percentage**).

[3]*Understanding Truth-in-Lending* (Washington, D.C.: Small Business Administration, November
1969).

7. The unpaid balance on which the finance charge was calculated.
8. The closing date of the billing cycle, and the unpaid balance as of that date (**new balance**).[4]

INSTALLMENT CONTRACTS

Installment credit must also provide certain information to the buyer under the truth-in-lending legislation. This information must be disclosed on a printed form (usually an installment sales contract) before the credit is extended. It must also be provided in the terminology, specified by the law, which is indicated below.

1. The cash price (cash price).
2. The down payment including trade-in (cash down payment, trade-in, or total down payment—as applicable).
3. The difference between the cash price and down payment (unpaid balance of cash price).
4. All other charges, itemized but not part of the finance charge.
5. The unpaid balance (unpaid balance).
6. Amounts deducted as prepaid finance charges or required deposit balances (prepaid finance charge) and/or (required deposit balance).
7. The amount financed (amount financed).
8. The total cash price, finance, and all other charges (deferred payment price).
9. The total dollar amount of the finance charge (finance charge).
10. The date on which the finance charge begins to apply (if this is different from the date of the sale).
11. The annual percentage rate, which must be expressed as a percentage after January 1, 1971 (annual percentage rate).
12. The number, amounts, and due dates of payments.
13. The total payments (total of payments).
14. The amount you charge for any default, delinquency, and the like, or the method you use for calculating the amount.
15. A description of any security you will hold.
16. A description of any penalty charge for prepayment of principal.
17. How the unearned part of the finance charge is calculated in case of prepayment. (Charges deducted from any rebate must be stated.)[5]

[4]Ibid.
[5]Ibid.

BAD DEBTS AND COLLECTIONS

Small business owners would like to collect all their credit accounts, but this is not possible. The amount of bad debts they sustain on credit accounts will depend mostly on how effective they are in selecting people to whom they will grant credit and in the efficiency of their collection methods.

Small business owners should keep good records of credit accounts. By dividing bad debts by sales, they are able to compute the bad debt ratio. They should calculate this ratio on a periodic basis in order to check the adequacy of their credit program. Once they have decided what is a realistic bad debt ratio for the firm, any significant shift in the bad debt ratio should be a signal that something is wrong. Small business owners should try to balance their credit policy so that they are not too restrictive and eliminate good customers or too lenient and have excessive bad debts.

Collection of overdue accounts requires considerable skill to balance effective collection without harming customer goodwill. If the small business firm initiates action too soon and with too firm a hand, it may lose many good customers. On the other hand, if it moves too slowly, while giving an impression of a lax attitude, it may never collect the account.

Collection timing and methods should vary to some degree with the credit record of the customer. However, a process of stages of collection methods should be employed in collection efforts. These stages should move from a soft approach to a final stern, legal approach.

COLLECTION MESSAGES

The four steps in collection messages are (1) reminder, (2) stronger reminder, (3) inquiry and appeal, and (4) legal ultimatum.

Reminder

Most overdue accounts are collected with the first letter and are probably due to customers' oversight or procrastination. These people are valuable customers so the reminder is intended to collect the money while retaining the goodwill of the customer. Consequently, the first message must start with the assumption that the customer fully intends to pay the bill but has overlooked it. The message must be very soft and must reassure the customer that the firm does not feel the individual is purposefully failing to pay the bill. The message should be a short note that includes something like "Have you overlooked us this month?"

Stronger Reminder

The second stage of the collection messages should, like the first, still assume the failure to pay is the result of oversight or procrastination. The firm is still trying to collect the bill but also keep the person as a customer. However, the message should be a little firmer. The phrase "overlooked" is still used but a definite request for payment should be included in the message.

Inquiry and Appeal

The third stage of the collection messages assumes that the failure to pay is not an oversight, but there is something wrong. The firm is still trying to collect the debt and retain patronage of the individual. The firm does not, at this point, assume the customer is a customer it does not want on a credit basis. Consequently, the message should try to find out what is wrong and at the same time increase the pressure to pay. It should contain such phrases as "What is the difficulty?" and "Your credit rating is valuable."

Legal Ultimatum

The small business must at this stage assume that the customer is not going to pay the bill unless force is applied. The firm also reaches the stage at which it must assume the customer is no longer a valuable credit customer but a "cash-only" customer. The message must have urgency and outline the action the firm will take if the debt is not paid at once. Phrases such as "turned over to a collection agency" and "This action will destroy your credit rating" should be included. The small business should then follow the action threatened if payment is not received.

TIMING OF COLLECTION MESSAGES

Credit customers differ and so should the timing of the collection messages. The person who has a good credit record should be given a longer period in the four stages of the collection process. On the other hand, the person who has a record of slow payment should receive the messages over a much shorter interval. In general, the first reminder should be sent when the debt is 4 weeks overdue. The Inquiry and Appeal message should be sent when the debt is 6 weeks overdue and the Legal Ultimatum when the debt is 10 weeks overdue. The debt should be turned over to a collection agency or attorney for legal action after five to six months.

DISCUSSION QUESTIONS

1. Why is retail credit important to most small business firms?
2. How are traditional 30-day charge accounts different from revolving charge accounts?
3. How does installment credit differ from charge account credit?
4. What are some of the ways small business firms finance 30-day accounts, revolving charge accounts, and installment credit?
5. How does a small business obtain information about potential credit customers?
6. What was the reason for Congress passing the truth-in-lending law?
7. How does the truth-in-lending law attempt to achieve its goal?
8. What is a bad debt ratio and how is it used?
9. Should the collection system for overdue accounts be the same for all customers?

STUDENT PROJECTS

1. Identify a store that uses:
   (a) 30-day charge accounts
   (b) Revolving charge accounts
   (c) Installment credit
2. Obtain a copy of a revolving charge account statement and an installment sales contract and check them to see if they meet the requirements of the truth-in-lending law.
3. Obtain a copy of a credit application form and analyze it to determine if you feel it does a good job of obtaining credit information.
4. Find out if your community has a Retail Credit Bureau and, if so, who owns the Bureau.

CASE A

SLOAN MUSIC STORE

Steve Sloan is in the process of opening a music store in a town of 30,000. His will be the only complete music store in the town. Steve will carry musical instruments, records, tapes, stereo sets and systems, and a broad range of music-related merchandise.

Steve is an accomplished musician and is knowledgeable about most of his products. He plans to carry a high-price and a low-price line in both instruments and stereo equipment. He has contacted the local high school band director and obtained permission to place instruments on display when the director meets with the parents of new band students each year.

The band director has told Steve that he must have some sort of financing available or most parents would not buy instruments from him. Steve agrees and feels that he must have credit available other than the few selected 30-day accounts he had planned on carrying. Steve has spent a big part of his funds for the store lease, remodeling, and initial inventory. He feels he has enough funds to provide working capital and support a few 30-day accounts.

He has agreed to pay you a fee if you will set up a credit system for him and advise him how he might obtain financing for customer credit.

Questions

1. What type of credit would you advise Steve to set up and for what types of merchandise would this credit be intended?
2. Will Steve have to pay any fees for any of the credit you have established?
3. If Steve carries the 30-day account credit as he plans, how can he find out about his credit customers?
4. What are the two main things Steve must tell his customers to comply with the truth-in-lending law? (Not all, just the two major items.)
5. Tell Steve about the bad debt ratio and how he should use it.
6. Generally, how should Steve go about collecting overdue accounts?

CASE B
LANCE BRIAN'S COZY CARPETS

Lance Brian is the sole owner of Cozy Carpets, which has been selling carpet and other floor coverings to building contractors for two years. He extends credit to these contractors and has had some problems in the past; however, he now has separated customers into those who are reliable in paying their accounts and those whom he requires to pay in cash. He feels there is very little he can do to improve his credit and collection practices.

Lance recently moved his business to a new location in an attractive building. It is on a major thoroughfare and surrounded several miles in each direction by residential housing that is about 4 to 10 years old. Lance has had few retail sales to individual home owners in the past, but now he feels the surrounding residential neighborhood could produce considerable retail sales. He realizes that he must have some kind of retail credit available since each sale represents several hundred and even thousand plus dollars. Lance has the capital to offer retail credit if he desires.

Lance has asked you to help him set up a retail credit plan.

Questions

1. Would you advise him to offer 30-day charge or revolving charge credit?
2. Would you advise him to use bank credit cards? Explain your reasons.
3. Would you advise him to offer installment contracts? Should he finance them himself?

SECTION
SIX
THE GOVERNMENT
AND SMALL BUSINESS

21
LEGAL CONSIDERATIONS

PREVIEW OF THIS CHAPTER

1. In this chapter, you will learn what the requirements are for a contract to be valid and enforceable in a court of law.

2. You will understand the various legal recourses available to a person when there is breach of contract.

3. You will find out why there is a Uniform Commercial Code, what it attempts to do, and what areas of commercial law it covers.

4. If you ever plan to start a small business, you will be interested to discover the different types of checks, how to minimize bad checks, and what to do when you receive a bad check.

5. You will learn how small businesses might use other negotiable instruments—certificates of deposit, money orders, letters of credit, and bills of lading.

6. You will find there are three different types of installment sales contracts, which are the best in terms of repossession, and how to go about repossessing merchandise.

7. You will learn that small businesses must have various types of permits and licenses in order to operate.

8. You will be able to understand these key words:

Contracts	Undue influence
Competent parties	Breach of contract
Consideration	Uniform Commercial Code
Legal purpose	Bad checks
Mutual assent	Chattel mortgage
Legal form	Conditional sales contract
Duress	Lease-purchase contract
Fraud	Licenses
Checks	Certificates of deposit
Money orders	Letters of credit
Bills of lading	

Small business firms exist in an environment governed by laws. In fact, business of any size could not exist without laws to set standards and requirements of conduct. Daily, the small business engages in activities that are governed by law. If the small business owner is to succeed, he or she must know his or her rights and responsibilities under the law.

CONTRACTS

The small business owner deals almost daily with some form of contract—written or verbal. For example, if a customer orders a sandwich in a restaurant, he or she and the business are entering into a verbal contract. The restaurant is agreeing to provide a sandwich and the customer is agreeing to pay the advertised price for the sandwich. Examples of contracts in written form would be leases, deeds, warranties, and installment sales contracts. Since small business owners are engaged in contracts on a continuing basis, they must know what is required for a contract to be valid and enforceable. They must also be aware of their rights in case the other party does not honor the terms of the contract.

REQUIREMENTS OF A VALID CONTRACT

Each state establishes its own laws concerning contracts. As a result, there are some variations in legal requirements for valid contracts in various states. However, the states do have the same basic requirements.

In order for a contract to be valid and enforceable in any state, it must meet the requirements of (1) competent parties, (2) consideration, (3) legal purpose, (4) mutual assent, and (5) legal form.

Competent Parties

All parties to a contract must be competent parties under the law. The law defines parties that are not competent as drunkards, convicts, insane persons, and persons who are below the legal age. Laws in the 50 states vary between 18 and 21 in terms of minimum legal age. Generally, persons under the legal age specified by the state can enforce contracts against adults, but adults cannot enforce contracts against them. An exception exists in many states when the contract is for necessities, such as food, shelter, clothing, and ordinary education.

The small business owner should be aware that, although the law declares that drunkards and insane persons are not competent parties, it does not automatically mean that the person who appears intoxicated or acts abnormal cannot be a party to a valid and enforceable contract. In general, a person must

This Agreement BETWEEN

as Landlord

and

as Tenant

Witnesseth: The Landlord hereby leases to the Tenant the following premises:

for the term of

to commence from the   day of   19   and to end on the

           day of   19   to be used and occupied only for

upon the conditions and covenants following:

1st. That the Tenant shall pay the annual rent of

said rent to be paid in equal monthly payments in advance on the   day of each and every month during the
term aforesaid, as follows:

2nd. That the Tenant shall take good care of the premises and shall, at the Tenant's own cost and expense make all repairs

and at the end or other expiration of the term, shall deliver up the demised premises in good order or condition, damages by
the elements excepted.

3rd. That the Tenant shall promptly execute and comply with all statutes, ordinances, rules, orders, regulations and requirements of the Federal, State and Local Governments and of any and all their Departments and Bureaus applicable to said
premises, for the correction, prevention, and abatement of nuisances or other grievances, in, upon, or connected with said
premises during said term; and shall also promptly comply with and execute all rules, orders and regulations of the New
York Board of Fire Underwriters, or any other similar body, at the Tenant's own cost and expense.

27th. Landlord shall not be liable for failure to give possession of the premises upon commencement date by reason of the
fact that premises are not ready for occupancy or because a prior Tenant or any other person is wrongfully holding over or
is in wrongful possession, or for any other reason. The rent shall not commence until possession is given or is available, but
the term herein shall not be extended.

And the said Landlord doth covenant that the said Tenant on paying the said yearly rent, and performing the covenants
aforesaid, shall and may peacefully and quietly have, hold and enjoy the said demised premises for the term aforesaid, provided however, that this covenant shall be conditioned upon the retention of title to the premises by the Landlord.

And it is mutually understood and agreed that the covenants and agreements contained in the within lease
shall be binding upon the parties hereto and upon their respective successors, heirs, executors and administrators.

In Witness Whereof, the parties have interchangeably set their hands and seals (or caused these presents to be
signed by their proper corporate officers and caused their proper corporate seal to be hereto affixed) this
day of   19

Signed, sealed and delivered

in the presence of

....L. S.

....L. S.

....L. S.

Figure 21-1 Sections of a standard lease form.

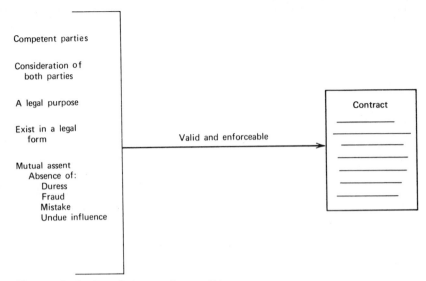

Figure 21-2 Requirements for a valid contract.

be adjudged by the courts to be a confirmed drunkard or insane before he loses his status as a competent party. Intoxication and abnormal actions are usually not a defense against a valid contract unless the actions are so extreme as to prohibit intelligent action.

Consideration of Both Parties

Both parties to the contract must give some form of consideration for it to be a valid enforceable contract. For example, a relative creates a contract in which he promises a young man that he will give him $5000 on his 21st birthday. This would not be an enforceable contract because the young man did not give any consideration in the contract. However, consideration does not have to be in the form of money or tangible goods. For example, if the relative mentioned above promised to give the young man $5000 on his 21st birthday if he would refrain from drinking intoxicating beverages, it would be an enforceable contract because the young man would give consideration by not drinking intoxicating beverages.

A Legal Purpose

Contracts must be for a legal purpose to be valid and enforceable. In other words, the law will not enforce a contract requiring an act that the law itself declares illegal. For example, if a political candidate agreed to pay a person to break into his opponent's home for material to use in the campaign against him, the burglar could not force payment of the fee because it was for an illegal purpose and, therefore, not a valid contract.

Mutual Assent

In order for a contract to be valid and enforceable in a court of law, it must have mutual assent from both parties to the contract. The law recognizes four areas that violate the concept of mutual assent: (1) duress, (2) fraud, (3) mistake, and (4) undue influence.

Duress   Duress exists when a person is forced by threat to enter into a contract against his will. For example, if a person threatens bodily harm to another person unless he signs a contract, the resulting contract would not be valid and could not be enforced under the law.

Fraud   Fraud exists when there is intentional misrepresentation of fact. If fraud is present in a contract situation, then the contract is not valid and enforceable. For example, if a person intentionally turns back the speedometer of an automobile that he is selling and intentionally represents it to have a lower mileage, he is intentionally misrepresenting the automobile. A contract signed under these conditions would not be valid and enforceable. However, it should be pointed out that, while the law declares fraud illegal, proving intentional misrepresentation in court is not always an easy task.

Mistake   When one party to a contract makes an obvious mistake and the other party to the contract is aware of the mistake and takes advantage of it, the contract is not valid and enforceable. For example, if a contractor bid on a job and in listing costs added them together wrong, the other party could not take advantage of it and make him perform the job at the miscalculated price.

Undue Influence   If one party to the contract has undue influence on a person because of their relationship and causes the other party to contract to his harm because of this relationship, it cannot be a valid and enforceable contract. For example, an agent that has his client sign a contract to perform in a nightclub he owns at an unreasonably low fee could not enforce the contract because of the undue influence he had as a result of their relationship.

Legal Form

Contracts may be in either verbal or written form with certain limitations specified by the states. Some states specify that all contracts involving real property (real estate) must be in writing. Some other states specify that all contracts involving sums of more than a specified amount ($500 is a common amount) must be in writing. Some require both to be in writing. For example, if one person verbally tells another he will sell him his golf clubs (personal property) for $200 and the other person accepts, it is a valid contract. On the other hand, if one person verbally offers to sell another person his home for $20,000 and the other person accepts, it is not a valid contract in states that require real property contracts to be in writing.

Most contracts are of the verbal variety, such as the earlier example of the person ordering food in a restaurant. While verbal contracts are valid and enforceable (with the exceptions noted above), they are sometimes difficult to prove in courts of law because of their verbal nature. Consequently, the small business owner should always insist on contracts of a significant value to be in the form of writing, regardless of state requirements for legal form.

RECOURSE FOR BREACH OF CONTRACT

When one party to a contract does not fulfill his part of the contract (breach of contract), the other party to the contract has certain rights of recourse under law. In courts of law, he may (1) force performance of the contract, (2) cause the contract to be discharged, or (3) collect damages resulting from nonperformance of the contract (see Figure 21-3).

Performance of the Contract

One party to a contract may go to court to force the other party to the contract to fulfill his part of the agreement. For example, Joe sold Don land and received payment for it. Then he changed his mind, tried to give the money back, and kept Don from entering the land. Don could go into court, prove his claim, and

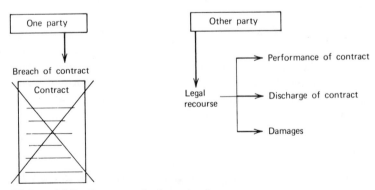

Figure 21-3   Recourse for breach of contract.

the courts would direct Joe to turn the land over to Don. If Joe still refused, he would be declared in contempt of court and liable for criminal actions.

Discharge of the Contract

If one party to the contract fails to perform his part of the contract, the other party is not obligated to fulfill his part. For example, if one person agrees to sell another an automobile and then does not give him the automobile, the other person is under no obligation to pay the purchase price.

Collect Damages

If one party to a contract suffers loss or damages as a result of the other party's not fulfilling his part of the contract, the injured party may recover damages in a court of law. For example, if a school hires a football coach and signs a contract for one year of employment and the coach is released from his duties after six months, the school must pay him wages for the remaining six months if he cannot find an equal position at another school.

UNIFORM COMMERCIAL CODE

Each individual state establishes its own laws (within the limits set by the U.S. Constitution and its state constitution) governing *intrastate* commerce (commerce within the state). The federal government establishes rules governing *interstate* commerce (commerce between the states).

Since each state establishes its own laws governing intrastate commerce, the early years of the United States witnessed a wide range of state statutes and judicial rulings. Conflicts and confusion were common because of the difference in state laws. In 1890, a move was initiated to encourage the states to adopt uniform laws governing commerce. By 1945, over 60 uniform statutes were formulated and adopted by a large number of states. In 1945, work was begun to combine all these uniform acts into a code encompassing the field of commercial law. In 1952, the Uniform Commercial Code was first published and then revised in 1958 to its present form. With the exception of the state of Louisiana, all 50 states have adopted the Uniform Commercial Code.

The general areas of law and some of the major provisions of each area that are included in the Uniform Commercial Code are:

1. *Sales.* Requirements of contracts—rights of seller and buyer.
2. *Commercial Paper.* Requirements of negotiable instruments including time, liability, acceptance, alteration, and delivery.

3. *Bank Deposits and Collections*. Banking practices such as cut of time for posting.
4. *Letters of Credit*. Rights and duties of bank, receiver, and customer.
5. *Bulk Transfers*. Provisions preventing dishonest merchants from buying large quantities of goods without paying for them and selling them to third parties.
6. *Warehouse Receipts, Bills of Lading, and Other Documents of Title*. Regulates documents of title to personal property entrusted to others for various reasons.
7. *Investment Securities*. Regulates registered and bearer bonds, stock certificates, and other investment paper.
8. *Secured Transactions, Sales of Accounts, Contract Rights, and Chattel Paper*. Legal aspects of pledges, assignments, chattel mortgages, liens, conditional sales contracts, leases, and so on.

CHECKS AND OTHER NEGOTIABLE INSTRUMENTS

Some of the negotiable instruments a small business is likely to come in contact with are (1) checks, (2) certificates of deposit, (3) money orders, (4) letters of credit, (5) bills of lading, and (6) warehouse receipts.

CHECKS

Almost all small businesses receive and issue checks drawn on banks almost every day. Businesses that receive checks usually have a problem with bad checks. Retail and service firms usually suffer more than other businesses from bad checks, but manufacturers and wholesalers also find them a problem. Good check cashing procedures and collection practices help reduce losses from bad checks.

Types of Checks

The basic types of checks are (1) personal checks, (2) two-party checks, (3) payroll checks, (4) government checks, (5) counter checks, and (6) traveler's checks.

Personal Checks   A personal check is a check made out by the individual signing the check and made directly to the small business. A small business should require positive identification on all personal checks. If the state issues driver's licenses with photographs, this is one of the best means of identification. If not, the store should require the driver's license and note carefully the signature and description of the person. Additional identification should also be required in the form of credit cards, government passes, or identification cards. Signatures on these should also be compared to the driver's license and the check.

Two-Party Checks A two-party check is a check made out by one individual to another individual who endorses it so it can be cashed by the small business. Generally, a small business should not accept two-party checks. The possibility of its being a stolen check or forgery is too great a risk.

Payroll Checks Payroll checks are issued by a business to an employee for his salary. They usually have the word "payroll" printed on them and often have the amount imprinted on the check by a machine. The small business should require identification as previously described. In addition, it generally is not a good policy to cash out-of-town payroll checks. Thieves sometimes steal blank payroll checks from firms and then pass them to small businesses in other towns.

Government Checks Government checks are checks issued by the local, state, or federal government. They may be for such purposes as wages, tax refunds, pensions, social security payments, welfare allotments, and veterans' benefits. It is not at all uncommon to find thieves that specialize in stealing government checks from mail boxes. In fact, in some metropolitan areas, stealing has become so common a practice that some banks will not accept government checks unless the person has an account in the bank. The small business firm should follow the same cautious identification procedure it uses with personal checks when accepting government checks.

Counter Checks Banks usually have checks with the bank's name on them placed on counters in the bank so depositors may use them to withdraw funds from their accounts without having to have their personalized checks with them. Unless the small business knows the customer well, he should not honor a counter check.

Traveler's Checks A traveler's check is a check sold by firms through banks to persons who do not wish to carry large sums of cash with them when they travel. The buyer signs each traveler's check in the presence of the bank teller and then must sign below the original signature when he cashes the check. A comparison of the two signatures identifies him as the owner. The small business employee or owner who accepts traveler's checks should *always* require the second signature in his presence and carefully check the two signatures.

Money orders may also be cashed as checks. Private firms, banks, and the

United States Postal Service issue money orders for a fee. Small business firms should not cash money orders because they are usually purchased to send in the mail and not for direct transactions.

In addition to careful identification, the small business owner or employee who is cashing the check should look for:

1. A difference in the written and the numerical amount on the check.
2. Proper endorsements.
3. Old dates or postdated checks.
4. An address of the customer and the bank.
5. Erasures and written-over amounts.

Types of Bad Checks

Checks may be bad because of (1) insufficient funds, (2) no account, (3) a closed account, or (4) forgery.

Insufficient Funds Checks that are returned from the bank marked insufficient funds should be redeposited a second time after the customer is notified. Most of these checks are collected. State laws and bank practices vary, but, generally, if the check does not clear the second time, the bank will no longer accept it, and it is the small business owner's responsibility to collect it.

If the small business owner is unable to collect the check and resorts to prosecution in the courts, he or she should check state law to determine what actions must be taken to prosecute. Most states require the business owner to send the check writer a registered letter and wait from 5 to 10 days for payment before suit is filed.

No Account When a check is returned from the bank marked "no account" there is almost no chance of collection. This is usually evidence of intentional fraud by the check writer. However, before notifying the police, an attempt should be made to contact the check writer just in case he or she has changed banks and inadvertently written the check on the wrong bank.

Closed Account A returned check marked "closed account" is usually the result of a person's changing banks and forgetting he or she has a check outstanding. Also, the bank may have closed the account because of too many overdrafts. It may also be fraud on the part of the check writer. Collection should be attempted first and then prosecution begun if collection fails.

Forgery The police should be notified immediately in cases of forgery. Forged checks are worthless and it would be rare indeed for collection attempts to be of any value. If the forged check is a U.S. government check, the small business should notify the nearest local field office of the U.S. Secret Service.

Small business firms should automatically stamp on the back side of all checks received the notation "for deposit only" and the name of the business. This prevents the checks from being cashed if stolen.

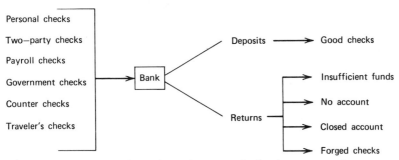

Figure 21-4 Types of checks and reasons for bank not accepting.

CERTIFICATES OF DEPOSIT

Certificates of deposit are documents that certify that a person has on deposit with a bank or savings and loan association a certain sum of money. The document also states the time the individual has agreed to leave the money on deposit until it matures. A person or business might have $1000 on deposit with a bank drawing 6½ percent interest and might have agreed to leave it on deposit for six months minimum time. It can be withdrawn, with the bank's agreement, before the six-month period is up, but the person will pay a substantial penalty.

MONEY ORDERS

In a sense, a money order is a check drawn up by a post office, bank, or express office and purchased by an individual. It is a promise the institution will pay a specific amount of money on demand to specific persons. Money orders are often used to avoid the delay in clearing a regular check since the receiver knows the post office, bank, or express office checks are good. The person or business pays the institution the amount of the check plus a small fee.

LETTERS OF CREDIT

A bank may issue a letter of credit requesting that money or credit be given a specific person. The bank then guarantees payment of the debt. Letters of credit are often used in international markets and markets outside the usual business area of the firm.

BILLS OF LADING

Freight carriers, such as railroads and truck lines, issue bills of lading to certify certain merchandise is in their possession and is being transported. Only special types of bills of lading are negotiable and they are called "Order Bills of Lading." The person or business whose name appears on the order bill of lading can endorse the shipment to another person. One way bills of lading are used is the circumstance of a business that ships goods but does not have a warehouse, starting a carload of freight across the country and then selling it before it reaches the original destination. The firm endorses the shipment over to the buyer and diverts the car to him/her. Order bills of lading are often used by middlemen in farm products. They purchase carload lots of farm products and then sell them while they are in transit.

WAREHOUSE RECEIPTS

When goods are placed in a public warehouse (a warehouse that stores goods for business firms and individuals), the owner receives a warehouse receipt for the goods. If he wishes to sell the goods, all he has to do is endorse the warehouse receipt over to the buyer, who then may claim the goods. Warehouse receipts are also used when a business borrows money and uses the warehoused goods as collateral. The warehouse receipt is signed over to the creditor until the debt is paid.

INSTALLMENT CONTRACTS AND REPOSSESSION

Installment sales contracts may exist in three basic types: (1) chattel mortgage, (2) conditional sales contract, and (3) lease–purchase.

CHATTEL MORTGAGE

Under the chattel mortgage contract, the title of the merchandise passes to the buyer at the time of the purchase. The contract is secured by the seller having a lien against the merchandise.

CONDITIONAL SALES CONTRACT

The conditional sales contract is the most common type used today. As the name implies, the sale of the merchandise is conditional on the buyer making payments on time and meeting other conditions. These contracts usually require the purchaser to insure the merchandise and pay all maintenance costs until the merchandise is paid for. The title to the merchandise does not pass to the buyer until all provisions of the contract are completed.

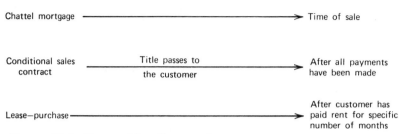

Figure 21-5   Types of installment sales contracts.

LEASE–PURCHASE

Under the lease-purchase type of sale, the merchandise is rented to the purchaser until he has made a specific number of payments. After he has made the specific number of payments, he receives title to the goods.

The conditional sales contract and the lease–purchase arrangement are superior to the chattel mortgage in terms of repossession of merchandise. State laws governing repossession of merchandise under all three types of contracts vary widely. However, the chattel mortgage contract is more time consuming and more expensive than the other two types of contracts in terms of repossession in most states.

The authors have known small business owners who repossess merchandise by going to the person's home, telling him or her they are there to repossess the merchandise, and then going into the house to take it back. *No small business owner should ever use this method of repossession.* Not only does it violate the rights of the customer, which can result in legal problems for the small business owner, but it can be very dangerous. Any small business owner who repossesses merchandise should first consult an attorney to learn the requirements of that state's laws and then carefully follow the requirements of the law.

LICENSES AND PERMITS

Most states and many local governments require businesses to obtain various types of licenses. In addition, state and local governments often require employees of small businesses to obtain permits, for example, health permits. Some of the licenses are for control purposes, as is the case of a health permit. However, many are for taxation purposes, such as city business permits.

Individuals interested in starting a small business should first check and determine what licenses and permits are required for the business. In some cases, these may result in their not being able to operate a business. For example, if an individual built a tavern and then could not obtain a liquor license for some reason, he or she could not operate the business. Persons buying a business should also make sure that licenses and permits of the business will transfer to them or that they will be able to acquire them after they have bought the business.

From this chapter, it can be easily seen that legal aspects of small business can be complex and differ from state-to-state. The small business entrepreneur would be well advised to contact an attorney when he or she is starting a business.

DISCUSSION QUESTIONS

1. Who are competent parties in terms of a contract?
2. Does a contract have to be in writing or may it be verbal?
3. What can a person do if another party does not honor a contract?
4. Do you consider the Uniform Commercial Code to be a good idea? Explain.
5. What types of checks would you advise a small business owner to accept?
6. How may a small business owner minimize bad check losses?
7. Which type of bad check returned by the bank is the most likely to be collected?
8. If you owned a department store, how might you use (1) certificates of deposit, (2) money orders, (3) letters of credit, and (4) bills of lading?
9. If you were a small business owner, which type of installment sales contract would you use? Explain.
10. How should a small business owner go about repossessing merchandise?
11. Why should a prospective small business owner investigate licenses and permits before he or she starts or purchases a small business?

STUDENT PROJECT

Obtain a copy of an installment sales contract (blank or completed). If it is a blank contract, fill in the contract with fictitious information as if you were buying an appliance.

1. Determine if the installment sales contract meets the various requirements of a valid contract.
2. Determine if it is a chattel mortgage, a conditional sales contract, or a lease-purchase agreement.

CASE A
SAM'S USED CAR LOT

Sam Perkins has just leased a vacant lot and built a small office on it. He plans to open a used car lot as soon as he can attend several wholesale automobile auctions.

Sam has a considerable amount of working capital, so he has decided to finance his own installment sales contracts in order to make what he considers an attractive interest rate.

Sam knows a good deal about used cars and their value and he feels he is a good salesman. However, Sam knows little about the legal aspects of operating a used car lot. Sam has asked you to help him by answering several questions.

Questions

1. Sam wants to know what he can do in terms of contracts to protect himself when he sells an automobile on the installment basis.
2. Sam has asked you what he should do if someone does not pay the installments on the purchase.
3. What type of contract would you tell Sam to use in his installment sales? Explain to Sam why you chose this type of contract.
4. Sam sells cars on Saturday when the banks are closed and he takes checks for down payments. Tell him (1) what type of checks he should accept and what type he should not accept; (2) what kind of identification he should require; and (3) what he should do if any are returned from the bank.
5. What should Sam do about repossessions?
6. What should Sam do about licenses and permits?

CASE B
REDELL'S APPLIANCE STORE

The Redell Appliance Store is owned and operated by Coy Redell. The store sells a well-known line of appliances—stoves, refrigerators, dishwashers, and others. It also has a complete service department for all the products it sells. Coy has been in business for 15 years and has been very successful.

Coy has been using a local bank to finance installment purchases for his customers. Since the business has been so profitable, Coy has quite a large sum of money accumulated in certificates of deposit in a local savings and loan association and he has been looking for some place to invest it to earn more money. One day while filling in a loan application for a customer, Coy realized that the interest rate on the installment contract was considerably higher than the amount he was earning with his certificates of deposit. He decided that he would start financing his own installment contracts with his savings.

Coy has asked you to help him. He has several questions he needs answered.

Questions

Coy's questions are the following.

1. What should I do to make sure I have valid contracts with my customers?
2. What can I do if a customer does not make his payments on the installment contract?
3. What kind of installment contracts should I use?
4. A banker friend told me the other day that my certificates of deposit are one form of negotiable instruments. Are there other negotiable instruments I can use?

22

GOVERNMENT CONTROL AND ASSISTANCE

PREVIEW OF THIS CHAPTER

1. In this chapter, you will discover that government control of business legislation is important to small business because it ensures a healthy competitive environment.

2. You will learn which are the primary controls of business legislative acts, what they prohibit, and what agencies administer them.

3. You will discover what the Occupational Safety and Health Act is and how it affects small businesses.

4. You will learn what effect consumer protection laws have on small business firms.

5. You will be interested to find that the Small Business Administration is the main governmental agency providing assistance to small business.

6. If you plan to start a small business, you will be pleased to learn that the Small Business Administration helps small business firms with loans, management assistance, training, set-aside contracts, and publications.

7. You will be able to understand these key words:

Interstate commerce	Federal Garnishment Law
Intrastate commerce	Unordered merchandise
Sherman Antitrust Act	Rule of reason
Clayton Act	Price discrimination
Federal Trade Commission Act	Tying contracts
Robinson–Patman Act	Intercorporate stockholding
Food, Drug, and Cosmetic Act	Interlocking directorates
Price fixing	False advertising
Monopoly	ACE
Occupational Safety and	SCORE
Health Act	Set-aside contracts
Consumer protection laws	Small Business Administration

| Cooling-off periods | Magnuson–Moss Warranty Act |
| Fair Packing and Labeling Act | University Small Business Institutes |

Government control of business is important to small business because it helps ensure fair competition for small business firms. The federal government also offers valuable assistance to small business firms.

Small business firms are seldom charged with violations of social control of business legislation. However, social control of business legislation is important to small business firms because they must have a healthy competitive environment in order to survive and prosper.

Without protective legislation, corporate giants, with their massive financial power, would have the ability to eliminate almost any small business. To illustrate, some large corporate chains in the early days of chain stores would establish a store in a small town and sell at or below cost until they had driven all competition out of business. After they had eliminated all competition, they increased prices above what they had originally been.

Many states have social control of business legislation, but the more important pieces of legislation regulating business are federal laws that apply to interstate commerce. Major federal social control of business legislation exists in the form of the (1) Sherman Antitrust Act, (2) Clayton Act, (3) Federal Trade Commission Act, (4) Robinson–Patman Act, and (5) Food, Drug, and Cosmetic Act.

SHERMAN ANTITRUST ACT, 1890

The Sherman Antitrust Act prohibits restraint of trade and monopoly in business.

The two main sections of the act read as follows:[1]

Sec. 1 Every contract, combination in the form of trust or otherwise, or conspiracy, in restraint of trade or commerce among the several states, or with foreign nations is hereby declared to be illegal. . . .
Sec. 2 Every person who shall monopolize, or attempt to monopolize, or combine or conspire with any other person or persons, to monopolize any part of the trade or

---

[1] United States Code, Title 15, Section 1-8.

commerce among the several states, or with foreign nations, shall be deemed guilty of a misdemeanor. . . .

The restraint-of-trade section of the Sherman Antitrust Act has usually been applied to price-fixing arrangements between firms. One of the more famous cases of application of the Sherman Act was the conviction of several electrical manufacturers in the 1960s. For the first time in the history of the Sherman Act, several executives of the electrical manufacturers were sent to prison under criminal prosecution of violations of the act.

The section of the Sherman Act prohibiting monopoly has been greatly eroded by the courts. In 1911, the Department of Justice (which is responsible for administering the act) brought suit against Standard Oil Company of New Jersey and American Tobacco Company. The government asked for and received a judgment that dissolved both companies into several smaller companies. (It is interesting to note that both Standard Oil of New Jersey and American Tobacco are larger companies today than were their parent companies before the 1911 dissolution decree.) However, the courts, in reaching their decision, established what is known as the "rule of reason." The rule of reason held there was cause for dissolution of monopoly only when "alarming and ungentlemanly conduct" and an overwhelming percentage control of the industry existed. The Department of Justice brought suit against United States Steel Corporation (which then controlled 75 percent of the steel industry) in 1912 asking for dissolution. In 1920, the United States Supreme Court ruled in favor of United States Steel claiming the Department of Justice had failed to prove unworthy motives, predatory acts, and overwhelming percentage control of the industry. The rule of reason has, for all practical purposes, eliminated the use of the monopoly section of the Sherman Act.

As mentioned earlier, the Sherman Act is administered by the Department of Justice. The Department of Justice may use either criminal prosecution or civil injunction under the law. Under criminal prosecution, persons may be subject to fines not to exceed $100,000 (corporations $1 million) and/or imprisonment of no more than one year. Civil injunctions involve asking the courts to issue a decree correcting the violation of the Sherman Act. In addition, individuals or businesses may institute civil proceedings to recover three times the amount of damages proved plus attorneys' fees from persons or firms guilty of violations of the Sherman Act.

CLAYTON ACT, 1914

The Clayton Act was intended to strengthen antitrust action by the federal government. It was intended to provide more specific legislation than was contained in the Sherman Act. The Clayton Act prohibits four practices of business: (1) price discrimination, (2) exclusive and tying contracts, (3) intercorporate stockholding lessening competition, and (4) interlocking directorates in competing corporations.

PRICE DISCRIMINATION

The Clayton Act prohibits price discrimination between different purchasers "where the effect of such discrimination may be to substantially lessen competition or to tend to create a monopoly in any line of commerce." This section was intended to prohibit a company from eliminating competition by selling at or below cost to selected customers. For example, one suit brought by the government charged that a manufacturer was selling spark plugs to automobile manufacturers at below cost in order to gain a large share of the replacement market (the government lost the suit because of the good faith provision discussed below).

The Clayton Act contained a provision that allowed price discrimination "when made in good faith to meet competition." The inability of the government to disprove good faith allowed almost a complete defense of this section of the Clayton Act. The inability of the Clayton Act to deal effectively with price discrimination led to the passage of the Robinson–Patman Act in 1936 (discussed later in this chapter).

EXCLUSIVE AND TYING CONTRACTS

The Clayton Act prohibits the following practices when their effect "may be to substantially lessen competition or tend to create a monopoly":

1. Tie-in sales—for example, the case of a mortgage company compelling home buyers to sign a contract to ensure their homes with a subsidiary of the mortgage company in order to obtain a home loan.
2. Exclusive dealerships that require the dealer to agree not to sell products of the seller's competitors.
3. Requirement contracts—a contract that requires a customer to agree to buy all future needs from the seller.
4. Full-line forcing—the practice of selling a customer a product only if he agrees to purchase other lines of merchandise from the seller.

INTERCORPORATE STOCKHOLDING LESSENING COMPETITION

This section of the Clayton Act prohibits a corporation from holding stock in another corporation when it would substantially lessen competition. For example, General Motors was forced by the courts to sell its stock in DuPont because DuPont supplied large amounts of paint to General Motors. The courts felt this intercorporate stockholding had the effect of lessening competition in the paint industry since General Motors used such vast amounts of paint.

Since the Clayton Act prohibited acquiring stock and not assets, many companies simply bought out the assets of competitors as a means of avoiding the act.

INTERLOCKING DIRECTORATES IN COMPETING CORPORATIONS

The Clayton Act prohibits a person from serving on the board of directors of two or more corporations that are or have been in competition if the effect could be to lessen competition. This section excludes banks, common carriers, and companies with capital of less than $1 million.

This section of the Clayton Act has not been as effective as intended by Congress since another person, such as a relative or employee, may serve on another board of directors and achieve the same results.

The Clayton Act is administered by the Federal Trade Commission with the following exceptions.

1. The Interstate Commerce Commission administers the Clayton Act when carriers are involved.
2. The Federal Reserve Board administers the act when banks are involved.

FEDERAL TRADE COMMISSION ACT, 1914

When the courts interpreted the Sherman Antitrust Act, they condemned unfair competition but declared the act did not make it illegal. Small business owners were concerned and demanded action from Congress. In response to public and small business pressure, Congress enacted the Federal Trade Commission Act, which contained the following provisions.

1. The Federal Trade Commission (FTC) was established to be comprised of five members appointed by the President for seven-year terms. No more than three members may be from the same political party.
2. Any unfair methods of competition were declared illegal.
3. The Federal Trade Commission was given power to issue cease-and-desist orders. These orders could be challenged in court by the defendant.
4. The Federal Trade Commission was empowered to collect information about business and its conduct that was to be made available to the President, Congress, and the public.

The Federal Trade Commission building in Washington, D.C.

The most important sections of the Federal Trade Commission Act were the section declaring unfair methods of competition illegal and the section giving the FTC the power to issue cease-and-desist orders. The broad nature of the provision declaring unfair competition illegal provides legal authority for the Federal Trade Commission to deal with all types of business activity that injure competition.

Before the passage of the Federal Trade Commission Act, any individual or business suffering loss because of antitrust violations had to proceed directly through the courts under the Sherman and/or Clayton acts. This often proved to be a long and expensive process. Under the Federal Trade Commission Act, individuals can file a complaint with the FTC and the commission has the power to issue a cease-and-desist order.

The Federal Trade Commission has become the primary agency enforcing antitrust legislation. Since it was formed, it has been empowered to administer the following acts.

1. The Clayton Act of 1914.
2. Parts of the Wheeler–Lea Act of 1938, which dealt with false advertising of food, drugs, cosmetics, and devices.
3. The Wool Products Labeling Act of 1939, which requires that all wool products except carpets, rugs, mats, and upholstering have a label attached that describes the kind and percent of fiber contained in the product.
4. Parts of the Lanham Trade-Mark Act of 1946, which allows the Federal Trade Commission to apply to the Commissioner of Patents for cancellation of trademarks which are deceptive, immoral, obtained fraudulently, and/or in violation of the Lanham Trade-Mark Act.
5. The McCarran Insurance Act of 1948, which regulates various activities in the insurance industry.
6. The Fur Products Labeling Act of 1951, which requires manufacturers to show on labels attached to garments the type of animal fur, country of origin, and specified processing information.
7. The Flammable Fabrics Act of 1953, which prohibits sale of highly flammable wearing apparel.

Some small businesspersons feel Congress has worked to their disadvantage several times in the past by making drastic cuts in the Federal Trade Commission budget. They feel this was motivated not by an attempt to reduce the taxpayer's burden, but by a desire to curtail the social control of business activities of the Federal Trade Commission.

ROBINSON–PATMAN ACT, 1936

The Robinson–Patman Act was passed to close weaknesses of the price discrimination section of the Clayton Act. The Robinson–Patman Act prohibits (1) price discounts that cannot be fully justified by lower costs to the seller, (2) selling private brands of a product that are identical to regular brands at a lower price, and (3) giving buyers proportionally unequal advertising and promotional allowances. One of the major strengths of the act was that it placed the burden of proof for justifying price differences on the seller. In addition, the act not only makes the seller guilty under the act in cases of price discrimination but it also makes the buyer guilty if he knowingly accepts a discriminating price.

The Federal Trade Commission may issue a cease-and-desist order when the seller is unable to show cost justification for price discrimination. The parties judged guilty may be subject to fines under civil proceedings and even subject to criminal action in certain instances. In addition, the act provides for any person injured by violation of the act to recover treble damages in civil actions.

FOOD, DRUG, AND COSMETIC ACT, 1938

Over 100 pieces of legislation to protect consumers from impure foods and drugs were turned down by Congress before the first one, the Pure Food and Drug Act, was passed in 1906. The Pure Food and Drug Act of 1906 was passed only after extensive publicity of abuses in the food and drug industry. The Pure Food and Drug Act of 1906 prohibited (1) the sale of food and drugs unsafe for human consumption and (2) false information from manufacturers concerning their product. The Department of Agriculture was responsible for administering the act. The act was weak and ineffective in protecting the consumer.

In 1937, a drug manufacturer sold a drug contaminated with poison, which resulted in 93 deaths. The resulting publicity and public reaction caused Congress to pass the Food, Drug, and Cosmetic Act in 1938. The Food, Drug, and Cosmetic Act of 1938 was considerably stronger than the 1906 act. The 1938 act prohibits (1) adulterated products, (2) misbranding, and (3) false advertising.

The Federal Trade Commission administers and enforces the false labeling and misbranding sections of the 1938 act. The Federal Trade Commission also has power to administer the prohibition of adulteration and false advertising; however, it has generally left these functions to the Food and Drug Administration of the Department of Health, Education, and Welfare, which also has enforcement power.

Figure 22-1 shows major business legislation.

OCCUPATIONAL SAFETY AND HEALTH ACT

There are about 13,000 deaths per year in the United States due to occupational accidents. In addition, there are about 2.2 million workers who sustain disabling injuries on the job. In an attempt to reduce deaths and injuries related to work, Congress passed the Occupational Safety and Health Act, which is administered by the Occupational Safety and Health Administration (OSHA). The act requires that all workers must be free from recognized hazards that could cause death or serious injury.

OSHA has considerable power to enforce compliance with the law. The law allows fines of up to $1000 for each violation and fines of up to $1000 per day unless the violation is corrected within a prescribed time. Also, if an OSHA inspector finds a violation he or she feels could cause death or serious injury,

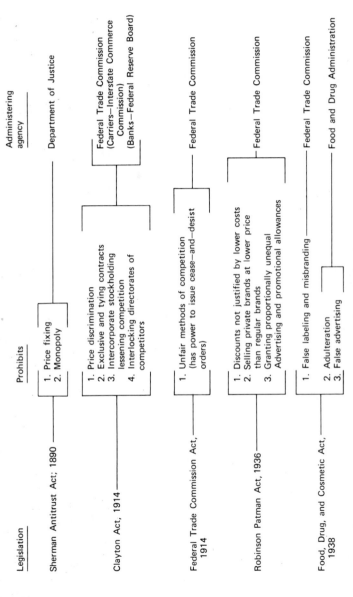

Figure 22-1 Major government control of business legislation.

the inspector can obtain a court injunction and have the business shut down until the violation is corrected.

Some businesses have maintained that some inspectors are overly zealous to the point of absurdity and/or do not have the knowledge necessary to perform their jobs realistically. In fact, many people in business have accused many of the government agencies of the same weaknesses. For example, one OSHA inspector ordered a manufacturer of pet sanitary litter to give all its employees a two-week mine safety course, at company expense, because it also owned a mine. Another agency was going to fine a person for flying a homemade helicopter six inches off the ground even though it was tied to the ground. They claimed he had failed to get FAA clearance. Publicity caused them to drop the case.

The small business owner should be aware of OSHA and the requirements for his or her type of business. The regulations cover, almost without exception, every type of business, even retail businesses. The requirements of OSHA can be very strict and most often expensive. For example, the law requires any business that uses hydraulic jacks to have them inspected and serviced every six months by a certified dealer.

The year before the law went into effect, 81.8 million people were employed. That same year there were 13,800 (0.017%) workers killed, and another 2.2 million (2.7%) sustained disabling injuries. In 1979, there were 98.5 million workers employed. Of these, 13,000 (0.013%) were killed on their jobs and 2.2 million (2.2%) sustained disabling injuries. This indicates a small decline, which could be due to OSHA.

CONSUMER PROTECTION LAWS

The number of so-called "consumer protection laws" has been growing in recent years. The small businessperson must be aware of these laws and regulations in order not to violate their provisions. Some of the more important ones to small businesses are discussed below.

COOLING-OFF PERIODS

This Federal Trade Commission regulation requires a cooling-off period in door-to-door selling if the purchase exceeds $25. The buyer has three business days to cancel a purchase by written notification. The salesperson is then required to pick up the goods or make arrangements, at his or her expense, for the return of the goods within 20 days, or the customer can keep the goods. The salesperson must return in full any payment or trade-in received in the sale. The salesperson must also cancel any credit note or mortgage involved in the sale.

This regulation also makes provision for cooling-off periods in cases where the buyer's home is used as security in a credit transaction (not original purchase). Major repairs and remodeling often involve a second lien on the home. The three-day period is required in these transactions and the creditor must give the buyer written notice of his or her right to cancel. Written notification is also required to cancel the purchase.

There are certain exceptions—purchases made entirely by phone or mail, purchases made in relation to earlier negotiations at a retail store, purchases of stocks and bonds from registered brokers, purchases of insurance, the rental of property, and parts and labor for maintenance and repair.

FAIR PACKAGING AND LABELING ACT

The Fair Packaging and Labeling Act of 1969 requires that any manufacturer or distributor of a consumer product must display prominently on labels the true net weight or volume of the contents. The law also prohibits such terms as "giant quart" or "jumbo pound." Under the law, a manufacturer can only advertise coupon offers or "cents-off" sales if the price is below the regular price. Any commodity labeled "economy size" or any other such term must be sold at a price that is at least 5 percent less than the per-unit of weight or volume price of all other sizes of the same product sold at the same time. Introductory price offers can last no longer than six months and may be used only for new products, products that are substantially changed, or products being introduced for the first time in a particular marketing area. Any manufacturer who elects to show the number of servings on his label must also show the amount of each serving.

This law also requires manufacturers to list on the label all of the ingredients of the product in decreasing order of weight for any nonstandard foods. The common name of the product and the name and address of the manufacturer must appear on the label of all goods except prescription drugs.

FEDERAL GARNISHMENT LAW

The Federal Garnishment Law of 1968 deals with an individual's wages being withheld for the payment of a debt. The federal law prohibits garnishments of more than 25 percent of an employee's disposable earnings (gross pay minus all deductions required by the law) in any one week or 30 times the federal minimum wage in effect at the time, whichever is less. The law also prohibits the employer from firing an employee because of one debt. The law does not prohibit firing if there are garnishments for two or more debts. If there is a state law covering garnishment of wages and it gives the debtor the better break, it is used instead of the federal law. Some states have laws prohibiting garnishment of wages and the federal law has no meaning in these states.

MAGNUSON–MOSS WARRANTY ACT

The Magnuson-Moss Warranty Act of 1974 provides that:

1. No company can be forced to offer a written warranty.
2. Every term and condition of the warranty must be spelled out in writing.
3. All warranties must be written in ordinary language instead of in "legalese."
4. Any written warranty must be labeled either "full warranty" or "limited warranty."
5. Full warranties require that:
   (a) Defective products will be fixed or replaced free including removal and installation if necessary.
   (b) They will be fixed in a reasonable time.
   (c) The customer does not have to do anything unreasonable.
   (d) The warranty covers any owner, not just the purchaser.
   (e) If the product cannot be fixed, the customer has the choice between a new one or his or her money back.
6. Warranties that do not meet all these requirements must be labeled "limited warranties."

MERCHANDISE, MAIL ORDER AND UNORDERED

Mail order firms must fill orders from customers within 30 days or offer the customers their money back. They must send customers a postcard allowing cancellation and the return of their money. If customers want their money back it must be returned promptly. This regulation does not apply to magazines.

Free samples and merchandise mailed by charitable organizations soliciting contributions are the only unordered merchandise that can be sent through the mails. Other than these two categories, any merchandise that is unordered may be considered a free gift by the receiver. It is illegal for the business to bill or dun the person receiving unordered merchandise.

GOVERNMENT ASSISTANCE TO SMALL BUSINESS

Many agencies of the federal government offer various forms of assistance to small business. For example, the Commerce Department will provide information and assistance to small businesses to help them engage in international trade. The Department of Health, Education and Welfare has had some programs to assist in the education of small businesspersons in good business practices. The Department of Labor has sponsored programs that provide assistance to businesses in poverty areas for training workers. The Office of Minority Business Enterprise in the Department of Commerce has sponsored programs designed to increase the number of minority small business firms. However, the bulk of government assistance to small business has come from the Small Business Administration of the Department of Commerce.

The Small Business Administration (SBA) was established by Congress in 1953 to "help small businesses grow and prosper." The SBA strives to achieve this goal by offering various services to small business firms. Without a doubt, the most important function of the SBA has been in their loan programs discussed in Chapter 7. The SBA also performs other valuable services to small businesses in the form of (1) management assistance, (2) training, (3) "set-aside contracts," and (4) publications. (See Fig. 22-2.)

MANAGEMENT ASSISTANCE

The SBA provides management assistance to small business firms in the form of (1) their own field representatives, (2) grants to consultants, (3) the ACE program, (4) the SCORE program, and (5) university Small Business Institutes.

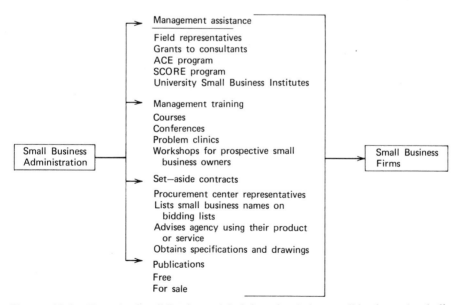

Figure 22-2 How the Small Business Administration helps small business (excluding loans).

Field Representatives

The SBA has 98 field offices spread out over the United States, Guam, and Puerto Rico. These field offices have field representatives whose primary function is to administer assistance to small businesses, particularly those with SBA loans. Although usually understaffed, these field offices provide valuable guidance in all phases of operations to small firms.

Grants to Consultants

The SBA provides funds, when they are available, to various types of consulting firms to assist loan recipients and other small businesses. The type of consulting sometimes varies from year to year, with such services as accounting and general business consulting being offered. The amount of funds made available for this type of service has been relatively small when compared to the amount of loans the SBA has outstanding. The SBA feels the program more than pays for itself in terms of improving the ability of loan recipients to repay their loans.

ACE Program

The ACE (Active Corps of Executives) program is one of the ways the Small Business Administration attempts to provide management consulting to small businesses. The SBA recruits persons actively engaged in small business, trade associations, major industry, professional fields related to small business, and educational institutions to join its ACE program. These volunteers provide free consulting (except for expenses that are paid for by the small business) to small business firms.

SCORE Program

The SBA forms SCORE (Service Corps of Retired Executives) chapters in cities and towns, consisting of persons who are retired from careers in business and business-related fields. These chapters include such persons as retired accountants, lawyers, engineers, economists, bankers, retailers, wholesalers, manufacturers, and educators. When a small business feels it needs help in solving problems or increasing efficiency of the business, it contacts the SBA field office, which in turn contacts the nearest SCORE chapter. The SCORE chapter then sends out one or more of its members who are best suited to help the small business. Today, there are more than 4000 SCORE volunteers across the country helping small business firms. SCORE services are free to the small business except that the small business pays the out-of-pocket travel expenses of the volunteer.

University Small Business Institutes

The SBA contracts with colleges to provide business consulting to small firms. The SBA pays the school a small sum (currently, $250 each) for each business consulted. The methods of providing the service varies from school to school. Sometimes the instructor is directly involved in the consulting with his or her students. Sometimes the consulting is provided entirely by students. The school is required to provide periodical reports to the SBA and provide both the business and the SBA copies of the consulting recommendations. The service is entirely free to the small business. This program is designed to provide assistance to small business firms and give students exposure to real business firms and their problems. Both authors are involved in this program at their colleges and feel the program is very beneficial to both students and small businesses.

MANAGEMENT TRAINING

The SBA provides management training through (1) courses, (2) conferences, (3) problem clinics, and (4) workshops for prospective small business owners.

Courses

The SBA cosponsors training courses for small business owners with educational institutions, SCORE chapters, and other civic organizations. Instructions are given by teaching staffs of colleges or other professionals. The small business owners who attend pay a small fee to cover expenses of the course, which usually consists of one day a week for several weeks.

The course may vary from general courses on policy and goals of small business to such specialized courses as bid preparation on government contracts or how to engage in export trade.

The SBA provides mailing envelopes and postage and helps with the publicity of the course. The institution provides the speaker and the room for the course.

Conferences

Conferences sponsored by the SBA are intended to help the small business owner with specific problems. They usually last only one day and cover such specialized topics as taxation. The SBA usually cosponsors these conferences with colleges, chambers of commerce, trade associations, and other civic groups. These conferences usually consist of a professional speaker, panel discussions, and question-and-answer sessions. The SBA provides mailing envelopes and postage for advertising the conference and helps with publicity.

Problem Clinics

The SBA also joins with cosponsoring institutions to offer problem clinics for small business owners. SBA contribution to the clinic is the same as for courses and conferences. The group of small business owners is led in a discussion of a common problem by a leader well versed in the specific problem. Problem clinics help small business owners exchange knowledge of a common problem and help them share in various methods of dealing with the problem.

Workshops for Prospective Small Business Owners

The SBA establishes workshops in cooperation with civic organizations in an attempt to help prospective small business owners understand the need for preparation before starting a new venture. SBA personnel or professionals hold a one-day session or several evening classes to instruct prospective small business owners in how to start a new business. Training materials are provided by the SBA to both the instructor and the prospective small business owners.

SET-ASIDE CONTRACTS

The federal government contracts with private business for billions of dollars worth of goods and services each year. The various purchasing agencies of the federal government set aside contracts on which only small businesses may bid in an effort to promote small business. The SBA has Procurement Center Representatives in major government procurement agencies to review and recommend additional set-aside contracts for small business. The Procurement Center Representatives also provide lists of small business sources to the procurement agencies and often recommend relaxation of restrictive specifications so that small firms may bid on them.

SBA field offices have personnel who help small firms in government contract bidding by performing such functions as advising which agency uses their products or services, helping them get their firms on bidding lists, and helping them obtain bidding specifications and drawings.

PUBLICATIONS

The SBA offers a wide range of both "free" and "for-sale" publications designed to help the small businessperson in a wide range of problems. Publications that are for sale are sold by the Government Printing Office at cost. Almost all free publications and some of the for-sale publications can be obtained from SBA field offices. The categories and one example of each of the publications are:

Free Publications	Example
Management Aids	*The ABCs of Borrowing*
Small Marketers Aids	*Interior Display: A Way to Increase Sales*
Small Business Bibliographies	*Photographic Dealers and Studios*

For-Sale Publications

Small Business Management Series	*Human Relations in Small Business*
Starting and Managing Series	*Starting and Managing a Small Shoestore*
Nonseries Publications	*Export Marketing for Smaller Firms*

A complete list of all publications, both free and for sale, can be obtained by writing one of the SBA field offices near you. The field offices and their addresses are:

SBA Field Office Addresses

Boston	Massachusetts 02114, 150 Causeway Street
Holyoke	Massachusetts 01050, 302 High Street
Augusta	Maine 04330, 40 Western Avenue, Room 512
Concord	New Hampshire 03301, 55 Pleasant Street
Hartford	Connecticut 06103, One Financial Plaza
Montpelier	Vermont 05602, 87 State Street, P.O. Box 605
Providence	Rhode Island 02903, 57 Eddy Street
New York	New York 10007, 26 Federal Plaza, Room 3100
Albany	New York 12210, 3100 Twin Towers Building
Elmira	New York 14901, 180 State Street, Room 412
Hato Rey	Puerto Rico 00919, Chardon and Bolivia Streets
Melville	New York 11746, 425 Broad Hollow Road
Newark	New Jersey 07102, 970 Broad Street, Room 1635

Camden	New Jersey 08104, 1800 East Davis Street
Rochester	New York 14014, 100 State Street
Syracuse	New York 13260, 100 South Clinton Street, Room 1071
Buffalo	New York 14202, 111 West Huron Street
St. Thomas	Virgin Islands 00801, Federal Office Building, Veterans' Drive
Philadelphia	Bala Cynwyd, Pennsylvania 19004, One Bala Cynwyd Plaza
Harrisburg	Pennsylvania 17101, 100 Chestnut Street
Wilkes-Barre	Pennsylvania 18702, 20 North Pennsylvania Avenue
Baltimore	Towson, Maryland 21204, 8600 La Salle Road
Wilmington	Delaware 19801, 844 King Street
Clarksburg	West Virginia 26301, 109 N. 3rd Street
Charleston	West Virginia 25301, Charleston National Plaza, Suite 628
Pittsburgh	Pennsylvania 15222, 1000 Liberty Avenue
Richmond	Virginia 23240, 400 N. 8th Street, Room 3015
Washington	D.C. 20417, 1030 15th Street, NW., Suite 250
Atlanta	Georgia 30309, 1720 Peachtree Road, NW.
Biloxi	Mississippi 39530, 111 Fred Haise Boulevard
Birmingham	Alabama 35205, 908 South 20th Street
Charlotte	North Carolina 28202, 230 South Tryon Street, Suite 700
Greenville	North Carolina 27834, 215 South Evans Street
Columbia	South Carolina 29201, 1801 Assembly Street
Coral Gables	Florida 33134, 2222 Ponce de Leon Boulevard
Jackson	Mississippi 39201, 200 East Pascagoula Street
Jacksonville	Florida 32202, 400 W. Bay Street
West Palm Beach	Florida 33402, 701 Clematis Street
Tampa	Florida 33602, 700 Twiggs Street
Louisville	Kentucky 40202, 600 Federal Place, Room 188
Nashville	Tennessee 37219, 404 James Robertson Parkway, Suite 1012
Knoxville	Tennessee 37902, 502 South Gay Street, Room 307
Memphis	Tennessee 38103, 167 North Main Street
Chicago	Illinois 60604, 219 South Dearborn Street
Springfield	Illinois 62701, 1 North Old State Capitol Plaza
Cleveland	Ohio 44199, 1240 East 9th Street, Room 317
Columbus	Ohio 43215, 85 Marconi Boulevard
Cincinnati	Ohio 45202, 550 Main Street, Room 5028
Detroit	Michigan 48226, 477 Michigan Avenue

Marquette	Michigan 49885, 540 West Kaye Avenue
Indianapolis	Indiana 46204, 575 North Pennsylvania Street
Madison	Wisconsin 53703, 122 West Washington Avenue
Milwaukee	Wisconsin 53202, 517 East Wisconsin Avenue
Eau Claire	Wisconsin 54701, 500 South Barstow Street, Room B9AA
Minneapolis ·	Minnesota 55402, 12 South Sixth Street
Dallas	Texas 75242, 1100 Commerce Street
Albuquerque	New Mexico 87110, 5000 Marble Avenue, NE.
Houston	Texas 77002, 1 Allen Center, 500 Dallas Street
Little Rock	Arkansas 72201, 611 Gaines Street
Lubbock	Texas 79401, 1205 Texas Avenue
El Paso	Texas 79902, 4100 Rio Bravo, Suite 300
Lower Rio Grande Valley	Harlington, Texas 78550, 222 East Van Buren
Corpus Christi	Texas 78408, 3105 Leopard Street
Austin	Texas 78701, 300 E. 8th Street
Marshall	Texas 75670, 100 South Washington Street, Room G12
New Orleans	Louisiana 70113, 1001 Howard Avenue
Shreveport	Louisiana 71101, 500 Fannin Street
Oklahoma City	Oklahoma 73102, 200 N.W. 5th Street
San Antonio	Texas 78206, 727 East Durango, Room A-513
Kansas City	Missouri 64106, 1150 Grand Avenue
Des Moines	Iowa 50309, 210 Walnut Street
Omaha	Nebraska 68102, Nineteenth and Farnam Streets
St. Louis	Missouri 63101, Mercantile Tower, Suite 2500
Wichita	Kansas 67202, 110 East Waterman Street
Denver	Colorado 80202, 721 19th Street
Casper	Wyoming 82601, 100 East B Street, Room 4001
Fargo	North Dakota 58102, 657 2d Avenue, North, Room 218
Helena	Montana 59601, 301 South Park
Salt Lake City	Utah 84138, 125 South State Street, Room 2237
Rapid City	South Dakota 57701, 515 9th Street
Sioux Falls	South Dakota 57102, 8th and Main Avenue
San Francisco	California 94105, 211 Main Street
Fresno	California 93712, 1229 N Street
Sacramento	California 95825, 2800 Cottage Way
Honolulu	Hawaii 96850, 300 Ala Moana
Agana	Guam 96910, Pacific Daily News Building

Los Angeles	California 90071, 350 South Figueroa Street
Las Vegas	Nevada 89101, 301 East Stewart
Reno	Nevada 89505, 50 South Virginia Street
Phoenix	Arizona 85012, 3030 North Central Avenue
San Diego	California 92188, 880 Front Street
Seattle	Washington 98174, 915 Second Avenue
Anchorage	Alaska 99501, 1016 West Sixth Avenue, Suite 200
Fairbanks	Alaska 99701, 101 12th Avenue
Boise	Idaho 83701, 1005 Main Street
Portland	Oregon 97204, 1220 South West Third Avenue
Spokane	Washington 99120, Courthouse Bldg., Room 651

DISCUSSION QUESTIONS

1. What does the Sherman Antitrust Act prohibit, and how effective is it?
2. Who may sue for violations under the Sherman Act?
3. What does the Clayton Act prohibit and is it effective?
4. What are the two most important parts of the Federal Trade Commission Act?
5. What are the major provisions of the Robinson-Patman Act?
6. Who administers the Food, Drug, and Cosmetic Act?
7. If you were a small manufacturer, would you be concerned with the Occupational Health and Safety Act? Explain.
8. Name at least one type of small business that could be affected by the following "consumer protection laws" and tell how it could be affected.
   (a) Cooling-off periods.
   (b) Fair Packaging and Labeling Act.
   (c) Federal Garnishment Act.
   (d) Magnuson–Moss Warranty Act.
   (e) Mail order merchandise.
   (f) Unordered merchandise.
9. What forms of management assistance does the Small Business Administration offer small firms?
10. How does the Small Business Administration assist small businesses in terms of goverment contracts?

STUDENT PROJECT

Take the list of Small Business Administration publications to a small business and find out which he/she thinks would be of interest to most small businesses.

CASE A

PULVER'S OFFICE SUPPLY

James Pulver has operated an office supply store in a town of 150,000 for 25 years. There is only one other office supply store in town and it has maintained good relations with James for many years. They meet about once a year and try to keep their prices in line with each other. They both feel there is enough business for both of them and there is no use "cutting each other's throat."

Recently, a chain of office supply stores was created and they have just established one of their stores in the same town in which James has his store. The new chain purchases a large volume of merchandise, and James has learned that they are selling some products cheaper than he can buy them. His business has fallen off drastically, and James is worried that he may not be able to stay in business much longer.

James does admit that the new store has better marketing and promotional practices and seems more efficient than his operation. He suspects that he may have been too lax about his business because of the lack of real competition.

Questions

1. Evaluate each of the following laws to determine if the new chain or James may be in violation of them.
   (a) Sherman Antitrust Act.
   (b) Clayton Act.
   (c) Federal Trade Commission Act.
   (d) Robinson–Patman Act.
   (e) Food, Drug, and Cosmetic Act.
2. If James finds out that the new chain is in violation of any of these laws, what would you advise him to do?
3. What assistance could James obtain to improve his business?

CASE B

FEDERAL TRADE COMMISSION EXPERT

Recently, you graduated from college, and you have just accepted a job with the Federal Trade Commission. The first day on the job you had several letters on your desk. A description of each letter is presented below.

Letter A   A small businesswoman writes that she recently sent out bid requests and received three bids, each of which quoted exactly the same amount, $2,416.52.

Letter B   A small businessman writes that he is having to pay almost twice the amount for a product than paid by a large competitor who buys from the same firm.

Letter C   A small businessman writes that he was forced out of business by a competitor who sold his product at below what he could produce it for; then, after he went out of business, the competitor raised his price.

Letter D   An individual writes that she bought a product that, according to the label, was supposed to weigh eight ounces, but it only weighed seven ounces.

Letter E   An individual complains that he bought a vacuum cleaner from a door-to-door salesman. He decided he didn't want it and asked for his money back. The company refused to refund his money.

Letter F   A worker writes that he was fired from his job because of a garnishment of his wages to pay a debt.

Letter G   A small businesswoman wants to know if her product warranty meets the full warranty or limited warranty requirements.

Letter H   A small businessman complains that he was sent equipment through the mail even though he had not ordered it. He does not want the equipment and the company is sending him nasty letters threatening to ruin his credit.

Letter I   A small businessman writes that he has heard the government provides assistance to small firms and he wants to know whom to contact.

Question

How would you answer each letter?

PHOTO CREDITS

Chapter 1 4: Judy Gurovitz/Photo Researchers. 9: Norbert Kleber/Photo Researchers. 19: Sybil Shelton/Monkmeyer. 26: Lucinda Fleeson/Stock, Boston.

Chapter 2 44 and 45: American Bank Note Company.

Chapter 3 61: McDonald's Corporation. 75: Carrel Corporation Public Relations.

Chapter 4 89: Bernard Pierre Wolff/Magnum. 97: Mahon/Monkmeyer.

Chapter 5 117: P. Vannucci/Leo de Wys. 119: Cary S. Wolinsky/Stock, Boston. 120 and 122: Ray Ellis/Rapho-Photo Researchers.

Chapter 6 146: Stanley Rosenthal/Leo de Wys. 152: Storebest Corporation. 156: Alon Reininger/Leo de Wys. 159: M. Schneit/Leo de Wys.

Chapter 7 175: Gregory A. Keller/Freelance Photographers Guild.

Chapter 8 193: Patricia Hollander Gross/Stock, Boston.

Chapter 9 228: Robert Hauser/Rapho-Photo Researchers. 236: Ray Ellis/Photo Researchers.

Chapter 10 262: Cary S. Wolinsky/Stock, Boston. 265: Mimi Forsyth/Monkmeyer.

Chapter 12 303 and 304: Sybil Shelton/Monkmeyer.

Chapter 13 315: Lowell Georgia/Photo Researchers. 325: Mimi Forsyth/Monkmeyer.

Chapter 14 332: Bruce Roberts/Photo Researchers. 342: Yvonne Freund/Rapho-Photo Researchers.

Chapter 15 358: Freelance Photographers Guild.

Chapter 16 388: Sybil Shelton/Monkmeyer.

INDEX